Democracy and the Courts

Democracy and the Courts

THE RISE OF JUDICIAL ELECTIONS IN THE ANTEBELLUM SOUTH

DAVID M. GOLD

THE UNIVERSITY OF SOUTH CAROLINA PRESS

© 2025 David M. Gold

Published by the University of South Carolina Press
Columbia, South Carolina 29208

uscpress.com

Printed in the United States of America

Library of Congress Cataloging-in-Publication Data
can be found at https://lccn.loc.gov/2025003001

ISBN: 978-1-64336-565-7 (hardcover)
ISBN: 978-1-64336-566-4 (ebook)

CONTENTS

Introduction 1

CHAPTER 1
The Southern Roots of the Elective Judiciary 15

CHAPTER 2
The South's Northern Tier 39

CHAPTER 3
The Reluctant Southeast 71

CHAPTER 4
The Old Southwest 95

CHAPTER 5
Explaining the Rise of Judicial Elections 131

CHAPTER 6
Electing the Judges 147

CHAPTER 7
Elected Judges and Judicial Review 163

CHAPTER 8
Retreat of the South 191

Epilogue: From Reconstruction to Jim Crow 201

Notes 233
Selected Bibliography 291
Index 305

Introduction

The elective judiciary is a distinctively American phenomenon that has always baffled foreigners. When the young Frenchman Alexis de Tocqueville visited the United States in 1831 and early 1832, he was astonished to learn that "[s]ome [state] constitutions provide for *election* of members of the courts and require them to submit to frequent reelection." Nearly half a century later, an English newspaper praised the new American president, Rutherford B. Hayes, for his opposition to the "mischievous system" of the elective judiciary, a question "about which there are not two opinions on this side of the Atlantic." "To the rest of the world," asserted a former state supreme court judge in 1988, "the American adherence to judicial elections is as incomprehensible as our rejection of the metric system." Twenty years after that, a *New York Times* headline noted that "U.S. voting for judges perplexes other nations."[1]

This odd practice of electing judges opens a window onto nineteenth-century American democracy. By the time Andrew Jackson became president in 1829, most citizens recognized as a basic tenet of the nation's political creed that the people should elect the "political" branches of government, the legislative and executive. Soon, this notion of popular sovereignty began to embrace the supposedly non-political judicial branch. During the run-up to the Mississippi constitutional convention of 1832, Henry S. Foote, coproprietor of the Vicksburg *Mississippian*, insisted "that the appointment of all important civil officers should spring from *direct popular agency*." Foote expressly included judges among the "important civil officers." In 1834, an Ohio legislative committee declared that "the people are qualified to exercise all the rights and privileges belonging to freemen," including the people's natural right, "essential to the very existence of a free government," to "appoint their own agents." At the Massachusetts constitutional convention of 1853, an advocate of judicial elections conceded that there was "no great evil existing under the present [appointive] system," but he wanted "to carry out the theory of our government in the fundamental laws." In short, there was an elemental American principle at stake. Even opponents of judicial elections acknowledged the right of the people to elect their judges; they rejected not the principle but the policy.²

Although judicial selection played a subordinate part in the larger wave of constitutional reform that swept across the nation in the mid-nineteenth century, it was hardly an insignificant issue. Constitutional convention delegates, lawyers, politicians, and newspaper editors argued passionately over the subject: Would elected judges be more or less susceptible than appointed judges to political influence? Would direct accountability to the people render judges partial in individual cases? Were the voters competent to choose their judges? And underlying it all, which method of judicial selection better comported with the principles of American republicanism?

The debate has continued to the present day. Before the Civil War, the arguments were largely theoretical, for the nation did not then have much experience with electing judges. Following the war and a quarter-century of the elective judiciary, the New York State Assembly impeached three judges on charges of corruption. One resigned, but the state senate convicted the others. Afterwards, New York attorney Dorman B. Eaton, who had a low opinion of the electorate, published a pamphlet entitled *Should Judges Be Elected?* "A few months since," he wrote,

> when the brazen demagogue faces of such infamous judges as have disgraced no civilized State since the days of Jeffreys and Scroggs looked down from our seats of justice upon a bar indignant and a people humiliated; a little later, when at a single legislative session, the unexampled number of five judges were awaiting trial for official corruption—a number greater than were arraigned in the whole period of appointed judges in this State from 1777 to 1846 . . . it might have been thought almost an insult to public sentiment to gravely debate whether judicial elections were a public blessing.

Eaton blamed the popular election of judges for the politicization of the judiciary, the demoralization of the bar, and all sorts of social evils.³

Complaints about judicial elections reached a critical stage during the Progressive Era. Chief Justice Emmet O'Neal of Alabama, for example, believed that the popular election of judges, together with the primary system of nominating candidates, impaired judicial independence by "inclin[ing] the judge to yield to popular passion and prejudice, to be swayed by every passing breeze of popular sentiment, and to allow his own reelection to exercise a controlling influence on his official conduct." To replace judicial elections, O'Neal endorsed a type of merit selection that would have combined the nomination of judges by legal experts with retention elections.[4]

On the other hand, North Carolina chief justice Walter Clark extolled the election of judges—he himself had been elected to the superior and supreme courts of his state—and he believed that judicial elections should be extended to the federal courts. Many of the federal judges, Clark wrote, were "appointed by corporate influences." Constantly rubbing elbows with "the wealthier classes," he continued, the federal judges were "under no obligations to the people and under every obligation to the classes." "[T]hey go upon the bench knowing what influence procured their appointment, or their confirmation, and usually with a natural and perhaps unconscious bias from having spent their lives in advocacy of corporate claims."[5]

The result of Gilded Age and Progressive Era ferment regarding judicial selection was a potpourri of state selection systems even more diverse than the hodgepodge produced by the reform movement of the mid-nineteenth century. That movement had left many states with wholly elective judiciaries and others with entirely appointive ones. In the latter category, legislatures did the appointing in some states, governors in others. A few states had mixed systems featuring appointed supreme court judges and elected lower court judges. In 1909, North Dakota added a new wrinkle by providing for nonpartisan judicial elections. Other states followed suit, with at least one (Ohio) continuing to have party nominations. Merit selection took a while to catch on, but in 1940 Missouri became the first state to adopt a commission plan of judicial selection. Under the plan, a nonpartisan commission of lawyers and laymen would submit to the governor three nominees for any judicial vacancy, except on some of the lower courts, from which the governor would have to make the appointment. A judge who wished to remain in office for a second or subsequent term would be subject to a retention election.[6]

Today, according to the Brennan Center for Justice, fourteen states use some form of merit selection to choose their judges, fourteen have nonpartisan elections, seven have partisan elections, ten employ gubernatorial appointment, two use legislative appointment, and four have hybrid systems. These numbers are only for the states' highest courts. Throwing in lower courts complicates the picture even further. All in all, when retention elections are included, close to 90 percent of state judges stand for election at some point in their judicial careers.[7]

Modern legal scholars and political scientists take the mode of judicial selection very seriously. Consider the titles of a few twenty-first-century books and articles on the subject: *Free to Judge: The Power of Campaign Money in Judicial Elections*; *In Defense of Judicial Elections*; "Judges as Politicians: The Enduring Tension of Judicial Elections in the Twenty-First Century"; "Judicial Elections: Recent Developments, Historical Perspective, and Continued Viability"; "Why state courts—and state-court elections—matter"; and "Voter Ignorance and Judicial Elections." In addressing such contemporary issues as the influence of money on judicial elections or the competence of voters to choose their judges, scholars sometimes seek to explain how we got where we are. "To understand the judicial election debate today," writes one, "it is important to appreciate both the history of judicial selection in the United States and the different judicial election methods used throughout the states."[8]

To that end, many students of judicial elections include overviews of the origins and early impact of judicial elections in their publications, often relying on the efforts of Kermit Hall, Caleb Nelson, or Jed Handelsman Shugerman to explain the rise of the elective judiciary.[9] The work of these three scholars is discussed in chapter 5. Here I wish only to point out that the "perennial" debate over judicial selection, as Charles Gardner Geyh describes it, entails understanding the origins of the elective judiciary. To get the history right, one must consider the regional diversity that characterized the movement toward the elective judiciary and the complexity of factors that shaped the beginnings of this peculiarly American institution.

Until 1846, only one state chose any of its judges, except those on the bottom rungs of the judicial ladder, by popular election. Instead, either the governor or the state legislature named the judges. In the latter case, senators and representatives typically met together to hold an election among themselves. However, when scholars, journalists, and other observers speak of an elective judiciary, they invariably mean judges who are chosen by the state's voters. Judges selected by the other branches of government are considered to be appointed. Between 1846 and 1853, the idea of the popularly elected judiciary spread like wildfire. States from the Atlantic to the Pacific, from the Great Lakes to the Gulf of Mexico, took the selection away from governors and legislators and gave it directly to the voters. New states entering the Union thereafter all likewise put their faith in the people.

The attempts of legal historians to explain this rise of judicial elections in the middle of the nineteenth century tend to focus on states that switched from an appointive to an elective system through the drafting of a new constitution by a constitutional convention. The scholars devote most of their attention to New York, three states of the Old Northwest (Ohio, Indiana, Illinois), and Kentucky. Of the states that failed to adopt judicial elections, only Massachusetts, where the convention delegates debated the issue, receives much notice.

This is an unfortunate oversight because New York and the Old Northwest cannot be taken as representative of the entire country. The story of the rise of judicial elections reveals significant regional variations.[10] Every New England state retained an appointive judiciary. Every one of the ten states that refused to adopt even a partially elective judiciary sat in the East. Seven of the states that accepted judicial elections for all their courts, and all three of the states that did so only for courts below the supreme court, were in the South. Almost every northern state that adopted judicial elections did so through a constitutional convention. Seven of the twelve southern states that made the change did so by way of statute or constitutional amendment. And only southern states backtracked before the Civil War. These facts cannot be explained if the investigation is restricted to a handful of states that followed similar paths to reform.

Some conditions that prompted mid-century constitutional reform movements in the North also contributed to crusades in the South. Maryland as well as New York had endured a fiscal crisis after improvident public spending on internal improvements. Alabama, like Ohio, suffered from an inefficient court system. Louisiana no less than Rhode Island had a malapportioned legislature. But the prevalence of these factors was not the same everywhere. Although some southern states racked up enormous public debt, relatively little of it stemmed from internal improvement fiascos. Legislative malapportionment figured far more prominently in the South than in the North. The extensive powers of southern justices of the peace and county courts gave rise to grievances that had slight analogs in the North. And southern reformers, unlike their northern counterparts, had to deal with slavery, which impinged on constitutional questions of all kinds. Because the switch to judicial elections was generally associated with other constitutional reforms, explanations for the change in a few northern states may not make sense for the South.

A close student of the spread of judicial elections in the mid-nineteenth century argues that the proliferation was largely responsible for a steep rise in the number of cases in which state courts declared statutes unconstitutional. His compilation of cases from the twenty-four states that had joined the Union before 1821 finds 119 such decisions rendered by popularly elected courts in the 1850s versus 58 cases from all state judiciaries, most of them appointed, in the 1840s. But 60 percent of the 119 decisions of elected courts in the 1850s emanated from three northern states. The twelve southern states included in the survey issued forty-eight decisions invalidating state or local laws. Thirty-six (75 percent) came from the elected courts of seven states; and of these thirty-six, thirty-one (86 percent) were rendered by the courts of three states. In the uneven distribution of declarations of unconstitutionality, at least, the North and South were much alike.[11]

Nevertheless, a study of the southern cases is worthwhile for several reasons. First, it reveals that factors other than the switch to judicial elections account for the increase in judicial activism in the 1850s. Second, the peculiar constitutional history of one state, Louisiana, in the middle of the nineteenth century provides a unique opportunity to compare the decisions of appointed and elected judges on the validity of the same constitutional provisions. Finally, developments in another southern state, Missouri, highlight the interplay of law and sectional politics on constitutional decision-making.

Defining the South

The inclusion in this study of Missouri and the other border states begs the question of what we mean by "the South." The 1840 census divided the country into five regions: New England, Middle, Southern, Southwestern, and Northwestern. In this arrangement, Delaware and Maryland were placed in the Middle category, Kentucky and Missouri in the Northwest. After the next national count, James De Bow, the superintendent of the U.S. Census, noted the difficulty of arranging the states into regions due to the territorial and population growth of the country and the addition of new states. It made no sense, he thought, to separate Kentucky and Missouri from Tennessee and Arkansas and throw them together with California and the Territory of Oregon. Nor was it rational to combine Maryland

and the District of Columbia with New York and Pennsylvania in the Middle States, for "they belong to the South." "Cannot some method be proposed," asked De Bow, "which, whilst it shall not obliterate the old distinctions now so much in use, will admit as elements of classification the great geographical divisions of the country, the Lakes, the Valley, the Gulf, the Atlantic, the Pacific, and also such as are political or social, as States or Territories, slaveholding or non-slaveholding States, &c.?"[12]

De Bow proceeded to do just that, creating a new scheme of three major regions (Eastern, Interior, and Western), each subdivided into north and south. In this arrangement, all the states of the future Confederacy belonged to a southern subdivision, with Maryland and Delaware in the Southeast, Kentucky and Missouri in the southern Interior.[13] To De Bow, ever the loyal southerner, slavery seemed to be the key distinction between North and South. He had no choice but to place the free state of California in the southern subdivision of the West; while the state's northern border is at approximately the same latitude as Chicago, its southern border adjoins Mexico. But there was no reason other than the existence of slavery to put Delaware in the South.

As the sectional conflict heated up after the Mexican War, with North and South quarreling over enforcement of the Fugitive Slave Law and the expansion of slavery to the new western territories, the categorization of states came increasingly to depend on whether they were free or slave. In 1850, in his last speech to the Senate, South Carolina's John C. Calhoun counted fifteen northern states and fourteen southern states, considering only Delaware to be "doubtful" or "neutral." To Calhoun, North meant free, South meant slave. Delaware was doubtful because free blacks there greatly outnumbered the tiny slave population and sentiment for emancipation was strong. But when the *Daily National Era* reported on a vote in the House of Representatives relating to the Kansas-Nebraska Bill in 1854, it divided the congressmen into two groups: those from the "free" states and those from the "South." As states where slavery was legal, Delaware, Maryland, Kentucky, and Missouri were southern states. From then on, newspapers generally referred to Delaware as a southern state. During the Civil War, De Bow's successor at the census, a Pennsylvanian, grouped the states in different ways for different purposes, but he generally refused to regard any of the border states as southern. Northern newspapers, though, continued to describe Delaware as a southern state, and after the war former Confederate vice president Alexander H. Stephens persisted in equating all the former slave states with the South.[14]

In this book, I follow the view of the 1850s that the South means the slave states, including the border states. This expansive definition of the South is appropriate not only because it conforms to the understanding of contemporaries during the rise of judicial elections but also because slavery affected the fate of the elective judiciary.

Defining the Judiciary

In a letter that nineteenth-century advocates of judicial elections cited repeatedly, Thomas Jefferson questioned the longstanding assumption that the people lacked the competence to elect qualified judges. "I do not know that this is true," he wrote in 1816, "and, if doubtful, we should follow principle." In Connecticut, Jefferson asserted, the people had been electing judges for two centuries, "with the most satisfactory success."[15]

Jefferson's characterization of Connecticut's experience contained an element of truth, but it presented an unrealistic picture. From an early date, Connecticut's General Court, the governing body of the colony, was a "curious jumble of legislature, police court and parent." Although there was a gradual separation of judicial functions from the other powers of government, the governor and members of the General Court (later, the General Assembly) continued to make up the membership of the courts. These judges were not elected *qua* judges; they were elected as legislators who also had judicial duties. The only judges whom the voters elected for the specific purpose of adjudicating disputes were the members of their town courts, tribunals having very limited jurisdiction.[16]

Two years after Jefferson wrote his letter, the first constitution of Connecticut did away with the last vestiges of judicial elections in that state by establishing a judiciary entirely separate from the other branches of government. There were, nonetheless, other examples of elected officials who had judicial responsibilities. In New York, most of the members of the state's highest court obtained their positions through election as senators; their judicial functions came with the job in much the same way that mayors in Ohio and Louisiana today have the authority to conduct mayor's courts. The legislators were not "real" judges; that is, they did not necessarily have legal training, and their chief function as public officers was not to resolve disputes between litigants.[17]

Something similar can be said about many lower court judges, including county court judges in the southern states and probate judges everywhere. In his 1816 letter, Jefferson complained that the justices of Virginia's inferior courts, appointed for life, were "the real executive as well as judiciary, in all our minor and most ordinary concerns," possessing the power to tax and to name key local officers. In most of the South, the county courts were the chief organs of local government. Probate judges had mostly ministerial duties (a characterization widely although not universally accepted). When the Illinois legislature conferred probate jurisdiction on specially designated justices of the peace, it expressly stated that these officers, in addition to the judicial powers they possessed as justices, had enumerated "ministerial powers," such as granting letters of administration, probating wills, receiving estate inventories, and so on. A Massachusetts lawmaker who in general opposed the election of judges favored the election of probate judges because their duties "were not in a great degree judicial, but were mainly administrative." The popularly elected inferior court justices of Georgia, sometimes recognized as the first true judges to be elected in the nineteenth century, had nonjudicial duties that may have outweighed their judicial ones.[18]

Justices of the peace exercised considerable judicial authority, but accounts of judicial elections rarely take note of them. The Ohio constitution of 1802 made justices of the peace elective. In 1804, the General Assembly defined the justices' jurisdiction. Under the statute, the justices could conduct arraignments; issue warrants, summonses, and subpoenas; and try minor criminal and civil cases. In Ohio and other states, delays in the administration of justice caused by a fast-growing population led the legislature to expand the justices' jurisdiction. In short, justices of the peace wielded real judicial power. If the story of judicial elections included them, it would begin at least as early as 1802.[19]

But, going by the neglect of justices of the peace in studies of judicial elections, historians do not typically regard justices as "real" judges. In this, they stand in company with John Marshall, who distinguished between untrained lay magistrates and true "judges of law." Justices often had administrative duties, such as issuing ferry licenses or laying out roads, that made them as much executive as judicial officers. Most justices lacked legal training. When residents of the Territory of Iowa petitioned Congress to increase the justices' jurisdiction because the higher courts were so far away, the Senate judiciary committee rejected their request. "Our justices of the peace," the committee noted, "are seldom very intimately acquainted with the common or municipal law; they are generally taken from the various pursuits of life, selected from the great mass of their fellow-citizens for their honesty and probity and not for their legal qualification to fill the station."[20]

The associate or "side" judges who in some states sat on higher-level trial courts also get scant mention in accounts of the rise of judicial elections. The Indiana constitution of 1816 and the Michigan constitution of 1835 provided for the election of associate judges. Typically, two associate judges, usually laymen, would sit alongside a professional presiding judge. In Indiana, for example, each circuit court consisted of a president judge and two associates. But although associate judges did occasionally exercise their judicial authority, they came to be widely regarded as expensive and "useless appendages" of the courts on which they sat. Years after the Michigan legislature eliminated associate judgeships, the great jurist Thomas M. Cooley recalled that the associates' "duty was to do nothing, and they did it faithfully." In other words, they were not "real" judges.[21]

We will see in the course of this book that these low men on the judicial totem pole, especially justices of the peace, did in fact play a role in the advent of judicial elections. The point here is to distinguish between them and the "real" judges at the center of the story. To maintain the distinction, *justices* as used herein refers to justices of the peace except when the context indicates otherwise. *Judges*, unless expressly identified as probate or county court judges, includes only members of higher courts whose functions were primarily judicial in nature.

Defining Democracy

In its 1964 decision applying the "one man, one vote" rule to state legislative districts, the United States Supreme Court observed that "[t]he right to vote freely for the candidate of one's choice is of the essence of a democratic society, and any restrictions on that right strike at the heart of representative government. And the right of suffrage can be denied by a debasement or dilution of the weight of a citizen's vote just as effectively as by wholly prohibiting the free exercise of the franchise."[22] These rights of suffrage and representation formed the basis of Jeffersonian constitutionalism.

Jefferson enshrined in the Declaration of Independence, as the foundational principle of American government, the tenet that governments derive "their just powers from the consent of the governed." Jefferson would have provided for the manifestation of that consent through universal or near-universal adult white male suffrage (what would later be called "free suffrage") and legislative representation based on something akin to "one-man, one vote" (or "equal representation"). He did not think it necessary that the voters choose all public officers; in his draft of a constitution for Virginia, the electorate did not even choose the governor or the senate. It was enough, thought Jefferson, that the people elect the equitably representative assembly that did the choosing.[23]

Judicial elections barely registered in the consciousness of people who lacked access to the ballot or fair representation in the legislature. They were too preoccupied with obtaining those more fundamental rights. The ladies who gathered at early women's rights conventions or who sent letters of support demanded enfranchisement, insisted that men could not adequately represent them, and claimed the right to hold office. They called upon natural rights, denounced taxation without representation, and modeled their statements of principles and grievances on the Declaration of Independence. The arguments presented by these women echoed those made by disenfranchised men in Rhode Island, underrepresented inhabitants of western South Carolina, and aggrieved citizens in several other states where government fell short of the Jeffersonian standard. Women and men who ran into resolute resistance in their struggle for free suffrage and equal representation had little energy to spare for the relatively minor cause of judicial elections.[24]

In the Age of Jackson, reformers would push for further democratization of their constitutions. Andrew Jackson entered the White House in 1829 obsessed with corruption in government and holding a set of political ideas that came to be called Jacksonian democracy. A jaundiced view of Jackson and Jacksonian democracy has taken hold among modern scholars. Historians have rejected the association of Jacksonianism with democracy because Jacksonian equality did not extend to women, blacks, or Indians and because Jacksonians "seldom advocated a radically egalitarian distribution of wealth." One scholar, recognizing that "democracy is not inherently progressive," remarks that Jacksonian democracy was defined as much by "[w]hite supremacy, the defense of slavery, and the ethnic cleansing of Native Americans" as by "the Bank War and mass politics."[25]

But the failure of Democrats to extend equality to women and racial minorities or to radically redistribute wealth does not mean that Jacksonian democracy was a fraud. When Jackson and his followers spoke of equality, they had in mind the political equality of different social classes. Jackson insisted that being of the lower classes did not preclude one from holding public office: "no one man has any more intrinsic right to official station than another." Nor did it deprive one of the right to the equal solicitude of government. "Just laws," he wrote in 1821, "can make no distinction of privilege between the rich and the poor." As president, Jackson announced that "the humble members of society, the farmers, mechanics, and laborers," had the same rights under the law as the rich and powerful. The egalitarian passion of Jacksonian Democrats led them to denounce the "aristocratic" elements in government, notably including officeholders who were not directly elected by the people. A denial that judges should be elected, editorialized a Democratic newspaper, was "a remnant of the old English aristocratic prejudice from which every American should seek to free his mind."[26]

To prevent the well-to-do and well-connected from bending government to their own advantage, Jacksonians sought to limit the scope of governmental authority. After the financial panic of 1837, mainstream Democrats, already hostile toward banks and their paper money, turned against corporations and against governmental interference in the economy. "The less government interferes with private pursuits, the better for the general prosperity," President Martin Van Buren, Jackson's handpicked successor, told Congress. Governmental attempts to aid and regulate private enterprise, he declared, had always proved injurious and inevitably resulted in the bestowal of special favors upon individuals or classes, leading to well-founded complaints of "partiality, injustice, and oppression."[27]

"[T]he first principle of our system," Jackson himself proclaimed, is *"that the majority is to govern."* The will of the majority became the guiding principle of the Democratic Party. The *Chicago Democrat* declared itself "ready to be advised and instructed by the party—the people themselves—*we will always obey the voice of the majority.*" "The democratick theory," intoned the New York *Evening Post*, "is, that the popular voice is the supreme law."[28]

To help ensure a government responsive to the will of people, Jackson urged rotation in office, which he regarded as "a leading principle in the republican creed." When Jackson uttered these words, he was thinking of administrative officials appointed by the president. But Jacksonians applied the principle to elected officials as well, favoring frequent elections and short terms of office. The *United States Telegraph,* Jackson's organ in Washington, lauded "[t]he frequency and freedom of elections, together with the direct responsibility of the elected to the people," as "the most striking characteristic of our government."[29]

To give an expanded electorate a more direct say in the choice of public officers, to put restraints on the possessors of political power, to foster transparency and accountability in government—these were all democratic goals, and often achievements, in the Jacksonian era. The spread of judicial elections can be appreciated only in the context of this prevailing democratic ethos of the time.

The term *democracy* and its various forms, such as *democrat* and *democratic*, appear frequently in this book. When referring to political affiliation—the Democratic Party—these words are capitalized. Otherwise, they begin with a small *d*. Most scholars capitalize both elements in the phrase *Jacksonian Democracy*, but because Jacksonian democracy was a capacious phenomenon that did not always have partisan implications, I have chosen to use the lower-case *d* unless a partisan meaning is intended.

It is common, when writing about public life in the mid-nineteenth century, to refer to the people's demands, to crusades or campaigns, to what the public or the voters wanted. The fact is, though, that we don't really know how much the general public cared about judicial elections or any of the other constitutional issues that made the news. We know from political party platforms and editorials in partisan newspapers where the parties stood on various matters (although even this knowledge is subject to the caveat that the parties were not monoliths), and we have the election results. But editors and correspondents often bemoaned the lack of public interest in constitutional concerns and the inadequate attention voters paid to judicial races. Constitutional convention delegates might remark upon the popular feeling among their constituents, but how many of them took pains to learn the sentiments of the mass of voters back home, as opposed to the opinions of their political or business associates or the more substantial of their neighbors? That is a matter of pure speculation. One thing we do know is that throughout the nineteenth century and into the twentieth, ballot issues involving the constitution often failed at the polls where the law required the approval of a majority of the people voting *at the election* and not just *on the issue*. A proposed amendment might receive the support of 75 percent of those voting on the question, but if most of the voters who turned out to elect a governor or president ignored the constitutional issue, the amendment would fail. So, the reader is hereby forewarned that any assertions made by anyone about popular demands in the mid-nineteenth century must be taken with a grain of salt.

CHAPTER 1

The Southern Roots of the Elective Judiciary

With the arguable exception of Connecticut, America's earliest foray into judicial elections occurred in Vermont during the American Revolution. Vermont's first constitution (1777) gave to the freemen of each county the power to elect the judges of the inferior court of common pleas, justices of the peace, judges of probate, and sheriffs, all to hold office during good behavior and "removable by the General Assembly upon proof of maladministration." A statute of 1781 provided for the election of the chief judge and four assistant judges of each county court by the freemen of the county. Another unusual feature of the constitution, borrowed from the Pennsylvania constitution of 1776, was the method of amending the fundamental law. The constitution created a council of censors, popularly elected every seven years. Among its other powers, the council could recommend amendments to the constitution and call a convention to act on them. The people elected the convention delegates. The council's proposals had to be "promulgated" at least six months before the convention met so that the people could instruct their delegates concerning them, but the amendments approved by the convention took effect without being subject to a popular referendum.[1]

The council of 1785–86 had misgivings about the election of judicial and other officers who could stay in office during good behavior, which potentially meant for life. The council proposed an amendment to give to the single-chamber General Assembly, acting in conjunction with the executive council, the power to choose annually all judges and the sheriffs. The censors believed the governor, executive council, and legislature to be "most competent" to choose judicial and executive officers, although they viewed the annual selection of these officers as a temporary expedient. The constitutional convention of 1786 adopted a revised constitution converting the judges and sheriffs into appointed officers.[2]

Vermont's short-lived experiment with judicial elections thus ended even before Congress recognized Vermont as a state in 1791. The United States entered the nineteenth century with no popularly elected judges. Georgia broke the pattern with a constitutional amendment in 1812. Georgia's constitution of 1798 was not notably democratic. It did not expressly limit the elective franchise to whites or males, but it did require voters to have paid all taxes due. There were property qualifications for holding legislative office. The system of representation, based on federal population (free persons, excluding Indians not taxed, plus three-fifths of slaves), favored the wealthier, slaveholding counties. The General Assembly chose most state officers, including the governor, as well as the inferior court justices who dominated local government. The judicial system included superior and inferior courts and justices of the peace. There was no supreme court on paper until 1835, when the General Assembly created one by constitutional amendment, or in practice until 1846.[3] By statute, the first five justices named in the governor's commission of justices of the peace in each county served as the justices of the county's inferior court. The General Assembly chose the justices, who held office during good behavior, and the superior court judges for three-year terms.[4]

The lawmakers could modify the constitution without calling a convention or putting a proposed alteration before the voters. In 1812, finding that "the term of good behaviour has a tendency to destroy that sense of responsibility which should ever be kept alive in a free country," they passed a constitutional amendment providing for the separate, popular election of justices of the peace and inferior court justices (they still were not called judges) for terms of four years. The amendment took effect upon its second passage by the requisite majority the following year.[5]

Students of Georgia's legal history mention the amendment without so much as speculating as to why it was passed.[6] The most likely reason, though, is that Georgians already had complaints about the justices similar to those later voiced by citizens in Virginia and North Carolina: that many were unfit for office, that they were chosen by legislators for political reasons, that they constituted an aristocracy. In 1795, a correspondent of the *Augusta Chronicle* complained that legislators handed out justiceships as rewards to friends or supporters, sometimes to individuals "little known either to God or man, unless it be for their ignorance, multiplicity, and disgrace to that office." In 1811, a grand jury presented a list of defects in the state constitution, the greatest of which was "the power that is lodged in the justices of the inferior court." The justices sat in the legislature, allowing them to fill numerous positions and "depriv[ing] the good citizens of this state from appointing their own county officers." They held office for life. They made laws "suitable to themselves," which they then acted upon as county justices. They exercised vast powers of local government. The list went on. As a remedy, the grand jurors recommended a constitutional amendment to allow the people to elect the justices of the inferior courts, justices of the peace, and militia officers.[7]

In 1799, the General Assembly had made various county offices (superior and inferior court clerks, sheriffs, coroners, county surveyors) elective. Because inferior court justices had administrative as well as judicial functions, such as issuing tavern licenses, overseeing the poor, appointing road commissioners, and levying taxes, the 1812 amendment represented the next logical step in the democratization of county government. It was also the first time since Vermont's short-lived experiment of the 1780s that any state made any part of its judicial system above the level of justice of the peace elective. But the Georgia amendment was hardly revolutionary. Inferior court judges were not "real" judges. Although usually men respected in their communities, they lacked legal training and, as a later governor commented, were not qualified to decide "complicated and vexed questions of law."[8]

Missouri

Less than a decade later, Missouri's first constitutional convention met to prepare for statehood. Missouri was ready. The population, recorded as 19,783 in 1810, more than tripled by 1820, and it would more than double again by 1830. The early settlers hailed mainly from Kentucky, Tennessee, Virginia, and North Carolina, but within a decade or so after statehood they would be joined by many newcomers from the Old Northwest and Europe. Most of the forty-one convention delegates came from the wealthy, conservative upper crust that had controlled the territory for years. The leading members represented St. Louis and other long-settled areas rather than the frontier. The convention approved the constitution with just one dissenting vote. It was not submitted to the people for ratification. In August, the voters elected state officers, and the government soon commenced operations, even though Congress had yet to approve the constitution. Congress finally assented in March 1821 and admitted Missouri to the Union.[9]

Notwithstanding the elitist character of the convention, the delegates produced a constitution that reflected Missouri's democratic political culture. Other states in 1820 had taxpaying or property qualifications for voting; Missouri's constitution conferred the franchise on all adult white male citizens. At a time when some states had grossly malapportioned legislatures, Missouri's constitution required that both the house and senate be apportioned according to the number of free white males residing in a county or district. A constitutional cap on the number of seats in the house of representatives, together with the requirement that each county have at least one representative, would result in a malapportioned chamber and in demands for redress in the fast-growing state. But the imbalance did not rest on rejection of the very principle of equal representation, as it did in some of the eastern states.[10]

The constitution provided for a popularly elected governor and lieutenant governor. The General Assembly chose the state treasurer, while the governor, with the advice and consent of the senate, appointed the auditor, secretary of state, and attorney general. Local voters elected county sheriffs and coroners. (The constitution was ambiguous on this point, but the General Assembly clarified the matter by statute.)[11] The judiciary consisted of a three-judge supreme court, a chancellor, circuit courts with one judge per circuit, inferior courts in each county, and local justices of the peace. The governor, with the senate's concurrence, appointed the supreme and circuit court judges and the chancellor, all of whom served during good behavior.[12] The constitution did not specify the appointing authority of the inferior court judges or justices of the peace, but the General Assembly quickly gave the governor the power to appoint the former and took upon itself the authority to name the latter.[13]

At the constitutional convention, Edward Bates drew up the article on the judiciary. A Virginian by birth, Bates had migrated to Missouri in 1814 at the age of twenty-one to join his older brother Frederick, a successful merchant, leading territorial official, and member of the St. Louis elite. Edward fell naturally into the same circle, studying law with a prominent attorney and hobnobbing with conservative businessmen and politicians. Soon after the constitutional convention Bates would become Missouri's attorney general and later, under Lincoln, attorney general of the United States.[14]

Bates and the other attorneys who dominated the convention proceedings found themselves at odds with Alexander McNair, a nonlawyer with democratic leanings despite a Federalist background. McNair had moved from Pennsylvania to Missouri in the early nineteenth century and secured military and civil appointments in the territorial government, including judge of the court of common pleas and quarter sessions. His career thus launched, McNair soon joined the St. Louis inner circle (the "little junto"). Having been at various times a trustee of the town of St. Louis, sheriff, US marshal, judge, and register of the United States land office, he was a natural choice of the junto for delegate to the constitutional convention.[15]

At the convention, Bates pressed for an independent judiciary that would serve as a check on the popularly elected branches of government. A group led by McNair may have argued for an elective judiciary with limits on the power of judicial review and against high salaries for the governor and judges. Bates prevailed, but McNair and his allies did not throw in the towel. McNair "let it be known" that he would run for governor even before the convention ended. In the August election, after campaigning vigorously in the rural areas, McNair crushed the territorial governor, William Clark of Lewis and Clark fame. The legislative elections also reflected popular dissatisfaction with the undemocratic features of the constitution. Many voters disliked the judicial article, with its high salaries, life tenure, appointed judges, and office of chancellor. Few men who had served as constitutional convention delegates won election to the General Assembly.[16]

Agitation for changes in the judicial provisions commenced immediately after the convention. The General Assembly could amend the constitution on its own, without calling another convention and without submitting amendments to the voters for ratification. The lawmakers had to pass an amendment by a two-thirds majority in each house, publish the amendment in the newspapers three times at least a year before the next general election, and then pass the amendment again by two-thirds majorities in the next General Assembly.[17]

In November 1820, the house voted on several proposed amendments. One would have fostered the elective principle, and cured a constitutional uncertainty, by requiring that sheriffs and coroners be popularly elected. The others would have made substantial changes in the judicial provisions. Among other things, the judicial amendments proposed to abolish the office of chancellor (an office toward which Americans harbored a longstanding hostility), prohibit the General Assembly from fixing a single location for supreme court sessions, eliminate the minimum salary for judges, limit judicial terms to six years, transfer the power to select judges to the General Assembly, and authorize the removal of judges from office on address of the legislature to the governor. A majority of the members present voted for each of the amendments. More than two-thirds of the members present voted to amend the provisions regarding the chancellor, judicial salaries and tenure, and the selection of judges. However, the constitution required the approval of two-thirds of all the members of each chamber, not two-thirds of those present. Due to absenteeism, not even the most one-sided votes in the house, 27–9, met the constitutional requirement.[18]

In the meantime, the senate was also considering amendments to abolish the chancellorship, repeal the judicial compensation floor, set judicial terms at six years, and give to the legislature the power to select judges. All these amendments passed the senate by nearly unanimous votes, and all failed in the house. As a Missouri historian commented, "The opposition of less than a dozen representatives . . . had thwarted not only the wishes of the legislature but those of the people of the State."[19]

In April 1821, after the General Assembly had adjourned *sine die* (indefinitely), Governor McNair called a special session of the legislature for June, ostensibly to deal with matters related to Missouri's distressing financial situation and its admission to the Union. (The state constitution directed the General Assembly to pass a law to prevent free blacks and mulattoes from entering the state, which antislavery congressmen found unacceptable. In February 1821 Congress approved Missouri's application for admission on condition that the constitutional provision would never be construed to authorize any law that violated the privileges and immunities clause of the United States Constitution.) The special session featured controversial debtors' relief legislation and the adoption of ten proposed constitutional amendments. The amendments included the abolition of the minimum salary for judges, transfer of the power to appoint judges and major executive officers from the governor to the legislature, and abolition of the office of chancellor. The proposed amendments did not include six-year terms for judges, but they did provide for the vacation of the supreme and circuit court judgeships at the end of the First General Assembly.[20]

It is not clear why amendments that had failed in the house at the regular session passed now. Perhaps attendance was better due to the crucial need to persuade Congress that Missouri should be admitted with the constitution adopted at the convention. In any case, the amendments would still have to be approved by the next General Assembly, after an intervening election, in order to take effect. By the time of the August 1822 election, the amendments had become linked to a furious battle over the debtors' relief legislation. Between February and July, three different circuit courts declared relief laws unconstitutional. The relief forces demanded an overhaul of the judiciary. However, the court decisions and a strenuous campaign by the anti-relief side, which portrayed the relief laws as a boon for speculators, deadbeats, and wealthy debtors, turned popular opinion against relief. The election resulted in a more conservative legislature. The new General Assembly ratified the amendments that abolished the office of chancellor, eliminated the minimum judicial salary, and vacated the judgeships; it failed to ratify the amendments that would have transferred the power to choose judges and executive officers from the governor to the legislature.[21]

Even if all the amendments had passed, they would not have established an elective judiciary. Providing for the popular election of judges would have been a radical action. Not one state at the time had an entirely elective judiciary, and few elected even lower-level judges. Taking the power to appoint judges away from the governor and giving it to the General Assembly, though, would have been a step toward popular control of the courts. The road to an elective judiciary began a few years later, when Jacksonians won a solid majority in the legislature, which they would maintain for many years. The invigorated Jacksonians set about trying, with some success, to further democratize Missouri's government.

In 1828, the senate judiciary committee, reporting on the expediency of reducing the terms of supreme and circuit court judges to not more than six years, found in favor of the idea, but it recommended terms of at least four years to preserve judicial independence. A constitutional amendment to establish four-year terms was introduced but did not pass. In its 1832–33 session, the General Assembly, perhaps emboldened by Mississippi's recent, pioneering switch to an all-elective judiciary, proposed constitutional amendments to give the legislature the authority to select supreme court judges, to give the voters the power to elect circuit court judges and court clerks, and to replace the good-behavior tenure of judges and clerks with six-year terms. A substantial majority of senators and representatives in the next General Assembly voted to ratify the amendments, but only the clerk amendment received the two-thirds majority of each house necessary for adoption. The opposition came from legislators who represented the longest-settled areas of the state, where anti-Jacksonians had their greatest strength.[22]

Although the General Assembly could not surmount the constitutional obstacles to creating an elective judiciary, it succeeded with lesser measures that required a simple legislative majority. By ordinary legislation the lawmakers provided for the popular election of county court justices and justices of the peace. When the General Assembly started creating probate courts for individual counties after 1835, it made the judgeships elective. Further progress toward the election of "real" judges would come in the 1840s, by which time Mississippi had had more than a decade's experience with an entirely elective judiciary.[23]

Mississippi

The "whole hogs" of Mississippi pioneered one of the most remarkable developments in American judicial history: the popular election of "real" judges. Before 1832, the only elected judicial officers in the country stood at or near the bottom of the judicial hierarchy. No state chose its entire judiciary, from justices of the peace to judges of the supreme court, at the polls. In 1832, Mississippi became the first to go "whole hog."

Congress created the Mississippi Territory, consisting of what later became the states of Mississippi and Alabama, in 1798, opening a vast new region to settlement. The "great migration" of the early nineteenth century brought thousands of settlers from the older eastern states. Planters and their slaves settled in the region around Natchez, the bustling Mississippi River port. Poorer people, who came in droves after the War of 1812 ended, settled north and east of the Natchez District. The white population of the western half of the territory, which became the state of Mississippi in 1817, rose from twenty-three thousand in 1810 to forty-two thousand in 1820 to more than seventy thousand in 1830, with no slowdown in sight. These small farmers, herdsmen, and lumbermen owned few slaves and had little affection for the Natchez elite who controlled the territory and then the state. A planter's daughter whose father had moved from Virginia to Mississippi would recall that "[t]he plainer classes in Virginia . . . recognized the difference between themselves and the higher classes, and did not aspire to social equality. But in Mississippi the tone was different. They resented anything like superiority in breeding."[24]

Mississippi's first constitution reflected the dominance of the aristocratic planters. It imposed a property qualification for service in the legislature: for a representative, 150 acres of land or an interest in real estate worth $500; for a senator, twice those figures. To qualify for governor or lieutenant governor, a person had to own 600 acres or have an interest in real estate worth $2,000. The propertied legislators appointed all the major state executive officers except the governor and lieutenant governor, all the judges and justices of the peace, and the attorney general and district attorneys. Judges held office during good behavior and appointed their own clerks. But the constitution had its democratic elements too. The qualified electors of the counties elected their sheriffs and coroners, and the constitution satisfied the fundamental criteria of Jeffersonian democracy: free suffrage and equal representation.[25]

By the time of Jefferson's death in 1826, the principle of free suffrage had been accepted, in practice if not necessarily in law, almost everywhere. In Mississippi, a would-be voter had to be either a taxpayer or an enrollee in the militia, but he did not have to own property. Early Mississippi statutes authorized cities and towns to impose poll taxes, and every white male between the ages of twenty-one and fifty had to pay a state poll tax. Moreover, all able-bodied free white men from eighteen to forty-five had to enroll in the militia. Such statutes effectively produced free suffrage. In any event, many local election officials may have disregarded the taxpayer requirement.[26]

Mississippi law did not explicitly state that the poll tax made a person a "taxable inhabitant" for suffrage purposes, but a rough calculation supports Alexander Keyssar's contention that it did. The United States census for 1830 shows a total state population of 136,621 and a white population of 70,443. Mississippi assessors reported 69,214 "free whites," of whom 37,226 were males. About half the state's population was under sixteen, giving 18,613 white males under sixteen, or an average of 1,163 for each year in that range. If we add 1,163 for each year of age from seventeen to twenty, we get 23,265 males under age twenty-one, leaving 13,961 men twenty-one and older. The assessors reported 14,821 taxable inhabitants. Most of these were probably white men owing the poll tax, a tax on land, or both. (Until 1839, control of land owned by women in Mississippi would have passed to their husbands upon marriage.) These are crude calculations, but they strongly suggest that the vast majority of white men were taxable inhabitants and therefore eligible to vote.[27]

Mississippi also approached the ideal of equal representation under its first constitution, notwithstanding the contention of a modern scholar that the constitution "gave Natchez a grossly disproportionate share of legislative representation."[28] The 1817 constitution based apportionment in the house on the number of free white inhabitants in a county but also guaranteed to every county at least one representative. The assurance of a representative for every county was common in the nineteenth century. The constitution also provided for separate representation of a city or town with sufficient population, which in practice benefited only Natchez.

The size of the house was limited to thirty-six members until the state's white population reached eighty thousand, after which the cap increased to one hundred. Apportionment in the senate would be according to the number of white taxable inhabitants in a district, with the number of senators to be fixed by the legislature at between one-fourth and one-third the number of representatives.[29]

The big potential problem with the plan of apportionment was the ceiling on the size of the house. With every county entitled to a representative, the steady creation of new counties would leave fewer representatives to apportion to the more populous counties already in existence. The house of 1825 had thirty-four members for twenty-one counties, with two from Adams County, in which Natchez was situated, plus one representing Natchez. Five years later the house had thirty-six members for twenty-six counties, with two from Adams County and no separate representation for Natchez. The Natchez members, by virtue of wealth, social position, or experience, may well have dominated legislative proceedings, but they did not have disproportionate representation in the house.[30]

In the senate, apportioned on the basis of white *taxable* inhabitants, wealth theoretically could have given Adams County increased membership. Indeed, Adams was one of just three counties to form a single-county senate district. But, as noted above, most white men were taxable. Furthermore, Adams County was the largest county in the state, with only one other county even close.[31] Population alone justified its senate representation.

The relatively democratic constitution of 1817 came under critical scrutiny in less than a decade. The issues that came up for discussion included the location of the state capital, which the constitution had temporarily designated as Natchez; the cost of annual legislative sessions; and the disposition of public lands acquired by treaty from the Choctaw and Chickasaw Indians. Judicial reform, though, rose to the top of the list. The growing population strained the judicial system. The constitution limited the number of superior and supreme court judges to eight but required a superior court to be held twice annually in every county. As the number of counties proliferated to accommodate all the new settlers, this arrangement became impractical. Some critics of the judiciary wanted to separate the supreme court from the superior courts (the judges of which, sitting together twice each year, made up the supreme court), while others sought to abolish the chancery court. Lifetime judicial appointments struck democratically minded citizens as a relic of monarchy. According to one historian, popular dissatisfaction with government focused on the county courts, the judges of which "composed an oligarchy ruling virtually independent domains."[32]

The beginnings of a constitutional reform movement coincided with the early years of the Jacksonian era. Jacksonian ideology amplified the complaints concerning the constitution. By 1830, there was pretty general agreement that the constitution needed reforming. Chancellor John A. Quitman that year pointed out that the ceiling on the number of house members, together with the requirement that each county have a representative, did not suit the needs of a state with extensive, newly settled lands. Quitman also objected to the constitution's limitation on the number of judges, called for the creation of a separate supreme court so that its judges would not be "bias[ed] toward former impressions," and expressed a preference for biennial instead of annual legislative sessions. Around the same time, attorney Robert J. Walker, the featured speaker at a public dinner in Natchez, suggested similar reforms as well as representation in the senate on the basis of the white population, an end to unequal taxation, procedural reform in the courts, and "elections by the people."[33]

The only method of revision authorized by the constitution was a convention, so the General Assembly placed the issue on the ballot for the election of August 1831. As the referendum approached, "A Citizen," writing in the conservative newspaper the *Natchez*, urged readers to shake off their apathy and pay attention to the issues. If the capital were moved, would the courts move too? Would Natchez lose the new Planters' Bank, the depository of state funds? A Citizen noted several judicial issues of particular interest: Would there be an independent supreme court? How would the judges be appointed and for what tenure? Would the separate chancery court and the Adams County criminal court be continued?[34]

Interest among the voters was low, but of those who cast ballots on the issue in August, 80 percent favored a convention. Then came the campaigns for seats at the convention, and Jacksonian populism emerged in force. A letter from "The People" to the Vicksburg *Advocate & Register* urged voters to support William J. Redd because of his devotion to republican principles and his belief that the sovereign people should elect "presidents, Governors, Judges, and all other officers." The Vicksburg *Mississippian*, too, pushed hard for the popular election of all civil officers, insisting that the people were fully up to the job. With regard specifically to the election of judges, the paper dismissed objections based on the novelty of the idea. "If every thing is to be rejected which bears not the stamp of *ancientness*, why not at once abandon all the comforts and refinements of civilized life . . . ?" After all, the whole American experiment in self-government was unprecedented, but no one proposed to abandon it. The true question to be decided by the people of Mississippi, said the editors, was not whether an elective judiciary was new but whether it was rational. On this score, they had no doubt. The people already, with their patronage, judged the competency and character of lawyers. The qualifications of a lawyer and a judge being essentially the same, the people were equally capable of determining the fitness of judicial candidates.[35]

"A Citizen," probably not the same one who had previously urged the voters of Adams County to wake up to the stakes involved in a convention, buttressed the *Mississippian's* case. "The constitution being the guard and protection of the people's rights," he declared, ". . . should be correct in principle, exact, and explicit, in its details, and purely democratical in its context." Because the people were "the only legitimate source of power" in a republic, they should choose their public officers, including judges. According to A Citizen, the adversarial electoral process would inform the voters of the merits and flaws of judicial candidates, as it did for gubernatorial candidates, and the people would then make a carefully considered choice. Other advocates of elections complained that life tenure was not only antirepublican but made judges lazy and irresponsible.[36]

Arguments for an elective judiciary based on republican principles and the people's competence would be standard fare in constitutional convention debates more than a decade later. So would the contentions now put forward in Mississippi against judicial elections. A writer for *The Natchez* maintained that for a judiciary to be "pure and impartial," it had to be independent, with judges who were not answerable for their decisions at the polls. Moreover, short terms of office, such as the five years that had been proposed, would not attract talented lawyers or give new judges time to gain the experience required for the best work. How could judges retain their integrity on the bench, wondered the writer, when half the suitors in his court had opposed him at the election, decrying his lack of ability or character, while the other half had praised him to the skies? When, moreover, his future election might depend on courting lawbreakers and vagabonds, "who exult in an opportunity to display their power at the polls"?[37]

Writing under the pseudonym Algernon Sidney, one opponent of judicial elections composed a multipart jeremiad warning of the dangers of an elective judiciary. He predicted that judicial elections would make the judiciary subservient to the dominant political faction at the time, a partisanship that would be reflected in the judges' official conduct. He cautioned that elected judges would tend to favor popular and influential litigants who appeared before him. In two of his essays, Sidney dissected Thomas Jefferson's letter of 1816 to Samuel Kercheval in which Jefferson had supported the idea of judicial elections. The sainted Jefferson's letter would be invoked again and again in future conventions. Sidney denied that the letter represented Jefferson's true position. In addition, Sidney challenged Jefferson's statement that Connecticut had had two centuries' experience with frequently elected courts.[38]

The question of judicial tenure proved controversial, causing disagreement even among opponents of judicial elections. One commentator favored appointment of judges by the governor (because he would draw judges from the whole state), with the advice and consent of the senate (which was more deliberate and coolly calculating than the house). However, he thought that lifetime appointments smacked of aristocracy. Another writer, calling himself Publius, insisted that tenure during good behavior fostered judicial independence. If judges were dependent on the legislature or executive, thought Publius, they would be too deferential to those branches and would hesitate to declare unconstitutional laws void. If judges depended on the people, they would be tempted to consult popularity in rendering decisions.[39]

The views of Chancellor Quitman are particularly interesting as he would frequently be cited by supporters of judicial elections in the mid-century constitutional conventions of other states. In a letter to the voters of Adams County, where he was campaigning for a seat at the convention, Quitman conceded the right of the people to elect their judges but denied the prudence of their doing so. A constitution, he insisted, is "intended for the benefit of the minority, to protect them against the action of the majority; to protect the weak against the strong, the poor and infirm against the rich and powerful. The judicial department is to apply these restraints. Is it not therefore improper . . . to place this department . . . under the influence and control of those who are to be restrained?" History showed that "in times of violent excitement, the many have abused their powers, and attempted to oppress and tyrannize over the minority." As examples, Quitman pointed to controversies in Kentucky over debtor-relief laws, in Georgia over the Yazoo land claims, in Alabama over usury. In all these cases, he continued, majorities were "ready to break down all constitutional restrictions, and invade the sacred rights of their fellow-citizens." It had taken a "firm, intelligent, and independent judiciary" to "check the mad career of grasping interest and ambition."[40]

At the convention, which met from September 10 to October 26, 1832, the delegates proved to be of one mind on various democratic reforms. They easily dispensed with property qualifications for officeholding, life tenures for all offices, and the taxpaying or militia qualification for voting. They also eliminated the cap on the number of representatives; with less unanimity, changed the basis of representation in the senate from free white taxable inhabitants to free white inhabitants; and switched from annual to biennial elections and legislative sessions.[41]

Judicial selection turned out to be a more contentious issue. One member of the convention divided his fellow delegates into three camps: "aristocrats," who opposed judicial elections; "whole hogs," who demanded the election of all judges; and "half hogs," who supported the election of county and circuit court judges but not supreme court judges. The judiciary committee, "much divided in sentiment," was the last committee to report. The majority proposed a court system consisting entirely of elected judges. At the top sat a separate, three-judge supreme court, called the high court of errors and appeals, the judges of which would be chosen for six-year terms. The legislature would establish judicial districts of from three to eight counties each, with every district served by a circuit court judge elected to a four-year term. Every county would have a probate judge, a board of police with administrative and limited judicial duties, and justices of the peace. The supreme court clerk would be chosen in a manner determined by law, but the lower court clerks, along with the attorney general and district attorneys, would be elected. The majority report did not provide for chancery courts, but this, according to the *Advocate & Register's* correspondent, was an accident. One of the committee members who favored courts of equity was absent when the vote on the subject was taken in committee. Had he been present, the vote would have been a tie, which the chair would have broken in favor of the courts.[42]

Quitman and Thomas P. Falconer submitted a minority report, attributed by the *Advocate & Register's* correspondent to Quitman. The report offered amendments to the existing constitution rather than an entirely new article on the judiciary. Quitman and Falconer concurred with the majority on the creation of a separate supreme court, and they would have retained the chancery court. However, they would have had the supreme court judges and chancellor appointed by the governor, with the advice and consent of the senate, to terms of six years. They recommended having circuit courts with judges appointed to six-year terms by the governor with the advice and consent of the representatives from the counties making up each circuit. The supreme court and chancellor would appoint their own clerks, but clerks of the lower courts would be elected. The report provided for probate courts but left the creation of other inferior courts to the legislature.[43]

The *Advocate & Register's* correspondent praised Quitman's report as a compromise between the pro- and anti-election camps. The appointment of circuit judges by the General Assembly, he suggested, had been plagued by logrolling, so that the people had sometimes been saddled with "some minion of power, who ha[d] never dwelt among them." By requiring the advice and consent of the representatives of the circuit, who would act under instructions from their constituents, this evil would be avoided, as would "the excitement which attends popular elections."[44]

Another member of the judiciary committee, Daniel Greenleaf, submitted a minority report of his own. He would have provided for a separate supreme court of from three to five members, popularly elected by district. The chancellor would be popularly elected to an eight-year term. Greenleaf proposed the creation of elected county courts, with the judges having four-year terms and the chief judge serving as the county probate judge. All judges would have to receive at least three-eighths of the votes cast to be elected. Greenleaf would have preferred that no candidate be elected with less than a majority. However, acknowledging the difficulty of securing a majority in many elections, he settled for a substantial plurality so that "the good sense and better judgment of nearly half of the people, would thus have to centre upon one man." The supreme court would appoint its own clerk, but all other court clerks would be elected.[45]

That a majority of the delegates favored the popular election of judges seemed obvious, but Nathaniel G. Howard, a half hog, nevertheless tried to amend the committee report. The attempt failed, 26–18, but Howard made one last try. Two days before the convention adjourned for good, he moved to amend the final document by providing for the election of supreme court judges by the General Assembly. This motion failed, too, by a vote of 25–19. Because the convention voted against submitting the final draft to a popular referendum, this vote ensured that Mississippi would become the first state to have an entirely elective judiciary.[46]

Missouri Again

Missouri nearly became the second. The Missouri constitutional convention of 1845 at one point voted for an all-elective judiciary, but ultimately it settled on elections for circuit court judges. This in itself would have been significant if the voters had not rejected the proposed constitution for other reasons. The convention nevertheless reveals the strength of pro-election sentiment in 1845.

Notwithstanding their defeat in the 1830s, advocates of judicial reform by constitutional amendment never gave up the fight. In 1843, they persuaded the legislators to adopt a proposed amendment to vacate the existing judgeships and limit judicial tenure in the future to ten years for supreme court judges and six years for circuit court judges. Whigs, who traditionally favored lifetime tenure, responded in the next General Assembly by urging that, if tenure were to be limited to a term of years, the constitution should be amended to let the people elect the judges; otherwise, the judges would be dependent on the executive. This bid failed, in part because some Democrats realized that popular elections might produce Whig judges. By the time the proposed tenure amendment came up for ratification in the next General Assembly, its prospects had become entangled with the matter of a constitutional convention.[47]

Judicial reform was only one subject, and not the most important, of constitutional revision in Missouri. Banking and, even more significantly, legislative representation generated more complaints. The constitutional requirement that every county have at least one representative could be squared with democratic theory as long as the number of counties remained small. However, as the legislature created more and more counties and the number of representatives threatened to bump up against the constitutional limit of one hundred, representation of the more heavily populated counties decreased in relation to the smaller counties.[48]

Whigs generally favored a convention, but the question divided the Democrats. The more radical, hard-money, antibank wing of the Democratic Party opposed the idea. The "soft" wing, which shared Whig views on financial matters, leaned in favor. One historian writes that the split among Democrats was primarily geographical, as Softs from under-represented areas favored reapportionment while Softs from the thinly settled, overrepresented areas opposed it. The two explanations are not inconsistent, since the lightly settled counties tended to favor hard money. Be that as it may, by 1843 support for a convention had reached a level sufficient to induce the General Assembly to put the issue to a popular referendum. The voters emphatically approved the call, which may have contributed to the defeat of the constitutional amendment then pending in the house. The purposes of the amendment, commented Democratic governor Meredith M. Marmaduke, were to make the judiciary more directly responsible to the people and to improve the bench by getting rid of dead wood. Nevertheless, Marmaduke suggested that the General Assembly might be wiser to leave changes in the judicial article to the coming constitutional convention. The house then rejected the judicial-tenure amendment, with more than half but less than two-thirds of the members voting for it.[49]

Since the beginning of statehood, a majority of legislators, and probably a majority of Missouri voters, had consistently favored the democratization of the judiciary. At the same time the principle of election of public officers had steadily gained ground. Limiting judicial tenure seems to have been a more important form of democratization than the method of selecting judges, but the election of sheriffs, coroners, court clerks, county court judges, probate judges, and justices of the peace, together with the majority vote in the General Assembly in 1833 in favor of electing circuit judges, indicates the weight that popular election carried in the public mind by the time the constitutional convention met.

Delegates to the constitutional convention would be chosen at the general election in August 1845. Although legislative apportionment was the dominant issue in discussions of the convention, some candidates for delegate also touted their positions on the election of judges. An advertisement endorsing Democrat Ezra Hunt, himself a judge, noted that in addition to favoring equalization of representation Hunt supported "the plan of electing Judges by the people—considering them the proper source of all power, and regarding them as fully competent to make the best selections for all posts of trust and honor." Democrats were not of one mind on the subject. The *Platte Argus* came out against the election of circuit court judges. The paper feared that judicial elections would either engender political partisanship in the selection of candidates or "draw forth a swarm of parrot-tongued pettifoggers, as candidates." In either case the cause of impartial justice would suffer. A pseudonymous writer to the *Democratic Banner* offered a two-fold response. First, argued T.S.R., if the judges turned out to be partisan, they would be no more so than those appointed by the governor—and at least the people "would have the man of their choice." Second, if the people were competent to elect legislators to make laws and governors to enforce them, they were equally capable of choosing judges to interpret them; after all, the people already elected justices of the peace and county court judges.[50]

T.S.R. "was no little astonished" that the Democrats of Platte County would oppose the popular election of judges. He noted that even Whigs seemed generally in support, although he questioned their motives, believing them to be in favor only so they could get their own men elected in some districts. In any case, it appears that judicial elections, at least at the circuit level, had widespread popular support.[51]

The convention met from November 17, 1845, to January 14, 1846. Delegate Miron Leslie, a prominent Democratic attorney, offered the first judicial plan. Under Leslie's proposal, the judicial system would consist of a supreme court made up of the circuit judges; circuit judges elected by an unspecified body of voters (presumably, either the electors of each circuit or the members of the General Assembly); and such inferior courts as the legislature might create. Judicial terms would be limited—Leslie left the number of years blank—justices of the peace would be elected, court clerks would be appointed by the courts, and the governor would be able to remove any supreme or circuit court judge on address of two-thirds of each house of the General Assembly. Later that day the judiciary committee, chaired by Ezra Hunt, reported that it was evenly divided between two plans, one to create separate circuit and supreme courts, the other to have the circuit judges meet together as a supreme court. Under either system the judges would be elected by the people. The committee asked for instructions regarding the scheme preferred by the delegates. A week later Hunt offered resolutions that there be separate circuit and supreme courts, the judges of each to be elected for limited terms, together with a probate and county court in each county.[52]

When the Leslie and Hunt resolutions came up for debate, the convention postponed discussion of Leslie's plan and turned to Hunt's. The delegates voted 43–16 that circuit judges be popularly elected. Edwin D. Bevitt, another Democrat, then moved to amend Hunt's plan to provide that the supreme court judges be elected by districts of equal population. The delegates agreed 29–25 to retain the popular election of the court but rejected election by districts, 31–23. After defeating, by a vote of 46–12, an amendment to have the supreme court judges chosen by the General

Assembly, the delegates seemed to have settled on the popular election of all judges.[53]

However, two days later the convention voted 39–21 to reconsider Bevitt's amendment. The close vote in favor of popular election appeared to be turning heavily against. A delegate then proposed that the supreme court judges be appointed by the governor with the advice and consent of the senate. Following a debate that focused on the number of supreme court judges and the length of their terms, the convention agreed that the supreme court would consist of three judges appointed by the governor for terms of twelve years. The final vote was 32–29, but it is hard to tell from the journal how many of the negative votes represented opposition to an appointed supreme court and how many indicated objections only to the specific form that the appointive system took.[54]

Notwithstanding the defeat of popular election of supreme court judges at the convention, the proposed constitution continued the trend toward democratization of the judiciary. It provided for the election of circuit court judges for six-year terms and abolished life tenure for the judges of the supreme court.[55]

The end of the convention in January 1846 brought the contest over ratification. The new constitution was doomed from the start. One-fifth of the convention delegates had voted against the draft, and eight refused to sign it. Even some of its supporters gave it only tepid praise. The *Democratic Banner*, for example, characterized ratification as the lesser of two evils. Opponents stressed the convention's failure to equalize representation in the legislature and the proposed constitution's provisions on banking and corporations. The subject of judicial elections played a minor role in the debate. At the August election, the voters sent the new constitution down to defeat.[56]

The setback for the cause of judicial elections proved to be temporary. Following the referendum, a reader of the *Boon's Lick Times* offered a list of three constitutional amendments he believed the people would support. The most important was a plan for legislative representation (the paper editorializing that no other changes should be attempted until representation was fixed), followed by the elimination of all provisions relating to banks, corporations, and internal improvements, and, finally, the popular election of judges. The legislature soon took these subjects under advisement. Representation received the lion's share of attention from the legislators and the press during the 1846–47 session of the General Assembly, but lawmakers also offered various amendments related to the courts. The house overwhelmingly passed an amendment to provide for the election of circuit judges every six years. A majority of senators favored the proposal as well, but not the necessary two-thirds. However, the General Assembly did adopt an amendment to limit the tenure of supreme court judges to twelve years and of circuit court judges to eight years. The next General Assembly ratified the amendment in January 1849 with little opposition.[57]

The 1849 amendment finally abolished life tenure for judges in Missouri, a longtime goal of judicial reformers. However, it left intact the gubernatorial power of appointment. But simultaneously with its adoption of limited tenure, the General Assembly took up the issue of judicial elections. On January 10, 1849, the house "debated at length" what one paper called "the most important subject before the House . . . introduced *this* session," the election of circuit judges. In February, Representative DeWitt C. Ballou introduced a proposal to elect the judges of the supreme court. Neither measure triggered much editorial comment. There was some debate among lawmakers concerning the circuit courts, but it did not involve the principle of election. Both proposals passed with minimal dissent in the house and none in the senate. The judicial amendments also reduced the tenure of judges at both levels to six years. Another amendment making elective the state executive offices (the secretary of state, attorney general, auditor, treasurer, and register of lands) progressed through the legislature at the same time. It, too, passed with little opposition.[58]

The amendments still had to be ratified by the next General Assembly, which did not meet until December 30, 1850, but ratification was a foregone conclusion. When the judicial election amendments came up for final passage in February 1851, only one member of either house voted against them. The executive election amendment passed as well. Because the amendments did not have to be submitted to the voters for approval, they immediately became part of the constitution.[59]

The South's Place in the Advance of Judicial Elections

The South did not stand alone in the early push for judicial elections. The first major debate over judicial elections took place at the New York constitutional convention of 1821. Although that controversy involved justices of the peace, the arguments pro and con adumbrated those that would appear in subsequent conventions in the Empire State and elsewhere. In 1846, New York would become the second state to adopt an

The Southern Roots of the Elective Judiciary 35

all-elective judiciary. Michigan took a small step toward the popular election of "real" judges in 1835 when its first constitutional convention provided for the election of county court judges. However, the territorial legislature had abolished county courts in 1833; the state legislature would not resurrect them until 1846. Iowans went further when their convention of 1844, held in preparation for statehood, proposed the popular election of district court judges. The voters defeated the constitution, but a second convention two years later drafted another constitution with the same provision. This time the electors ratified the document (three months before New Yorkers ratified their new constitution.)[60]

Why did Mississippi, Missouri, Michigan, Iowa, and New York, and not any of the other twenty-four states that belonged to the Union by the end of 1846, pave the way for judicial elections? History is full of contingency and chance. For example, many of Mississippi's leading politicians chose not to run for convention delegate in 1832 because they were busy seeking other offices to be filled at the same election, leaving the way open for "[l]ower-level backbenchers and Whole Hog outsiders" to win seats instead. The result was a narrow victory for judicial elections. Had the timing of the election of delegates been different, Mississippi might have retained an appointive judiciary.[61]

Every state had its own political dynamics and particular circumstances that affected the fate of judicial elections. The important question for understanding the rise of judicial elections is not what happenstance brought them about in any given state but what the far-flung states of Mississippi, Missouri, Michigan, Iowa, and New York had in common that made them likely locales for the switch in judicial selection (bearing in mind the rejection of Missouri's constitution at the polls).

One key shared feature was the phenomenal demographic growth in the five states. In Mississippi and Missouri, the spectacular rise in population upset constitutional arrangements for legislative representation and exacerbated conflicts between urban and rural areas. In those states and New York, growth overwhelmed judicial systems that were constrained by constitutional limits on their size and burdened by duties constitutionally imposed. Michigan and Iowa, as territories preparing for statehood, would have to keep these experiences in mind in framing their own constitutions.

The multitudes who flocked to New York City and St. Louis, to the Mississippi back country and the plains of Iowa, were not aristocrats. They were poor Irish immigrants, landless men, farmers looking for larger or fresher holdings, young lawyers and doctors escaping the competition back home. Whether they ended up as Democrats, Whigs, or something else, Jacksonian egalitarianism appealed to them. The states and territories west of the Appalachian Mountains were especially open to change. Tradition, including the tradition of respect for venerable appointed judiciaries in some of the eastern states, had a hard time taking hold where the population not only grew rapidly but moved about constantly—and the West had a highly mobile population.[62]

A leading historian of judicial elections dismisses Mississippi as a "laboratory with no prestige"[63] and instead, along with many other observers, credits New York with starting the judicial-elections crusade. But if we view the crusade, as it pertains to "real" judges, as a movement building momentum through the Jacksonian era, the wave rolled from West to East—from Mississippi, Missouri, Michigan, and Iowa to New York. It is New York that appears to be an anomaly. Indeed, of the sixteen eastern states, ten never adopted judicial elections at all in the antebellum period, one did so only for its lower courts, and two backtracked before or during the Civil War. The western states did not need New York to lead the way.

In addition to booming populations, the pioneering states shared a Jeffersonian constitutional culture. All enjoyed more or less free suffrage and equal representation. It is true that even constitutions that allowed all white men to vote, without property or religious qualifications, could restrict suffrage in various ways. Long residency requirements, for example, could exclude many men from the franchise, especially given the highly mobile nature of the population. Citizenship requirements kept many immigrants from the polls. But the elimination of property qualifications had extended the franchise to the vast majority of white men.

Legislative apportionment in the five states failed to provide truly equal representation, but it approached the Jeffersonian ideal. The common constitutional mandate that every county have at least one representative, while democratic in the sense of ensuring that all parts of a state had a voice in the legislature, caused serious deviations from the principle of equality, especially when the constitution placed a ceiling on the number of representatives. Slave states that used the federal basis of apportionment (counting three-fifths of slaves in the population on which representation was allotted) skewed representation in favor of slaveholding counties. Still, constitutions that made population the primary criterion for apportionment acknowledged the fundamental significance of equal representation. When small-county Democrats in Missouri argued that they needed to have their own representatives to watch over their interests, an embarrassed Democratic convention delegate lamented, "I find my own political friends advocating aristocratic doctrines—and my Whig friends advocating the pure doctrines of democracy." "All whigs and democrats," commented a Missouri newspaper, "seem to regard [equal representation] as the very life boat of our government."[64]

By the time of the Iowa, Missouri, and New York constitutional conventions, most states had thrown off suffrage restrictions and had accepted some form of population-based legislative apportionment. Reformers in states that had done neither had bigger things to worry about than the popular election of judges. They were fighting for the more elemental aspects of democracy. In fact, demands for an elective judiciary did not significantly contribute to the calling of a constitutional convention anywhere. Judicial elections typically came about in states where most people took the Jeffersonian standard of basic democracy for granted but had other grievances—a system of representation made obsolete by demographic developments, overburdened courts, out-of-control public debt—great enough to drag judicial elections in their wake.

CHAPTER 2

The South's Northern Tier

The four slave states that would refuse to secede on the eve of the Civil War ranged from tiny, three-county Delaware on the Atlantic to big Missouri, with more than one hundred counties, lying west of the Mississippi. These border states did not constitute a distinct region the way New England or the Old Northwest did. Virginia separated Delaware and Maryland from Kentucky and Missouri, and even Kentucky and Missouri, separated from each other by the Mississippi River, barely adjoined. But the presence of slavery in all four gave them enough of a southern social and cultural caste to prompt southerners to claim them as sister states.

The border states exemplify the west-to-east course of the movement toward judicial elections. Although Missouri did not adopt an elective judiciary until 1851, the state had been moving in that direction since the 1830s, if not before. Kentucky made the transition at its constitutional convention of 1849–50 and Maryland at its convention of 1850–51. Delaware's proposed constitution of 1853 provided for judicial elections but lost at the polls for other reasons.

Some historians have attributed the constitutional reform movement of the mid-nineteenth century to the state fiscal crises that followed the financial panics of the late 1830s, which in turn stemmed from extravagant state spending on poorly planned internal improvement projects.[1] Although the role of the fiscal crises has been overstated,[2] there is no question that they contributed significantly to public discontent with existing constitutional arrangements in New York, Ohio, Indiana, Illinois, and Michigan. In this regard, Kentucky and Maryland resembled those northern states. But neither Missouri nor Delaware suffered from similar financial catastrophes. Delaware had no public debt at all. Rather, the reform movements in the border states were impelled by more characteristically southern grievances: undemocratic local government in Kentucky and legislative malapportionment in Missouri, Maryland, and Delaware.

To be sure, these problems were not unique to the South. In Massachusetts, for example, complaints about legislative apportionment helped trigger a constitutional convention in 1853. But the complainants there were not from growing, underrepresented parts of the state. Rather, they were small-town folks who feared being overwhelmed by the rising urban areas if representation were according to population.[3] Many southern states faced the opposite situation. Lopsided legislative apportionment led to demands for a fairer system of representation based on population. As discussed in the previous chapter, malapportionment, more than any other issue, drove the constitutional reform movement in Missouri.

Gripes about local government also could be heard in the North. For instance, in 1848 the Vermont council of censors, a body elected to recommend amendments to the state constitution, urged that more local officers be elected and that the territorial jurisdiction of justices of the peace be reduced.[4] But northern justices of the peace and local courts had nowhere near the authority of their southern counterparts. County and township government in the North was generally in the hands of elected officers. By the mid-1840s, even justices of the peace were elected except in New England (and Rhode Island was an exception to the exception). The uprising against county courts that occurred in Kentucky and Virginia could not have occurred in the North.

Kentucky

The settlers of Kentucky during the American Revolution were mostly poor people in search of land or escapees from the tribulations of war. Many of the immigrants who arrived after the Revolution came from a higher social class. Among the latter was George Nicholas, scion of a prominent Virginia attorney and himself a lawyer, law professor, and legislator. Nicholas moved to Kentucky in 1789. When the proponents of statehood needed the guidance of a man trained in law and politics, they turned to Nicholas, who became the dominant figure at the Kentucky constitutional convention of 1792.[5]

Nicholas has been called an accommodationist, one who sought to blend the interests of the elite with the democratic aspirations of the majority. The constitution produced under Nicholas's guidance reflected his accommodationist beliefs. Its democratic features included free suffrage; apportionment of the house of representatives according to the number of free male inhabitants in each county; and the popular election of sheriffs and coroners. Its undemocratic sections provided for the indirect election of the governor and senators and the appointment by the governor, with the advice and consent of the senate, of most public officers (although the state treasurer was to be chosen by the General Assembly).[6]

Notwithstanding the elective offices of sheriff and coroner, county government was not democratic. Kentucky had begun its political life as a county of Virginia, where county courts dominated local government. Kentucky inherited the Virginia system. The county courts, composed of appointed justices of the peace, who also made up the courts of quarter sessions (courts that met four times annually in each county), had jurisdiction over civil matters not expressly vested in the court of quarter sessions and over probate and guardianship matters. They admitted deeds and other writings to record and heard all cases involving roads and mills and anything else they already had cognizance of before Kentucky became a state. In its first session, the General Assembly authorized the county courts to appoint tax commissioners and to lay out taxing districts. Three years after that, the legislature imposed a wide range of administrative duties on the county courts: superintending the inspection of agricultural products, regulating ferries, providing for the poor, erecting and maintaining public buildings, and more.[7]

In the first few years of statehood, the population exploded, tripling between 1790 and 1800, and conflict between ordinary folks and the "aristocracy" of planters and businessmen grew. John Breckinridge, a leading lawyer and planter in the prosperous Bluegrass region, exemplified the social division when he described the Green River country to the southwest as being "filled with nothing but hunters, horse-thieves & savages . . . where wretchedness, poverty & sickness will always reign." Every branch of government managed to make itself unpopular. The court of appeals, the state's highest court, so antagonized Kentuckians with a decision upsetting land titles that the legislature took away its jurisdiction over such cases and tried to remove two of the judges from office. Gubernatorial candidates and senators battled over a disputed election for governor. The senate came to be regarded as an undemocratic "rich man's club."[8]

Popular pressure brought about a second constitutional convention in 1799. The delegates quickly drafted a new constitution that retained free suffrage; extended apportionment in accordance with population to the senate; provided for the direct election of the governor and senators;

limited the governor to one term at a time; and watered down the veto so that it could be overridden a simple majority of each house. In other words, the new constitution embodied the essentials of Jeffersonian democracy.[9]

However, compromises diluted these democratic gains. The economically dominant "aristocrats" probably would have retained their political ascendancy in any case, but a switch from ballots to oral voting no doubt eased their concerns about the preferences of their clients and dependents. The slaveholders' fears for the security of their human property were allayed by a prohibition of any law providing for the emancipation of slaves without either the owners' consent or payment to the owners of "a full equivalent in money" prior to emancipation. The constitution changed the basis of legislative apportionment from the number of adult "free male inhabitants" to "qualified electors," a change that excluded recent immigrants from other states.[10]

Local government became less democratic. The county courts received constitutional status, their justices having tenure during good behavior. Every sheriff was now to be appointed by the governor from two county court justices recommended by his fellow justices. Similarly, whenever a county needed a surveyor, coroner, or justice of the peace, the county court would send two nominees to the governor, who would choose between them to fill the office. In short, the county courts became more powerful and self-perpetuating by constitutional provision. And the constitution itself became more difficult to amend. The new constitution took effect without being submitted to the voters for ratification.[11]

The constitution of 1799 lasted for half a century, but not because the citizens loved it. By the 1840s, complaints about the constitution had grown to serious proportions. Later in the century, Bennett H. Young, a prominent Kentucky lawyer, would enumerate seven major issues: slave emancipation, the selection of public officers, the use of state credit for internal improvements, the organization of the court system, dueling, legislative apportionment, and public support for common schools. One contemporary reform agenda adopted at a public meeting urged the following changes: abolition of all life tenures; "making *all* officers of the government (from the highest to the lowest grade) elective by the people"; having biennial legislative sessions; "some modification" of the county court system; securing and perpetuating the common school fund; and an amendment procedure by which all proposed changes would be submitted to the people. The meeting approved the last proposed reform, along with a pro-emancipation resolution, only after its opponents were asked to leave. This occurred after the voters had endorsed the calling of a convention in two successive referenda, as required by the constitution. In both 1847 and 1848, more than two-thirds of the voters favored the call.[12]

The question of slavery worked its way into every aspect of the convention debate. Kentucky had an active emancipationist movement in the 1840s. It would prove far too weak to get an emancipation clause into the constitution, but it stoked fear among the proslavery forces. During the period leading up to the convention, the Friends of Constitutional Reform, an anti-emancipation organization, insisted that the people had called for a convention in order to create a government more responsive to them, not to free the slaves. Whigs, who tended to be both more cautious than Democrats about altering the constitution and more favorable toward emancipation, implied that Democrats advocated radical reforms in order to protect slavery.[13]

But the demands for democratization were genuine. According to Young, the 1849 convention "came together with the almost unanimous purpose, and with instructions from the people to abolish all provisions for patronage and to remit all elevation of office to the people themselves." Under the existing constitution, the governor appointed all the state's judges and hundreds of other officeholders. With twenty or more appointed officials per county, over two thousand officeholders owed their positions to the governor. Because the Whigs regularly won gubernatorial races, most of the appointees were Whigs. The courts had patronage power, too. The courts appointed their own clerks who held their offices indefinitely during good behavior, making the clerkships plum positions often granted to the judges' relatives and friends. Counties became fiefdoms under the control of the county courts, as the judges perpetuated themselves in office and sold other offices to the highest bidders. One Kentucky historian wrote that "[t]hese absolute powers, coupled with official independence, produced so much nepotism and favoritism, and so grave did this abuse become, that . . . it affected the respect of the people for the judges themselves." Worse yet, "the open bargain and sale" of public offices turned the system of appointments into a "vast mart for the sale and retention of official plunder."[14]

The abuse of patronage was not the only judicial problem. Circuit court decisions in criminal cases could not be appealed, which not only produced inconsistencies among the circuits but gave the circuit judges, already beyond popular control due to their lifetime appointments, absolute power over "questions of life and liberty."[15]

The matter of apportionment throws some light, however obliquely, on the subject of judicial selection. The constitution apportioned the house according to the number of qualified voters in each county or district. (By the time of the convention, the city of Louisville qualified for separate representation in the house.) The Ohio River counties and Louisville, which were growing faster than the rest of the state, wanted representation to be based on the entire white population, including women and children, and not on the number of voters. In the debates at the convention, the delegates would argue over who would gain and who would lose from basing representation on the total white population, with statistics on the number of children in different counties being tossed about. The real issue, though, was that the northern counties, swelling with immigrants, favored emancipation. A delegate from northern Kentucky insisted that his part of the state would protect slavery, but members from the slaveholding counties would not be mollified by such assurances.[16]

The struggles over emancipation and representation necessarily involved the question of majority rule. Proslavery convention delegates, although they would succeed on these issues, repeatedly warned of the tyranny of the majority. When Archibald Dixon introduced an amendment to the bill of rights asserting "[t]hat absolute, arbitrary power over the lives, liberty, and property of freemen, (except for crimes,) exists nowhere in a republic—not even in the largest majority," the debate quickly devolved from abstract principles to proslavery denunciations of majoritarian threats to property in slaves. The convention adopted the amendment by a vote of 55–34.[17]

Given this fear of majorities, it is not hard to imagine a concern lurking in the minds of proslavery delegates that a popularly elected judge might not be committed to the judicial protection of slave property. Garrett Davis, a proponent of slavery and the convention's most outspoken opponent of judicial elections, claimed that the Ohio General Assembly, under the influence of popular agitation, had recently elected an abolitionist judge who had pledged to declare the state's fugitive slave law unconstitutional. In a debate over a proposition to allow the legislature to remove a judge from office by a majority vote of each house, William C. Bullitt, a major slaveowner who objected to judicial elections in principle, argued that the proposal would eliminate the judicial veto over unconstitutional acts of the legislature, for a judge who struck down a statute could promptly be removed by the same majority that had passed the law. This fear of legislative majorities could well have carried over into a dread that an emancipationist majority of voters might elect likeminded judges. If proslavery delegates did not make that argument explicitly, it may have been because, like Bullitt, they recognized the popularity of judicial elections among their constituents.[18]

Whatever suspicions proslavery delegates may have harbored concerning the popular election of judges, the incorporation of judicial elections into the constitution was never in doubt. However, a debate on its propriety did arise in connection with other matters: Should judges be removable from office by means other than impeachment? If so, what should be the process of removal? What should be the tenure of elected judges? If tenure were to be a term of years rather than during good behavior, should judges be eligible for reelection upon the expiration of their terms? In discussing these questions, the delegates marshalled many of the same arguments that members of other conventions deployed in debate over judicial elections. As one delegate remarked, "the principle of re-eligibility [is] inseparable from, and identical with, that of the election of the judiciary."[19]

The most impressive speech on the elective judiciary came from Whig Garrett Davis, a former state representative and congressman and future United States senator. In a two-hour oration that would occupy eleven pages in the published report of the debates, Davis took a stand directly against judicial elections. He began with a lecture on the nature of constitutional government. The great advantage of the American system of government over all other forms, said Davis, was "the division of government into departments, and its distribution among various officers and classes of officers, who shall co-ordinate, and who shall be a check against the encroachment of each other. These form a protection to the people, and to the rights which are reserved by the constitution for the people, and which are not at all intended to be given into the political scheme." The people could not be trusted with unchecked power, and they knew it. That was why they declared certain rights to be inalienable and placed them beyond the reach of a political majority.[20]

By way of example, Davis raised two specters then troubling Kentucky. Suppose, he said, that every adult male in the state should resolve that the slaves should be emancipated without compensation to the owners. What would be the effect of the resolution? "It would be unconstitutional, and it would be void; and a judiciary, able, understanding the principles of the constitution, impartial, independent, would rise above the raging storm, and would not allow this great principle in the constitution to be violated, that the people of the state of Kentucky cannot wrest from any man his property, without just compensation being made to him." Or suppose that the influx of Catholic immigrants should swell to such an extent that Catholics would become the majority and then, in obedience to their "despotic religion," attempt to suppress Protestantism. The constitutional principle of freedom of conscience would stand in their way.[21]

An elective judiciary, Davis continued, would inevitably be a political judiciary, as (he claimed) the examples of Mississippi and New York had demonstrated. Judicial candidates would be chosen by the parties in the same way as candidates for other offices were nominated: by party "cabals and juntos . . . not for their virtue, intelligence or legal attainments, but because of their political popularity and availability." And when the courts were filled with party hacks, "what then becomes of the protection which the constitution and laws promise the citizen?"[22]

Davis had delivered an "able and powerful speech," a "speech of transcendent ability," but one witness doubted "that there is another man in the convention who will vote against the election of judges." Davis's discourse, declared delegate Silas Woodson, when stripped down to its essentials, was nothing more than an effort to demonstrate "man's corruption and incompetency for self-government." But depictions of the appointed judiciary as a noble body of honest and principled men above the political fray could not overcome public disgust with the patronage system. The "practical question," argued Woodson, was whether the governor had "more discernment, more purity, more intelligence than one-half the voting population of Kentucky." With an eye on the "arrogant and sycophantic" men who constantly beset governors for office, the "lazy, idle, noisy partizans, who infest the country," Woodson insisted that the people could be trusted more than the governor to know who was most fit for judicial office.[23]

Given the extent of revulsion toward government in general and patronage in particular, there was no chance of defeating the elective system. The initial report of the Committee on the Court of Appeals, Kentucky's highest court, provided for the election of four judges, one from each of four appellate districts into which the state was to be divided. (The committee subsequently submitted a slightly amended report that required the approximate equality of the districts in voting population and the election of court of appeals judges and clerks by ballot, as opposed to *viva voce* [vocally].) The report also included the election of a court clerk for each district. The committees on circuit courts and county courts similarly recommended the popular election of judges, court clerks, state attorneys, justices of the peace, and constables. Due to problems with the completion of the report on circuit courts, the delegates ultimately decided that the three judiciary committees should be consolidated into one. The joint committee retained judicial elections in all cases. Every time a section of the report that made the judgeships elective came before the convention for consideration, the members adopted it without debate or a recorded vote.[24]

Even skeptics supported judicial elections. Elijah F. Nuttall, a staunch Democrat who described himself as "one of the people, a demagogue, if you please," opposed the elective judiciary in principle but vowed to vote for it because that was what his constituents demanded. At the same time, he backed the proposal to allow the legislature to remove a judge by a majority vote. Before the convention, Nuttall had not favored judicial elections "until the popular clamor . . . had swept over this commonwealth, and had swept off every man who was disposed to stand up for the independence of the judiciary. . . . We all had to give way." Now he was bound by his constituents to vote for judicial elections, but he still regarded such elections as far more dangerous than the removal of judges by a simple legislative majority.[25]

Although the delegates agreed on creating an elective judiciary, they disputed the manner of election. Kentucky had had *viva voce* voting since 1799, but when Charles A. Wickliffe submitted the report on the court of appeals, he stated that the committee favored voting for judges by secret ballot. The report did not specify the method of voting, said Wickliffe, only because the committee thought it best to await the reports of the other judiciary committees. A debate of sorts, consisting of remarks scattered throughout the proceedings, pitted pro-ballot delegates who worried that a judge might be biased against litigants who were known to have opposed his election against anti-ballot delegates who thought the *viva voce* mode more manly and voting by ballot degrading. The Committee on Miscellaneous Provisions recommended *viva voce* voting in all elections. When the report came before the convention, William Preston, who had previously urged that judicial elections be by ballot, moved an amendment to allow the legislature to prescribe the method of voting. The motion failed, 68–22. The constitution would require that in all elections, "votes shall be personally and publicly given, viva voce," with an exception limited to individuals who could not speak.[26]

The constitution as finally drafted worked a radical democratization of Kentucky's government. Most public officers, including judges, would now be elected by the people for specified terms, none more than eight years (judges of the court of appeals). The new constitution attempted to impose state fiscal responsibility with a debt ceiling, a requirement that taxes be levied to pay for any obligations incurred, and a ban on the lending of state credit to any individual or corporation. It sought to hold the General Assembly more accountable with biennial sessions, a limit to the length of sessions, and a requirement that every bill deal with one subject only. These and other changes made the document far more democratic than its predecessors. In a referendum on ratification in May 1850, 78 percent of the voters approved the new constitution.[27]

The conversion of Kentucky to an elective judiciary was in part a bottom-up affair. At the time of the constitutional convention, Kentucky enjoyed the essentials of Jeffersonian democracy—free suffrage and equal representation. But Jefferson would have been appalled by the undemocratic nature of local government, as were most Kentuckians. The desire to democratize the "aristocratic" county courts, reinforced by disgust with gubernatorial patronage, fueled the constitutional reform movement. It is possible that even without these causes the demands of emancipationists or the rising public debt would have led to a constitutional convention and, as an adjunct of other reforms, an elective judiciary. But in the actual Kentucky of the late 1840s, the elective judiciary was more than an abstract principle. The people especially loathed the appointment of judges who constituted their local governments. The argument that judges were different from other public officers and had to be insulated from popular influence might have carried more weight had county government been more accountable to the people. As it was, the title of "judge" had lost its aura of sanctity.

Maryland

In Maryland, as in Kentucky, a multiplicity of complaints led to a midcentury constitutional convention. A reform agenda of 1845 included: (1) the annual election of the governor and the popular election of all public officers except judges; (2) a complete revamping of the insolvency and debt laws; (3) an end to private legislation and the enactment of a general incorporation law; (4) a separation of the duties of clerks of courts and registers of deeds, with registers elected every year or two; (5) a reorganization of the court system, abolition of the offices of chancellor and attorney general, and the creation of the office of county prosecutor; (6) the annual, popular election of the secretary of state and state treasurer; and (7) remodeling of the Baltimore City Court and abolition of "the system of planting justices of the peace all over the city." Several of the agenda items included state salaries for public officers, apparently in the belief that the officers were overpaid.[28]

Two issues conspicuously missing from this list were the public debt and malapportionment of the legislature. Historians would later attribute the calling of the convention to these causes more than any other. Public debt and legislative apportionment headed the roster of reform topics recorded by James Warner Harry in his early-twentieth-century study of Maryland's constitution. According to Harry, the called-for reforms included "a change in the system of representation in the House of Delegates; limitation upon the power of the General Assembly to contract debts, or pledge the public credit; reduction in governmental expenses; the right to elect all local county officers; a reform of the judicial system, and especially a constitutional convention, elected directly by the people for the express purpose of framing a new constitution."[29]

How important each of these questions was in the calling of the convention is hard to gauge. A few days before a referendum held in 1850 to ascertain the "sense of people . . . as to the expediency of calling a [constitutional] Convention," one newspaper complained that while everyone agreed on the need for a convention, no one ever explained why. Historian Fletcher M. Green ascribed the "real beginnings" of Maryland's mid-century constitutional reform movement to the high debt and taxation resulting from internal improvement disasters. The problem of public debt did indeed amount to a calamity. Incurred mostly from state participation in failed internal improvement projects, the debt had become unsustainable by the early 1840s, causing a suspension of interest payments on state bonds and bringing Maryland close to outright repudiation. By 1848, though, the crisis had largely passed. The system of representation in the General Assembly, on the other hand, remained a leading cause of discontent.[30]

Maryland underwent a constitutional transformation in 1836–37 that moved the state in a democratic direction. Constitutional amendments passed in 1810 had established free suffrage and abolished property qualifications for holding office, but malapportionment of the legislature had only gotten worse. The constitution of 1776 allotted to each county four members in the house of delegates, which, due to the rapid population growth of Baltimore and the Western Shore of the Chesapeake Bay, produced a growing imbalance. Two electors from each county chose the senators, so in the senate, too, the smaller counties wielded disproportionate power. The relatively small slaveholding counties were loath to yield any of their muscle lest the antislavery west and north somehow interfere with their human property.[31]

After surviving threats of extra-constitutional action, denounced by an anonymous opponent as a "revolutionary scheme," the Whig conservatives in the General Assembly agreed to several important reforms. These included apportionment of the house that took population into account, although Baltimore would have no more delegates than the largest county (which, in turn, was capped at six delegates) and even the smallest counties had three delegates; direct election of senators; popular election of the governor (theretofore chosen by the legislature); abolition of the governor's council (an executive body that, among other things, had to consent to gubernatorial appointments); and the subjection of gubernatorial appointments to the advice and consent of the senate.[32]

The reforms dampened discontent for a time, but they weren't enough. Between 1830 and 1850, Baltimore's population grew 110 percent while that of the rest of the state increased by only 13 percent. In 1850, Baltimore's inhabitants made up 29 percent of the state total. What the city wanted was representation according to population. The Baltimore city council, grieved at the "peculiar hardship" borne by Baltimore as a result of "unequal and unjust" laws, insisted that "representation according to population, is the creed of republicans; the only true and safe basis of government; and ought to be enjoyed by every American." "[T]he design of much the largest number of those, who are pressing this subject of a [constitutional] convention," declared one group of Maryland legislators, "is to change the basis of representation from the present mixed basis of population and territory, to one founded exclusively on numbers."[33]

Where in all this was the elective judiciary? In 1845 and 1846, when constitutional conventions elsewhere were considering the subject, the Whig *American Republic* inveighed against the popular election of judges, and the neutral *Baltimore Sun* published a column by an anonymous author opposing judicial elections. However, the idea seems not to have excited much interest thereafter until after the referendum of May 1850 approving the constitutional convention. (In 1849, though, the Baltimore Murray Institute, an organization formed to promote knowledge, morality, and religion among Baltimore's young men, invited the public to attend a discussion of the question, "Should Judges of the Courts be elected by the People?") During the summer and fall of 1850, the *Sun* advocated judicial elections. Some Whigs remained dubious. A Whig convention in Harford County, for example, adopted resolutions opposing judicial elections but favoring the election of clerks and registers. But the Whig candidate for governor that year came out for the election of "all officers by the people."[34]

Before the convention got fairly under way, Maryland newspapers anticipated easy acceptance of the popular election of local officials but thought that judicial elections would meet stiff resistance. It is certainly true that the reforms demanded by a significant portion of the population did not include an elective judiciary. At least two delegates, George Brent and John F. Dent, insisted, less plausibly, that representation was not a significant issue either. Reform of the system of representation definitely meant a great deal to Baltimoreans. Brent's and Dent's constituents, though, may have seen such reform as a threat. Brent hailed from Charles County and Dent from St. Mary's County, jurisdictions in the extreme southern part of the state where slavery flourished. For them, apportionment solely on the basis of population meant subjecting slaveholders to the tyranny of the majority. "It becomes us then of the southern and less populous counties of the State," proclaimed Dent, "to guard now, while we have it in our power to do it, against this tyranny of which we are warned, and which may, and I verily believe will, come upon us in the course of time, if we neglect now to hold on to that power or such a part of it as will enable us to protect our interests. I mean the institution of slavery."[35]

The fear of a majoritarian menace to slavery made its way into the debate over judicial selection. The most notable defense of an appointive judiciary came from Ezekiel F. Chambers, the chief judge of the state and a slave-owning convention delegate from Kent County. In company with opponents of judicial elections elsewhere, Chambers maintained that one vital purpose of an independent judiciary was the protection of individuals from popular passions. Judicial protection, he declared, extends to "[t]hose who are peculiarly exposed, whether by reason of infirmity of character, physical or moral; from the want of pecuniary means, or popular favor; or from any other cause; aye, even from deformity or depravity of moral principle—all, who are especially obnoxious to the excited passions or prejudices of others." To carry out this "high and moral obligation," a judge had to be independent, that is, free from "all other influences." His tenure of office had to "depend, not on the frowns and smiles of those upon whose rights he may pass judgment, but upon his faithfulness and firmness—*upon his 'good behaviour.'*"[36]

Of those who believed that judges should be dependent upon the sovereign people Chambers asked, "Will it be pretended, much less will it be believed, that each man for himself, investigates the facts of the case; and with a full understanding of them, and of the obligations of the law, calmly decides upon the moral conduct of the judge, and regulates his vote accordingly?" Everyone knew that the voter's decision "will be the result of prejudice, or interest, of excited feelings and passions." Moreover, the typical voter's decision was not really his own. There were men of influence who controlled dozens of votes. In litigation between a popular, well-to-do man and a poor or unpopular one, an elected judge could hardly be expected to remain impartial.[37]

So far, Chambers's argument, lengthy and coherent as it was, consisted in substance of the standard fare at midcentury constitutional conventions. But Chambers then turned judicial independence into a defense of slavery from abolitionist attacks. Chambers expressly denounced the fanaticism of abolitionism. After reciting the horrors of the French Revolution, he declaimed: "[W]e need not go abroad to find instances of popular delusion. . . . What makes us tremble for the very existence of our institutions. . . ? Is it not the delusion, the excitement, the frenzy, the madness of our people? . . . What is abolitionism doing, at this moment?" (Just days before Chambers spoke, the trial of fugitive slave Thomas Sims had concluded in Boston. Abolitionists had tried to help Sims escape. Three months before that, Boston abolitionists had succeeded in rescuing another fugitive slave.) How independent could a judge be when he was reliant on such a people? Fortunately, said Chambers, adverting to several federal judges, the country had "firm and faithful judges, independent of all popular clamor; holding their 'commissions during good behaviour'; who standing on the rock of real independence, have fearlessly opposed the storm. This you could never rationally expect from one, who depended, for his official life and character, upon popular favor."[38]

Notwithstanding the anticipation of difficulties for the elective judiciary at the convention and the strenuous opposition of Chief Judge Chambers, the delegates easily approved judicial elections. The judiciary committee provided for elected judges in its report, with terms of office set at ten years (two years for justices of the peace). Delegates who opposed judicial elections tried unsuccessfully to amend the report. One proposal would have given the selection of judges of the court of appeals to the General Assembly. It lost by a vote of 53–17. Another would have given the choice to the governor, with the advice and consent of the senate. It failed, 45–18. A third proposed amendment sought to have the legislature send to the governor three nominees for each position on the court, one of whom the governor would appoint. It, too, lost by a lopsided vote. When it became obvious that assaults on the elective judiciary had no prayer of success, skeptics tried lengthening the tenure of office to fourteen or twenty years or even during good behavior. These efforts also went for nought. For all the debate on judicial selection, the outcome was never in doubt. Under the new constitution, Marylanders would elect their "real" judges for ten-year terms. They would also elect their court clerks, orphans' court judges, registers of wills, justices of the peace, constables, sheriffs, and county prosecutors.[39]

The election of judges had not, in and of itself, been a compelling reason for calling the convention. It had been part of a larger demand for democratization of the constitution, which meant, among other things, giving the people the power to choose public officers of every description and at every level of government. While the choice of secretary of state and state treasurer stayed in the hands of the governor and legislature, respectively, most state and local offices remained or became elective. The convention also adopted a host of other democratic reforms. It created a fairer system of representation in the legislature, although Baltimore still got short-changed. It reduced the terms of senators from six years to four; limited the General Assembly's power to create debt, prohibited the creation of state debt for internal improvements, and barred the state from lending its aid or credit to private companies; and required that corporations be formed under general incorporation laws rather than by special legislation. All in all, concluded James Warner Harry, the new constitution "was remarkable for its extremely democratic features." The people ratified it by a vote of 29,025 to 18,616. Majorities in eight major slaveholding counties, unassuaged by a provision that prohibited the legislature from abolishing slavery, voted to reject the constitution.[40]

Delaware

In 1853, Delaware voters did something unique: they killed a proposed state constitution replete with democratic reforms, including an elective judiciary, and thereby thwarted the only real possibility that the state would adopt popular elections as the means of choosing its judges. Voters in Missouri, Iowa, and Wisconsin had previously defeated constitutions that provided for elected judges. However, in all three cases the elective judiciary soon became law, by virtue of a constitutional amendment in Missouri and through the redrafting and approval of constitutions in Iowa and Wisconsin. Only in Delaware did the concept die aborning.

Throughout the first half of the nineteenth century, the more conservative of the major political parties—the Federalists, National Republicans, and Whigs—dominated Delaware's politics. The state went against Andrew Jackson in the presidential election of 1832 and for the Whig candidate in every subsequent presidential election through 1848. Only once during the 1830s and 1840s did Delaware's voters send a Democrat to Congress. Even after intraparty dissension over slavery and prohibition sent Delaware Whigs down to defeat in 1850, foreshadowing the party's demise a few years later, Whigs regained control of the house and elected a substantial majority of delegates to the 1853 constitutional convention.[41]

Delaware should have been primed to reject judicial elections. Ultimately, it did, but only because so many voters objected to the proposed constitution for other reasons. But why did the convention produce a constitution that embodied much of the Jacksonian agenda, including an elective judiciary, in the first place? The answer lies in the accommodation of Delaware's conservatism to the democratic tendencies of the times.

To begin with, Whigs were not the hidebound Federalists of Democratic fantasies. They founded their party in opposition to the "executive tyranny" of Andrew Jackson, and they liked to refer to themselves as the "true democrats." The Whig Party prided itself on "its steady and habitual submission to law—its deference for vested rights—and abhorrence of all violent and disorderly attempts to alter or overthrow existing institutions," but it was not averse to change that was orderly and "intelligent."[42]

Beyond that, Whigs could see that the nation was increasingly democratic, as evidenced by the spread of elections. Just as Whigs had to adopt Democratic organization and tactics—"*They* set us the example of organization," declared a group of Illinois Whigs in 1840; "and we, in self defence, are driven into it"—so they had to accept popular sovereignty in the selection of public officers. In a state controlled by National Republicans, a constitution shaped largely by the "conservative, careful, cautious, and conciliatory" National Republican and future Whig leader

John M. Clayton in 1831 provided for the popular election of sheriffs and coroners. Around the country in the 1820s and 1830s, states were making county commissioners, assessors, justices of the peace, and other local officers elective. It was a trend the Whigs could not resist if they hoped to win election to higher offices.[43]

Finally, by the time Delaware's constitutional convention met on December 8, 1852, the Whigs had to face the unpleasant fact that the Democrats had made significant inroads into the Whig supremacy in the state. Kent County still seemed to be reliably Whig, but Sussex County had gone Democratic in the last three gubernatorial elections and three of the last four congressional elections. New Castle had seen a see-saw battle for ascendancy during the 1840s. In 1850 and 1852, though, the county had voted for the Democratic congressional and gubernatorial candidates and in 1852 for the Democratic candidates for congressman and president. It is true that in 1850 a temperance candidacy, and not a swing toward the Democrats, had probably cost the Whigs control of the General Assembly and led to a second straight loss in the race for governor. It is also true that the party revived somewhat in 1852, regaining the state house of representatives and bringing Sussex back into the Whig fold. But the Whigs could not have been overly sanguine, especially in light of the national party's disastrous showing in the 1852 presidential election. The Democrats' gains may have had more to do with national issues, particularly those involving slavery, than with Jacksonian ideology; but to the extent that party ideology entered into the constitutional convention debates, the Whigs could not afford to slight Democratic sentiments.[44]

The Democratic agenda for the convention did, in fact, conform to traditional Jacksonian thought. Party meetings in Dover (Kent County) and Wilmington (New Castle County) called for free suffrage, the abolition of property qualifications for office, the popular election of public officers, and a variety of other reforms. One difference between the Kent and New Castle resolutions was that only the latter demanded representation in the General Assembly according to population. On this vital issue, regional differences outweighed partisan ones at the convention. New Castle stood to gain, and Kent to lose, from representation by population.[45]

Delaware's constitution of 1831, the one in effect when the convention of 1852–53 met, fell short of the Jeffersonian standard of democracy. It required voters, except in their first year of eligibility, to have paid a "county tax" within two years preceding the election. Each of the state's three counties had three senators and seven representatives in the legislature until these numbers might be changed by a two-thirds majority of each house of the General Assembly. Despite a growing disparity in population among the counties, no change ever took place.[46]

In practice, the taxpayer qualification may not have restricted suffrage much. The constitution did not define "county tax." There was a poll tax on free white males, enacted as part of a state law that imposed property taxes and required assessors to make their returns to the levy courts. These "courts" were actually the taxing bodies for the counties. The poll tax probably fell within the definition of "county tax," so that anyone who paid the poll tax would have met the taxpaying prerequisite for voting.[47]

Representation proved to be a thornier problem. The years following the adoption of the constitution saw a growing disparity in population between New Castle County, home of Delaware's largest city, Wilmington, and the other two counties of Kent and Sussex. During the 1830s, New Castle grew by 11 percent as Kent and Sussex shrank. By 1850, Sussex had still not recovered, while nearly 47 percent of the state's people resided in New Castle. The constitutional scheme of legislative representation thus put New Castle County at a relative disadvantage.

By 1845, arguments were appearing in the newspapers for the necessity of a convention to fix the flaws in the 1831 constitution. A writer signing himself "Equal Rights" complained that the governor had too many public offices—for clerks, registers, prothonotaries—at his disposal. Such a broad power of appointment, he insisted, was antirepublican; if the voters were competent to elect governors and congressmen, they could elect local officers as well. When Democrat William Tharp broke the Whig grip on the governorship in 1846, he urged the legislature to give the people a chance to express their wishes, through a referendum, on the calling of a convention.[48]

Whigs, too, especially in New Castle County, demanded a convention. On March 5, 1847, the editors of the *Blue Hen's Chicken & Delaware Democratic Whig* of Wilmington announced, "We shall place CONVENTION at the head of our paper and never take it down until the people triumphantly carry a Convention and reform the constitution of the State—giving the people more power and the demagogues and office holders *less*." The same issue reported on a debate in the house over a convention bill, a debate that culminated in the defeat of the bill by a vote of 15–5.[49]

Neither Governor Tharp nor the proponents in the legislative debate specified the reforms they thought a convention should address. However, in 1849, Delaware's largest paper declared: "We go for convention and reform—for rotation in office—for representation according to population—for doing away all life tenures—for lowering salaries—for education—for abolishing useless offices—for law reform, and settling differences by arbitration—and for all sorts of useful laws and reforms beneficial to the people." It was an agenda to delight Democrats. On January 19, 1850, a Democratic meeting in Dover specified some additional reforms: an end to the "odious and corrupting" taxpayer qualification for voting, the abolition of property qualifications for office, the popular election of most public officials, and the prohibition of lotteries. In March, the *Blue Hen's Chicken* explicitly endorsed the popular election of judges for limited terms. The General Assembly that year took up the convention issue in earnest. The house and senate each passed a bill to put the convention question before the voters, but the differences between the bills could not be reconciled before the legislature adjourned.[50]

Notwithstanding the *Blue Hen's* reformist zeal,[51] Whigs, who had long controlled the General Assembly, were less inclined than Democrats to seek major changes in the constitution. In 1850, unusual turmoil in the state's politics, due to a split among Whigs over the proposed Compromise of 1850 and the opposition of temperance men to Whig leader John M. Clayton, gave the Democrats temporary control of state government. The Democrats pressed their advantage. In his final address to the legislature, outgoing governor Tharp observed that the "general agitation" of the convention question for the last several years had put the issue before the legislators "with an almost commanding claim upon its attention." Without recommending specific changes in the constitution, Tharp emphasized "the advance of popular rights" since the adoption of the existing constitution and the need to bring government closer to the people.[52]

On January 21, 1851, the new governor, William Ross, also a Democrat, recommended in his inaugural address that the legislature quickly pass a bill to determine the will of the sovereign people on the subject of a convention. The house complied the next day, and the senate followed suit. The statute set the referendum for November 4, 1851, despite a constitutional requirement that the election be held in May.[53]

Notwithstanding the "agitation" noted by both Governor Tharp and the referendum statute, as well as the eight months that pro- and anti-convention forces had between passage of the bill and the referendum to make their pitches to the citizenry, as of early October the people had still shown little interest in the subject. The *Blue Hen's Chicken* attributed the lack of excitement to the fact that there were "no officers to elect" and therefore none of the usual "run[ning] around, canvassing, soliciting, and urging men to the polls." Still, pointing to the "vast importance" of the subject, the paper exhorted the voters to turn out.[54]

For the *Blue Hen's Chicken*, of New Castle County, the issue of greatest importance was representation in the General Assembly. The paper labeled it "rank injustice" for a vote in one county to carry more weight than a vote in another. The only "just rule" of representation was population. If as a result the largest geographical unit ended up with the largest number of offices, that was "nothing more than Justice."[55]

In November, the voters approved a convention by a vote of 3,335 to 1,231. However, the existing constitution required the approval of a majority of citizens having the right to vote for state representatives, not a majority of those who actually turned out to vote. The number of eligible voters was around twelve thousand. The favorable vote at the November election therefore fell far below the constitutionally mandated majority. The General Assembly nonetheless proceeded to provide for a convention, asserting in the statute that the people had the right to call a convention and that the referendum was "the only proper evidence of the will of a majority of the citizens of the State." Whigs, led by Senator Clayton, raised a storm of protest against the statute's constitutional shortcomings. A resident of New Castle County, Clayton avowed his support for legislative representation according to population but declared that he would not pursue that goal by violating the constitution.[56]

While Clayton was denouncing the Democrats' improprieties in arranging for the convention, his adversaries were announcing their aims for constitutional revision. A meeting of Wilmington Democrats adopted resolutions demanding free suffrage, so that white males could vote "without the inspection or surveillance of Assessors or Tax Collectors"; the creation of single-member legislative districts of approximately equal population; popular election of public officers; judicial reform; the elimination of property qualifications for public office; restrictions on the growth of the free black population of the state; the establishment of the executive veto to control the "madness of legislation"; fairer taxation; and a return to annual elections (and thereby shorter sessions) for the legislature.[57]

The judicial reforms sought by the Wilmington Democrats included more terms of court and the abolition of life tenure, which together would make the administration of justice "more economical and convenient" and would reduce the suspicions of unfairness and bias that naturally "arise upon the adjustment of conflicting interests, when the power deciding is subject to no human accountability." The resolutions did not explicitly endorse judicial elections, but their recommended judicial reforms and advocacy of popular election of public officers in general pointed in that direction.

The statute providing for the election of convention delegates allotted ten delegates per county, a violation of the very principle of representation according to population that motivated the reformers of New Castle County. Moreover, the law provided for the election of delegates by hundreds (the Delaware equivalent of towns) rather than by counties, another breach of both the existing constitution (in the eyes of Whigs) and of the rule of equal representation (since the hundreds varied greatly in population). The Democrats may have hoped that the election of delegates by hundreds instead of counties would have allowed them to take delegates away from the dominant Whigs. If so, the plan didn't work, as the Whigs won eighteen of the thirty seats.[58]

The convention met briefly in December 1852 but convened for its real work in March 1853. The Whigs renewed their assault on the convention as unconstitutional, and three of their delegates resigned, but other Whigs remained and participated fully in the proceedings. On the great issues of suffrage and representation, the convention gave Jeffersonian democracy a partial victory. In Section 1 of its initial report, the Committee on the Right of Suffrage recommended abolition of the taxpayer qualification for voting and of the property requirement for holding office. After some discussion about the report's other provisions, especially the residency requirement, the committee of the whole accepted Section 1 by a vote of 15–8.[59]

The next day, though, the convention recommitted the report to the committee of the whole. Whig Daniel Corbit moved to reinsert the requirement that the prospective voter have paid a county tax within two years before the election or, if the voter had not been regularly assessed, be required to pay a $1.50 poll tax. "I consider," explained Corbit, "that every man who is protected by the government should contribute something, however small the sum may be, to the support of that government." His amendment would address the complaint that citizens had been left off the assessment lists. As to the taxpayer requirement itself, Corbin thought there had been "little or no complaint."[60]

Democrat Martin D. Bates objected to Corbit's proposal on the grounds that it would promote fraudulent voting by men who were ineligible for other reasons—out-of-staters, for example—and would place too much power, and temptation to corruption, in the hands of the tax collectors. After James R. Lofland, a Whig, dismissed his concerns, Bates added that the qualification constituted a disenfranchisement of the "poor, unfortunate, or sick" man who was unable to pay a tax. He was, he declared, "utterly averse" to the principle. And yet it was the "principle only" for which Lofland professed to contend, however unpopular it might be. The committee of the whole rejected Corbit's amendment and then readopted the first section of the report.[61]

Lofland also objected to abolishing property qualifications for office. "If you do away with them," he insisted, "you remove a great incentive to industry and exertion." Land in Delaware was "as cheap as dirt," he asserted, implying that anyone who refused to make the effort to acquire it didn't deserve to vote. Moreover, interests in property were entitled to protection. If landless men sat in both houses of the legislature, they would naturally want to shift the burden of taxation to landholders. Richard N. Merriken argued for the voters' freedom of choice, allowing them to determine a candidate's qualifications for themselves. The committee of the whole sided with Merriken, 18–7.[62]

On the matters of suffrage and qualifications for office, then, the delegates' one-sided votes displayed a distinct leaning towards Jeffersonian democracy. The debate over representation, however, revealed only lukewarm support for the Jeffersonian principle. There seemed to be a general consensus that New Castle County was entitled to more representation than Kent or Sussex, but the delegates from the latter two counties had no intention of letting New Castle have the kind of power that would come from representation according to population. The initial report of the Committee on the Legislative Department conceded ten representatives to New Castle, while Kent and Sussex would have seven apiece. Each county would have four senators. The legislature would be able to add to the total number of representatives (and reapportion them) and of senators upon a two-thirds majority vote of the members of each chamber.[63]

The members from New Castle could not have been surprised. United States senator James A. Bayard, Delaware's most powerful Democrat, denounced the report as hardly a reform at all. Bayard missed most of the convention, but he dominated the discussion of representation. "I take it for granted," Bayard told his fellow delegates, "that no man in this assembly . . . will, for a moment, deny the principle, *that the great basis of a republican government is, that every freeman stands in the community with equal civil and political rights.* . . . If this principle be true, can any gentleman give me a reason why it should not prevail throughout, as well in reference to the very highest right of all, the right to be represented, as to the mere right of voting personally?" In colonial days and the early days of the republic, Bayard noted, an apportionment that gave each county the same number of legislators caused no great hardship because the counties were roughly equal in population. But a great inequality had since developed, making a new scheme of representation imperative.[64]

In place of the committee report, Bayard offered a detailed plan that divided the state into districts of approximately equal populations for the election of both senators and representatives. He enumerated the districts and explained how he had arrived at them. If his plan were implemented, said Bayard, it would have the additional benefit of destroying "all county feeling in reference to State legislation."[65] This was a radical suggestion. Americans were still, and would long remain, attached to their villages, towns, and counties, which made truly equal representation impossible to achieve.

Bayard was probably correct in saying that none of the delegates would deny his basic principle. There were those elsewhere who continued to condemn representation by population as the tyranny of the majority. In Delaware, though, even delegates from Kent, the smallest county, while refusing to support Bayard's proposal, conceded the justice of representation according to population. One of them, Caleb Smithers, would subsequently argue against giving New Castle as many representatives as Kent and Sussex combined because New Castle would then "have the decided advantage over either of the other counties, where a question of interests were at stake."[66]

In presenting his plan, Bayard alluded to the rumored fear of people in Sussex that New Castle was imbued with "a spirit of fanaticism" that would threaten the security of property in slaves. Sussex, the southernmost county, held two-thirds of Delaware's small slave population. To allay this concern, however unjustified it might have been, Bayard offered to insert into the constitution a prohibition of statutory emancipation without the owner's consent. The proposal failed to win over any of the Sussex delegates. When Bayard formally offered his plan to the convention, the members chose to vote on it, paragraph by paragraph. The first paragraph proposed the establishment of fifteen districts from which the voters would elect seventeen senators and thirty-four representatives. The convention rejected it 19–8. The only yes votes came from the seven New

Castle delegates still at the convention and from one maverick from Kent. The second paragraph, which set forth the districts, lost 20–6. Two of the New Castle delegates, one of whom had already questioned the accuracy of the districts, opposed it.[67]

Several delegates from Kent claimed to object to the size of the legislature in Bayard's measure, while another, Caleb Smithers, insisted that he would not allow New Castle to dictate to Kent whether or how his county would be districted. (Smithers here echoed the sentiments of his political forebears at the national constitutional convention of 1787, where the delegates of tiny Delaware sought to protect their state from being completely dominated by the bigger states.) Neither Bayard nor his fellow New Castle delegate Benjamin T. Biggs bought these explanations. Lashing out at his opponents in evident anger and frustration, Bayard declared:

> Men will seldom relinquish power even for the sake of principle, but I hope and I believe gentlemen will find, that in a republic, a principle which no man on this floor dares deny, will finally triumph. No man here pretends to deny the equal, civil, and political rights of every citizen, no matter in what part of the State he may reside; yet gentlemen here vote down a proposition to secure the enjoyment of that right. . . . What is the fact with regard to gentlemen here? You represent land and not men.[68]

Biggs still professed a belief in the "liberality and charity" of the Kent and Sussex men. "Never until the vote taken this morning," he averred, "have I been led to believe that they felt any disposition whatever to prevent New Castle county being fully represented . . . according to her population." But now he wanted to know "on what kind of meat these men in Kent or Sussex county have fed that they have grown so great. They have got the power and they wish to retain it."[69]

Bayard, seeing no prospect of success at the convention, announced that he would take his case to the people and oppose the constitution. He left the convention in a huff. Further attempts would be made to approach equal representation, but the final result was unsatisfactory. The convention settled on a house of twenty-nine members (twelve from New Castle, eight from Kent, and nine from Sussex), and a twelve-member senate (four from each county). This scheme gave New Castle, with 47% of the state's population in 1850, 41 percent of the representatives and 33 percent of the senators. It would take a two-thirds majority in each chamber to increase the number of representatives or senators. Growing New Castle—its share of the state's population would be 49 percent in 1860—would not be satisfied with this arrangement.[70]

By the key measures of suffrage and representation, Jeffersonian democracy had not fully prevailed at the convention. The constitution incorporated free suffrage, but representation remained unequal, although less unequal than under the 1831 instrument. New Castle received a somewhat fairer share of representatives, and the constitution allowed not only a small increase in the number of representatives but also a reapportionment (one that would have been unlikely to occur, since it would have required the cooperation of at least eight members from Kent or Sussex in the diminishment of their own power). But no one refuted the principle of equal representation; its opponents failed to make any principled arguments against it. In that sense, Jeffersonian democracy ruled the convention.

Judicial reform occupied a lot of the delegates' attention. Delaware had entered the nineteenth century with a complex judicial system for such a small state. As a Delaware judge said in 1897, "A judicial system which supplied two co-ordinate courts of civil jurisdiction, comprising nine State judges, inclusive of two chief justices and a chancellor, was necessarily cumbersome and disproportionate to the limited area and population of such a State as Delaware." The main purpose of Delaware's constitutional convention of 1831 had been to reorganize the judiciary, which the convention had done. The new constitution reduced the number of state judges from nine to five: a chief justice, a chancellor, and three associate judges (one from each county), all appointed by the governor to hold office during good behavior. These five individuals constituted, in different combinations, a court of errors and appeals, a superior court, a court of chancery, an orphans' court, a court of oyer and terminer (a criminal court), and a court of general sessions of the peace and jail delivery.[71]

One controversial feature of the new system was the quorum requirement for the superior court, which had both original and appellate jurisdiction and was the chief trial court. It consisted of the chief justice and the two associate judges who did not reside in the county in which the court was sitting. Two judges made a quorum, which meant that at least two judges had to preside over every trial. This two- or three-judge tribunal was controversial at the 1831 convention and thereafter. At the 1853 convention it took up a great deal of the delegates' time and energy, far more than the question of judicial selection.[72]

The first report of the judiciary committee at the 1853 convention found the existing court system defective. The committee saw no need for three judges sitting together in either the superior court or the court of general sessions. It objected to appeals being heard by a panel that included the judge who had sat in the case below. The committee's recommendations included, among other things, reducing the number of judges to four, having cases heard by single judges, precluding judges from hearing appeals from their own decisions, and gubernatorial appointment of judges for terms of ten years, with the judges being eligible for reappointment.[73]

At the same time, the committee on appointments and tenures expressed a decided preference for the popular election of most public officers and the abolition of life tenures. While its first report focused on executive officers, the committee's guiding axiom—that all power emanates from the people, who should not have a third party interposed between them and their agents—could be applied to judges as well.[74]

The judiciary committee's report sparked a minority report and intense debate, especially over the proposed single-judge system. The committee produced a revised report that retained gubernatorial appointments for ten-year terms. The first official action involving judicial elections came with a motion by Whig Benjamin Biggs, offered at fellow Whig Lofland's suggestion, that the committee of the whole recommit the report to the judiciary committee with instructions to report amendments providing for the popular election of judges for fixed terms and for the abolition of the chancery court. The conservative Lofland seems an unlikely instigator of the motion. His purpose, however, was to get some proposition in writing for the consideration of the delegates. The idea of an elective judiciary must have been floating around the convention. Lofland wanted to know what he was up against.[75]

On April 12, the committee of the whole took up the judiciary committee's report. Biggs withdrew his resolution so that the committee of the whole could discuss the judiciary committee's report and consider any amendments that might be offered. When the resolution providing for the appointment of judges by the governor came up, a lively debate ensued over judicial salaries, special judicial elections, and other court-related issues. No one objected to the reduction of tenure from life to a term of years, although one delegate expressed a preference for longer terms.[76]

James H. Smith, a Democrat, moved to amend the resolution by replacing appointment with election. The debate on Smith's motion followed the path that had already been marked out many times in other states. Whig Corbit opposed the motion on the grounds that election would leave the selection of judges to politicians, who would let party considerations override the public interest. Delaware's experience with executive appointments, argued Corbit, had been good, with governors reaching across party lines to find the best men for the job. That would not happen if the choice were left to the people.[77]

Caleb Smithers, also a Whig, riposted that the governors themselves were not always such good men. Therefore, the choice of judges might just as well be entrusted to the people as to the governors. It was not the most inspiring defense of judicial elections. Smith himself barely rose to the occasion, saying that he was not "disposed at present to attempt to show that the people are equally, if not more competent than a Governor, to make good selections for this important station." He was willing to let the committee of the whole decide the matter as it would and take it up again when the delegates met in convention.[78]

Biggs began the next day's discussion by describing the question of judicial selection as "the most important" that had yet come before the delegates. To accept judicial elections, he cautioned, meant "to launch out in a field of untried experiment," at least as far as Delaware was concerned. For government to move on "prosperously and advantageously, bringing justice to all and every man," an "able and effective judiciary" was essential. Biggs announced that he would vote for the amendment, both because all appointments should emanate from the sovereign people and because the people, who elected the governor, were no less competent than the governor to choose their judges. Biggs denied that popular election would destroy judicial independence. For the most part, he observed, governors appointed members of their own party to the bench, often "as a reward for party services previously rendered." In reality, judges were appointed by party caucuses, without regard to competency.[79]

By 1853, many states had made the switch to an elective judiciary, including Delaware's neighbors Pennsylvania and Maryland. Biggs called upon their example. He predicted that if the convention did not make the judiciary elective now, the question would be back before another convention within ten years. The people were ready for judicial elections, said Biggs. They were the ones most interested in an impartial judiciary, unaffected by partisan feeling. In support of his argument, Biggs read from Thomas Jefferson's 1816 letter advocating judicial elections; adverted to Quitman of Mississippi, who had originally opposed such elections but had changed his mind based on experience; and on the success of the elective judiciary in other states, especially New York. Biggs concluded by asserting that the incorporation of judicial elections into the draft constitution would attract to the polls thousands of voters who might not otherwise opt to ratify the instrument.[80]

Biggs's oration concluded the debate on whether judges should be "elected by the people." Corbit moved to amend Smith's resolution by retaining gubernatorial appointment but "by and with the advice and consent of the Senate." The motion failed, 18-8, bringing the original proposition up for a vote. It passed, 16-10. Although neither party voted uniformly on the question, the Democrats leaned strongly in favor of elections, while the Whigs provided most of the opposition. Significantly, even if the three Whigs who had resigned from the convention had been present and had voted against elections, the amendment would still have passed.[81]

The delegates had committed to the principle of judicial election, but there were still questions to decide. Should the people choose their judges at general or special elections? Should judges be elected on a statewide or county basis? Should they be eligible for reelection?

Bates, a Democrat and chairman of the judiciary committee, argued that special judicial elections would reduce the influence of politics on the outcome. State and county elections, he contended, "excite[d] a high degree of party feeling," something from which judges "should be kept ... as free as possible." Moreover, separating the election of judges would keep the list of names on a general election ticket down to a reasonable length. The only argument Bates claimed to have heard against special judicial elections was the cost, but he doubted its validity. The convention had already settled on ten-year judicial terms of office. The savings gained by adding judgeships to the general election ballot once every ten years would be minimal. In any event, Bates cautioned the convention not to be penny wise and pound foolish. "[M]ixing up the election of judges with strictly party elections" was such a bad idea that Bates, who favored an elective judiciary, said he might have to move for a reconsideration of the vote on popular judicial elections if the committee of the whole insisted on electing judges at general elections.[82]

In the discussion that followed, the opponents of special judicial elections raised various objections: that turnout at special elections was low, that the cost and inconvenience of special elections were high, that the people were worn out with numerous elections, that judges were going to be party men regardless of how they were selected. One delegate contended for the election of judges at general elections but on separate tickets; it lost on a tie vote. Ultimately, the committee of the whole narrowly defeated the idea of special elections.[83]

In its revised report, the judiciary committee recommended that Delaware have five appointed judges: a chancellor, a chief justice, and three associate judges. Each of them might come from any part of the state. The associates, though, were appointed for particular counties; after being commissioned, an associate judge had to reside in the county for which he had been appointed. After the convention decided upon judicial elections, the question arose whether the people of each county should be able to elect their own associate judge. Smithers offered an amendment to that effect. After some debate, he modified his proposal to require only that the judges elected by the voters of any county reside in that county after being commissioned. The convention adopted the amended amendment.[84]

When the convention took up the final revision of the constitution, Lofland moved to undo the Smithers amendment. Smithers objected, explaining that having each county elect its own resident judge would likely result in having the judiciary manned by members of both political parties. If the judges were elected on a statewide basis, he continued, the dominant party would probably have all the judges, resulting in a "political court." Furthermore, added Biggs, the people of each county knew whom they preferred for judge; they should not have the voters of the other counties making the decision for them. Corbit and Smith countered that since all the judges would sit in the court of oyer and terminer and the court of appeals and hear cases in which the whole state was interested, the people of the whole state should elect them. Lofland's proposal lost by a vote of 14–10.[85]

The judiciary committee's report had made judges eligible for reappointment. Corbit, who never liked the idea of an elective judiciary to begin with, now moved to make judges ineligible for reelection. His motive, he said, was to protect judicial independence by eliminating political temptations. Bates dismissed Corbit's contention, claiming that the best lawyers would not sacrifice a lucrative practice for a single, ten-year term, which in turn would limit the people's choices in a state as small as Delaware. He further maintained that a judge seeking reelection would be more likely to rely on his reputation for impartiality and integrity than to appear before the voters as a corrupt man. The committee rejected Corbit's amendment by a wide margin.[86]

The final revision of the constitution provided that "[t]he Chancellor and the other Judges shall be elected by the people, and shall respectively hold their offices for the term of ten years, if so long they shall behave themselves well, and shall be eligible for re-election." The chancellor and chief justice would be elected on a statewide basis; the other judges would be chosen by the voters of the counties in which the judges resided.[87] The constitution said nothing about either the date of election or staggering of terms, leaving all five judges to be chosen on the same day, once every ten years, at a general election.

The final document approved by the convention for the most part shared the democratizing tendencies of the constitutions of other states adopted in the middle of the nineteenth century. The delegates eliminated the taxpayer qualification for voting and property qualifications for holding office. They abolished life tenures and provided for the popular election of judges and other officers (not including the secretary of state) who previously had been appointed. In altering the procedures for amending the constitution, the delegates sought to avoid controversies of the type that had rocked their own convention; they authorized the call of a convention by a majority of those voting at each of two consecutive general elections rather than by a majority of all eligible voters at a single special election.[88]

The delegates adopted other reforms that may have been inspired as much by the example of other states as by experience in Delaware. These included restrictions on legislative authority and requirements for legislative procedure that were popular with Jacksonian Democrats. One notable section of the proposed constitution prohibited the creation of state debt except to defray the expenses of government; barred the state from lending its credit to private enterprise; and outlawed state involvement in the construction of internal improvements[89]—all this even though Delaware had no state debt. New procedural provisions directed the reading of every bill three times on three different days and limited every local or private law to one subject described in the bill's title.[90]

The major failing of the 1853 convention was the apportionment scheme, which satisfied no one. It gave populous New Castle County more members in the house of representatives, which was an advance for democracy, but not enough to approximate equal representation. It left the senate as malapportioned as before and made no provision for reapportionment in the future. The flawed plan of representation, combined with the continued insistence of many Whigs that the convention was illegal, doomed the constitution. Three Whigs who had been elected delegates had refused to serve because of the convention's alleged unconstitutionality. Two more who had served refused to sign the final document on the same grounds. Lofland also refused to sign, but did not give a reason. Democrats Bayard and William C. Lodge denounced the apportionment plan as an insult to New Castle.[91]

The constitution's prospects did not improve between the end of the convention and the ratification referendum in October. The most prominent leaders of both parties, Clayton of the Whigs and Bayard of the Democrats, opposed the constitution. Advocates of ratification sometimes resorted to half-hearted endorsements ("half a loaf is better than none") that were not likely to inspire support at the polls. In the end, all three counties voted against ratification. Statewide, about 64 percent of the voters voted no. The elective judiciary did not play much of a role in the ratification debate. To both supporters and opponents of the constitution, it was just one among many changes from the old constitution, and far from the most important.[92]

The reform movement did not end with the defeat of the constitution. Life tenures remained unpopular. An act to reduce judicial terms to twelve years passed the legislature with the necessary supermajorities in 1857 and 1859, but the governor withheld his approval. (The constitution required the governor's "approbation" for proposed constitutional amendments to take effect.) The elective judiciary also had some support, especially at the Democratic *Delaware Inquirer* of Wilmington, but not enough to get beyond the talking stage.[93]

Of the four border states, Missouri, in the trans-Mississippi West, had the most democratic political culture. There is an aura of inevitability around its switch from an appointive to an elective judiciary, notwithstanding the defeat of the proposed constitution in 1846. The legislature wasted no time in addressing the root cause of that defeat, the convention's failure to fix the state's apportionment problem. Soon after passing a constitutional amendment to create more equal representation, the lawmakers, with near-unanimity, provided for the election of executive and judicial officers. It took the issue of representation to propel the constitutional reform movement forward—as it did in Maryland, Delaware, and to a lesser but still significant degree in Kentucky—but judicial elections seemed naturally to accompany that greater democratic reform.

Missouri differed from the other border states in slavery's apparent lack of influence on constitutional deliberations. The cause of emancipation had lost steam in Missouri by 1845. When delegate Thomson Ward felt obligated to introduce a petition on the subject of abolition that had been sent to him, he said that he hoped it would not be read. Ward asked for, and got, a unanimous vote to that effect.[94] That was the last the convention heard of abolition or emancipation. Nor did the subject crop up in the subsequent push for the adoption of judicial elections by constitutional amendment. The conventions in the other border states took place after the Mexican War, when American possession of a vast western domain to which slavery might spread aggravated sectional tensions. Convention delegates from slaveholding counties, more conscious than ever about perceived majoritarian threats to slavery, brought their concerns into debates on representation and judicial selection. With the arguable exception of Delaware, they could not stem the democratic tide in the border states, but similar fears would have repercussions further south.

CHAPTER 3

The Reluctant Southeast

Before James De Bow took charge, the United States Census defined the South as Virginia, North Carolina, South Carolina, Georgia, and Florida. De Bow added Delaware and Maryland, a debatable decision based on the legality of slavery in those states. Assigning Delaware and Maryland to the border region leaves us with a geographically coherent and indisputably southern unit of five southeastern states.

In this Southeast, Florida was a latecomer. In the other, older states, where the fast-growing western Upcountry clashed with the constitutionally privileged eastern Lowcountry, demands for basic democratic reforms overshadowed proposals relating to judicial selection and every other aspect of constitutional revision. North Carolina and South Carolina never came close to adopting an elective judiciary. Virginia did so only because compelling circumstances based on the state's place within the Union pushed a reluctant planter aristocracy into acceding to a package of concessions that included judicial elections. In Georgia, superior court judges became subject to popular election, but the supreme court remained appointive. In both Virginia and Georgia, widespread dissatisfaction with the appointed local judges who dominated county government probably contributed to the adoption of elections for higher court judgeships as well. Only Florida, a new frontier state, followed a route to the elective judiciary resembling that taken in western and border states.

Virginia

In his *Notes on the State of Virginia*, published in 1786, Thomas Jefferson revealed his deep disenchantment with his state's constitution, which he thought contained a half-dozen "capital defects." The first such defect was the severe restriction of the suffrage. "The majority of the men in the state, who pay and fight for its support," wrote Jefferson, were "unrepresented in the legislature" because they could not vote. The second major flaw was the unequal representation of those who could vote. The constitution allotted two representatives per county, with certain boroughs and cities having one representative apiece. As a result, the small eastern counties had greatly disproportionate power; the nineteen thousand "fighting men" living below the falls of the rivers had half the senate and almost half the house. "These 19,000 therefore, living in one part of the country, give law to upwards of 30,000 living in another, and appoint all their chief officers executive and judiciary."[1]

The imbalance in representation would only get worse, and it would have grave consequences. In 1816, a meeting of prominent western and northern Virginians described representation in their state as "an absolute mockery of the principles of free government." They called for a convention to formulate a plan of action. In August, a convention of delegates from thirty-three western counties met at Staunton to consider amendments to the constitution. In a memorial to the legislature, the convention declared that the "first and fundamental principle of republicanism"— that "the will of the majority should be the law of the land"—"does not exist" because a minority living in one section of the state had the government in its hands.[2]

In that same year, Jefferson was still excoriating the constitution for its sanction of a restricted suffrage and unequal representation. He had other concerns as well. The county courts exercised tremendous powers; they were "in truth our principal executive and judiciary." Made up of justices of the peace appointed for life by the governor, the county courts filled their own vacancies, perpetuating their political orientation and sometimes family dynasties. In such circumstances, charged Jefferson, the county court became "the most afflicting of tyrannies, because its powers are so various, and exercised on everything most immediately around us"; militiamen and taxpayers were governed by men not of their choosing. The solution he suggested was the selection of judges by an electorate consisting of all men who served in the militia or paid taxes.[3]

Complaints about the "aristocratic" constitution and petitions to the legislature to call a convention piled up for years to no effect until 1828, when the General Assembly finally agreed to let the voters decide on a convention. The people voted in favor, and the convention duly met in 1829–30. It proved a disappointment to western reformers. To conservative easterners, it was unthinkable that a man could have a "permanent interest in the well being of the community" without acquiring enough land to qualify for the franchise. Reform-minded westerners found it equally incomprehensible that ownership of land was a prerequisite to love of country and an interest in good government. On the question of representation, the West insisted that as the people were "the only legitimate source and fountain of political power," representatives must be apportioned according to the white population, not according to wealth, sectional interests, or counties. Conservatives, fearful of majoritarian assaults on property, especially in the form of taxation on slaves, rejected the rule of "King Numbers" and insisted that property as well as people be represented.[4]

The results of the debates were the slight expansion of the electorate and a redrawing of house and senate districts that modestly increased western representation, with a promised decennial reapportionment, within limits, beginning in 1841. A leader of the disadvantaged western portion of the state thought the new constitution was not much of an improvement because it left the "odious despotic aristocracy" of the East in control. The constitution, writes a modern scholar, was out of touch with the democratizing tendencies of the age, "antediluvian, even in terms of its own times." It retained property qualifications for voting. It left the selection of all major state officials, including the governor, to the General Assembly. Courts appointed their clerks, justices of the peace appointed constables, county courts nominated sheriffs to be commissioned by the governor. Judges held their appointments during good behavior, meaning, in most cases, until they resigned or died (although they could be removed by a two-thirds vote of each house of the legislature).[5]

Over the next twenty years both the total population and the free population of Virginia, excluding the counties that would make up the future state of West Virginia, grew by 8 percent; the population of the West Virginia counties grew by 71 percent. The persistence of western underrepresentation in the legislature kept the campaign for constitutional revision alive. Easterners had good reason to fear fair representation for western Virginians. The mountainous West cared less for slavery and more for internal improvements and public education than did the plantation society of the politically dominant Tidewater and Piedmont regions. Eastern slaveholders worried that the West, with a majority of the state's white population, would lay heavy taxes on their slave property to finance transportation projects and public schools for the benefit of the West. The General Assembly's failure to implement reapportionment in 1841 as required by the constitution ratcheted up demands for another constitutional convention. Years of pressure finally led to the convention of 1850–51, called with the support of eastern conservative leader

Henry A. Wise, the Democratic *Richmond Enquirer*, and various easterners who sought constitutional reforms unrelated to representation. With the national crisis over slavery at a fever pitch, Wise, anxious to mollify Virginia's westerners in order to unify Virginians in support of slavery, urged reform of suffrage and representation.[6]

Virginia's unity was in fact threatened. By 1830, the future West Virginia, by virtue of geography and political orientation, had developed a distinct identity and a population larger than that of several states.[7] At the time of the 1829–30 constitutional convention, western Virginians inside and outside the meeting hall had raised the specter of secession from Virginia if their demands were not met. When the final draft of the constitution came up for approval at the convention, the Trans-Allegheny delegates opposed it virtually unanimously. When the voters weighed in, those in the Trans-Allegheny counties overwhelmingly voted no. Renewed suggestions of secession received serious consideration.[8]

Wise, running for delegate to the 1850 convention from Virginia's Eastern Shore, announced a program to warm the hearts of westerners: free public education for all, from primary school through college; suffrage for every white male citizen who bore arms, worked on a public highway, or paid a state or county tax in the year preceding the election; representation apportioned according to the number of legal voters in a district; internal improvements for the mutual benefit of East and West, but subject to the requirement of a supermajority of each house to approve a loan, tax, or appropriation bill; biennial legislative sessions to reduce the number of laws and the cost of doing legislative business; the popular election of every state and local officer from governor to constable and of all judges and justices; and the abolition of the county courts. "There is no question," wrote Wise, "of the right and competency of the people to elect their Judges as well as other officers."[9]

The notion of an elective judiciary was novel. Virginia newspapers had reported on the adoption of judicial elections by the New York convention of 1846, but at that time there did not seem to be much inclination in Virginia to follow suit. In 1850, though, with the Virginia convention in view, newspapers printed editorials, letters, and circulars addressing the issue, some from candidates for seats at the convention. Those who favored the popular election of judges insisted that, as "all power is vested in the people," the people had a right to elect their judges directly or to delegate the power of appointment to others. And as the people had the capacity to choose judges, and as no one had a deeper interest in selecting meritorious candidates, they would be best off making the choices themselves.[10]

The most thoughtful opponents of judicial elections did not deny the right of the people to elect judges but emphatically denied the propriety of their doing so. Judges, asserted one critic, were not the servants of the people but of justice. Selection by the legislature might occasionally be tainted by "party excitement," but party excitement was far hotter among large masses of people. Moreover, experience had already demonstrated that political canvassing for judicial posts had a baleful effect. "Even now in the infancy of the system [in other states]," wrote this objector, "a judge has to prove to the people, that a decision he has made is *sound law*; it is but a step further to require of judges *pledges* to certain legal opinions; and then the law will change with every moon, or at least with every change in the strength of the parties *pro* and *con* any particular set of legal doctrines." A judge involved in a closely contested race would be tempted to decide pending cases in favor of the parties having the greater political influence. In short, judges would become similar to politicians, undignified "wooer[s] of the popular favor."[11]

Advocates and opponents of judicial elections agreed on one thing: the county courts needed to be abolished or reformed. The *Staunton Spectator* editorialized that the county court system was the chief target of complaints about the judiciary. The paper opposed judicial elections for the higher courts, believing that judges, unlike legislators, had to be guided not by the popular will but by "the law and the testimony," by "right, justice and good conscience." But the "highly aristocratical" county courts were different. A "self perpetuating corps of officers of any kind" had no place under a republican government. The *Spectator* might have added that the particular "corps of officers" who made up the county courts had numerous nonjudicial functions. As one candidate for delegate opined, "the justices should be periodically elected by the people, clothed as they are with the power of taxation for county purposes." Another candidate proposed doing away with the county courts altogether, replacing them with "county police, composed of commissioners elected by the people."[12]

At the convention itself, judicial elections took a distant back seat to legislative representation in the attention of the delegates. The law apportioning delegates had been rigged to favor the East, but everyone recognized that the West would have to be granted greater representation.

The result was an apportionment that, for the time being at least, gave the West control of the house and the East control of the senate, with a complicated scheme for future reapportionment that augured well for the West. Another compromise gave eastern slaveholders a cap on the taxation of slaves. Most of the delegates took free suffrage and the popular election of the governor as givens.[13]

The idea of an elective judiciary received relatively little discussion. Notwithstanding the judiciary committee's initial report, which recommended that the judges of the supreme court of appeals be chosen by the General Assembly, it seems to have been assumed early on that all judges would be elected. In a speech in February on the controversial subject of the basis of representation, long before the issue of judicial elections was decided, western delegate William Lucas observed that "we nearly all, are now at last, in favor of giving the election of all officers to the people."[14]

A separate committee handled county government, including the county courts. The hostility of western delegates toward the county courts was palpable. Lucas railed that the "sectional minority east," by controlling the legislature, held in its hands not only the election of state officers but even "that of justices of the peace . . . constituting our county courts which decide, manage and control everything belonging and appertaining to county police and levies, and so even our purse strings." James Neeson denounced the "odious and irresponsible county court," while James E. Stewart inveighed against the "corrupt and overbearing" despotism of the county courts. All three men hailed from counties that would later belong to the state of West Virginia.[15]

The majority report and one of the minority reports of the Committee on County Courts and County Organization retained the county court, while another minority report proposed its abolition. All three, however, provided for the election of justices of the peace, so that the county courts, if preserved, would be elected by local constituencies. The convention subsequently agreed to retain the county courts and voted for the election of the justices of the peace, who would constitute those courts. Thus, even if the plan of legislative representation adopted by the convention failed to satisfy the West, the inhabitants of that region at least gained control over their local governments. The general notion of popular election of public officers had broad support at the convention, enthusiastic in some cases and grudging in others, but the idea that judges should be elected may have been rooted in resentment of the county courts.[16]

The constitution produced by the convention went a long way toward satisfying the demands of reformers. It embraced (almost) free suffrage; gave the West fairer if not yet equal legislative representation; and extended popular election to the governor, lieutenant governor, board of public works, judges and justices, attorney general, court clerks, prosecuting attorneys, county surveyors, sheriffs, constables, commissioners of revenue, and overseers of the poor. At the ratification election in October 1851, both East and West approved the constitution; the combined margin was nearly 7–1. The cause of judicial elections, not especially strong on its own, had benefited from the broader democratic reforms brought on by sectional conflicts both within Virginia and between the free and slave states.[17]

North Carolina

Virginia presents an instructive comparison with neighboring North Carolina. Despite numerous similarities between the two, North Carolina remained one of the ten states that did not adopt judicial elections before the Civil War. North Carolina had an undemocratic first constitution much like that of Virginia, with restricted suffrage, malapportionment of the legislature, a General Assembly that appointed all the important state executive and judicial officers, and powerful, unelected county courts.[18] Also like Virginia, it had a growing western Upcountry whose desire for internal improvements was thwarted by the eastern planters who controlled the legislature. Frustrated westerners finally threatened to take extralegal action. "If the General Assembly does not submit the inequalities of our constitution to the people in some formal mode," warned one newspaper, "we of the west are determined to go to work without the behest of that body." Under the specter of revolution, and with eastern demands for a charter for a Raleigh-to-Wilmington railroad that the West would support only if the people were permitted to vote on a constitutional convention, the lawmakers finally agreed to a referendum. Voting along sectional lines, the electorate approved, and a convention met in 1835.[19]

The law authorizing the referendum expressly limited the convention, should one be called, to the consideration of specific propositions. It directed the delegates to provide for senate districts that were laid out according to state taxes paid. House districts were to be based on their federal populations (free persons plus three-fifths of slaves); but each county was to have at least one representative. The convention would have discretion to eliminate separate representation for borough towns. The law allowed for a number of other discretionary amendments, including the popular election of the governor and modification of the religious test for office-holding.[20]

Operating under these restrictive instructions, the convention made the requisite changes in representation, provided for the popular election of the governor, and liberalized the religious test. Retaining taxes paid as the basis of senate apportionment favored the East. So did the counting of slaves in determining representation in the house, although the West would nevertheless now have a small majority in that chamber. A new real-property requirement for suffrage in senate elections would reduce the electorate by the late 1840s as the economy changed. The popular election of the governor meant little because the governor had slight power under the constitution both before and after 1835. Overwhelming support from the West resulted in ratification of the constitutional reforms, but the changes failed to end the sectional conflict.[21]

As in Virginia, the General Assembly showed some enthusiasm for state-backed railroads after the convention, but the fruits of this new zeal were small, and the failure of some of the roads left the state with unexpected liabilities. Nevertheless, in the late 1840s Democrats joined Whigs in advocating more public support for internal improvements, and in the 1850s many Whigs displayed their democratic bona fides by joining Democrats in a push for free suffrage. Western Whigs also pressed for a referendum on the calling of a constitutional convention that would change the basis of representation in the senate from property to white population. Eastern Whigs saw a change in the basis of senatorial representation as a threat to property, to the interests of slaveholders, and to the political power of the East generally. Democrats denounced the referendum proposal as a majoritarian threat to the "vested rights of minorities" and to the constitution itself, which specified how a convention could be called. They were content to trumpet their devotion to free suffrage (which would pose no threat to their slave property as long as the East retained its advantage in the legislature) and to let the Whigs fight among themselves over representation. Free suffrage finally became a reality with a constitutional amendment in 1857; the convention movement died from astute Democratic politicking.[22]

Through all this constitutional ferment, the cause of judicial elections made little headway. By 1850, North Carolina newspapers had been reporting on the adoption of judicial elections in other states for several years. In 1846, the *North Carolina Standard*, published by Whig-turned-Democrat William H. Holden, reprinted an article that praised the working of the elective system in Mississippi. The next year another Democratic paper, noting that New York and Illinois had switched to elective judiciaries, suggested that "if the plan works well, all the States ought to adopt it." The real push came early in 1850 when Holden turned from simply reporting to strongly advocating the switch. At their state conventions in June, both parties included planks in their platforms regarding judicial elections, although, as the Democrats gleefully pointed out, the Whigs simply called for taking the sense of the people on the question whereas the Democrats manfully declared that judges ought to be elected. On the other hand, the Whigs also wanted the legislature to get the people's sentiments on the election of the state treasurer, state comptroller, secretary of state, justices of the peace, "and other State officers."[23]

Democrats sometimes questioned the sincerity of the Whigs in supporting judicial elections, complaining that the Whigs were trying to ride this Democratic "pony" into office. "Some of the most liberal Whig papers . . . have raised their standard in favor of this measure," said the *Goldsborough Patriot*. "But that it had its origin with the Democrats, we think none will deny."[24]

Why the Democrats themselves called for judicial elections at this time is not clear. There does not seem to have been a public clamor for a change in judicial selection. When Holden published his call for popular election, he argued from general principles, not from any specific problems in North Carolina. When the Whig *Raleigh Star* declared for the popular election of judges and justices of the peace, it grumbled about logrolling in the General Assembly and unqualified magistrates (justices of the peace) in many counties, but again without particulars. There were, no doubt, grounds for complaint; in 1848, there had been a nasty internecine spat among legislative Whigs over seats on the supreme and superior courts, with a handful of Democrats deciding the supreme court election and a few disgruntled Whigs handing the superior court seat to a Democrat. But advocates of the popular election of judges and other public officers rarely particularized their indictment.[25]

The Democrats won big in the 1850 elections, but they did not push a judicial election amendment through the legislature. Getting constitutional amendments passed was not easy. The 1835 constitutional convention had filled a gap in North Carolina's fundamental law by creating procedures for amending the constitution. The General Assembly could call a convention by a two-thirds favorable vote in each house; or it could adopt an amendment by a three-fifths majority in each house, pass it again by a two-thirds majority following legislative elections, and then submit the proposed amendment to the voters. Through the latter process, the lawmakers and the voters secured free suffrage in 1857, doubling the number of citizens who could vote for senator and creating, in the words of John V. Orth, "a republic of tax-paying white males twenty-one years of age or older." But the elective judiciary remained beyond reach.[26]

Advocates of popular judicial elections continued to agitate for change throughout the 1850s. In 1851, when suffrage reformers were trying to get a constitutional convention called, members of the state house of commons, as the house of representatives was then called, unsuccessfully sought to add a recommendation that judges, justices of the peace, and the top state executive officers be elected by the people. One member called it "singular that the people should have no voice in the election of the highest officers of the State" and declared that "[n]o tyranny was more galling than judicial tyranny." In an address to the people of the state, a meeting of western legislators, most of them Whigs, charged that the legislature had often been the scene of intrigues where judges had been chosen to serve party purposes rather than the interests of the people. But critics rarely, if ever, pointed to specific instances of "judicial tyranny" or other problems with the courts.[27]

Such interest as there was in judicial elections may have stemmed from gripes about the local courts. The address of the western legislators passed quickly over the election of judges and state executive officers but hammered on the election of justices of the peace. In North Carolina, the governor, upon the recommendation of the General Assembly, appointed justices for life. The justices constituted the county courts, known as courts of pleas and quarter sessions. The county courts, in addition to their probate and other judicial duties, largely governed their counties. They had general supervision over roads, ferries, and bridges; appointed commissioners to lay off rivers; licensed peddlers; had custody of weights and measures; established county fairs and appointed fair commissioners; appointed the county coroners; and had numerous other powers and responsibilities. The justices formed wealthy, powerful oligarchies that largely controlled life in their counties.[28]

The western legislators called the appointment of justices of the peace by the legislature "worse than a farce." Members who wanted certain men appointed, often for political purposes, simply handed in the names to be read by the clerk. "Nobody hears the names, or cares to hear them." That an appointee was unfit for the office made no difference. The address listed the numerous important powers exercised by the justices, including the imposition of taxes "much more heavy than those imposed by the Legislature." "If they tax the people," asked the western lawmakers, "ought not the people to elect them?" There was, they said, no constitutional amendment more necessary for the public good than this. But by 1854, the suffrage amendment had garnered the support of both parties, so that, in good Jeffersonian fashion, a broad electorate would soon be choosing the legislators who would be selecting the judges. Once that happened, the arguments for judicial elections lost some of their punch. Despite efforts to keep the reform movement alive, antebellum North Carolina would see no further changes to its constitution.[29]

With Virginia and North Carolina sharing so many features in their constitutional development, why were the outcomes for judicial elections so different? Perhaps the most important answer lies in the distinctive identity of Virginia's western Upcountry. Western Virginia—even leaving out the Shenandoah Valley and accounting only for the future state of West Virginia—had about 31 percent of Virginia's white population in 1850 and nearly 40 percent of its territory. With few slaves and a long border with the free states of Pennsylvania and Ohio, West Virginians had strong political, cultural, and economic affinities for the Midwest and the mid-Atlantic states. Even their attitudes toward marriage differed from the rest of Virginia's.[30] If Virginia were to retain its great influence in the affairs of the Union at a time of intense conflict between North and South and of growing talk of secession in the southern states, it could not afford to lose West Virginia. Concessions had to be made; at the convention of 1850–51 they were made, under the leadership of easterner Henry A. Wise.

North Carolina's western population outnumbered the East's as early as 1830, but the state lacked a powerful commercial class interested in bringing the East and West together. Whereas Virginia had six towns with white populations exceeding five thousand in 1850, including Richmond (15,274), Wheeling (11,179), and Norfolk (9,075), the biggest town in North Carolina, Wilmington, had just 7,264 total inhabitants, nearly half of them slaves. No other town had more than three thousand white residents.[31]

North Carolina also lacked an eastern leader of Wise's caliber to overcome the East's resistance to concessions on the key issue of representation. Like West Virginians, North Carolina's westerners developed a sense of themselves as a people distinct from the easterners; unlike West Virginians, their orientation was toward the South.³² In the great national contest, North Carolinians of the East and West shared a southern identity. Eastern Carolinians did not have to appease their western fellow citizens to keep them from a political separation. (Not that North Carolina had Virginia's pretensions to preserving great influence in national councils.) In short, easterners in North Carolina lacked the incentives of Virginia's easterners to conciliate their West. Judicial elections were a side issue in Virginia, one more plum to mollify westerners; in North Carolina, they were not even that.

South Carolina

In South Carolina, judicial elections never stood a chance at all. South Carolina also had an East-West rift and arguably the least democratic constitution in the nation. Already in the eighteenth century the white population of South Carolina's western Upcountry far exceeded that of the aristocratic Lowcountry, which had disproportionate representation in the legislature. The constitution of 1790 specified what localities would have what numbers of senators and representatives, with no formula for accommodating changes in population or the movement of people. Voters had to meet a property-holding or taxpaying qualification. Representatives had to own five hundred acres of land and ten slaves or real estate worth 150 pounds sterling, free of debt; senators, a freehold estate (usually meaning a full ownership interest in real property) worth three hundred pounds sterling, clear of debt. The requirements were higher if the representative or senator did not live in the district from which he was elected. The property-holding requirement was significantly greater for the governor and lieutenant governor. The state residency requirements for all these officers were considerable (ten years in the case of the governor and lieutenant governor). The constitution left to the legislature complete power to establish a judicial system, but it stipulated that judicial tenure would be during good behavior. The legislature appointed the superior court judges, commissioners of the treasury, the secretary of state, and the surveyor-general. All other officers would continue to be appointed "as hitherto," unless the legislature directed otherwise.³³

The constitution of 1790 put almost the entire power of the government into the hands of the legislature. In turn, the property tests for officeholding and the scheme of representation, which favored small, Lowcountry parishes, put legislative power into the hands of a slaveholding,

Lowcountry aristocracy. Upcountry folks naturally felt aggrieved. However, as cotton cultivation and slavery spread to the Upcountry, a nouveau-riche elite emerged there that felt a kinship with the older, aristocratic class of the low-lying rice-growing region. The relatively small South Carolina Upcountry lost its democratic zeal with the desertion of its local elite and the appearance of black slaves. In the so-called compromises of 1808 and 1810, the Lowcountry planters agreed to constitutional amendments that granted nearly equal legislative representation to the Upcountry and abolished the property qualification for voting. But the equality of representation proved illusory as slavery encroached on the Upcountry and the territory of the white belt shrank. Moreover, the aristocrats, "bound together by kinship, economic, political, and cultural ties," controlled both the Upcountry and the Lowcountry, and South Carolina retained the nation's highest property qualifications for holding office.[34]

Notwithstanding this upper-crust consensus and the alleged cooling of the Upcountry's democratic ardor, many westerners remained disgruntled with their unequal status. A lengthy article in the Upcountry *Southern Patriot* in 1852 complained that the upper portion of the state paid more taxes and had more whites, more slaves, and more territory than the lower portion but was grossly underrepresented in the senate. Some of the small eastern parishes had "not population and taxation enough to give them one Representative in the House," argued the paper, yet they had "an equal influence in the Senate" with the large Upcountry election districts of Edgefield, Pendleton, and Spartanburg, "whose wealth and population entitle them to five, six, and seven Representatives. Is such a government worthy of the name republic?" Senate representation was not the westerners' only complaint. They also pointed to the hardships that large political and judicial districts imposed on courts, litigants, and witnesses.[35]

In 1852, a movement to divide the districts of Edgefield and Barnwell took off. Both districts, separated from Georgia by the Savannah River, occupied middle ground between the Lowcountry parishes and the Upcountry districts. Edgefield straddled the fall line commonly used to distinguish the Up- and Lowcountry; Barnwell adjoined Edgefield on the latter's southeastern border. "Harper," in the first of a series of pro-division articles for the *Edgefield Advertiser*, criticized the enduring intransigence of the "aristocratic tyrants" in the legislature in refusing past petitions for division. The obduracy of the parishes, wrote Harper, had driven the Edgefield divisionists "to side with the Mountain Districts, where disaffection to the Parishes is spreading fast and wide." On the other hand, Harper thought it necessary to pen his articles in order "to arouse the Up-Country from a lethargic dream."[36]

Harper was interested chiefly in the system of representation in the legislature, but he claimed that rustics from Barnwell to the North Carolina line were being marshalled for a united "demand on the Barons for a new charter":

> The division of Barnwell, Edgefield and Pendleton—the re-organization of the basis of Representation—giving the election of Presidential Electors to the people—erecting a better Free School System—establishing a Penitentiary—putting down the Militia System—publishing an edition of the Laws which common people can read and understand, and indeed, a departure in several directions, from what is erroneously called "the settled policy of the State," because it is in reality only "the settled policy of the Parishes," may soon be expected.

The divisionists were divided among themselves. Some of the Edgefield divisionists, perhaps attracted too much to the lifestyle and social status of the Lowcountry planters, displayed insufficient sympathy for the inhabitants of the mountain districts. One of the latter warned, "If the Divisionists of Edgefield are not cooperating with the Divisionists of the 'up country,'—laboring to obtain a balance of power in our Legislature by dividing the larger Districts, and thereby gaining a Senator for every new District," then the mountain people would support neither the division desired by Edgefield nor the latter's candidates. The author of this caution called for other reforms as well, including the popular election of judges and other public officers.[37]

Nothing came of all these demands. South Carolinians had been distracted from a discussion of state concerns by the great national conflict over slavery; but, wrote Harper, "as we are at peace now with our mortal enemy—Uncle Sam" (this was about three months before President Franklin Pierce signed the incendiary Kansas-Nebraska Act), the time was right for a discussion of state affairs. It was wishful thinking. As long ago as the 1790s, by which time the clash between the Upcountry and the Lowcountry had already appeared, political theorists in South Carolina had argued that a mere numerical majority had no special right to rule and that wealth and property had a claim to representation in government. John C. Calhoun's *A Disquisition on Government*, published shortly before the eruption of the divisionist controversy, similarly contended for representation of diverse interests rather than just numbers of people. During the polemics on division, the *Southern Quarterly Review* published a defense of South Carolina's political philosophy, lauding the state's existing system of government as ideal. Calhoun's theory of "concurrent majorities" was employed to defend South Carolina's interests as a state from supposed depredations by the federal government. When the Kansas-Nebraska Act reignited the fight over slavery, any reform based on the rights of a numerical majority lost all chance of success. With no democratic movement to carry reforms in its wake, the scattered sparks of interest in judicial elections died out.[38]

Georgia

After the amendments of 1811–12 providing for the popular election of justices of the peace and inferior court judges, further democratization of the Georgia constitution came slowly. Amendments in 1824 and 1835 transferred the choice of governor to the voters and eliminated the property qualifications for election to the house and senate. After much agitation, an extralegal constitutional convention, and two authorized conventions, all focused on representation, the General Assembly in 1843 finally reformed legislative apportionment; but it did that to reduce the size of the legislature so as to enhance efficiency and save money, not to equalize representation. A newspaper exulted that the "measure will no doubt bring about a new era in the history of Georgia legislation." However, as the governor pointed out in his inaugural address, the amendment would "not affect the principle of Representation."[39]

In 1847, the state's newspapers and legislators suddenly showed substantial interest in extending popular election to supreme and superior court judges, prosecutors, and state executive officers. A bill to transfer the selection of superior court judges to the people lost in the house by just six votes. The movement for popular election continued in the next biennial session. As with the 1812 constitutional amendment making the inferior court justices elective, the reasons for this newfound concern are obscure. Complaints about "trafficking for offices at every tavern and boarding house" and about logrolling in the legislature surfaced during the debate over an election bill in 1849, but the newspapers had had little bad to say about the superior courts before then.[40]

What is clearer is that by 1847 the proposal to adopt judicial elections was in line with a growing trend. Constitutional conventions in Missouri,

Iowa, New York, Illinois, and Wisconsin had recently approved the election of some or all of their states' judges, and in Ohio the rising Democratic star Clement Vallandigham had spoken out powerfully before his fellow state representatives in favor of judicial elections.[41]

In Georgia, the arguments pro and con were generally the same as those made elsewhere. The Augusta *Daily Constitutionalist* noted the principal objections made by election opponents: that elections would tempt candidates into "demagogueism, and discreditable electioneering appeals for the popular suffrage"; that the "adroit electioneerer" would prevail over better qualified but less popular men; that successful candidates, in making decisions, would favor those who helped get them elected; that a desire to curry favor among the voters would lead corrupt judges to "pander to popular prejudice," while "fear of popular indignation" would overawe weak judges. The paper rejected all the charges, insisting, first, that the people were more intelligent and virtuous than opponents of elections gave them credit for; and second, that corruption and weakness were failings of human nature that could afflict any judge, regardless of how he had been selected. Moreover, election advocates asserted, appointment by the General Assembly had not been a resounding success. A representative complained on the floor of the house that legislators, in appointing judges, had engaged in "enormities and outrages" that would "disgrace a brothel." The sins committed by appointed judges, he claimed, included drunkenness, political favoritism, and "gross violation of official duty."[42]

But there was an added dimension to the debate. The ambiguous wording of the constitution gave rise to a dispute over the legislature's authority to adopt judicial elections by statute. The constitution provided that superior court judges "shall be elected," without saying by whom. Those who believed the legislature had no power to change the system of selection by statute insisted that the constitution inferentially imposed the duty of appointing the judges on the General Assembly. The constitution provided for the legislative selection of the judges of courts above and below the superior courts, they argued; the only reasonable interpretation was that it had meant for the lawmakers to appoint all judges. Furthermore, the framers of the constitution had, "by contemporaneous exposition" (presumably meaning their actual practice), shown that they intended for the legislature to be the appointing authority. If that were not so, they would have drafted a bill in the first post-convention legislature to put popular elections into effect. Those who contended that the General Assembly could make the superior courts elective by statute pointed out that the constitution did not expressly confer the appointing power on the legislature and, therefore, that the people had not delegated it.[43]

Ultimately the lawmakers decided on a referendum to measure public sentiment on the question. As in other states, the voters showed far less interest in the issue than did newsmen and politicians. The turnout was low, but those who did vote overwhelmingly favored election. In 1852, the General Assembly enacted the popular preference into law.[44]

During the public debate over electing superior court judges, the idea of making the supreme court elective received very little notice. Perhaps the reason was that the superior court judges were elected by district, so that the electorate was more likely to know them than they were to know the judges of the supreme court. That argument was made in other states. Another reason may have been the newness of the supreme court. Established by constitutional amendment in 1835, the court did not begin to function until 1846 because a longstanding hostility to the very idea of a supreme court kept the legislature from passing a law necessary to implement the amendment.[45]

The situation soon changed. A bill introduced during the 1853–54 legislative session sought to amend the constitution to make supreme court judgeships elective. To take effect, a proposed amendment had to pass each house of the General Assembly by a two-thirds majority in two successive sessions. The *Albany Patriot* optimistically predicted that there would not be much opposition, but the bill failed to get a two-thirds majority in the senate. In the 1855–56 session, a bill to make various changes to the judicial system, including the election of supreme court judges, did receive the requisite majorities. It again passed the house with a constitutional majority in 1857, but several senators argued against some features of the proposed amendment and succeeded in talking it to death. The senate postponed the bill indefinitely by a vote of 61–28, reconsidered that vote, and indefinitely postponed it again. After the first postponement a newspaper correspondent noted that public hostility toward the bill had been so vehement in some counties that "opposition to it had been made the test question for election." Unfortunately, the writer did not say what features of the bill had stoked such antipathy. The supreme court remained appointive until 1896.[46]

The absence of more-significant constitutional issues may help account for the failure of efforts to make supreme court judgeships and other state officers elective. (A constitutional amendment of 1855, however, did provide for the popular election of the state's attorney and local solicitors. This amendment, which modified a previous amendment of the same section passed in 1843, aligned with a nationwide switch from appointed to elected prosecutors.) The constitutional tumult of the 1830s had not resolved the burning issue of representation, but as it turned out, due to the constitutional requirement that every county have at least one representative and to the spread of slavery throughout the state, the actual apportionments made were fundamentally fair, notwithstanding the use of the federal basis. In December 1849, while the lawmakers were heatedly arguing over the election of superior court judges, the *Southern Banner* of Athens called for a constitutional convention to switch to the white basis. But there was no larger outcry over apportionment or other important constitutional reforms. The election of supreme court judges had no coattails to ride.[47]

When Georgia made its superior court judges elective, it joined Arkansas and Alabama as the only states that, prior to secession, appointed their supreme courts while electing the rest of their judiciaries. And it was the only state that made one of its higher courts elective by statute.

Florida

Notwithstanding its location south of Georgia and its long Atlantic coastline, Florida is often regarded as part of, or akin to, the Old Southwest. Its panhandle extends westward along Alabama's southern border almost as far as Mississippi. When a convention drafted a constitution for Florida in 1838, the delegates used Alabama's "thoroughly democratic" constitution as their chief model. Florida then was frontier territory, where thousands of migrants not wedded to the institutions they had known in their home states were creating "new social and cultural arrangements." In no other southeastern state was the atmosphere more conducive to constitutional innovation.[48]

Florida's constitution of 1838 boasted important democratic features more characteristic of the Southwest than the Southeast. It imposed no taxpayer qualifications for voting or holding office and expressly prohibited property qualifications for either. To vote, a person had to be enrolled in the militia unless exempted by law, a requirement that posed no impediment to voting since by statute all able-bodied white males from eighteen to forty-five years of age had to enroll unless exempted. The governor and legislators would be popularly elected, as would circuit court clerks. True, the General Assembly would appoint all judges, state officers, and solicitors and provide by law for the selection of justices of the peace, probate officers, and county commissioners; but Floridians could reasonably expect that the legislature would make most local officers elective since by 1838 they were already electing them.[49]

The constitution also did away with the powerful, appointed county courts, which had been heavily criticized as overbearing and unrepublican. In 1843, federal judge William Marvin, whom the territorial legislature had appointed to prepare the Revised Statutes of Florida, described the county courts as "a useless appendage of our judicial establishment." Noting that the superior courts and justice courts were "fully competent" to handle the judicial business of the county courts, Marvin recommended that boards of county commissioners be elected to transact county business and that county probate officers be appointed. Florida's first General Assembly provided for the election of county commissioners and other local officers and for the appointment by the governor of probate judges.[50]

In one important respect, however, the Florida constitution recalled the aristocratic constitutions of the older southeastern states. It provided for apportionment of the legislature on the basis of the federal formula (the number of free white inhabitants plus three-fifths of the number of slaves in a county or senate district), with each county entitled to at least one representative. The three-fifths clause gave disproportionate representation to the slaveholding planters of Middle Florida, a growing region that slanted sharply toward the Whigs. The entitlement of every county to a representative benefited the smaller counties, which had fewer slaves and tilted toward the Democrats. This offsetting of inequalities, which may have been the result of a compromise at the convention, seems to have left most Floridians more or less satisfied with the apportionment scheme, as control of the General Assembly swung back and forth between the parties. There would be little agitation over representation before the Civil War.[51]

The constitution described a judicial system composed of a supreme court, courts of chancery, circuit courts, and justices of the peace, plus corporation courts if the legislature chose to create them. However, for the first five years of statehood, and beyond if the legislature did not decide otherwise, the supreme court would consist of the circuit court judges, of whom there would be at least four. Chancery (equity) courts were to be created by the General Assembly at its discretion. Supreme and circuit judges would hold office during good behavior.[52]

Florida had to wait more than six years before being paired with a free territory (Iowa) for admission to the Union. By the time Congress granted statehood to Florida in 1845, the constitution was already outdated. Between 1830 and 1840, the total population grew by 57 percent, with the rate of increase of slaves outpacing that of whites. In the 1840s, the population grew even faster, but now the rate of growth for whites far exceeded that for slaves. As in other frontier territories and states, the white newcomers tended to gravitate toward the political party that espoused equality and democracy. The inchoate two-party system of proto-Whigs and proto-Democrats of the 1830s solidified after the constitutional convention. Upon the close of the convention, a group of leading "Democratic Republican Citizens," professing the "Jeffersonian Republican faith" and "ardent support" for President Van Buren's administration, formally organized as a party. They called for the creation of committees of correspondence in every county, a central committee for the state, and an address to like-minded Floridians "in relation to the various political topics requiring discussion and action." The Whigs, on the whole wealthier, more conservative, and less imbued with party spirit, had dominated the territorial government before the convention. Now they watched with dismay as their rivals won control of the government in the early 1840s. They learned the hard way that to compete on even terms they would have to imitate the Democrats' party organization and appeal to the democratic sentiments of the voters.[53]

The Democrats won the first state elections in 1845 and 1846. In his annual address to the General Assembly in November 1846, Governor William D. Moseley called upon the legislature to adopt constitutional amendments to provide for biennial instead of annual legislative sessions, to reduce the residency requirement for suffrage from two years to six months, and to provide for the election of circuit court judges to terms of five to ten years. As already observed, Floridians were accustomed to electing their local officers from territorial days. The *Pensacola Gazette* had described those who had filled the territory's appointive posts as "broken down and noisy politicians," and territorial governor Richard K. Call had called for making those posts elective where possible. Thus, although the election of judges was still a novelty, Moseley's 1846 recommendation could not have come as a shock. Nevertheless, the lawmakers did not act on it during that session.[54]

Moseley repeated his proposal in his 1847 annual message. "It is difficult to account for the existing anomaly in our State Constitutions which forbids to the people a voice in the selection of those of their public servants who, perhaps, of all others, have the most to do with taking care of their interests," said Moseley. He called the existing method of selection "manifestly a system opposed to the spirit of our free institutions." The governor urged prompt action. Once the initial five-year term was up, he warned, judges would be appointed for life, with the result that the "undoubted right" of the people to elect their judges would be "virtually nullifie[d]." The General Assembly, now in the hands of the Whigs, again declined to act.[55]

In his final annual address in November 1848, Moseley made one last pitch for judicial elections, "one more effort to excite public attention to this striking anomaly in our institutions." The need to "excite public attention" suggests that the public was not particularly interested in the subject. The General Assembly, still controlled by the Whigs, also remained unimpressed. At the end of the session, the Democratic *Floridian & Journal* called the passage of laws to provide for the election of probate judges and the register of public lands "a considerable advance of the popular principle [and] a strong index of the growing disposition to submit all offices to the same ordeal." However, the house had checked the "progressive spirit" by voting down a bill for the election of the circuit court judges. But the paper promised that Democrats would continue to press for judicial elections and that the majority of the people would demand it.[56]

Moseley's term as governor ended in 1849. During his tenure, the General Assembly had amended the constitution to switch from annual to biennial legislative sessions, reduce the terms of circuit court judges from life to eight years, and ease the requirements for suffrage by lowering the minimum period of residence in the state from two years to one and eliminating the need to be enrolled in the militia. Given the General Assembly's failure to approve judicial elections, the election of a Whig as governor in 1849 and continued Whig control of the General Assembly might have portended ill for the prospect of judicial elections. Indeed, although Governor Thomas Brown devoted a considerable portion of his first address to the legislature to reform of the judiciary, he said nothing about judicial elections.[57]

But times had changed. By the time Brown sent his message to the General Assembly on November 25, 1850 (due to the switch to biennial sessions, there was no 1849–1850 session), at least a dozen states had swapped or were in the process of swapping election for appointment as the method of judicial selection, in most cases for all of their courts. These included the southern states of Texas, Alabama, and Arkansas.

Mississippi, of course, had long boasted of its elective judiciary. In Louisiana in 1845, James Brent had strenuously argued for judicial elections, flourishing before his fellow convention delegates a letter from Mississippi's John A. Quitman, a former opponent of elections, proclaiming the Mississippi experiment "eminently successful."[58] The rush was on, and judicial elections were no longer a party issue.

In November 1850, after the Democrats had gained a small majority in each house of the legislature, Whig senator Jesse J. Finley introduced a bill to make the judiciary elective. On December 9, the Committee on Amendments and Revision of the Constitution, chaired by Finley, issued an enthusiastic report in favor of passage. Four days later the bill passed the senate unanimously. The house judiciary committee also reported in favor of the bill, adding that the members regarded the proposed amendment "as demanded by public opinion." Again, the bill passed unanimously. The next General Assembly approved the amendment with just one dissenting vote.[59]

The judicial election amendment did not pass alone. It was accompanied by an amendment to make solicitors elective, which easily sailed through the legislature. The General Assembly of 1852–53 also passed, with little opposition, an amendment transferring the selection of the secretary of state, the state treasurer, the state comptroller, and court clerks from the legislature to the voters. However, that measure ran into trouble in the subsequent General Assembly. By a 3–2 vote the senate Committee on Revision of the Constitution recommended the bill as "wise, proper and just." The minority objected that voters scattered across such a large state could not know the qualifications of the candidates and that the constitution should not be tampered with in the absence of serious grievances. When the bill came before the full senate needing a two-thirds vote for passage, it did not even muster a majority.[60]

There is no obvious reason why the General Assembly of 1854–55 should have defeated a proposal to make state executive offices elective after the 1852–53 legislature had passed both that measure and an amendment making judges elective with little dissent. The 1854 elections did not significantly alter the partisan composition of the General Assembly. One major event that occurred between the end of the 1852–53 session and the opening of the 1854–55 session was the passage by Congress of the Kansas-Nebraska Act. This legislation incorporated the principle of popular sovereignty, allowing the people of territorial Kansas and Nebraska to choose for themselves whether or not to permit slavery. Conservatives had always doubted the wisdom of "king numbers." After the act passed, southerners rallied to the defense of slavery and denounced popular sovereignty as embodied in the measure. The *Florida Sentinel* noted that the act's northern Democratic supporters had claimed that popular sovereignty would keep the territories free. This type of majoritarianism had no appeal in the South. Perhaps the reaction against popular sovereignty encouraged Florida's state senators to oppose the extension of the elective principle to state executive offices.[61]

Florida's constitution of 1838 failed the test of Jeffersonian democracy, at least on its face, because it favored wealthy slaveholders in the apportionment of the legislature. However, that affront to democracy was counterbalanced, at least to some extent, by the requirement that every county have at least one representative. In any event, there does not seem to have been any public uproar over the apportionment scheme. Generally speaking, in states where no one felt the need to crusade for such basic constitutional rights as free suffrage or equal representation, it took some other major impetus for constitutional revision, such as reining in spendthrift legislatures, to create a movement strong enough to draw judicial elections into its vortex. In Florida, the impetus appears to have been simply a belief that the constitution of the new state should embody democratic principles. Judicial elections came to Florida during a further democratization of an already democratic constitution.

CHAPTER 4

The Old Southwest

Charles S. Sydnor, southern born and bred, began his scholarly career as a neo-Confederate historian. The neo-Confederates glorified the antebellum South as an idyllic civilization led by cultured aristocrats in which the slaves were well cared for and content. They blamed Yankee abolitionists for bringing on the Civil War and for fomenting racial hatred with Reconstruction. But populist governor Theodore Bilbo's politically motivated purge of many of Sydnor's colleagues from the faculty of the University of Mississippi in 1930 awakened Sydnor to the splintered nature of southern society and to the blinkered character of neo-Confederate history. The reorientation of Sydnor's scholarly thinking led to his award-winning book *The Development of Southern Sectionalism: 1819–1848*. As described by historian Fred Arthur Bailey, the book "chronicled the transformation of the South from a land of national, respected, and progressive leaders—Washington, Jefferson, Madison, Monroe—to a region of lesser demagogues dedicated primarily to the defense of slavery and sectional pride."[1]

Sydnor thought that the South began to lose its respectability in the 1830s, just when the mixed blessing of democracy (mixed, because it could empower demagogues such as Bilbo) reached new heights in the Old Southwest. By 1837, the governments of four states—five if we include the then-independent Republic of Texas—were "thoroughly democratic." "In each of these states—Alabama, Mississippi, Tennessee, Arkansas, and Texas—the governor was popularly elected, there was universal manhood suffrage, legislative apportionment in both houses was based on white population, with provision for periodic reapportionments, and county government was democratic." (Sydnor omitted the adjective "white" in describing suffrage, but even that discriminatory word had its democratic aspect. Basing apportionment on the white population reduced the representation of plantation owners in the legislature.) One state of the Old

Southwest does not appear in Sydnor's list: Louisiana. Even there, though, Sydnor thought that "democracy was closely approximated" with the adoption of a new constitution in 1845.[2]

Sydnor neither used the term "Old Southwest" nor enumerated the states that the Southwest comprised. The Old Southwest is a vaguely defined region that, by one account, stretches from somewhere in western Georgia to the Mississippi River and from the Tennessee River to the Gulf of Mexico. In another telling, it includes "some combination" of Virginia, Kentucky, North Carolina, South Carolina, Tennessee, Georgia, Alabama, Mississippi, Louisiana, Arkansas, and Texas. Literary scholar James H. Justus wrote that while "the Old Southwest did have boundaries—give or take a state or two," "[l]atitude in terminology" did not bother early observers of the region. However, for this study of state and regional constitutional change in the mid-nineteenth century, we need to pin the boundaries down. The most convenient contemporary categorization is the one used in the federal census of 1850, which puts Alabama, Arkansas, Louisiana, Mississippi, Tennessee, and Texas in the Southwest. These states made up the West of the future southern confederacy.[3]

The Southwest, although undoubtedly southern, was also western. Every state west of the original thirteen, north and south, made its judiciary at least partly elective before the Civil War. In the Old Southwest, Mississippi, Louisiana, Tennessee, and Texas included all their courts in the judicial transformation. Alabama and Arkansas excluded their supreme courts. As we saw in chapter 1, Mississippi, with its mushrooming population and egalitarian ethos, led the charge in 1832.

Four states of the Old Southwest moved to judicial elections by way of constitutional amendment, which means that there was no big tome of convention debates to serve as a source of enlightenment on the motives and reasoning of the reform's backers and opponents. Amendments had to go through the legislature and in most states a popular referendum as well; but legislative journals did not record debates, and newspaper coverage of amendments was far less intense than reporting on conventions. Furthermore, even in the two southwestern states that transformed judicial selection through a constitutional convention, the conventions did not retain the services of an official reporter. This paucity of convenient primary sources has no doubt contributed to the neglect of the southwestern states by historians of judicial elections. Nevertheless, the story can be pieced together.[4]

Arkansas

The record for Arkansas is particularly skimpy. Arkansas entered the Union in 1836 with a democratic political culture. Its population was small, comparable to that of Texas but nowhere near those of the other southwestern states. A remote and rugged land located west of the Mississippi, the territory of Arkansas had just 30,388 inhabitants, white and black, in 1830. The great migration that washed over Alabama and Mississippi did not reach Arkansas with the same force, although some easterners kept going all the way across the river. The biggest contingent of immigrants came from Tennessee. The population grew fast, more than tripling by 1840 and then more than doubling again, to almost 210,000, by 1850. But by the latter year, Arkansas remained the least populous state in the Old Southwest, about one-fifth the size of Tennessee.

In the democratic conditions of frontier Arkansas, the state convention of 1836 produced a democratic constitution. It provided for universal white male suffrage, legislative apportionment based on the white male population (although each county in existence when the constitution took effect was entitled to at least one representative), and no property or tax-paying requirement for holding office. However, the constitution barred atheists from public office. Judges and state executive officers other than the governor would be appointed by the legislature, but the people would elect most local officials, including justices of the peace. The justices also served as the county courts, together with a presiding judge in each county elected by the court who also served as the probate judge. These courts exercised most of the powers of local government.[5]

Notwithstanding the popular nature of the constitution, a dominant planter class emerged over time. It "coalesced over the course of a generation from a variety of elements: sons of planters of the Old South on the make in the West, frontier lawyers and doctors, land speculators, and self-made men, elevated from the yeomanry." The yeoman farmers enjoyed a "steady if hollow acknowledgment of yeoman respectability and equality." But the differences between the planters and yeomanry were not sufficiently great or deeply rooted to disturb the general social harmony or the overall satisfaction with the state's constitutional arrangements. The first constitutional amendments, aside from one concerning banks, seem to have been aimed at practical judicial problems. One gave the General Assembly the power to compel judges of one judicial circuit to hear cases in another, a second allowed the legislature to expand the jurisdiction of justices of the peace, and a third stated that judges and other public officers having specified terms would remain in office until their successors were chosen and qualified.[6]

The bank amendment of 1846 stemmed from bad experiences with state investments in the two banks that were authorized by the constitution, a state bank and "one other banking institution, calculated to aid and promote the great agricultural interests of the country." In 1841, the state's entire outstanding debt of $2,676,000 was due to these investments. That year, the *Arkansas State Gazette* editorialized, "We believe that the people of Arkansas would stand direct taxation *for State purposes* as cheerfully as any people in the Union; but that we should be taxed to pay the debts of the most *aristocratic* monopoly of land holders in the United States is unbearable." The General Assembly of 1844-45 passed an amendment to prohibit the creation of any banks in the future, and the next legislature ratified it. The constitution did not require that the amendment be submitted to the voters for approval.[7]

Inevitably, even in a state as relatively free of social conflict as Arkansas, other complaints about the constitution arose. In 1844, Senator David Maxwell presented a citizens' petition asking for seven specific constitutional amendments. Three would have enhanced the separation of church and state. The others proposed to prohibit the state from pledging its credit or faith, eliminate the legislature's power to create or charter banks, require a two-thirds majority of each legislative chamber rather than a simple majority to override a gubernatorial veto, and improve the procedure for amending the constitution. The petition also contained a number of other suggestions, including the popular election of the presiding judges of the county courts.[8]

Except for the prohibition of new banks, nothing came of these proposals at the time. The petition had been signed by just seventeen individuals in three counties, and the newspapers gave no indication of agitation for reform. However, during the 1846 session of the General Assembly, legislators introduced numerous constitutional amendments. On November 16, Senator Thomas Newton offered a resolution to provide for the popular election of the presiding judges of the county courts and of county prosecuting attorneys. The next day, Senator Richard C. Byrd moved a substitute resolution embracing eight amendments. The substitute proposed to add the election of circuit court judges; prohibit the General Assembly from electing any of its members to other offices; limit the length of legislative sessions; limit the membership of the senate and house to eighteen and fifty-four, respectively, until the state's population reached five hundred thousand; and allow the legislature to create judicial circuits having any number of counties. All the amendments were referred to a select committee of seven senators that included both Newton and Byrd. The committee endorsed all eight amendments and added two more, one to modify the constitution's provisions on taxation, the other to allow the General Assembly to create new counties of any size from three existing ones.[9]

The senators squabbled over the amendments involving the sizes of the two houses, taxation, and the size of counties, but the election amendments cruised through with no opposition and then passed the house as well. Altogether, the legislature passed seven of the ten amendments reported by the select committee, two (on taxation and counties) in modified form. The proposals on the sizes of the house and senate and on the length of legislative sessions failed. The next General Assembly ratified the five amendments that provided for popular elections, empowered the legislature to create judicial circuits with any number of counties, and barred legislators from appointing their house and senate colleagues to public office.[10]

The election of circuit court judges, presiding judges of the county courts, and county prosecutors was so generally accepted that there seems to have been no debate on the subject in the legislature of 1848–49. The senate votes on final passage of the amendments were 21-2 (circuit court judges), 23-1 (prosecutors), and 25-0 (county judges). Nor was there much discussion in the newspapers, although the *Washington Telegraph* did carry an exchange on the subject. Responding to pro-election articles, the editors warned, "Bring [judges] down at the feet of the people; send them about through the circuit, like so many beggarly mendicants, electioneering for a reelection to their places, and where is their independence then?" In the absence of a crusade for wholesale constitutional revision or complaints specifically about the courts, it is hard to assign a reason for the change in judicial selection, other than that the principle of selecting public officers by popular election was in the air everywhere. But in Arkansas its application was limited to local officers. The day after the senate ratified the five amendments of 1848, Senator G. W. Clarke proposed to amend the constitution to provide for the election of state executive officers. It received little attention. And few people at the time seem to have been interested in the election of supreme court judges.[11]

That would soon change. For the time being, given the early establishment of local democracy in Arkansas and the national trend toward the election of most local officers, a move to make county court judges elective conformed to the spirit of the age. The county court, held by the presiding judge and two justices of the peace, was the main agency of local government. Its statutory "powers and jurisdiction" included "all matters relating to county taxes, disbursement of money for county purposes, and in any other case that may be necessary for the internal improvement and local concerns of the county." The court had oversight of roads and bridges and the supervision of paupers. It granted various business licenses, appointed the judges of elections, audited and settled claims against the county, had management of county property, and ordered the erection of county buildings.[12] It is probably safe to assume that the presiding judges, who also served as the probate judges, dominated the county courts, in which case it could hardly be a cause of wonder that the people wanted the power to elect them.

The circuit court amendment was a more significant innovation. The circuit courts were purely judicial bodies, with extensive original and appellate jurisdiction. As of December 1846, when the General Assembly passed the amendment providing for the election of circuit court judges as the first step in the amendment process, only the constitutions of Mississippi, Michigan Iowa, and New York provided for elected "real" judges. In the latter two states, the first judicial elections were still months away. Michigan had just held its first elections for the recently created county courts the month before. The election of prosecutors, too, was uncommon at the time. Before 1846, only four states had elected prosecutors.[13]

Perhaps Arkansans saw the change to elective circuit court judges and prosecutors as the completion of local democracy. Unlike the supreme court, which was primarily an appellate court and sat only in Little Rock, each circuit court had to hold two terms in every county in its circuit every year. Even folks who were not already personally acquainted with the judges and prosecutors had opportunities as attorneys, litigants, witnesses, or observers to get to know them on the socially important court day. The supreme court lacked that closeness to the people. Arkansas political scientists Diane D. Blair and Jay Barth observed that for small farmers "state government was irrelevant at best, irritating and intrusive more often.... [T]hey were doubtless anxious to stay at arm's length from an expensive and seemingly unnecessary relationship."[14]

The supreme court's distance from the people may or may not have played a part in the omission of the court from the 1848 amendments, but the enthusiasm for the popular election of public officers soon caught up with that tribunal. In a letter to the *Washington Telegraph* in July 1848, "One of the People" endorsed the election amendments, arguing that they would keep candidates for office from flocking to the state capital "like carrier pigeons" to market themselves to legislators and would encourage officers to serve the people well in the hope of getting reelected. The same considerations, said the writer, would apply to supreme court judges and state executive officers. In November, the governor, in his address to the legislature, recommended extending the elective principle to the supreme court judges and other "public functionaries" and suggested that a convention would be a better method than piecemeal amendments for dealing with this and other constitutional issues.[15]

Throughout the 1850s, supporters of elections kept pushing for additional constitutional amendments or a convention. In 1850, a senate committee reported a resolution for the election of supreme court judges and state executive officers. The full senate passed a similar resolution in 1852 and again in 1857, while the house did likewise in 1854. The principle of popular election obviously had great support, but the senators and representatives couldn't get their legislative act together. Finally, in 1859, the General Assembly passed an amendment to provide for the election of the secretary of state, auditor, treasurer, and attorney general, but the secretary of state failed to publish the resolution as required by the constitution. In 1860, the house passed the resolution again by a large majority, but the senate rejected it. A separate resolution to provide for the election of supreme court judges received a majority in the house but less than the two-thirds necessary to send it to the senate.[16]

The voters never got to express their sentiments on the issue directly. Even if an amendment had gotten the requisite majority in one General Assembly, been properly published, and then received a two-thirds majority in each house of the next General Assembly, the measure would have become part of the constitution without a referendum. The closest the people came to having a direct say was their vote on the calling of a constitutional convention in 1854, authorized by the legislature the year before. The *Arkansas State Gazette and Democrat*, which devoted a column or more of many weekly issues to the proposed convention beginning at least as early as February 1854, set forth a list of "[s]ome of the more important points requiring reformation": (1) the extension of the elective franchise (an odd suggestion given the existing free suffrage, as a rival paper pointed out); (2) judicial reorganization to make the administration of justice simpler, faster, and cheaper; (3) removal of the prohibition of banks; (4) reduction of the size of the legislature in order to "secure cheaper, more expeditious, and wiser legislation"; (5) the direction of public funds toward improvements "of a general and permanent character" instead of "local and temporary objects" (which sounds like a complaint about logrolling); and (6) the election of all public officers for short terms to replace "that miserable system of juggling necessarily attending the election of officers by a few, which has filled our public stations with incompetent men, and brought ruin upon the State."[17]

Although elections came last on this partial list, the *State Gazette* later noted that "the necessity for a convention was urged through the columns of this paper, and one of the main reasons for holding one, was to make our State more thoroughly democratic, by letting the people resume into their own hands, the election of all their officers." The newspapers carried some debate over the pros and cons of electing supreme court judges, but how much the issue meant to voters is impossible to say. What we do know is that they didn't care enough to vote for a convention. The final tally stood 10,997 for a convention and 15,847 against. Apart from one amendment dealing with one county, no further amendments were adopted and no conventions held before the Civil War.[18]

Alabama

When the great migration to Mississippi began in the early nineteenth century, a planter elite already dominated life in and around the thriving river port of Natchez. Alabama had nothing quite like the Natchez aristocracy. It did, however, have its own stupendous in-migration that dwarfed that of Mississippi. According to the 1810 census, the white population of what would become the state of Mississippi numbered about twenty-three thousand, while that of the future Alabama fell short of 6,500. Ten years later, Alabama had more than eighty-five thousand white residents, twice the number of Mississippi's white population and more than Mississippi would be able to claim in 1830. Mississippi's white population tripled between 1810 and 1830; Alabama's increased by a factor of nearly thirty, to over 190,000. The tremendous influx into Alabama from the southeastern states included many planters and their slaves (slaves would constitute nearly two-fifths of the state's population in 1830), but ordinary folks also came in throngs. When Alabamians wrote a constitution in 1819, the document reflected the democratic sentiments of these yeomen and subsistence farmers. Besides, even the aristocracy "was not at all aristocratic in the political theories it accepted."[19]

At the constitutional convention of 1819, a Committee of Fifteen produced a first draft of a constitution. The committee consisted of eleven lawyers, three physicians, and a merchant. Most of them doubled as planters, and the planter counties had a disproportionate share of the members. The draft required membership in the militia for voting and used the federal ratio (whites plus three-fifths of slaves) for apportionment. The convention rejected both. When conservatives sought to allot one senator to each county, regardless of population, the delegates rejected that, too. The constitution as ultimately written based legislative representation in both houses on the white population; enfranchised all adult white males who had lived in the state for one year and the voting district for three months; imposed no property, taxpaying, or religious qualifications for holding office; gave the appointment of executive and judicial officers to the legislature rather than to the governor; and made sheriffs and court clerks elective. It was a remarkably democratic document.[20]

The constitution created a judiciary consisting of a supreme court, circuit courts, and justices of the peace. It expressly bestowed upon the General Assembly the authority to establish chancery and probate courts. The judges of the circuit courts would also serve as the judges of the supreme court until such time as the legislature chose to create a separate supreme court. Except for its power to issue certain remedial writs, the supreme court had only appellate jurisdiction. At the convention, the Committee of Fifteen recommended life tenure for judges. A proposed amendment to limit judicial tenure to six years lost, 25–18. However, the constitution conferred on the legislature the duty to decide on the manner of appointment and terms of office of justices of the peace.[21]

From the moment the constitution took effect, proponents of limited judicial tenure sought to amend it. They succeeded in 1830, assisted by the unpopularity of a supreme court decision. Advocates of the change insisted that it would make judges more responsive to the will of the people, while opponents feared a loss of judicial independence. The voters ratified the amendment by more than 3–1.[22]

By the mid-1830s, perhaps inspired by the passage of the amendment limiting judicial tenure or by the new constitution of Mississippi, some Alabama legislators had begun agitating for the popular election of judges.

The people had been electing their justices of the peace since 1823. The next target was the county court, a tribunal established when Alabama was part of the Mississippi Territory. The county court, presided over by a single judge, had civil and criminal as well as probate jurisdiction. It also had a wide range of nonjudicial duties: overseeing the construction of the county courthouse and jail; appointing county surveyors and treasurers and recommending for gubernatorial appointment coroners, auctioneers, and notaries public; licensing and regulating taverns; working with elected commissioners of revenue and roads in supervising roads, bridges, and ferries.[23]

In 1842, Representative William O. Winston of DeKalb County proposed a constitutional amendment to raise the jurisdiction of justices of the peace in civil cases from fifty dollars to two hundred dollars and to give the selection of county court judges, who were not always lawyers, to the voters. The first part of the amendment, said Winston, was meant to make justice cheaper and more convenient. The second part represented "the true democratic doctrine, that the people should choose for themselves." The legislature, Winston argued, usually did not know the character and qualifications of the men it elected and often chose a person the people of the county did not want. The house, after amending the resolution to reduce the justices' jurisdiction to one hundred dollars, adopted the first part of the resolution 66–27 and then the second part by a vote of 79–17.[24]

In a letter to the *Wetumpka Argus*, J.G. endorsed the election of county court judges. There was no good reason, he thought, for legislators from all over the state to be choosing local officers in whose qualifications and integrity they had no interest. The practice was both antirepublican and debased. "There is nothing in any government so corrupting as the power of bestowing offices," wrote J. G. "I am sick of every year's report of the scramble made for office, at every meeting of the Legislature." Far better would it be if the candidates presented themselves directly to the people, who would then learn of their merits and faults. The people might err, but then they might err in the election of legislators too.[25]

In response to J. G., "A Friend of the Constitution" objected to the expansion of the justices' jurisdiction. Many justices, he noted, "know but little about the law, and are wholly incompetent to discharge the duties that will devolve upon them." The proposed change would result in expensive, time-consuming appeals, which in turn would place the debtor class of "honest laboring farmers and mechanics" at the mercy of their creditors. The election of county court judges would provide no offsetting benefit, "Friend" contended, because the legislature generally chose competent individuals to man the courts.[26]

Another commentator suggested doing away with the county court system entirely, claiming that the people had "universally repudiated" it but pointing to no particular flaws in the system.[27] Nothing in the newspapers supported the notion of a universal repudiation of the county courts, and the voters rejected the proposed amendment. Whether the rejection was due to the county court portion of the measure or opposition to the broadening of the jurisdiction of justices of the peace is unknown. Given the general trend of the times toward more popular elections, it may be that insufficient faith in the abilities of the justices of the peace to handle larger cases tipped the vote toward defeat of the amendment.

In the meantime, dissatisfaction with the judicial system, at least among lawyers and politicians, was growing. Governor Henry W. Collier, a former chief justice of the supreme court, outlined the judiciary's defects in an address to the General Assembly. The county court judges, lacking "professional qualifications," could not deal "understandingly" with the "exceedingly abstruse and comprehensive science" of the law, claimed Collier. He recommended that the common law jurisdiction of the county courts be taken from them. He also suggested that the dignity of the circuit courts be elevated by reducing the number of circuits and raising the salaries of the judges, and he made detailed recommendations for improving the chancery courts. In general, Collier sought to raise the judiciary's level of professionalism and efficiency. His proposed reforms, the governor believed, would reduce the labors of the supreme court, which were "unsurpassed by any other appellate court [of like size] in the Union."[28]

The public had been hearing similar messages for at least twenty years. Beginning in 1829, if not before, advocates of judicial reform had argued that a separate supreme court would mean a better, more respected supreme court, one with the time to explore and decide upon the grave questions of law that came before it. Governor Gabriel Moore urged the General Assembly to create either a separate supreme court or a separate court of chancery on the ground that the existing delays of justice amounted to a denial of justice. After a debate in the legislative session of 1831–32 during which the question of judicial elections seems never to have arisen, the lawmakers established a supreme court of three judges appointed by the legislature to six-year terms.[29]

The agitation for judicial reforms in the 1840s received a boost from dissatisfaction with the workings of the county courts in probate matters. In July of 1847, a legislative candidate wrote to the Huntsville *Democrat* that the probate court required some modification "and perhaps a thorough revision." In December, Whig senator James W. McClung, one of the leading political figures in the state, introduced a bill to create elected probate courts. A similar bill was introduced in the house. The *Independent Monitor's* correspondent at the capital reported that the bill, intended to replace "our present awkward organization," would likely pass, disappointing the many office-seekers who had hoped to be appointed to the county courts by the legislature. But Whig representative Joseph W. Taylor objected to the bill on both constitutional and practical grounds. Taylor did not address the question of whether the election of judges was a good idea in principle. However, he insisted that probate courts were "inferior courts" under the constitution—that is, true courts whose powers were not "merely ministerial"—and that their judges therefore had to be elected by the General Assembly.[30]

While the probate court bill was progressing through the legislature, Representative Benjamin F. Porter, a former judge, introduced a resolution to amend the constitution to provide for an entirely elective judiciary, Representative I. W. Garrott (not Senator William H. Garrett, as reported by the *Independent Monitor*) introduced a resolution to transfer the power to elect circuit court judges to the people, and Senator Jefferson Buford also offered a judicial election amendment. In January, Porter's resolution was referred to the judiciary committee with instructions to report on the popular election of the secretary of state, state treasurer, and state comptroller. McClung, Porter, Garrott, and Buford were all Whigs at the time. Whether some political motive lay behind their proposals, or the resolutions represented a populist "spirit of change," or something else prompted the interest in judicial elections is unclear. In March 1848, the General Assembly passed a resolution to give the people the power to elect circuit court judges and the judges of the probate and other inferior courts (but not chancellors).[31]

Passage by a two-thirds majority vote in each house was just the first step in the constitutional amendment process. The voters had to approve the amendment and then the next General Assembly had to ratify it by another two-thirds majority. Apparently, the electors agreed with the newspaper correspondent who wrote that "whatever may be the necessary evils attendant on popular elections, they can never equal those of the present system." They approved the judicial elections amendment by "a very large margin." The ensuing General Assembly ratified the amendment and then promptly replaced the county courts (and the clerks of those courts) with an elected probate judge for each county.[32]

An unnamed prominent lawyer criticized the probate court statute for making only one minor change in the court's jurisdiction (transferring the usually simple common law cases to the circuit court) and otherwise leaving the vitally important probate and guardianship powers of the court untouched. Although the critic did not mention the fact that the probate judge would be popularly elected, he did stress the need for judges to be well-versed in the law—an implied criticism, perhaps, of the new mode of selecting the judge.[33]

Some democratically inclined citizens were not satisfied with the extension of popular election to probate and circuit judges. During the 1849–50 session, Whig senator William M. Murphy introduced resolutions for the election of supreme court judges and chancellors by district, the state attorney general, and county prosecutors. Many otherwise influential newspapers pushed for a constitutional convention in the early 1850s, urging among other things the popular election of supreme court judges, but the people overwhelmingly defeated the call in 1852. According to the Huntsville *Southern Advocate*, the heavy anti-convention vote did not mean "that the people are pleased with the present constitution; but simply that they prefer it with its acknowledged defects to incurring the expense and dangers of a convention with plenary powers."[34]

Why Alabamians so enthusiastically embraced the election of probate and circuit court judges but not judges of the supreme court or state executive officers is hard to say. The elective judiciary rarely, if ever, stood alone as an issue worth fighting over. In other states with democratic or semi-democratic constitutions, deep and widespread discontent over other things—malapportionment of the legislature, a broken judicial system, a bankrupt system of internal improvements—brought about constitutional conventions and wholesale constitutional revision. Judicial elections rode along with a broad transfer of power to the people. But Alabama did not experience such popular dissatisfaction with its constitution. The apportionment scheme caused no popular angst. The state had few significant internal improvements, and banks rather than the legislature bore the brunt of the blame for the state's financial woes after 1837.[35]

The judiciary, as we have seen, did give rise to complaints about delays in the administration of justice and unqualified county court judges. But unlike the constitutions of some other states, Alabama's fundamental law included an amendment process that obviated the need for a convention. The first amendment reduced judicial terms from life to six years. Then, by statute, the General Assembly created an independent supreme court. When enough people thought that biennial legislative sessions would be better than annual sessions, they amended the constitution to accommodate that desire too. But when a convention proposition made the ballot in 1852, the voters turned it down. There simply was no great demand for sweeping constitutional change, and that might have doomed the elective supreme court.

It is possible, of course, that if the voters had had a chance to express themselves on the selection of supreme court judges and state executive officers, they would have opted to elect them. After the institution of six-year judicial terms, though, complaints about the supreme court seem to have been rare. The court's chief problem was overwork. The solutions proposed (by Governor Collier, for example, in 1849) involved a restructuring of the lower judiciary. The county court, and then the probate court, were closer to home. The trend throughout the country during the Jacksonian era was toward the popular election of more local officers. By the time of the judicial elections amendment, Alabamians were already electing their sheriffs, justices of the peace, constables, tax collectors, and commissioners of revenue and roads.[36] It was natural that they should want to elect the county courts, which had administrative as well as judicial functions. When the legislature abolished the county courts, those administrative duties were transferred to the elected probate courts and county commissioners.[37]

The circuit courts, although not local tribunals in the same sense as were the county courts, were still far closer to home than the supreme court. Unlike the roving supreme court judges of other states, who had to hold trial terms in every county or district, the Alabama supreme court was primarily an appellate court holding sessions at the seat of government. After the creation of a separate supreme court in 1832, the judges did not travel even in the capacity of circuit judges. However, the circuit courts held sessions twice annually in each county within their circuits, so the people had opportunities to become familiar with the judges of those courts. Moreover, as a legislator observed during the debate over the establishment of a separate supreme court, "It is in the Circuit Courts chiefly that the great majority of cases must be finally decided in which the people are interested. These courts must pass upon our rights of life, property and reputation." In short, the adoption of elections for the circuit court judges can be seen as a logical extension of the democratization of local government. There was no crusade to revamp state government that might have carried the election of state officers, including supreme court judges, with its current.[38]

Texas

Texas was an anomaly when it joined the Union on February 19, 1846. It had never gone through a territorial phase. Located in what was then the far southwestern corner of the United States and developed by immigrants from Tennessee, Missouri, and other western slave states, Texas had been an independent republic for a decade after breaking away from Mexico. As citizens of a sovereign nation, Texans had been living under a constitution drafted by Americans and based on American models.

The republic's constitution, hastily drafted in 1836 in the midst of the revolt against Mexico, embodied the democratic values of the American Southwest. It conferred the right of suffrage on every adult citizen, not expressly excluding women.[39] Senate districts had to be "as nearly equal in free [white] population . . . as practicable." The framers neglected to state how the representatives would be apportioned, except to require that each county have at least one. Congress, as the legislature was called, would elect the supreme and district court judges, while the president, with the advice and consent of the senate, would appoint the heads of executive departments. Except for district court clerks, who would be elected by the voters of each district, the constitution did not specify how local governmental officers would be selected. However, Congress passed laws providing for the popular election of justices of the peace, sheriffs, coroners, and constables. Congress also established county courts, each consisting of a congressionally-appointed chief justice (who also served as the county probate judge) and two associate justices chosen by the local justices of the peace from among their number. The voters elected the clerks of the county courts. In short, the republic's founders created a good Jeffersonian constitution.[40]

In 1845, following years of agitation from Texans and American Democrats, the U.S. Congress voted to annex Texas. At the Texas constitutional convention, called that year to prepare a constitution for statehood, the presiding officer, former chief justice of the republic Thomas J. Rusk, cautioned against the introduction of "new and untried theories." Rusk urged the delegates to concentrate on admission to the American Union and to leave amendments to the "experience and intelligence" of future Texans. For the most part, the delegates heeded Rusk's advice. The new instrument kept free suffrage (limiting the "qualified electors" to males) and equal representation. Altering somewhat the appointing authorities, it gave to the governor the power to appoint the judges of the supreme and district courts, the attorney general, the secretary of state, and notaries public and to the legislature the power to choose district attorneys and the state treasurer and comptroller. In accordance with existing practice, the constitution empowered the people to elect their local sheriffs, coroners, constables, and justices of the peace. In compliance with a constitutional directive, the legislature quickly established probate courts, with judges chosen by the voters.[41]

The method of selecting the "real" judges stirred some controversy. After the San Augustine *Red-Lander* came out in favor of judicial elections while the convention was in progress, the *Texas National Register* of Washington published a lengthy rebuttal. "[W]e profess to be good democrats and true," wrote the editors, "we entertain . . . the maxim *vox populi, vox dei* [the voice of the people is the voice of God], but we should look upon the introduction of such a system, not as the extension of democratic principles, but as the establishment of mobocracy." The paper favored executive appointments (to avoid the logrolling involved in legislative appointments) and terms long enough to allow for stability in the law, the benefit of experience for the judge, and the attraction of the best men.[42]

In a subsequent issue, John S. Ford, who would soon purchase the *Register*, recited the litany of contentions against judicial elections that were already becoming common in the United States. If the people elected the judges, Ford wrote, the judges would feel dependent upon them. Judicial decisions would "assume a hue and coloring from popular opinion." The judge "would be constantly called on to decide delicate questions of right between individuals, who have a voice in his election" and would be under obligations to his supporters. Candidates who excelled at electioneering and gladhanding would defeat better-qualified candidates who lacked electioneering skills. The week after that, the paper condemned "constantly recurring appeals to the ballot box."[43]

At the convention itself, the judiciary committee report proposed that the judges of the supreme court and district courts be appointed by the governor, with the advice and consent of the senate. A substantial minority of delegates, although nothing close to a majority, objected. Delegate

William C. Young offered a substitute for the pertinent section of the committee report to give the selection of the judges to the legislature. James S. Mayfield then sought to modify Young's proposal so as to make those judges elective. Mayfield's amendment lost by a vote of 38–19, and then Young's substitute lost 33–24. Another delegate tried again with a substitute section that would have provided for the popular election of supreme court judges to six-year terms and district court judges to four-year terms, shorter terms in each case than those established in the committee report. The convention rejected the substitute without a roll-call vote.[44]

The delegates also engaged in an extended discussion over the method of selecting state executive officers, particularly the secretary of state. The report of the committee on the executive provided for the popular election of the secretary, treasurer, and comptroller. The arguments for and against popular election echoed many of those made in the connection with the selection of judges. The convention ultimately rejected the election of these officers, but the elective principle would soon prevail.[45]

At the first session of the state legislature, a proposed constitutional amendment to make the judiciary elective died in the house judiciary committee, but not before a minority report made the familiar arguments for popular election. Among other things, the minority insisted that the only method of judicial selection consistent with republicanism was "to give the people, themselves, immediately and directly, the election of their officers." Although the amendment failed in 1846, the trend toward democratization could not be stopped. In the next legislature, during which signers of the minority report from the previous session chaired the judiciary committees of both chambers, a popular election amendment passed with just nine dissenting votes in the two houses combined. The measure provided for the election not just of judges but also the attorney general, district attorneys, the state comptroller, the state treasurer, and the commissioner of the general land office.[46]

The quick about-face on popular elections may not have surprised anyone. While convention president Rusk was no fan of popular elections for either judicial or executive officers, he seems to have recognized that once Texas began functioning as a state, constitutional amendments would be a distinct possibility. Texas had experienced its own great migration of land-hungry arrivals, at first mostly small farmers from Tennessee, Missouri, Kentucky, and Arkansas, and later on Gulf-state immigrants who brought their slave culture with them. Between the first state census of 1847 and the federal census of 1850, the population grew by 50 percent.

As in other western states, the political ferment attendant upon this rapid growth bolstered the Jacksonian leanings of the state. Oran Roberts, an early Texas judge, many years later attributed the turn towards judicial elections in part to concerns about Governor George T. Wood's judicial appointments. That seems unlikely. Wood took office on December 21, 1847. The joint resolution to amend the constitution was introduced on January 11, 1848. It is possible that, in the short interval between Wood's inauguration and the resolution's introduction, complaints about Wood's judicial appointments (if he made any during that period) not only arose but proved serious enough to provoke a response; but it's a stretch. By January 11, it must have been clear to everyone that such a measure was in the offing. Roberts's further observation that elections were more in tune with "the general principles of a democratic republican government" is a better explanation for the pursuit of an amendment to make both judicial and executive offices elective.[47]

To become law, the amendment had to go before the voters and then be passed again by a two-thirds majority in each house of the following legislature. After the referendum but before the official returns were in, the *Democratic Telegraph and Texas Register* made light of the whole issue. "We voted for the amendment," wrote editor Francis Moore Jr., "but we considered it a matter of very little importance whether the people elected the Judges or the governor whom the people had elected appointed them." But Moore acknowledged that other papers regarded the amendment as "very important." The referendum resulted in a whopping approval, 15,852–3,139. The following legislature ratified the result by a combined vote of 58–5. The amendment thereupon became part of the constitution in January 1850.[48]

Tennessee

"The writing of new more egalitarian constitutions has often been viewed by historians as one of the hallmarks of the Jacksonian era, and Tennessee's new document fits fairly well into this interpretation." This is historian Paul H. Bergeron's assessment of the Tennessee constitution of 1835. Tennessee's first constitution (1796) was more democratic than that of North Carolina, the model on which it was based. It extended the suffrage to "freemen," including free blacks (or so it seemed until the state supreme court decided in 1838 that "freemen" meant free whites) and based apportionment on taxable inhabitants (which, because of the poll tax, previously enacted by both the territorial and the state governments and mentioned in the constitution, probably did not make representation terribly unequal). On the other hand, the constitution included property qualifications for holding office in the state legislature or as governor and required a belief in God to hold any office. The voters elected the governor and state legislators, but the General Assembly appointed other state public officers while county courts appointed the chief local officers. Judges, justices of the peace, state attorneys, and court clerks had tenure "during good behavior." The constitution left the establishment of a judiciary largely to the legislature, which never succeeded in creating an efficient court system, and it required that land, whether developed or undeveloped, be taxed uniformly, regardless of value, except for a ceiling on the taxation of town lots. The tax provision would prove to be a boon for the owners of high-value land.[49]

Tennessee's population more than sextupled between 1800 and 1830, creating the usual pressures for change. Widespread unhappiness with the judiciary generated a strong court-reform movement. In the state's early years, the courts faced all the same problems encountered by courts in other states: crowded dockets, politically charged controversies, disputes over judicial review. In 1829, state senator Adam Huntsman studied the condition of the judiciary in depth and reported it to be "the most expensive and least efficient of any in the United States." The General Assembly passed a law that, among other things, added a fourth judge to the supreme court, penalized judges financially for absenteeism, and provided for an official court reporter.[50]

Inefficiency was only one of the problems troubling the Tennessee judiciary in the Age of Jackson. One student of Tennessee's constitutional history noted that the years leading up to the 1834 constitutional convention were "characterized by every form of breakdown in the judicial system and deep public discontent. . . . [E]ach session of the general assembly was besieged with applicants for judgeships or unsuccessful litigants seeking redress. This along with the rigid personalities of some judges . . . resulted in a spate of largely politically-motivated impeachments." Anti-court sentiment "reached its nadir in 1831 when the legislature examined the state of the judiciary, found it sorely deficient, and nearly removed all chancellors, circuit and supreme court judges." The people wanted greater accountability on the part of judges, a demand that may have been fortified by the supreme court's decisions in politically sensitive cases. In 1831, the supreme court, having claimed the power of judicial review as early as 1812, struck down a law that gave the state bank special remedies against defaulting debtors. In 1834, the court invalidated a statute that denied equitable remedies to manumitted slaves. These interferences with public policy enacted by the people's representatives perhaps bolstered a more general demand for greater control over the judiciary, especially in the form of limited tenure.[51]

Scholars disagree over the relative importance of judicial problems in the calling of the constitutional convention of 1834. One historian writes that public disgust with incompetent judges who had tenure for life led to the convention. According to another student of Tennessee's constitutional history, the "prime impetus for constitutional change" was the old constitution's land tax clause; judicial problems came second. A third scholar lists both judicial problems and the land taxation system, along with several other matters, as "[a]mong the chief causes of dissatisfaction" with the constitution. In any case, defects in the judicial system clearly loomed large in the public mind.[52]

In the months leading up to the convention, advocates and opponents of judicial elections debated the merits of an elective judiciary in the newspapers. The arguments of the opponents ranged from the reasonable to the fevered. One candidate for a seat at the convention, R. L. Cobbs, argued that a popularly elected judge might be swayed in his decisions by the ability of litigants to deliver votes. Another, R. M. Burton, maintained that a judge elected in a close contest would know who were his friends and who his enemies and would not be likely "to hold the scales of justice impartially in his hand." Elected judges "would be influenced by public opinion, party excitement and the popular clamor of the day." A "wild, visionary and maddened Democracy is abroad in the land," cried Burton, "under the fascinating pretence, of putting everything in the hands of the people ... which if made to prevail, will plunge this country into a whirlpool of confusion and of endless misery."[53]

When Burton flung out this dire warning, he thought that judicial elections might actually come to pass. In favoring the appointment of judges and attorneys general (prosecutors) by the legislature, he wrote, he acknowledged that he stood "opposed to what is considered by some the popular doctrine of the day." He need not have worried. At the convention, several proposals to create an elective judiciary failed. One such motion lost 48–8. According to a student of Tennessee's constitutional history, the convention's refusal to allow the popular election of judges and state attorneys was the only respect in which it failed "to make the

Constitution sufficiently democratic to meet the wishes of the people." However, the delegates did abolish life tenure in favor of twelve-year terms for supreme court judges and eight-year terms for other judges. The fixed terms of office accorded with the prevalent Jacksonian democracy, although they were longer than many Jacksonians would have liked.[54]

The new constitution, which the voters ratified by a nearly 2½–1 margin in 1835, presaged the democratic reforms of other states' mid-century conventions in other ways as well. The proposed constitution dropped property qualification for voting and both the property and religious qualifications for holding office. Some important local offices—justice of the peace, sheriff, county trustee, and county register—became elective. Property, both real and personal, would be taxed according to value, and legislative apportionment would be based on the number of qualified voters rather than taxable inhabitants in each county or district.[55]

In 1847, after years of quiescence on the subject, Tennessee Democrats began pushing again for the election of judges and other public officers. The absence of activity before then perhaps can be ascribed to a wait-and-see attitude following ratification of the new constitution and the abolition of life tenure. The convention of 1834 having rejected judicial elections, there was no point in rushing into the still-novel idea until the solution to the accountability problem adopted by the convention had been tested. Furthermore, although Andrew Jackson, the great Democratic hero, called Tennessee home, the state was a bulwark of the Whig Party from 1835 to 1853. The constitution's cumbersome amendment process required that any proposed amendment first be passed by a simple majority in each house of the legislature, then be passed again by a two-thirds majority of each house in the next General Assembly, and finally be ratified by the voters. No amendment providing for judicial elections could get through the General Assembly until the Whigs—more conservative than the Democrats, less enamored of popular elections, and more concerned about judicial independence from political agitation—could be brought on board.[56]

A peculiar provision in the Tennessee constitution may also have affected the timing of the renewed effort to secure an elective judiciary. The constitution prohibited the legislature from placing constitutional amendments on the ballot more than once every six years. According to Democratic state representative Edwin Polk in 1848, the last ballot issue had been passed by the legislature of 1843–44. The next possible time for a referendum on an amendment, said Polk, would be 1850, and for that to happen the process would have to begin in the 1847–48 legislative session.[57]

The examples of other states—Iowa, New York, even Missouri and Wisconsin despite the defeat of their proposed constitutions at the polls—may have inspired the drive for a judicial election amendment, a drive possibly bolstered by a desire among Democrats to oust Whig officeholders. There was certainly a perception that corruption infected the process of appointing men to office. In March 1849, the Democratic *Nashville Union*, disgusted by the sight of judicial aspirants hanging around the legislative lobbies and intriguing with lawmakers, complained that the process of election by the legislature had "degenerated into a species of *log-rolling* and *bargaining*." A nineteenth-century Tennessee historian, commenting on the "legislative legerdemain" that resulted in an unlikely choice for a United States senator in 1845, wrote that the appointment provided "insight into the tortuous methods to which unscrupulous politicians with small talents resorted in those days, in the hopes of defeating the will of a majority whose assent and approval they could never hope to achieve by the strength of their character, the force of their intellect, or the importance of their public services."[58]

There were, at the same time, calls for other court reforms. The *Union* complained that a "system of absurd forms and intricate pleadings, derived from the spirit of feudalism" closed the doors of legal knowledge to the people. Since 1845, there had been efforts in the legislature to reduce the number of judicial circuits and the number of terms held annually in each circuit. The proposals were offered as cost-saving measures, but opponents contended that the reductions would actually increase costs and impose undue burdens on the judges.[59]

In October 1847, Democratic representative David W. Ballew introduced a resolution to amend the constitution to provide for the election of circuit court judges and circuit attorneys general and the appointment of a state attorney general by the legislature. Ballew justified his proposal on both theoretical and practical grounds. As a matter of principle, he said, the election of judicial officers by the legislature violated the constitution's separation of powers. As a practical matter, the election of public officers took up weeks of the lawmakers' time every session, delaying the business of legislation, prolonging sessions, and creating ill will among the throngs of disappointed aspirants for office. It would be better, maintained Ballew, to give the choice of circuit judges and attorneys general to the voters of each circuit. They were familiar with the candidates and had only the public good as their aim. To the objection that judges should not be involved in electioneering, Ballew replied: "If the judicial ermine ought not to be soiled by electioneering—much less should it be stained by artifice and intrigue," which typically accompanied elections in the legislature. Noting that Mississippi and New York elected their judges, and that Tennessee voters chose their justices of the peace with no adverse consequences, he insisted that the "spirit of the age and the genius of our people" demanded popular election. And, of course, there was an appeal to the people's pocketbooks. Sessions prolonged by weeks for the selection of public officers increased expenditures "exorbitantly," said Ballew, whereas the voters could elect the officers in one day "without any cost to the State."[60]

During the debate over Ballew's proposal, Whig William W. Pepper offered an amendment to provide for the popular election of virtually all public officers in the state, including not only supreme court judges but even the officers of the penitentiary and lunatic asylum and others "not herein specified." Ballew believed it was a partisan proposal designed to defeat his resolution. The chief question, apparently, was why Ballew had not included the supreme court judges. Ballew explained that he had omitted them out of concern that the measure might then fail. Half a loaf, he thought, was better than none. But he had no objection to the popular election of the supreme court and in fact regarded his measure as the first big step in the march of judicial reform. Ballew then reiterated the financial benefits of his proposal, providing dollar amounts that he supposed were "far too moderate."[61]

The house rejected Pepper's amendment and passed Ballew's resolution, but the senate, by a 13–12 vote, effectively killed the resolution by postponing consideration until the next General Assembly. In 1849, Democratic governor William Trousdale, remarking upon the "strong conviction pervading the public mind" that the method of selecting judicial officers had to be changed, urged the legislature to adopt constitutional amendments providing for the popular election of judges and attorneys general.[62]

In October 1849, Democratic representative Jacob Adcock introduced a resolution to amend the constitution along the lines of Ballew's proposal of the previous session. Judiciary committee chairman Edwin Polk, who had delivered a ringing endorsement of Ballew's resolution, returned a committee report that encapsulated the arguments of that speech. Unlike the masses in England centuries ago, when the practice of appointing judges took root, declared Polk, modern Americans had been "enlightened by the influence that free institutions always give to the human intellect." The people, the source of all political power, knew full well that their own welfare depended on the intelligent use of their power. If they were competent to elect the president, governor, and legislators, then of course they were competent to elect judges and prosecutors. Polk condemned the existing system of legislative appointment as the worst of all possible systems, for it gave the authority to select judges to a small body of men, offering "great inducement for combinations and influences to operate." A large electorate was less susceptible to partisan intrigue.[63]

Moreover, even with good intentions, legislators from one area of a large state could not know the merits of candidates from other areas. Dismissing the concern that elected judges would favor their associates and supporters, Polk pointed out that all judges had "personal and political friendships," regardless of how they were selected. He noted that Mississippi and New York had already adopted judicial elections and that Pennsylvania was in the process of doing so. And naturally Polk wound up his brief by declaring that such elections accorded with the American system of government.[64]

One representative later tried to amend Adcock's resolution by providing for the popular election of the state treasurer and secretary of state, but those suggestions fell flat. Polk offered an amendment of his own that cleaned up the language of the original resolution, added the election of supreme court judges, reduced the terms of the latter to eight years, and directed the General Assembly to establish a day for the election of judges and attorneys general that would be different from the day for the election of state and county officers.[65]

The house accepted Polk's amendment and then passed the resolution by a vote of 51-16. The senate further amended the resolution with a provision to create a new county and then voted separately on the various parts of the resolution. They approved the election of supreme court judges 18-7, the election of lower court judges and attorneys general 22-3, and the rest of the amendment 18-7. When the house refused to concur in the senate alteration, the senate receded. The first step in the constitutional amendment process had been completed.[66]

Back in September, before the start of the 1849-50 legislative session, the *Union* had complained that only one Whig paper had come out forthrightly for a popular election amendment.[67] Many Whigs soon jumped on the judicial election bandwagon. The impetus for the amendment came from the Democratic-majority house, but the resolution still had to get through the senate, where the Whigs had a 14–11 majority. A united Whig Party could have stopped the amendment, but too many Whig senators either believed in an elective judiciary or dared not risk the wrath of their constituents. All the opposition to the amendment came from Whigs, but half of the Whigs voted for the election of supreme court judges and all but three for the election of lower court judges. The house vote told a similar story. The Democrats had a slim majority, but the amendment passed overwhelmingly. The elective judiciary had become too popular to resist.[68]

The proposed amendment still had two hurdles to jump. It needed the approbation of two-thirds of the members of each chamber in the 1851–52 General Assembly, and, if it received that, the approval of a majority of the voters who voted for representatives in the 1853 general election. The hurdles proved to be very low. Only one member of either house voted against the amendment, Democratic representative Humphrey R. Bate, who called the election of judges "monstrous madness." As election day approached, the Democratic *Fayetteville Observer* urged its readers to vote for "this really republican measure," while the Whig *Nashville Gazette* held that popular election would "infuse a high confidence in the tribunal among the people." The voters ratified the amendment handily. Thus, with little controversy and without benefit of a constitutional convention, the Tennessee judiciary became elective.[69]

Louisiana

Charles Sydnor omitted Louisiana from his list of southwestern states that had become democratic by the late 1830s. Sydnor thought that in Louisiana "democracy was closely approximated" only in 1845. To be eligible to vote in Louisiana before then, a person had to have paid a state tax within the six months preceding the election or have purchased land from the United States. In the absence of a state poll tax, this requirement may have barred many residents from voting. As late as the 1840s, nearly half of the adult white men in the state could not vote. There were property qualifications for the offices of state representative, senator, and governor. Representation in the senate was according to districts fixed in the constitution, regardless of population. The General Assembly chose the governor from the two candidates receiving the highest totals in a popular vote. The governor, with the advice and consent of the senate, appointed the secretary of state, the attorney general, and all judges and sheriffs. The legislature appointed the state treasurer. Judges held office effectively for life ("during good behavior"). The constitution could be amended only through a cumbersome process. First, the General Assembly had to pass a law specifying the changes sought and scheduling a popular referendum on the calling of a convention. If a majority of voters approved a call, another vote would be held the next year. If a majority still favored a convention, the lawmakers had to schedule a convention at their next session and provide for the election of delegates.[70]

"The framers of the first Louisiana constitution," wrote historian Judith K. Schafer, "did not create a democratic document; they forged a government designed to keep themselves and those like them in power." "Themselves and those like them" meant, for the most part, the New Orleans merchants and southern Louisiana sugar planters who would favor the Whigs when that party arose in the 1830s. But immigration from the eastern states and abroad posed a problem for the dominant classes in the southern part of the state. Most of the domestic newcomers settled in northern Louisiana, a region of small farms, while foreign immigrants congregated in New Orleans. Neither group had much in common with the Whig elite of merchants, bankers, and sugar planters; both groups generally favored the Democrats.[71]

Andrew Jackson carried Louisiana in the presidential elections of 1828 and 1832, and the state by the mid-1830s found itself surrounded by Mississippi, Arkansas, and the Republic of Texas, all with constitutions far more democratic than its own. "The tendencies of the age," wrote one Louisiana pamphleteer, "are decidedly revolutionary"; there was a worldwide desire to simplify government, "secure effectually the political rights of the mass," and make those in power directly responsible to the people. The "government by gentlemen" established by the 1812 constitution became ever harder to defend. Sooner or later the Whigs would have to yield to the pressure for reform. In the presidential election campaign of 1840, Whigs everywhere took the opportunity to blame the Democratic administration in Washington for the hard times. If ever the Whigs of Louisiana could reap some benefit from inevitable constitutional reform, 1840 was the time.[72]

Still, unlike the strongly proconvention Democrats, the Whigs sent at best a "mixed message" on the calling of a convention. A bill introduced in the senate, which had a 9–8 Democratic majority, early in 1841 proposed to give the electorate an opportunity to call a convention to amend the constitution in the following respects: to reduce the tenure of judges from life to a term of years; to establish universal white manhood suffrage; to provide for more equal representation in the legislature, according to population; to provide for the popular election of sheriffs and other parish officers; and to provide for the direct popular election of the governor. The Whig-controlled house stripped away the bill's "ultra radical features" so that the bill as passed stated the purposes of the convention as being to provide more specificity regarding the qualifications of electors, a more equal system of representation, the direct election of the governor, modifications of the supreme court's jurisdiction and places of sitting, and an expansion of the preamble to refer to a part of the state that had once belonged to territorial Florida.[73]

In the first referendum on the calling of a constitutional convention, held in 1842, 76.9 percent of the voters favored a convention. The Whig bastion of South Louisiana produced a 2-1 proconvention majority. In Greater Orleans, nearly half the voters approved. Popular enthusiasm for constitutional change only increased thereafter. In the second referendum in 1843, 80.2 percent of the voters, including 63 percent of those in Greater Orleans, approved the call.[74]

During the long approach to the convention, public discussion focused on democratization of government. Whether issues other than those listed in the legislation could even be considered by the convention was a controversial matter much debated in the press. One such issue raised by Democrats was the popular election of judges. The notion that judges should be appointed for set terms rather than for life had been aired often enough that it was no longer startling and could even be endorsed by Whigs. But when the Democrats of Monroe resolved that "[a]ll judges, as well as clerks and other officers of the State, shall be elected or appointed for a limited period of years," the mere possibility that such language could be construed to favor the election of judges made the Whigs of New Orleans apoplectic. They condemned the resolution as proof that Democrats sought to embody "doctrines the most radical and subversive of rational liberty" in the constitution. During the campaign for seats at the convention, many Democrats backed off from the elective judiciary. Still, when the voters elected a bare majority of Whigs to the convention, one Whig editor breathed a sigh of relief. Counting forty-eight conservatives among the delegates, he was satisfied "that none but changes absolutely necessary will be made in our Constitution—that the Judiciary will not be elective by the people—thus securing to us one of the greatest boons we were struggling for."[75]

The convention, which met from August 5 to August 24, 1844, and then from January 14 to May 16, 1845, decided that it had plenary power and was not limited to the subjects listed in the legislation that put the question of a convention before the voters. That meant that the delegates could bring up internal improvements, judicial elections, or any other issue they desired. Yet, despite the state's recent financial difficulties and defaults, internal improvements barely figured in the debates. One delegate, referring to the New Orleans & Nashville Railroad debacle, asserted that the governor's veto of the bill authorizing bonds for the project was "the first check on the wild spirit of internal improvements" and would have saved Louisiana more than half a million dollars had it been sustained. Other delegates mentioned "wild and visionary schemes" and the "spirit of speculation." But there was little debate concerning internal improvements because the real problem had been property banks.[76]

The planters in the booming cotton economy of the Southwest needed credit, so the relevant states chartered banks and supported them with stock subscriptions and bond sales. Louisiana, with its big commercial center of New Orleans in addition to cotton and sugar plantations, "plunged deepest." As in other southwestern states, the capital for the expanding banks was supposed to come from mortgages on slaves and land, but in the end most of it came from state bonds or bank bonds guaranteed by the state. And much of the bank credit went to bank directors and officers and their associates who used it to speculate in public lands. Fluctuating cotton prices portended trouble for the banks and the states even before the Panic of 1837, but the Panic wiped out the region's prosperity. Banks failed, leaving the states with bond obligations they had trouble meeting.[77]

In the early 1840s, Louisiana was awash in debt. Nineteenth-century historian Charles Gayarré wrote that "[a]t the beginning of the year 1839 the State owed to the Banks $75,000; at the beginning of 1841 the debt amounted to $850,000; and it was generally believed at the time . . . that the members of the Legislature, in their private capacity, owed to those institutions about one million of dollars." Moreover, the state had issued $24,450,000 of bonds on behalf of banks, and in 1843 it defaulted on $1.273 million in bond interest payments. During the depression that followed the financial panic, banks found themselves unable to pay specie for their obligations. Many banks had to forfeit their charters.[78]

The convention responded harshly to the debt and banking problems. The new constitution prohibited the state from subscribing to the stock of any corporation or joint stock company. It barred the legislature from "pledg[ing] the faith of the State for the payment of any bonds, bills, or other contracts or obligations for the benefit or use of any person or persons, corporation, or body politic whatever." It imposed a state debt ceiling of $100,000 that could not be exceeded unless the legislature provided for payment of the principal and interest by taxation. And the constitution prohibited the creation, renewal, or extension of any corporate body with banking or discounting privileges. The delegates adopted all these restrictions without much discussion.[79]

While the debt crisis was of immediate concern, the judiciary presented problems of longer standing. As in many other states, judicial backlogs frustrated everyone involved in the system. The three-man supreme court was required to hold sessions in two different locations each year. The state's rapidly growing population and a penchant for appealing lower-court decisions led to a steadily increasing caseload. Health troubles and disagreements among the judges exacerbated the problem, as did the large number of lawsuits stemming from the Panic of 1837. Even the court's procedural rules slowed down the disposition of disputes.[80]

The convention addressed these issues by creating the office of chief justice to deal with administrative functions, limiting terms of office to eight years for supreme court judges and six years for district court judges, fixing respectable judicial salaries, and modifying the supreme court's jurisdiction. The creation of fixed judicial terms, while providing a means of forcing infirm judges off the bench, also tempered the "aristocratic" nature of judicial office and could thus be seen as a democratic reform. However, it did not go far enough to satisfy the Democratic Party. During the campaign for the election of convention delegates, both parties had retreated from their more extreme positions, which among Democrats included the popular election of judges. But the idea of popular election of public officers remained powerful. With little debate, the convention provided for the election of justices of the peace, district court clerks, sheriffs, and coroners, all previously appointed.[81]

Some Democratic convention delegates refused to abandon the notion of an elective judiciary. On April 22, 1845, as the convention neared its end, Democrat James F. Brent, a young lawyer from Rapides Parish, proposed that the four judges of the supreme court be elected by district. In support of the motion, fellow Democrat Amasa Read urged the convention not to be influenced by the "unaccountable sanctity enveloping the judicial ermine, as moss covers the time beaten temples of antiquity." In the selection of officers under a republican government, said Read, "*vox populi vox dei*." The judiciary had become "corrupt and irresponsible," and it was "high time to cleanse the Augean stables" by letting the people draw the line. If the people could be trusted to elect men to frame a constitution and make laws, and to choose doctors, lawyers, architects, and others to work on their behalf, Read argued, then they could be trusted to elect judges. Read quoted the testimony of judges William L. Sharkey and Robert H. Buckner of Mississippi on the success of the elective judiciary in that state and predicted that the day would soon come when every state would follow Mississippi's example.[82]

Brent argued that for democratic government to work well, it had to have the "respect and affections" of the people. The more the people participated in government—"the more they are taught to believe that it is *their* government"—the more effectively the government would function. Brent denounced the "wealthy and aristocratic classes" for clinging to the executive appointment of the judiciary in order to save themselves "from a fancied and imaginary peril." If, as the Louisiana bill of rights declared, "all power is inherent in the people," then to deny the right of the people to elect their officers was to attack the fundamental principles of popular government. And if the right of election were conceded, then to oppose judicial elections on the grounds of expediency was to suck all the meaning out of a merely theoretical right.[83]

To the argument that popular election would destroy the independence of the judiciary, Brent declared that in a republic there was no need for a judiciary independent of the people. "According to the theory of our government," he said, "there is no power in the State antagonistical to that of the people." The convention had already decided against life tenure for judges, so that they could no longer be "irresponsible despots." Now it was necessary to make them accountable. But to whom? Here Brent insisted on judicial independence—not from the people but from the other branches of government. "Our only safety," he contended, "consists in keeping each of the departments separate from, and independent of the others." The "true and proper independence of the judiciary" was one that kept "the balance wheel of our political system" free from the control of the legislature and the executive.[84]

Brent recognized the necessity of judicial review:

> The constitution assigns to each of the departments, its respective duties; and it says, "thus far shalt thou go, and no farther."

> The judiciary is relied upon, not only to decide disputes among citizens, but to keep the other departments from shooting madly from the spheres allotted to them. It is its duty to decide whether the laws enacted by the legislature, and approved by the governor, are constitutional, or not. If constitutional, to enforce them; if not, to avoid them and set them at naught.[85]

Brent raised the specter of a judge unwilling to set aside an unconstitutional law for fear that it would cost him reappointment by the governor or legislature. "Is this the kind of independent judiciary," he asked, "to which you wish to surrender the lives, the liberties, and fortunes of our people?" To those who demanded a judiciary "independent of popular clamor," Brent retorted that he would rather have a judiciary reflect popular feeling than be subject to "legislative clamor, venality and corruption" or "executive power, tyranny and usurpation."[86]

Opponents of judicial elections worried that the people would not choose good judges. Brent did not share this concern. In the first place, he believed that legislatures and governors often filled judgeships with political cronies, regardless of their abilities or character. Secondly, he thought that the people, out of self-interest, would elect good men. "Now who has such a deep and abiding interest in the appointment of a good judge as the people among whom the judge is to act?" he asked. "If a bad judge be selected, who suffers from his dishonesty, his incompetence and his reckless disregard of justice, but the people who live under his jurisdiction?"[87]

Thanks to the example of neighboring Mississippi, Brent was able to call upon experience in support of an elective judiciary. Adding to the evidence offered by Read, Brent read a recent letter he had received from former Mississippi governor and judge John A. Quitman. Quitman had opposed the introduction of the elective judiciary in 1832, but he had since changed his mind, concluding that "the experience of electing judges by the direct votes of the people, has proved eminently successful in our State." Brent also quoted Jefferson's letter of 1816 approving of judicial elections. Nevertheless, Brent's motion stood no chance of adoption. To go from an appointive system that gave judges life tenure to popular elections for fixed terms would have been a radical step—far too radical, no doubt, for the majority Whigs to swallow. No one bothered to speak against Brent's motion, and it lost 40–20.[88]

Despite the convention's failure to adopt judicial elections, the new constitution went some way toward satisfying the demands for more popular government. It abolished property and taxpaying qualifications for voting, gave judges fixed terms of office rather than tenure during good behavior, and made justices of the peace, district court clerks, sheriffs, and coroners elective. One aristocratic delegate complained, "We have an election for almost every thing, from a sheriff down to an inspector of pork!" But representation remained a contentious issue. Under the new constitution, representation in the senate was based on total population, including slaves, which meant that the slaveholding planters could block any legislation that threatened their interests. The constitution also guaranteed at least one representative for each parish, a boon to the rural districts, and placed caps on the number of representatives and senators New Orleans could have, regardless of its population. All this might have been a blow to the Whigs, but the constitution also required two years of residence in the state, without interruption of more than ninety days, to qualify for the franchise. This would most likely cut down on the number of transient worker voters, the majority of whom probably would have voted Democratic.[89]

The voters ratified the new constitution by a vote of 12,277 to 1,395, but the huge victory did not indicate widespread enthusiasm for the document. To many, it was better than the 1812 constitution but still seriously flawed. Critics complained of the instrument's residence requirements for holding office, establishment of a supreme court with an even number of judges, and limits on the frequency and length of legislative sessions. The Whig merchants of New Orleans could not abide the restrictions on banking and on public aid to railroads. Some Democrats, too, including farmers and planters hurt by the constriction of currency and credit, saw the need for relaxation of the constitution's banking restrictions. Louisiana's transportation system was abominable. The roads were "so poor as hardly to deserve the name" and the railroad system limited to a few short lines. The agitation for railroad construction intensified in the mid-1840s, as Louisianans and other southerners sought by commercial ties to link the fortunes of the South and the West. A convention held in New Orleans in January 1852, with hundreds of delegates from eleven states in attendance, endorsed public aid to railroad corporations. Resolutions offered by James Robb of Louisiana and adopted by the convention called a system of railroads through the South and Southwest "an object of such importance, as to justify and require a liberal application of the resources of the states interested in these works." The resolutions also asserted the right of cities, counties, and parishes, with the approval of their inhabitants, to subscribe to the stock of railroad companies.[90]

In 1849, the *Daily Crescent* started pushing forcefully for judicial elections. "[T]he selection of men to fill offices of honor and profit can never fail to excite sympathies and awaken passions," read an editorial in the paper. "Hence the intrigue and bargaining for place, when places are in the gift of a governor or a legislature. Hence the necessity for calling in the whole people—who will not sell and cannot be swindled out of their own interests—to perform this vital function of government—the selection of agents fitted for properly administering the laws." A few weeks later, the editors, upset by a decision of the Louisiana Supreme Court, insisted upon the necessity of judicial elections to make the judiciary "obedient to the public will."[91]

Not everyone favored judicial elections, of course. According to a writer to the New Orleans *Courier*, it was "well known that all the Whigs, and even some of the democrats" of Franklin in the sugar-planting belt of southern Louisiana, opposed the elective judiciary. But the Whig candidate for lieutenant governor in 1849 asserted that both Whig and Democratic opponents of judicial elections in 1845 had since discovered that the system of gubernatorial appointments was rife with political partisanship and now favored an elective judiciary. The Whig *Southern Sentinel* boasted that the Whig candidate for governor supported the "liberal and enlightened principle" of an elective judiciary.[92]

Legislators of both parties heeded the calls for change. In 1850, with each party in control of one house, a Democratic senator and a Whig representative introduced a measure calling for a constitutional convention. Antibank Democrats, including Governor Joseph M. Walker, feared that a convention would undermine the banking restrictions adopted in 1845. The bill passed the house with the support of about 60 percent of the members of both parties, but only four senators resisted a motion to table. In the meantime, the legislature gave the required three-fifths majority to proposed constitutional amendments to reduce the residency requirements for voting and to make elective the posts of supreme and district court judges, district attorneys, the attorney general, secretary of state, state treasurer, and state superintendent of public instruction. Judicial terms of office would be reduced to four years. The terms of the other officers would be two years. One newspaper observed early in 1850 that in the previous election both parties "were so liberal upon this question [of an elective judiciary], that . . . neither party would *dare* retreat from it." Now, in the legislative halls, "they must *'face the music'* . . . whether they like it or not."[93]

In 1851, largely as a result of Democratic divisions over the Compromise of 1850 and the desirability of banking reform, the Whigs gained control of both legislative chambers. The General Assembly again passed the resolution to make more offices elective, as the constitution required for placement on the ballot, but the matter quickly became moot when the legislators passed a convention bill. A Whig newspaper exulted that the convention would produce reforms "indispensable to the future progress and social and political welfare of the State—the most prominent being an Elective Judiciary, a safe and judicious mode of Banking, a Homestead Exemption bill, a liberal system of Internal Improvements, a better method of Public Education, &c." The voters approved the measure and elected a large majority of Whig convention delegates.[94]

At the convention itself, suggests historian Wayne M. Everard, "[l]egislative apportionment was perhaps the most bitterly debated" issue. The question once again was whether representation should be based on total population or eligible voters. Advocates of total population won out. According to Schafer, the convention's adoption of total population (slave and free) as the basis for representation in both houses of the legislature could have given a Whig alliance of black-belt planters and New Orleans merchants control of the legislature for years to come, if the national Whig Party had not disintegrated for other reasons. But Michael F. Holt contends that the Whigs at the convention, in their anxiety to get rid of the restrictions on the chartering of banks and state funding of internal improvements, entered a "Faustian bargain" that handed future control of the legislature to the Democrats. Holt observes that the use of total population as the basis of representation benefited both the Whig sugar planters in the southern part of the state and the Democratic cotton planters elsewhere but also diminished the influence of the Whig bastion of New Orleans in the legislature. Furthermore, the new constitution eliminated the two-year residency requirement for voting, which probably increased the Democratic vote in New Orleans.[95]

It is not clear why the Whigs, who had a nearly 2–1 majority of the convention delegates, would have needed to strike a deal with the devil. In their push for public aid for railroad construction, they enjoyed the hearty support of a considerable number of Democrats. Deal or no deal, the fact is that the convention both eliminated the obstacles to state funding of internal improvements and extended the democratic reforms of 1845. The delegates opened up new banking opportunities for the financing of railroads and expressly authorized the legislature to incur up to $8 million in debt to aid private companies formed for the purpose of constructing internal improvements. A Democratic delegate considered this measure to be the "one great and controlling desire of the whigs of New Orleans" and as "graft . . . solely for the promotion of speculators," but a significant minority of Democrats voted with the Whigs on banking and internal improvements. The proposed constitution essentially incorporated the democratic amendment resolution recently adopted by the General Assembly by eliminating the two-year residency requirement for voting and by making elective a slew of additional offices, including judgeships and the major state executive positions.[96]

The convention seems to have accepted judicial elections without much discussion. The judiciary committee's report, as amended by the convention, provided for the election of both the supreme court and inferior courts. There is no indication in the convention journal or in the newspapers of any opposition. The delegates did demonstrate some disagreement on related issues such as the number of supreme court judges, the length of judicial terms of office, and judicial salaries, but none of the proposed substitutes for sections of the committee report challenged the principle of judicial elections.[97]

After the convention but before the popular vote on ratification, Democrats who opposed the proposed constitution made a fuss over the section that based representation in the house on total population, including slaves, as it had been in the senate since 1845. They argued that the new apportionment would foster a planter nobility. The provision was controversial at the convention, but the split among the delegates had been more along sectional than party lines. A majority of Democrats had actually voted in favor of it. The Whig delegates of Orleans Parish voted for the apportionment 16–10, despite having a low concentration of slaves, because the constitution removed the ceiling on the size of the city's legislative delegation, and they believed that the city's rapid growth would allow it to outpace the rural slave-owners' representation. The voters ratified the constitution on November 2 by a vote of 19,850 to 15,833.[98]

In 1845, Louisiana had been the last southwestern bastion of the old conservatism that denied the principles of free suffrage and equal representation. Through a decade-long process that included two constitutional conventions, the state moved toward Jeffersonian democracy. The tension between the democratic impulses of the people at large and concerns among slaveholders for the safety of the slave system produced a compromise that fell short of equal representation. Yet, the transformation of the Louisiana constitution was remarkable. "The Constitution of 1845 was radical and progressive to a great extent," said delegate Andrew S. Herron at the 1852 convention, "but the objection to it was that it did not go far enough." Now, Herron continued, the delegates were "making a Constitution for the people. . . . The Constitution ought to bear radicalism on its face."[99] In its broadening of the elective franchise and giving to the expanded electorate the power to choose virtually all of its public officers, judges included, the constitution of 1852 represented the triumph of radical democratic ideals.

CHAPTER 5

Explaining the Rise of Judicial Elections

Every so often, there appears a new attempt to explain the great transition from appointive to elective judiciaries in the mid-nineteenth century. For many years, the predominant view credited—or blamed—Jacksonian democracy. In 1873, prominent New York lawyer and civil service reformer Dorman B. Eaton, who disliked the elective judiciary, pointed to the democratic tide that had swept his state in 1846. "It was a period favorable to radical theories and rash experiments," he wrote. There was much in New York's political and legal systems that had needed reforming, Eaton conceded, but the method of selecting judges was not among them. He insisted that the elective judiciary had been adopted by the state's 1846 constitutional convention without much thought. Rather, "[i]t floated in on the rush of the stream of revolution."[1]

Eaton's assessment long remained the usual explanation for the spread of the elective judiciary. Progressive Era critics of judicial elections, including such legal luminaries as Harlan Fiske Stone and Learned Hand, agreed with it, as did such prominent professors of law as Evan Haynes and James Willard Hurst. Hurst attributed the swing toward judicial elections to Jacksonian democracy's insistence on greater popular control of public offices. It was, he claimed, an emotional, "scantly deliberated" development. Haynes placed the rise of the elective judiciary in the context of democratic movements and humanitarian reforms in Europe as well as America, but he concurred that the change had little to do with the merits of popular election. It resulted, he thought, from "ebullient enthusiasm" and a "violent swing toward the democratization of government."[2]

Most commentators on the rise of judicial elections simply wagged their fingers at Jacksonian democracy, without subjecting the phenomenon to serious scholarly scrutiny. That changed in the later twentieth century with the work of Kermit L. Hall and Caleb Nelson. Contrary to the antipopulist critics of judicial elections, Nelson contended that the switch to the elective judiciary came after deliberate, intelligent consideration of its merits. "[O]pposition to the reform was potent," Nelson noted, "and the arguments on both sides were sophisticated; in several state conventions, in fact, the debates over the elective judiciary were so long that they prompted time limits on speeches." Viewing the development in historical context and analyzing the arguments put forth by supporters and opponents of judicial elections at the mid-century constitutional conventions, Nelson concluded that a "general suspicion of official power," a suspicion rooted in American history and characteristic of Jacksonian democracy, had motivated the constitutional reform movement, of which the elective judiciary was one component.[3]

The populist element in the "general suspicion of official power," though, must not be underestimated. Its force appeared repeatedly in the angry rhetoric employed by constitutional convention delegates, especially in states where massive internal improvement projects had crashed and burned, leaving huge public debt as their legacy. The conventions in the Old Northwest bristled with hostility toward state legislatures. It was to that branch of government, declared an Illinois delegate, that "we trace all our evils. If we had had no Legislature for the last twelve years we would now be a happy and prosperous State." A member of the Indiana convention complained of public offices becoming "the mere foot-ball of contending political parties"; of politicians pushing for local expenditures just to enhance their own power; of "hosts of contractors, bankers, stock jobbers, brokers, corporation mongers, gamblers, speculators, and petty office holders, rioting upon the spoils of the State, and united to support the powers which most favored themselves." In Ohio, a convention delegate cried that his constituents had been "taxed, and re-taxed, and overtaxed year after year . . . and have never received anything in return. And sir, we ask now that debt-contracting, loan laws, and money squandering may forever be put an end to—that the whole system may be dug up by the roots, and no single sprout ever permitted to shoot up again."[4]

Side by side with the "suspicion of official power" described by Nelson there stood a long tradition of active government, advocated during the Jacksonian era primarily by the Whig Party. The Whig philosophy, wrote Horace Greeley, editor of the Whig *New York Tribune*, "regards Government with hope and confidence, as an agency of the community through which vast and beneficent ends may be accomplished." There were Democrats, too, who supported publicly-subsidized internal improvements, a system of tuition-free common schools, and even prohibition. Although Whigs usually provided the main opposition to judicial elections, many Whigs, and some Democrats, voted for judicial elections without sharing the broader animus against government.[5]

Nelson, like other modern scholars, relies on the records of just a few states, in Nelson's case Massachusetts, Kentucky, New York, Illinois, Indiana, Iowa, and Ohio. Although common themes reverberated everywhere, there were, as we have seen, significant regional variations in the movement for an elective judiciary. Scholars have paid little attention to the South, states that adopted judicial elections by amendment rather than a constitutional convention, and states that rejected judicial elections (other than Massachusetts). What drove the reform movement in New York and the Old Northwest did not necessarily drive the movement in Virginia or Georgia.

In his tirade against the elective judiciary, Eaton asserted that New York's adoption of judicial elections in 1846 had induced other states to fall into line. This notion has had a long life. A century after Eaton's pamphlet appeared, a commentator asserted that the change in New York "set off a chain reaction." Jed Shugerman writes that "[a]fter New York, constitutional conventions and judicial elections swept the country, demonstrating the power of bandwagons and the cascade effect." The evidence for this copycat theory usually consists of states and dates—New York came first, and everyone else followed. Mississippi, which switched to an elective judiciary in 1832, is ignored or dismissed as an outlier of little significance.[6]

While constitutional convention delegates in various states did cite the New York example, sometimes positively and sometimes negatively, discussions of New York took up very little time in the debates. Moreover, election proponents made just as much use of Mississippi, which, having gone to judicial elections in 1832, had had far more experience with the elective system. Mississippi figured in the debates at the New York convention, with opponents of judicial elections deriding the precedent set by "the repudiating, assassin, slave state of Mississippi" and supporters defending the Mississippi judiciary for standing up "against the acts of unfaithful agents who have brought the state into debt and dishonor" and for protecting the interests of the yeomanry. It could not have hurt the reformers' cause to have had the Empire State on their side, but the precedent had little impact.[7]

The first serious alternative to the "stream of revolution" and "chain reaction" explanations for the rise of an elective judiciary came from the pen of the distinguished legal historian Kermit L. Hall in 1983. According to Hall, the change in judicial selection came about because "moderate" lawyers at the state constitutional conventions sought to achieve conservative ends using radical means. Lawyers made up a large percentage of the convention delegates, and they dominated the committees that drafted the judicial articles of the proposed constitutions. Hall divided them into three groups. First, there were radicals who wanted to take control of the judiciary away from party leaders and give it to the people by shortening judicial terms and making judges face the voters. They hoped by doing so to curtail judicial review. Then there were conservatives who wanted a judiciary that was free from the influence of popular prejudices and passions and unafraid to protect property rights and preserve social stability. Conservatives opposed popular elections. They preferred that judges be appointed for long terms or during good behavior. Finally, wrote Hall, there were the moderates, lawyers who shared the conservatives' vision of an independent judiciary but who saw the need, in an increasingly democratic political culture, to root judicial authority in popular legitimacy. They argued that popular elections would enhance the power and prestige of the judiciary and encourage judges to stand up to legislatures.[8]

Nelson criticized Hall's analysis on the grounds that "the switch to the election of judges was as much a popular reform as a lawyer's reform. . . . Hall's lawyer-delegates simply reflected the popularity of the reform." He also disagreed with Hall's position that proponents of elections sought to check popular majorities as represented in the legislatures. (These proponents would have been Hall's moderates. Hall argued that radicals "urged popular election as a restraint on the independence and power of the judiciary.") Rather, insisted Nelson, pro-election delegates "wanted to check legislatures precisely because they were *not* reliably majoritarian." The reformers had come to distrust all government and sought "to rein in . . . all the people's agents" in every branch of government.[9]

But there are more fundamental problems with Hall's argument. When Hall used the terms "radical," "moderate," and "conservative," he meant them in a political sense—at the constitutional conventions, "the fate of the elected judiciary" lay in the hands of "[p]olitical moderates composed of Whig and Democrat lawyer-delegates." In Hall's usage, though, anyone who opposed judicial elections was *ipso facto* a conservative; anyone who favored judicial elections for the purpose of restraining the judiciary (rather than the legislatures, as Hall said the conservatives and moderates wanted) was a radical; and those who supported judicial elections but sought by their rationales and complementary measures to strengthen the courts was by definition a moderate.[10]

Hall grouped Michael Hoffman of New York with the moderates when in fact Hoffman was a leading radical—deeply suspicious of corporations and "monopolies," wary of banks and their "soft money" notes, opposed to public debt, devoted to the ideals of equality and of popular but limited government, and unafraid to advocate measures, including constitutional change, to address the crisis of democracy he believed had arrived. As Jed Shugerman points out in his criticism of Hall's argument, the leaders of the fight for judicial elections in New York, including Hoffman, "were mostly 'radicals' or populists, not leaders of the profession." Hall described Samson Mason of Ohio as a moderate for arguing that the elective principle and a restructured court system (presumably the one offered in the majority report of the judiciary committee, which Mason signed) promised "swifter justice . . . greater economy . . . and a judiciary accountable to the people." But these were also the goals of radical Rufus P. Ranney—"a good representative of the Locofoco, destructive agrarian party," in the eyes of a fellow delegate—who rejected the majority report and offered a plan of his own. The "eminently conservative" Peter Hitchcock, on the other hand, signed the majority report. In Wisconsin Edward Ryan, a radical Jacksonian Democrat, opposed an elective judiciary. The judgments of a court, he contended, were not supposed to represent the will of the people; they were supposed to be the results of an interpretation and application of the law. Judges had to "stand on the eternal rock of right, unswayed by all the clamorous waves of opinion." In short, Hall's categorization of radicals, moderates, and conservatives based on their stances toward an elective judiciary is problematical, to say the least.[11]

Furthermore, Hall's evidence is suspect. His article is rife with erroneous citations. In some cases, the error lies in the lack of a relationship between statements in the main text and the cited sources.[12] In other instances, direct quotations simply do not appear in the cited sources. For example, the language attributed to Samson Mason, above, for which Hall provides a citation, is not at the cited page or anywhere else in the debates of the Ohio convention.[13] To take just one more illustration, Hall quotes delegate "Abner" (actually Edward) Keyes telling the Massachusetts convention that the "judiciary are so weak" because they "depend on the legislative branch for their appointments." "Elect your judges," Keyes allegedly continued, "and you will energize them, and make them independent, and put them on a par with the other branches of government." The quoted language cannot be found anywhere in the three volumes of Massachusetts debates.[14]

Notwithstanding the perceptive critiques of Hall's contentions by Nelson and Shugerman, Hall's explanation for the switch to the elective judiciary has remained influential to the present day.[15]

The most recent and most sophisticated explanation for the rise of judicial elections is that of Shugerman, who locates the roots of judicial-selection reform in the financial panics of 1837 and 1839 and the depression that followed. Shugerman frames his argument within a three-part model of historical causation: "long-term *preconditions*, midterm *precipitants*, and short-term *triggers*." The precondition, he writes, was democratic ideology. Precipitants included the financial panics, the state fiscal crises that followed, and "systematic abuses of the appointment process." The triggers were the constitutional conventions in New York in 1846 and in other states thereafter. "Without the precipitants and triggers," writes Shugerman, "it is less likely that there would have been constitutional conventions proposing broad changes to state courts in the 1840s and early 1850s."[16]

The success of the Erie Canal, Shugerman maintains, inspired New York and other states to indulge in an internal improvement "binge." Public funding of roads, canals, and railroads resulted in enormous public debt, as poorly planned enterprises failed. The panics and ensuing depression drove many states to default or to the edge of bankruptcy and caused huge increases in taxes. Popular antipathy toward public subsidization of economic development led to demands for constitutional conventions to curtail legislative power. New York led the way with its convention of 1846. Delegates to the New York convention demanded judicial elections because elected judges would be more independent than appointed judges and therefore more willing to resist the legislature. Other states, stirred by New York's example, also opted for elective judiciaries. Just about everywhere the pro-election convention delegates got what they wanted as the number of statutes declared unconstitutional soared.[17]

Shugerman hedges his bets at various points. For example, he writes that "[t]he movement for judicial elections required a constellation of forces to line up" and that "economic depressions do not ordinarily lead to more support for judicial review and judicial power." Still, he insists that the depression following the Panic of 1837 was "the most significant factor of all leading to the conventions and the adoption of judicial elections" and that the reformers "intended elected judges to stand up to the legislatures."[18]

Shugerman's understanding of the rise and impact of judicial elections is intellectually satisfying on its face. It ties elections to specific economic and political developments. It provides a concrete foundation for the increase in the number of cases in which courts struck down statutes. Based on a close study of constitutional convention debates and an extensive review of state court cases, the economic crisis theory links more aggressive judicial review to the adoption of judicial elections and explains how and why the two phenomena arose when they did. As the newspapers used to say, this is "interesting if true." But there are problems with the argument, especially with regard to the precipitants and trigger, as well as with the positions of convention delegates regarding judicial review.

The economic "precipitant"—the states' financial disasters—generated a great deal of public hostility toward state legislatures, and it is no surprise that these calamities have been credited with bringing about constitutional conventions. However, the fiscal debacles were just one source of dissatisfaction and rarely the most important. Convention delegates in states that had suffered severely from internal improvement schemes remembered the pain and sought to prevent its recurrence. Even states that had not accumulated huge public debt took a lesson from the experiences of others and adopted constitutional provisions designed to forestall its acquisition. But that was not why the conventions were called. In some states, notably Delaware, Maryland, Missouri, and Virginia, the greatest grievance was malapportionment of the legislature. In others, including Ohio (where anger over failed internal improvement projects ran high) and Tennessee, unhappiness with the organization of the courts weighed more heavily, as did discontent over the undemocratic nature of local government in Kentucky, Virginia, and other southern states. The independent republic of Texas, the territories of Iowa and Wisconsin, and the war prize California held conventions to draft constitutions for admission to the Union. Even in New York, a contemporary observer attributed the convention primarily to "the enormous evils which existed in the administration of the law," while delegates at the convention itself asserted that "the reconstruction of the judicial system was the chief reason for calling the Convention."[19]

Some states embraced judicial elections and publicly supported internal improvements simultaneously. Louisiana is a good example. The southwestern states did not invest heavily in internal improvements in the 1830s, at least not in comparison with the states to their north and east. They had numerous natural waterways, a sparser taxable population, and few compunctions about taking federal aid from the sale of public lands or other sources. As we saw in chapter 4, however, Louisianans' passion for railroads ramped up at the same time as their interest in judicial elections. The constitutional convention of 1845 imposed severe restrictions on banking and the creation of public debt while rejecting judicial elections, but just seven years later another convention eased the banking restrictions, authorized state loans for internal improvements, and embraced judicial elections. The newfound zeal for both state-supported internal improvements and judicial elections does not square with the notion that conventions adopted the elective judiciary in order to restrain fiscally irresponsible legislatures.

In Missouri, too, the legislature had been reluctant to sponsor internal improvements. In 1836, Democratic Governor Lilburn W. Boggs pressed the lawmakers to promote internal improvements, especially railroads. "If we would apply the incentive to industry—if we would give life and vigor to agriculture and commerce—if we would cheapen transportation, facilitate intercourse, and place our State upon the vantage ground now occupied by some of the other States," Boggs told the lawmakers, "we must adopt a system of internal improvements. . . . [N]ow is a suitable time for us to commence." Boggs had plenty of support for his dream, especially in St. Louis, where railroad enthusiasts thought the new form of transportation essential to their city's future as a leading trade center of the Mississippi Valley.[20]

Few legislators, though, shared St. Louis's ardor. They chartered a host of railroad companies but, wary of raising taxes or incurring debt, refused to give them state aid. The General Assembly created a board of internal improvements in 1839, but that body issued only one report before the legislature abolished it in 1841. An attempt to create a new board in 1845 received a brusque dismissal in the senate. By the time the constitutional convention met in 1845, Missouri had done next to nothing in the way of constructing or financing internal improvements. But soon after the convention, Missourians of both parties hopped aboard an internal improvements bandwagon. Railroad boosters in and around St. Louis launched a campaign for federal assistance and raised private capital for a railroad to the Pacific. Ultimately, they concluded that state funding would be needed if St. Louis were to retain its position as the preeminent commercial center of the Mississippi Valley. Whigs and Democrats alike discovered a new fondness for state aid to private enterprise. The General Assembly caught the railroad fever and in 1851 granted two railroads a total of $3.5 million in bonds. It was a cautious beginning of a policy of state aid that would see increasing assistance during the 1850s. And it happened in the same year in which a constitutional amendment gave Missouri an elective judiciary.[21]

Shugerman devotes considerable space to the "trigger" for judicial elections, the New York convention of 1846, but his argument seems to be based on correlation, not causation. In any event, as discussed above, New York did not play a large role in the debates of other states' conventions, and the New York example was used by opponents as well as supporters of the elective judiciary. The trend toward elections of all sorts, not just for judges, grew steadily throughout the Jacksonian era, without the aid of a New York trigger. Developments in Iowa, Wisconsin, Illinois, Arkansas, and Missouri in the mid-1840s, not to mention the Mississippi precedent of 1832, suggest that the spread of judicial elections would have happened even without the New York example.[22]

Perhaps the biggest question mark about the economic crisis explanation is its assertion that constitutional conventions approved judicial elections for the purpose of strengthening judicial review. Hall and Nelson, too, write that pro-election delegates at the conventions sought to fortify judicial review in order to check irresponsible legislatures. There is some evidence in the published proceedings of the conventions to support this notion. Michael Hoffman of New York advocated judicial elections as a means of ensuring judicial independence from the legislature. Ohio convention delegate Samuel Humphreville commented on the difficulties of getting a court chosen by the General Assembly to declare a law unconstitutional. He expressed the hope that popularly elected judges would show their independence in their decisions. In Georgia, which did not have a mid-century constitutional convention, an essayist for a newspaper wrote that a judge dependent on the legislature for his position would need "nerves of steel and an iron will" to hold unconstitutional "any favorite object of legislative will."[23]

But these were isolated instances, and one can find comments going the other way. A pro-election delegate at the Kentucky convention insisted that the judiciary's "vast power ... of striking every act of the legislature dead" required legislative checks on judicial power. In Ohio, the chairman of the committee on the legislature declared that the committee had reported one proposed provision for the express purpose of *preventing* a presumptuous supreme court from assuming the power to declare laws unconstitutional.[24]

Arguments for and against judicial elections were more likely to focus on judges' impartiality with regard to litigants than on judicial review. Opponents of judicial elections worried that elected judges would not be able to resist partisan popular prejudice and passion. Could they remain impartial when the people wanted to see a criminal defendant hang? Would they risk abuse from the press and the possible loss of office in a libel suit brought against a partisan newspaper? Would not the partisan need of judicial candidates to pander to the voters turn the aspirants into scroungers after votes, soiling the judicial ermine in the political muck? "We have heard of Lynch law," declaimed Chief Judge Chambers of Maryland, ". . . Yet popular prejudice against an individual, does not forfeit his claim to the benefits of the law. . . . [W]hat can you in such a case expect from your Judge 'dependent upon the people?'"[25]

There is, to be sure, a degree of validity to each of the explanations offered for the rise of the elective judiciary. In many states, populist fervor drove a constitutional reform movement that, while rarely directed at judicial selection, had the election of all public officers as a key component. Much of the popular outrage, particularly in the Old Northwest and the Mid-Atlantic states, focused on legislatures that had plunged the states into badly planned and ruinous internal improvement projects. The reforms that followed sharply diminished the legislatures' power, including the power of appointment. Yet when the subject of judicial elections elicited discussion in the newspapers or at constitutional conventions, the debates typically included thoughtful arguments pro and con. Lawyers always figured prominently in these debates, and although the pro-election disputants were not necessarily political moderates, they did argue that elections would enhance the legitimacy of the courts in the eyes of the public. None of this would have happened in the absence of a prevalent democratic ideology that proved hard to resist even when the holders of power did not share it.

Perhaps the biggest obstacle to any attempt to explain the sudden shift to judicial elections is the size and diversity of antebellum America. States that differed from one another in their constitutional and political histories, geographies, demographics, and economies could not have followed identical paths even to a common end. Some states never reached that end. In the face of these factors, it may be imprudent to offer an overarching explanation for the advent of judicial elections. However, based on the history related in the foregoing chapters, I offer four observations.

First, Eaton had a point when he charged that judicial elections were swept in with the "rush of the stream of revolution." The elective judiciary was never an idea important enough to prompt the calling of a constitutional convention. In Mississippi, it became a hot-button issue only after the campaign for seats at the convention began. In New York, it was not a high priority for the strange-bedfellow convention alliance of Whigs and radical Democrats. Eaton underestimated the intellectual seriousness of the case for judicial elections, but he was right when he wrote that at the New York convention "there was no real debate on the subject." He understood that the elective judiciary was a side issue in the constitutional revolution of the mid-nineteenth century and that it took some larger reform campaign to bring it into existence. The elective judiciary turned into a subject of heated debate at some conventions because to lawyers it was a matter of the utmost importance. However, as the low turnout at judicial elections would show, the voters at large did not care much about how judges were chosen.[26]

What voters did care about, reasonably or not, was the power of government to do harm. The widespread disgust with government that characterized mid-nineteenth-century politics, especially in New York and the Old Northwest, found expression in calls to limit legislative authority —authority to contract debt, finance internal improvements, enact "special legislation" for the benefit of banks and other corporations, grant divorces, create new counties, pass laws by logrolling and other unseemly practices. Reformers also sought to curtail or eliminate the power, whether lodged in the legislature, the governor alone, or the governor in conjunction with the senate, to appoint public officers. When newspaper editors or public meetings presented their recommendations for constitutional reform, they often had the popular election of public officers at or near the top of their lists. In Ohio, newspaper editor Samuel Medary urged "[t]he election of ALL OFFICERS BY THE PEOPLE!" Illinois Democrats wanted "to place the election of every officer in the hands of the people." In Michigan, the Democratic *Detroit Free Press* demanded "the election of all officers by the people," while the Whig candidate for governor declared that he would "approve of such an amendment as would fully convert the appointing power ... into an election by the people."[27]

Notwithstanding the far-reaching changes wrought by the Mississippi constitutional convention of 1832, Eaton's "stream of revolution" flowed mainly through the North. Certainly, there were southerners who wanted sweeping reform. An Arkansas paper endorsed "the election of all officers by the people," while citizens in Kentucky called for "making *all* officers of the government (from the highest to the lowest grade) elective by the people." In Arkansas and Kentucky, as in Ohio, Illinois, and Michigan, the insistence on popular election of public officers was part of a longer agenda pushed by convention advocates; in none of these states did anyone focus on the election of judges. But in most of the South, the revisions that followed these demands for reform were more conservative than the radical revamping of government that occurred in New York and the Old Northwest.[28]

The transition to the elective judiciary itself was more conservative in the South. In Georgia, it came by way of statute and was limited to the lower courts. In Alabama, Arkansas, Florida, Missouri, Tennessee, and Texas, it came through constitutional amendments, and in Alabama and Arkansas it excluded the supreme court. Although the judicial election amendments all had companion amendments providing for the popular election of additional public officers or other constitutional revisions, none amounted to a revolution in state government. Even in Louisiana, where a limited "revolution" occurred at the 1845 constitutional convention, judicial elections did not come about until another convention met seven years later. The long-term trend toward democratization of government made the switch to the elective judiciary possible, but the rush of revolution was more characteristic of New York and the Old Northwest—and, to a lesser extent, the border states—than of the South as a whole.

Longer judicial terms of office also revealed the South's relative conservatism. Of the nine southern states that made their highest courts elective before the Civil War, only Mississippi, Missouri, and Texas established terms as short as six years. The mid-century conventions or amendments in Florida, Kentucky, and Tennessee all set the terms of supreme court judges at eight years, in Louisiana and Maryland at ten, and in Virginia at twelve. Eleven free states adopted judicial elections for their highest courts before the outbreak of hostilities. Ohio had the shortest terms of office, just five years. Supreme court judges in California, Indiana, Iowa, Kansas, and Wisconsin had six-year terms, Minnesota judges seven-year terms. Only Illinois, Michigan, New York, and Pennsylvania went beyond seven years, and Pennsylvania alone afforded its supreme court judges double-digit terms (fifteen years, as before its judicial-elections amendment).[29]

A second observation, related to Shugerman's precondition, is that states in which the citizenry generally shared Jeffersonian democratic principles switched to judicial elections. (Northern New England proved an exception to the rule.[30]) The few states where powerful segments of the population did not share the Jeffersonian ideal either did not switch to judicial elections or did so only under the threat of upheaval. After the proudly undemocratic potentates of South Carolina's Lowcountry coopted influential Upcountry opponents in the early nineteenth century, constitutional reformers in the Palmetto State lacked the strength to force further change. Virginia's aristocrats were no less conservative, but, faced with the threat of secession by a large and growing Upcountry at a time when unity seemed essential, they made significant democratic concessions that included an elective judiciary. In Maryland, which also fell short of the Jeffersonian ideal, a state reform convention heard talk of revolution if the General Assembly persisted in refusing to call a constitutional convention, and the governor warned that "unless the wishes of the people, in this behalf, are satisfied, the sanction of the Legislature will not much longer be invoked." The legislature soon put a convention referendum to the voters. The convention that followed adopted judicial elections and other democratic reforms.[31]

My third observation concerns demographics. The rise of urban centers and the settlement of new areas upset constitutional arrangements for legislative representation, generated regional demands for internal improvements, and posed conundrums for political parties. Intoxicated by visions of endless progress, many states that experienced rapid growth embarked on imprudent economic development schemes that produced massive public debt. Judicial systems, constrained by constitutional limits on their size and burdened by duties constitutionally imposed, could not keep up. These and other problems associated with growth created dissatisfaction with government and pressures for constitutional revision, in the absence of which judicial elections probably would not have come about.

Most of the states that, in the mid-nineteenth century, either switched from appointed to elected courts or provided for judicial elections in their original constitutions had undergone dramatic demographic developments in the previous twenty or so years. In the Northeast, people were moving from farms and villages to burgeoning commercial centers. In the Southeast, the growth of the western Upcountry far outpaced the stagnating eastern Lowcountry. But the truly spectacular increases occurred in the West. Of the ten states that rejected judicial elections entirely, all of them in the East, not one doubled in population between 1830 and 1850. Connecticut, Delaware, New Hampshire, Vermont, North Carolina, and South Carolina were among the most slowly growing states in the country. The populations of Maine, Massachusetts, New Jersey, and Rhode Island increased by 46–63 percent. In contrast, every state outside the territory of the original thirteen—that is, every western state plus Florida—more than doubled in population except Kentucky, Tennessee, and Mississippi. But Mississippi's white population had quadrupled in the two decades before its constitutional convention of 1832. Every one of these "nonoriginal" states adopted judicial elections, although Alabama and Arkansas, along with Iowa until 1857, kept their supreme courts appointive.

Of the six nondoubling states that moved to the elective system, two—New York and Pennsylvania—nevertheless saw extraordinary growth in the 1830s and 1840s. Just their *increases* in raw numbers would have placed each of them among the eight largest states in 1850. Tennessee's increase, excluding slaves, while not so dramatic, still was more than the total 1850 populations of five other states. The white populations of Tennessee and Kentucky, roughly three-quarters of a million each in 1850, and of Virginia, at nearly nine hundred thousand, were among the largest in the country. Maryland was a slow-growth state, but constitutional revision there was driven largely by Baltimore, which more than doubled in population between 1830 and 1850 and by the latter date was the second-biggest metropolis in the United States.

The success of the movement for judicial elections in the fast-growing states was not just a matter of numbers. The millions of people who moved to northeastern cities, settled the southeastern Upcountry, and migrated west were mostly of the poor and middling sorts, folks who naturally took democracy to heart. They had no great regard for town representation as seen in Vermont or the lifetime judicial tenure so respected in Massachusetts,[32] and they possessed no ingrained sense of deference to "aristocrats." These democrats viewed public officers, including judges, as their agents, to be chosen by themselves.

Finally, the shift to judicial elections was in some measure a bottom-up reform. It began with justices of the peace in several states and inferior court judges in Georgia. The first major recorded debate over judicial elections, which occurred at the New York constitutional convention in 1821, involved justices of the peace. Mississippi's radical step of creating an entirely elective judiciary in 1832 had been preceded by an act providing for the popular election of justices of the peace.³³ Complaints about the powerful, unelected, self-perpetuating county courts in Virginia carried more weight at that state's constitutional convention than did grievances about the selection of higher court judges. That was true of Kentucky, Mississippi, Arkansas, and Alabama as well. Before the New York convention of 1846 settled on the election of all the state's judges, the denizens of Indiana and Michigan elected associate judges in their trial courts; voters in Missouri, Illinois, and other states elected probate judges; and the new Iowa constitution provided for the election of district court judges. This was Jacksonian democracy in action—democratizing the government closest to the people then moving up to the higher offices until the radical becomes the norm.

CHAPTER 6

Electing the Judges

In the spring of 1847, the editors of the *New-York Daily Tribune* bemoaned the insufficient interest shown by the general public in New York's forthcoming first judicial elections.[1] A letter to the editor warned that "the friends of an Elective Judiciary have more and more reason to be alarmed at the general apathy which prevails upon the subject." The day after the election, the *New York Herald* reported that the election for judges had "passed off in a spiritless manner." If not for an intraparty tiff among Whigs regarding candidates for district attorney, remarked the paper, the "very small" number of votes cast in the city in the most important election in the state's history "would scarcely have exceeded those usually thrown for school commissioners." Moreover, those who did vote kept in office the same judges who had been in office before the election. "It is not a little singular," observed the *Sunday Dispatch*, "that in this first selection of judges under the new constitution, there has been, in fact, no change in the judiciary. The judges under the old constitution are, by the direct sanction of the people, the judges under the new."[2]

The situation in New York was not unique. Before and during the various state constitutional conventions, newspaper editors and correspondents and convention delegates expended a great deal of time and energy arguing the pros and cons of different methods of judicial selection, of long and short tenures of office, of election of judges by district and election at large. As it turned out, the people didn't much care. After judicial elections became law, newspapers often lamented the voters' lack of interest in judicial contests. A Louisiana paper decried the people's "shameless want of interest in the election of judges . . . ever since they have acquired the right of electing them." Other Louisiana papers noted the "extreme apathy" among the populace when it came to electing judges. Moaned one paper, "people do not and will not take an interest in Judicial Elections."[3]

A Tennessee critic of judicial elections complained that few people knew anything about the merits of candidates for the supreme court and therefore the masses, "as a general thing, have staid at home without knowledge of or interest in the subject." Even in large towns, he noted, the polls sometimes did not even open. The 1855 election went so quietly that, one newspaper speculated, perhaps half the people did not know there was a contest. According to Kermit Hall, only 10 percent of the eligible voters cast ballots.[4]

Opponents of the elective judiciary had warned that judicial candidates would demean themselves by wallowing in the political mire. Advocates did not so much deny that partisan politicking would inhere in the election of judges as insist that it would be no worse than what went on with gubernatorial and legislative appointments. A newspaper in Pennsylvania, where the governor appointed the judges, remarked that "[t]he Governor is always influenced in his appointments by party distinctions, or the preferences of favoritism, and in that respect a change [to judicial elections] would make no difference, or if any, it would be a favorable one, as the choice of the people would then be consulted, instead of the selections of sectionally interested parties, or the peculiar wishes of the Governor." In Ohio, where the General Assembly chose the judges, a paper asked, "Does not a whig Legislature uniformly appoint whig judges and a democratic Legislature appoint democratic judges? The people, then, could be no worse in this respect than the Legislature, and they have motives to do better, which the Legislature has not."[5]

Some southerners hoped for better results from judicial elections. After Georgia's first elections for superior court judges, one paper crowed that the results demonstrated the people's capacity to choose their own judges. "In the strongest Democratic Circuits, Whigs have been chosen, and *vice versa*," commented the *Georgia Telegraph*. "In every instance the choice has alighted on upright and capable men." But partisanship was present from the outset. Although many judicial aspirants announced their candidacies in brief, nonpartisan notices in the newspapers, others were nominated by local party conventions. In 1858, a Democratic candidate defended party nominations, noting that when the legislature appointed the judges the party in power had usually chosen men from its own ranks and that "the same preference for political friends" was "strictly observed" in the appointment of US Supreme Court justices.[6]

One way to alleviate the partisanship intrinsic to judicial elections, thought reformers, was to set different dates for judicial and general elections. The New York judicial elections of 1847 took place in June; the general election occurred in November. Virginia's constitution of 1850 prohibited the holding of judicial elections within thirty days of any election for president, Congress, or the General Assembly. In Alabama, Arkansas, Louisiana, and Tennessee, too, judicial elections and general elections were held at different times. In Georgia, the legislature originally had judicial elections take place at the general election but soon moved them to another month. Missouri's constitution set the dates for both general elections and judicial elections as the first Monday in August; but with the first election of judges taking place in 1851, judicial terms being for an even number of years, and other state and federal officers being chosen in even-numbered years, regular judicial elections would occur in off years.[7]

The result of such schemes may have been less to reduce the politicking involved in judicial elections than to dampen voter turnout. "May we not safely say," wrote one Virginia skeptic, "that the people are very much annoyed now with the necessity of electing their State and federal law-makers? We constantly hear complaints that the voters will not, to the neglect of their private affairs, come to the polls; and many of those who do go, often go grumbling. If they are wearied now, what will they do when they have two elections in one year[?]" But if the election of judges took place at the same time as the election of other officers, he continued, "experience teaches us that there will be but one ticket for all those on the same side, and the whole must be endorsed or none. . . . [T]he mass of the people [will not] have anything to do with the choice of judge, or any other officer; for the ticket will have been formed by the wire pullers and managers, long before an opportunity has been given the people of even bestowing a thought upon the subject."[8]

The writer's prediction that voters would vote for all the candidates "on the same side" was borne out by election returns in Ohio and Indiana, where judicial elections coincided with general elections and voters tended to vote straight tickets. In those states, judicial candidates won when their party carried the state and lost when their party as a whole lost. Indeed, in every supreme court race in those states in the 1850s, the vote totals for each of the candidates closely tracked the votes received by the candidates for state executive offices.[9]

Mississippi voters exhibited similar tendencies. Comparing the vote totals for the high court of errors and appeals and state executive officers is difficult because the three judges were elected by district. However, the voters of the state at large chose the chancellor for a six-year term at the general election. In 1845, the Democrats swept all the state contests. The

Democratic candidates for governor, secretary of state, attorney general, auditor, and treasurer received between 27,164 and 28,310 votes. Three candidates, two Democrats and one Whig, vied for the office of chancellor. The combined total for the Democrats was 27,377, comfortably within the range of votes for the Democratic candidates for executive offices. The Whig votes for the executive offices ranged from 10,916 to 18,640. The Whig candidate for chancellor received 12,558 votes. It appears that most Democratic voters voted straight tickets, while Whigs either voted straight tickets or regarded some races as hopeless causes.[10]

In 1851, in the midst of a national crisis over slavery, the Whig label lost much of its meaning in Mississippi; the contending parties were the Union and State Rights parties, although newspapers often identified the Unionists as Whigs and the State Righters as Democrats. In a tight race that drew more votes than any other, Henry S. Foote, the Union candidate for governor, outpolled his State Rights opponent, Jefferson Davis, 29,358–28,359. In the other contests for executive offices, all won by Unionists, the Union vote ranged from 27,875 to 28,221, the State Rights vote from 25,084 to 25,523. Newspapers generally tried to keep the race for chancellor nonpartisan, usually leaving the candidates' names, Charles Scott and John I. Guion, off the state tickets. Judging by the results, though, most voters knew where the two stood—not on equity matters but on federal-state relations. Scott and Guion were both old Whigs, but Guion, who had recently served as governor following his predecessor's resignation, had become a fervent State Righter. Scott, the Union candidate, won 28,513–24,192.[11]

In Ohio and Indiana, supreme court races were openly partisan and always contested. In other states, judicial candidates sometimes ran unopposed. The Virginia constitution of 1850 divided the state into five sections, in each of which the voters elected one supreme court judge. In the first judicial elections, incumbent judges faced no opposition in two sections; in a third section, a challenger to the incumbent did not appear until the last moment. When popular elections took effect in Texas in 1851, the three incumbents faced only one opponent. When they resigned and ran again in 1856 so that they could accept a salary increase, they had no practical opposition. In Tennessee's first supreme court election, the three incumbents ran unopposed. In a subsequent election to fill a vacancy, the Democratic candidate had no opponent until a Know Nothing candidate entered the race at the eleventh hour. In Missouri in 1855, a highly regarded Whig attorney who had the support of the court's two

Democratic judges won a special, uncontested, and generally ignored election for an open seat.[12]

The dearth of public interest in judicial elections induced some rethinking about the wisdom of separating judicial from general elections. A Louisiana Democrat complained that while his party, in the spirit of the constitution's intent to keep judicial elections "aloof from . . . the political contests of the day," had refrained from making nominations, the Whigs had taken advantage of public indifference to organize a partisan turnout and win. The only way to save the electoral system, he wrote, was to hold all elections at the same time to boost the vote for judges and to have party endorsements to give the voters confidence in the suitability of the candidates.[13]

Unlike this Louisiana commentator, who believed that every supreme court judge in his state owed his nomination and election to "political considerations," a Tennessee observer thought that public indifference was the only thing that had kept supreme court races from "degenerating into mere political contests." But the Tennessean had little hope for the future. "We have not, as yet, met in party conventions and made party nominations," he noted. "We have not enjoyed the rare pride of beholding our candidates for judicial honors, riding over the State and over their respective districts, bearing the banners and advocating from the stump, the tenets of their respective parties." But, he predicted, "we shall soon exult in the glorious privilege of having justice administered by a partisan judiciary."[14]

In the Old Northwest, the nominating process was blatantly political from the beginning, as were the races themselves. State party conventions nominated the supreme court judges, who then were elected by the voters of the entire state. The partisan newspapers printed the party nominations in every issue from the time of the conventions to the day of election. The editor of the *Indiana State Sentinel* insisted that it was "just as necessary to have Democratic Judges to administer the laws, as to have Democratic Legislators enact them." "[T]hat's our doctrine," he declared, "and we have the boldness to avow it."[15]

In the South, candidates typically made known their availability for judicial office by publishing notices in the papers. That did not keep politics from intruding into the contests, as the Louisiana Democrat quoted above observed, but at least it nodded to the ideal of a nonpolitical judiciary. By the end of the 1850s, though, Louisiana's judicial candidates were announcing their readiness to serve subject to the decision of a party convention—a district convention in the case of associate judges, since they were elected by district. Everywhere, except in extraordinary cases, party affiliation would prove to be the most important determinant of a judicial election.[16]

Scholars have sometimes asserted that the transition to judicial elections encouraged judicial activism—the elected judges struck down more statutes than had the appointed judges who had come before them. One writer credits the judges' new electoral accountability. Another suggests that judicial elections might have "produced new types of judges," men who were more comfortable engaging in the political process and more inclined to intervene in politics than their predecessors had been. A third proposes that the experience of running in elections might have disillusioned the judicial candidates with democracy, leading to a countermajoritarian turn in their thinking and a greater inclination to invalidate legislation.[17]

If most voters were apathetic toward supreme court elections, except when partisan considerations led them to vote for judicial candidates along party lines, they surely did not cogitate about a candidate's notions of judicial review when casting their ballots. Whether judges, once elected, thought about the people's preferences is another question. At the Ohio constitutional convention delegate Charles Reemelin declared that if popular opinion had controlled the supreme court, "we would have had less subservient tools to the money power of this State." A Vermont proponent of judicial elections imagined that "if we can have judges *from* the people, they will be very likely to think *with* the people . . . and our laws will be judicially sustained." Modern-day law professor Jed Shugerman, on the other hand, contends that constitutional reformers sought an elective judiciary in order to make judges independent of state legislatures and thus *more* likely to invalidate legislation. Elections, he writes, "would embolden judges by providing them with popular legitimacy; and voters would reward judges who defended popular constitutional rights and punish those who did not." In either case, the argument rests on the assumption that judges would render decisions with reelection in mind. But how much weight would a judge give to the opinion of a public that either did not vote in judicial elections or voted along party lines?[18]

The assumption depicts judges in an unflattering light, as calculating politicians who, when appointed, sought to please the appointing authority and when elected sought to satisfy the electorate. But while advocates of elections sometimes spoke as though a judge were simply another politician, most convention delegates and newspaper editors, whether or not they favored judicial elections, recognized that judging was different from legislating. Southern commentators believed that judges should be above politics. A correspondent of an anti-election newspaper observed, "[W]e are accustomed to regard a partisan judge as a moral monster," while a pro-election paper intoned, "The office of Supreme Judge is one of great responsibility, and those who compose that court should be men divested of all selfishness, all ulterior political purposes, and all party animosities." "We are all proud to know," wrote a third commentator, "that our judges now occupy, in public estimation, a position on the same platform with the ministers of the Gospel. The people regard them as a peculiar class of officers—as separate and apart from other men. We would blush to see them noisily mingling in politics."[19]

Of course, such views were not restricted to the South. A writer in *The New Constitution*, a pro-election Ohio paper, insisted that even judges who had been active political partisans before taking the bench under the appointive system had never had their integrity questioned. "[T]here is a concentrated weight of responsibility upon a judge," he wrote, "a character of honesty and integrity to sustain, that the most violent partisan will not dare to disregard." The notion that judges calculated the political advantages of deciding on the constitutionality of statutes goes against this deeply ingrained conception of the judicial role.[20]

The very ability of judges to make such fine calculations is doubtful. When judges were appointed by the governor or chosen by a joint ballot of the house and senate, they would have had to predict the party of the governor or the makeup of the legislature several years down the road. When they were popularly elected, they would have had to foresee the forces that ruled the parties and the voters. Either would have been an exceedingly difficult task in the topsy-turvy political world of the 1850s.[21]

It seems highly unlikely in any event that an aspiring judge's attitude toward judicial review would have made a difference to his selection. In states where the lawmakers had appointed the judges, the nominating arena moved from the legislature to party conventions, which had become entrenched in American politics beginning in the late 1830s. Party conventions "countered the image of closed, restricted, elite-dominated decision making associated with the legislative nominating caucus," but party leaders "were always fully entwined in the organs of political decision making, be they smoke-filled rooms, caucuses, or conventions." Judges got appointed, or nominated and elected, on the basis of their political leanings, personal friendships, and professional qualifications, not on their theories of judicial review. There might be exceptions, especially in connection with slavery or prohibition, but then the question was more political than judicial and was unrelated to the method of judicial selection. If Ohio had never adopted judicial elections, the same Republicans who denied Joseph Swan renomination in 1859 because of his position on the Fugitive Slave Law could have prevented his reappointment by the General Assembly.[22]

While as a general rule politics proved more potent than judicial philosophy in determining who sat on a state's supreme court, the influence of partisanship varied from state to state. In the North, judicial races were openly partisan. In some southern states, it is harder to pin down the politics of judicial selection, but benches tended to reflect the prevailing partisan patterns. Virginia's first judicial elections, as noted above, featured seriously contested races in only two of the state's five sections. The elections resulted in a court consisting of four Democrats and one western Whig.[23] A few months earlier, a Democrat had won the state's first popular gubernatorial election and his party had carried thirteen of Virginia's fifteen congressional districts.[24] The voters may or may not have known about or paid attention to the party associations of the judicial candidates, but it is surely no coincidence that the court's composition generally mirrored the political orientation of the various sections and of the state as a whole.

Under Louisiana's first constitution, supreme court judges had lifetime appointments. Early in 1839, though, when the court was under severe criticism for its inefficiency, two of the three members of the court, Henry Carleton and Henry A. Bullard, submitted their resignations. The governor appointed Pierre Adolph Rost and George Eustis to their places, but by the end of June they had quit as well. In August, George Strawbridge and Alonzo Morphy replaced Rost and Eustis. Strawbridge however, wanted only to clear the docket in his district. He soon resigned to be replaced by Bullard. In the meantime, the General Assembly expanded the court's size to five. In the winter of 1840, Edward Simon and Rice Garland joined Morphy, Bullard, and chief judge François Xavier Martin on the bench.[25]

The supreme court entered the 1840s, then, with an incumbent chief judge, a former judge with a new appointment, and three new members. Then the constitution of 1845 vacated all the seats and reduced the term of office to eight years. In 1846, a new four-man court, including Rost and

Eustis, took over. Before their terms expired, another new constitution ousted all the judges again and put the choice of judges into the hands of the electorate.[26] All of this extraordinary activity, combined with the difficulty of identifying the political affiliations of some of the judges, makes for unreliable comparisons with judicial selection in other states.

Once elections took effect, though, a more-or-less normal pattern could be seen, at least in the results. The 1852 constitution provided for a chief justice to be elected by the voters of the entire state and four associate justices to be elected by districts. The initial terms of the associate justices were staggered, so that one member of the court would be elected every other year; thereafter, all the justices would have ten-year terms. There seems to have been an effort to minimize political partisanship in the selection of judges. The constitution required that judges be chosen at separate elections. Contenders announced their candidacies by putting ads in the papers, without mention of parties. The party state conventions declined to nominate candidates for the supreme court, and the newspapers called on voters to elect the best men without regard to partisan considerations. The nonpartisanship of the races, the special election date, and the general public disinterest in judicial contests combined to produce a low turnout.[27]

Yet the results still showed the power of political affiliation. The Whigs had been strong in 1852, with a large majority of the delegates at the constitutional convention that year. But their very successes—the writing of a new constitution and the acceptance by Democrats of internal improvements and other elements of the Whig program—deprived them of their chief state issues. In November, their presidential candidate, Winfield Scott, lost badly. In the state elections on December 27, the Democrats took all six state offices on the ballot and won a big majority in the legislature, and the following March they crushed the dispirited Whigs in the New Orleans municipal elections. In April, notwithstanding the supposedly nonpartisan nature of judicial contests and the presence of at least five well-qualified Whigs in the races, the Democrats took every supreme court seat.[28]

The Whigs soon disappeared as a major party in Louisiana, replaced by the nativist American or Know Nothing party. In 1855, when the Know Nothings were at the height of their popularity and politically potent in New Orleans, Chief Justice Thomas Slidell resigned from the supreme court. Edwin T. Merrick, one of the defeated Whig candidates for the court in 1853, won an election to fill the vacancy. Merrick may or may not have formally joined the Know Nothing Party, but he had the endorsement of the Know Nothing *American Patriot*, which called him "the great pioneer of the cause of Native Americanism in our State." That same year, Alexander M. Buchanan, who in 1853 had won the election for associate justice in the first supreme court district, which included part of New Orleans, had to run for reelection because he had drawn the two-year term on the new court. Now the *Opelousas Patriot*, another Know Nothing paper, identified him as the candidate having American Party support. He, too, won.[29]

In 1857, a contest for associate justice took place in the second district, which included the rest of New Orleans. The *New Orleans Crescent* initially discounted charges that James L. Cole was running as a Know Nothing and incumbent James N. Lea as a Democrat—both, it said, were independent and well-qualified—but soon a correspondent of the *Crescent* joined others in accusing the Democrats of running Lea as a political partisan. On the other hand, the *Houma Ceres*, which leaned toward the Know Nothings, endorsed Cole. Cole won. After the election, the *Crescent* decried the fact that judicial elections inevitably involved "political partiality." The political partisanship involved in judicial elections could no longer be disguised. In 1858, after Henry M. Spofford resigned from the bench, a Democratic convention nominated Thomas T. Land for the open seat. The American Party having precipitously declined in influence, Land's opponent ran as an independent candidate. Land prevailed. The next year, a race for associate justice from another district again featured a Democratic nominee and an independent, and again the Democrat won.[30]

The importance of political affiliation in judicial selection before as well as after the institution of judicial elections is clear in the case of Tennessee. The 1835 constitution created a supreme court of three judges, appointed by the General Assembly for twelve-year terms. One judge had to come from each of the three Grand Divisions of the state—East, Middle, and West. Two of the four incumbents in 1835 chose not to seek reappointment. In their steads, the General Assembly, which had an Anti-Jackson majority, unanimously selected Jacksonian William B. Turley from West Tennessee and Anti-Jacksonian William B. Reese from the East. This display of bipartisanship did not carry over to the Middle Division, where both Nathan Green Sr. and John Catron of the old four-member court resided. The lawmakers could not retain them both. In October, the Tennessee House of Representatives passed a resolution endorsing Hugh

Lawson White for the presidency. Catron, a longtime Jackson loyalist, supported Jackson's choice, Martin Van Buren. When it came time to appoint the judges, the General Assembly named Green, a Whig but not active in politics, by a vote of 71–27.[31]

Green, Reese, and Turley made up the supreme court until 1847, when their twelve-year terms expired. The Whig-controlled legislature[32] retained Green and Turley, who were often at odds but who both had acquired excellent reputations as judges. Reese retired, and the legislature replaced him with another Whig, Robert J. McKinney.[33] Turley resigned in 1850 to accept the judgeship of a newly created trial court.[34] This time the Democrats had control; they replaced Turley with Democrat Archibald W. O. Totten.[35] When Green resigned in 1852, the Whigs were back in the saddle. The Whig governor appointed former Whig congressman Robert L. Caruthers[36] to fill the vacancy until the end of the next legislative session.[37] In 1853, the General Assembly, with a Whig majority on a joint ballot, elected Caruthers to the seat until the popular election under the constitutional amendment could be held.[38]

Thus, with the exception of Turley, the General Assembly consistently appointed judges affiliated with the party of the reigning legislative majority.

When popular elections took effect in 1854, the three incumbent judges, two Whigs and a Democrat, all ran for election for what were now eight-year terms. Although the voters of the entire state elected all three judges, each of the state's three grand divisions had to be represented on the court. McKinney was the candidate for East Tennessee, Caruthers for Middle Tennessee, and Totten for West Tennessee. All ran unopposed. The only other supreme court elections during the decade resulted from vacancies. When Totten resigned in 1855, Governor Andrew Johnson appointed fellow Democrat William R. Harris to fill the vacancy until the election later that year. Harris went on to defeat a Know Nothing at the polls. Three years later Harris died in a steamboat explosion. Once again, a Democratic governor, Isham G. Harris, the deceased judge's brother, appointed a Democrat, Archibald Wright, to fill the vacancy until a special election could be held. In that election Wright ran unopposed until a Know Nothing candidate entered the race at the last possible moment. The public showed little interest in the contests. In the lackluster race of 1858, the polls in one Nashville ward did not even open. Notwithstanding the absence of public interest in the supreme court races, the results reflected larger political trends in Tennessee. Both before and after the arrival of judicial elections, the supreme court judges almost always belonged to the party that controlled state government.[39]

In Missouri, too, political association was key to electoral success in judicial races, but the disarray in the Democratic party complicated the issue. The Missouri General Assembly had trouble electing a United States senator in 1851. After twenty-four ballots, a member offered a resolution declaring that an election at the present session was impossible because the Whigs outnumbered both the partisans of Democratic US senator Thomas Hart Benton and the anti-Benton Democrats and therefore would not go over to either; the Bentonites had a majority within the Democratic Party and could not, "contrary to the usages of the Democratic party, go over to the minority of that party, or to the Whig party"; and the anti-Bentonites, "upon principle," could not join with the Whigs and would not act with the Bentonites. Ultimately, with the support of the anti-Benton Democrats (whose "principle" finally gave way), the Whig candidate prevailed on the fortieth ballot.[40]

The deep rift within the state's Democratic Party between Benton's supporters and opponents meant that there were essentially three major parties in the state: the Benton Democrats, the anti-Benton Democrats, and either the Whigs (until 1854) or the Know Nothings (after 1854). The animosity between the two wings of the Democratic Party sometimes simmered at a temperature low enough to enable cooperation; but when it flared it gave the Whigs power out of proportion to their numbers.

For the most part the Democratic division did not affect appointments to the supreme court. Before the constitutional amendment of 1851, Missouri's governor appointed the state's judges, subject to confirmation by the senate, and they held office during good behavior until they reached the constitutional age limit of sixty-five. With the governor's chair and the senate controlled by Democrats throughout the 1840s, the two Democratic camps cooperated sufficiently to ensure that Democrats of some stripe would hold all three supreme court seats. As of 1840, the supreme court had two judges appointed in the 1820s (Mathias McGirk and George Tompkins) and an anti-Benton Democrat (William B. Napton) appointed by a Democratic governor in 1839. When McGirk resigned in 1841, a different Democratic governor named another anti-Benton Democrat, William Scott, to replace him. Tompkins reached the age limit for office in 1845, to be replaced by yet another anti-Benton Democrat, Priestly H. McBride, appointed by a Benton Democrat.[41]

In 1849, the General Assembly passed a constitutional amendment reducing the terms of supreme court judges to twelve years. The amendment also vacated all the existing judgeships, giving Governor Austin A. King, a Benton Democrat, the opportunity to appoint an entirely new bench. King kept Napton on the court, but, in the words of one newspaper correspondent, he "decapitated [Scott and McBride] without ceremony." In their places, King appointed John F. Ryland, a Benton Democrat, and James H. Birch, an anti-Benton Democrat. That is how the court stood until the first judicial elections in 1851.[42]

Judicial elections took place in off years, which may have dampened the partisanship that accompanied campaigns for governor, the state legislature, and Congress. In the 1850 elections, the split in the Democratic Party produced mixed results for the usually dominant Democrats. Benton Democrats won a plurality in the senate. Whigs attained a plurality in the house and a majority of the state's congressional seats. But anti-Benton Democrats far surpassed Benton Democrats in the house, winning almost as many seats as the Whigs.[43]

The parties did not hold conventions to nominate men for judicial office. Instead, the office seekers announced their candidacies in the papers, without specifying the party to which they belonged. The Hannibal *Western Union*, for example, carried the message: "We are authorized to announce the Hon. JOHN F. RYLAND as a candidate for Judge of the Supreme Court of Missouri at the next August election." James H. Birch submitted a more elaborate statement, still without mentioning his party: "THE undersigned, respectfully announcing himself as a candidate for the position he at present occupies upon the bench of the Supreme Court, deems it not immodest to refer citizens of the State, with whom he may be unacquainted, to the authorized reports of his official opinions, and add, in the same connexion, that if continued in his station, he will devote to its duties his exclusive consideration."[44]

Newspapers exhorted the voters to support judicial candidates on the basis of their "character, abilities, and moral integrity" rather than their politics; as one correspondent pointed out, it was the partisan nature of gubernatorial appointments that had led to the elective judiciary in the first place. But a skeptical Napton wrote in his journal, "It is said that politics is not to have any influence upon these elections. *We shall see.*" The same partisan newspapers that urged the electorate to vote for judicial candidates on the basis of their legal qualifications nevertheless identified the candidates' parties. "A Democrat" charged that the Whigs had deliberately solicited men to run until they had exactly three candidates for the three supreme court seats, whereas the Democrats had done no such coordinating and therefore had twice as many candidates.[45]

In truth, the two camps of Democrats acted as separate parties, each of which also came up with three candidates. Birch ensured this by withdrawing from the race to avoid splitting the anti-Benton vote. In announcing his decision, Birch observed that judges had political philosophies that determined their positions on constitutional matters ("the purposes and the powers of governments"). In this sense, judicial candidates "are regarded as politicians, and the Court to which they aspire, a political tribunal of last resort." Birch saw these views as entirely proper. As an anti-Benton Democrat, he wanted to give anti-Benton judicial candidates the best chance of controlling the court. His departure left three Whigs, three Benton Democrats, and three anti-Benton Democrats in the race.[46]

In August 1851, the voters, reflecting this confused situation, elected as supreme court judges a Whig (Hamilton Gamble), a Benton Democrat (Ryland), and an anti-Benton Democrat (Scott). One paper interpreted the result to mean that "neither party voted upon party grounds." Napton, however, blamed his fourth-place finish, close behind Scott, on the collaboration of Whigs and Benton Democrats against him. Gamble resigned in 1854, and Whig Abiel Leonard, a highly regarded attorney, promptly became the leading candidate to replace him. Leonard publicly agreed to serve provided he not be a party candidate. On January 1, 1855, with the support of the court's two Democratic judges, Leonard won a special election for the seat without opposition. Not surprisingly, the public showed little interest in the election.[47]

Because the constitutional amendment of 1851 had reduced the term of office to six years, another election took place in 1857. By this time Benton's political career was over—he had finished a distant third in the 1856 gubernatorial contest—and the Whig Party was breathing its last. Moreover, there was a gubernatorial election due to a resignation, which no doubt increased public interest in the poll. Democrats won the governorship and two of the supreme court seats. John C. Richardson, a candidate favored by the nativist Know Nothings, who were then enjoying a short-lived popularity, secured the third supreme court post. The next year, Democrats won the great majority of both state and federal legislative contests, and in 1859, after Richardson resigned, the Democratic attorney general cruised to victory in the race for his seat to create an all-Democratic court.[48]

For all the pious declarations of nonpartisanship as an ideal in judicial elections, politics intruded into the selection of Missouri's judges both before and after the switch to elections. Legislators, newspaper editors, voters, and the candidates themselves may have wanted judges to possess good character and legal qualifications, but it was impossible to keep party considerations out of the contests. What elections did accomplish, though, was to open the supreme court to non-Democrats.

The arrival of judicial elections did not bring new types of men to the bench or awaken judges to political realities of which they had not been aware before. The rise in the number of cases in which courts held statutes unconstitutional cannot be explained by either the elected judges' greater comfort with the democratic political process or their growing disenchantment with it. Everywhere legislators, newspaper editors, and voters wanted judges to possess good character and legal qualifications—the newspapers, almost all of them highly partisan, lauded the character, experience, and ability of their parties' candidates, and sometimes of the opposing candidates as well—but even where these qualifications were not evenly balanced, party generally trumped all else. In newspaper commentary, a candidate's position on judicial review rarely, if ever, received notice. In the isolated instance when an editor or correspondent mentioned the candidates' leanings on a constitutional issue, it was not to affirm or question the power of judicial review but to encourage voters to ensure that the right person exercised the power.[49] If voters paid little attention to judicial races, except when they coincided with elections for other high offices, and if party leaders usually determined who the nominees would be, then it may reasonably be said that, in the matter of judicial selection, the great constitutional upheaval of the mid-nineteenth century had little effect on the composition of the bench.

CHAPTER 7

Elected Judges and Judicial Review

In the 1820s and 1830s, Maine was possibly "the hardest drinking state in the Union." In Portland and Waterville, townspeople took a rum break twice each weekday. Rum peddlers covered the campus of Waterville's Baptist college. The secretary of the state temperance association reported in 1832 that Maine had two thousand saloons and other establishments that sold intoxicating liquor, one for every 225 men, women, and children in the state. In 1837, Edward Kent, the mayor of Bangor, offered the following resolution at a meeting of the local temperance association: "Resolved, That we deem it both constitutional and expedient to repeal the present license law, and substitute instead, a law which shall *prohibit* the sale of ardent spirits except for medicinal and mechanical purposes." "[T]he sanction or influence of legal authority," Kent told the city council, "should never be given to a traffic, which fills our jails with criminals, our almshouses with paupers, and our whole land with want and misery." Leading the national antiliquor crusade, Maine in 1851 became the first state to enact a statewide prohibition law.[1]

In 1859, Kent the prohibitionist, now a member of the state supreme court, struck down a legislatively prescribed form of complaint for a liquor law violation as a denial of due process. His decision was one of four rendered by the Maine court in the 1850s that invalidated legislation. The court's total for the previous decade had been zero. In New England as a whole, the six high courts struck down laws just twice in the 1840s but thirteen times in the 1850s. Seven of the thirteen stemmed from the anti-liquor crusade.[2] In all six states, the judges obtained their judicial positions by appointment.

Legal scholars have long noted the mid-nineteenth-century increase in negative judicial review by state courts. ("Negative judicial review" is the exercise of judicial power not just to pronounce upon the constitutionality of legislative acts but to strike them down as unconstitutional.) Although researchers rarely agree on the numbers of cases in the states studied, they all point to the same rising trend. In 1916, James M. Rosenthal compiled the pertinent decisions in Massachusetts to that date, discovering only one such case before 1847 but thirteen from 1847 to 1857. The next year, Edward S. Corwin reported finding four instances in New York in the decade 1831–1840, eighteen from 1841 through 1850, and thirty-four from 1851 through 1860. In 1962, Elijah W. Miles wrote that the Indiana Supreme Court of the 1850s "assumed an almost uncompromising attitude toward the legislative branch of government," striking down statutes more than thirty times between 1851 and 1860 compared to six times in the three-and-a-half decades of statehood before then. Twenty-first-century scholars report similar findings. In an eight-state study, Richard Drew counted twelve declarations of unconstitutionality in the 1830s, thirty-one in the 1840s, and ninety in the 1850s. Jed Handelsman Shugerman's more comprehensive tally for the twenty-four states that had entered the Union by 1821 produced, for those three decades, totals of forty, fifty-eight, and 149.[3]

Investigators have offered various explanations for the undeniable upsurge in negative judicial review. Corwin attributed the increase in New York mostly to conflict between a conservative bench and a reformist legislature. Morton J. Horwitz, citing Corwin's figures, saw the growth of negative judicial review as a symptom of a "shift from 'political' to formal legal criteria" by a judiciary determined to thwart legislative redistribution of wealth. Miles ascribed the increase in Indiana in part to "a wave of reform" sweeping across the state. This wave, he wrote, led to more laws and "many more opportunities to pass on the validity of legislation."[4]

Drew suggested yet another explanation for the upswing in invalidations of legislation, contending that the ongoing, passionate partisan competition between Whigs and Democrats beginning in the 1830s fostered judicial independence; where competition was the greatest, the incidence of negative judicial review was the highest. Drew made no extravagant claims for his findings, stating only that "party competition offers at least a partial explanation for the expansion of judicial power" and acknowledging "other relevant differences among the states that might affect their courts' activism, such as economic development, population size, etc." Among these other possibilities was the institution of judicial elections, which might have "produced new types of judges," men who were more comfortable engaging in the political process and more inclined to intervene in politics than their appointed predecessors had been. About the same time that Drew threw out this suggestion, Larry Kramer observed that the "slight upsurge in state court constitutional activity in the 1840s and 1850s [was] facilitated by the fact that the state judiciaries had become electorally accountable," and Kermit L. Hall asserted that, as reformers intended, "the incidence of judicial review soared . . . as elected judges replaced appointed ones."[5]

The connection between judicial elections and judicial review achieved a full-fledged exposition a few years later at the hands of Jed Handelsman Shugerman. As we saw in chapter 5, Shugerman argues that the improvident internal improvement programs pursued by many states in the 1830s and the economic crisis that followed led to demands for a more independent judiciary that would rein in irresponsible legislatures. According to Shugerman, delegates at the numerous constitutional conventions of the mid-nineteenth century pushed for judicial elections that would free judges from dependence on the other branches of government and encourage more aggressive judicial review. The plan succeeded, he writes, as elected judges proceeded to strike down more legislation.[6]

Certainly, there were more instances of negative judicial review in the state courts after the adoption of judicial elections than before, but the distribution of the cases among the states was uneven. Shugerman reports that 119 of the 149 decisions in the 1850s came from elected courts; but just two states (New York and Indiana) accounted for half of that total.[7] Some states that switched to judicial elections saw little or no increase in the ensuing decade, while invalidations of legislation rose in Maine and other states that retained appointive judiciaries.

An analysis of the figures for just the southern states reveals similar confusion. To give himself a sufficiently long time for state-by-state comparisons, Shugerman considered only states that had joined the Union by 1820. That eliminated three of the fifteen southern states: Arkansas, Florida, and Texas. For present purposes, we may also disregard Mississippi, which changed to an elective judiciary in 1832 and kept it through the antebellum period. (The Mississippi Supreme Court never struck down more than two statutes in a decade.) Of the remaining eleven states, six made their judiciaries entirely elective in the early 1850s (Kentucky, Louisiana, Maryland, Missouri, Tennessee, and Virginia), while five retained appointive supreme courts (Alabama, Delaware, Georgia, North Carolina, and South Carolina).

The six elective supreme courts struck down laws seventeen times in the 1840s and thirty-five times in the 1850s. (The latter total omits four decisions rendered by the old appointed courts before the adoption of judicial elections but includes four "transition" decisions rendered after the constitutional change was made but before the first elections. Shugerman adds transition cases to the total decided by elected courts because the judges were facing election. This is a dubious proposition—some judges did not run for election—but it makes little difference here.) That is a doubling of negative judicial review, made more significant by the fact that the elected judges did not take office with the turn of the decade. Tennessee's first judicial elections took place only in 1853. On the other hand, just two states (Louisiana and Tennessee) account for 66 percent of the instances of negative judicial review in the 1850s, with another 23 percent coming from Missouri. The number of such cases doubled in Tennessee, tripled in Louisiana, and octupled in Missouri. But the four invalidations of laws from Kentucky, Maryland, and Virginia combined were two fewer than the number the appointed courts of those states had issued in the 1840s.

This wide variation among the elective states should be enough to cast doubt on the idea that judicial elections made for negative judicial activism. The numbers for the five appointive states add to the skepticism. The supreme courts of those five states declared six statutes unconstitutional in the 1840s, thirteen in the 1850s. North Carolina, which did not even have elected justices of the peace let alone judges of the supreme court, had no cases of negative judicial review in the 1840s but five in the 1850s.

Is it nevertheless possible that the switch to judicial elections accounts for the extraordinary increases in judicial review in Tennessee, Missouri, and Louisiana? The only way to know is to examine the decisions. As the Maine liquor cases noted at the beginning of this chapter show, controversial political issues such as prohibition could contribute to an upswing in negative judicial review even in states with appointed courts. The decisions in Tennessee, Missouri, and Louisiana reveal other factors as well that better explain the rise in negative judicial review, notably precedent established by predecessor courts and a profusion of new constitutional provisions.

Tennessee

Tennessee had an unusual history of judicial review. Courts there claimed the power to strike down unconstitutional laws as early as 1804, but, as in other states, they wielded it sparingly at first. In the 1830s, though, the supreme court lost some of the reticence that continued to prevail elsewhere. While, according to one count, no other state had more than four decisions declaring statutes unconstitutional in the 1830s, Tennessee had twelve. That number dropped to six in the 1840s, then rose to thirteen in the 1850s.[8]

The early 1830s witnessed a battle between the courts and the legislature on an important matter of public policy: the conflict between whites and Indians over land titles. Under an agreement with the federal government, Tennessee acquired title to land previously ceded to the United States by the Cherokee nation. However, certain lands within the cession were by treaty reserved for Cherokee families. In 1826, the Tennessee court ruled that title to land under the reservation prevailed over title to the same land granted to an individual by the state of North Carolina. (The grant was based on a filing made in 1783, before North Carolina ceded its western territory, which later became the state of Tennessee, to the United States.) The decision implied that Tennessee titles would be similarly subordinated. The General Assembly responded by adopting a series of resolutions authorizing the state to appeal any "reservation cases" involving Tennessee titles to the US Supreme Court.[9]

In 1830, the court formally extended its ruling to Tennessee titles. In his opinion, Judge Catron threw back the legislature's challenge. "That the resolutions were intended to dictate to this court the course of future decision, we will not suppose," he wrote, "as this would be an attack upon the independence of the judiciary." The next year the court affirmed its independence by striking down several statutes unrelated to the Cherokee land question and again deciding against the state when the state tried to dispose of reserved lands to which Cherokees claimed title.[10]

As tensions between the court and legislature mounted, the Nashville Bar Association urged the judges to resign. The association presented its suggestion as a way to pressure lawmakers to adopt court reforms that would ease the burdens on overworked judges. Others, however, saw the recommendation as a legislative attack on the court. Objecting to a proposal to get rid of the judges by abolishing the court, state representative David W. Dickinson stoutly defended judicial independence and hinted at the "true cause" of the attempt "to repeal . . . judges out of office." "Men who from any motive take the lead in any measure of an unconstitutional character," declared Dickinson, "never forgive the judges who declare it so."[11]

The crisis soon passed. The General Assembly passed court-reform legislation in 1831, and the new constitution of 1835 gave the court constitutional protection as a separate and equal branch of state government. The result was that long before judicial elections came to Tennessee, the people and their elected representatives acquiesced in the supreme court's belief that the court had "the duty ... to denounce as unconstitutional all laws which come directly and obviously in conflict with the constitution" and that unconstitutional laws were void.[12]

Tennessee's first elected supreme court judges, Robert J. McKinney, Archibald W. O. Totten, and Robert L Caruthers, took office in 1854. McKinney had been on the court since 1847, Totten since 1850. Both men, as appointees of the General Assembly, had written opinions declaring statutes unconstitutional before the voters approved judicial elections in 1853. Caruthers, appointed in December 1852, soon joined in an opinion by Totten invalidating a statute. To sustain the thesis that elected judges were more inclined than appointed judges to strike down legislation, one would have to believe that these incumbents changed their approaches once the constitutional amendment passed. Such cynicism would hardly seem justifiable, especially regarding McKinney. McKinney declared a statute unconstitutional before the judicial election amendment was even introduced, and he dissented from a holding of unconstitutionality when adoption of the amendment looked inevitable.[13]

Tennessee did witness an increase in negative judicial review in the 1850s, but the raw numbers tell a misleading tale. The old appointed court rendered two of the decisions before the adoption of judicial elections. Of the remaining ten, one held a statute unconstitutional only as applied to a contract that predated the law's enactment.[14] Precedent controlled the outcome of at least two other cases. In one the judges simply reaffirmed a recent holding of the appointed court.[15] The other, *Mayor and Aldermen of Alexandria v. Dearmon*, rested on an older decision. In *Dearmon*, the court struck down a law that singled out for punishment the sheriff of one particular county for failure to hold the annual election for town officers on time. The court ruled the statute unconstitutional on due process and equal protection grounds, although the constitutional clause did not use those terms. Rather, it prohibited the government from depriving a person of life, liberty, or property "but by the judgment of his peers, or the law of the land," which language, said the court, barred the enactment of private or partial legislation. The judges found the case to be squarely within the principles of *Budd v. State* (1842), in which the court had said:

If the felony affected only all the clerks of all the merchants of Nashville, or of Davidson county, or of Middle Tennessee; would that, in either case, be "the law of the land"? It is believed, none would so contend. And, why not? Simply because the law of the land is a rule alike embracing, and equally affecting all persons in general, or all persons who exist, or may come, into the like state and circumstances. A partial law on the contrary embraces only a portion of those persons who exist in the same state, and are surrounded by like circumstances. If peculiar felonies, affecting all the people, or certain of the public officers, of East Tennessee, only, were held to be "the law of the land," it would be difficult to say for what object that clause was inserted in the bill of rights.

Given the clear, strong precedent of *Budd*, a case decided long before the first serious consideration of judicial elections in Tennessee, the court could hardly have decided *Dearmon* other than as it did.[16]

The elected judges relied on the holdings of their appointed predecessors in yet another case, although the precise point of law differed. The Tennessee constitution imposed various general and special restrictions on the General Assembly's power to create new counties. The general provisions established a minimum area and voting population and prohibited the legislature from drawing a new county's border less than twelve miles from the courthouse of an old county from which the new county was taken. One of the special provisions barred the General Assembly from reducing the voting population of Marion or Bledsoe County to less than one thousand when creating a new county. The old court, in opinions by McKinney and Totten, had twice invalidated legislative violations of the twelve-mile limit. In *Gotcher v. Burrows* (1848), McKinney condemned the subterfuge by which the legislature had tried to evade the distance requirement—first creating Grundy County out of Warren and Coffee counties, and then, in a subsequent act, annexing more of Coffee County to Grundy. Ten years later, in *Marion County v. Grundy County*, Caruthers cited *Gotcher* in denouncing similar legislative trickery intended to skirt the territorial and population requirements.[17]

Because Tennessee adopted judicial elections by means of a stand-alone amendment, not a constitutional convention, there was no plethora of new provisions for the elected court to construe in the 1850s. As late as 1858, though, the supreme court had to decide a case of first impression under the 1835 constitution. Tennessee's first constitution (1796) had said little about the judiciary, leaving the creation of courts and their jurisdiction to the legislature. For much of the period between the creation of the supreme court in 1810 and the constitutional convention of 1834, the court had original jurisdiction in equity cases. The convention enshrined the supreme court in the constitution itself and expressly limited its jurisdiction to appeals. When Caruthers and A. O. P. Nicholson compiled the Tennessee statutes then in force in 1836, they omitted an 1829 law that authorized chancellors to transfer certain cases to the supreme court in the belief that the new constitution had rendered the law invalid.[18]

Nevertheless, the supreme court had continued to accept equity cases on transfer. The constitutional clause restricting the supreme court's jurisdiction to appellate matters went on to allow the court "such other jurisdiction as is now conferred by law." The judges seem to have assumed that this provision permitted them to continue to accept equity cases on transfer. Apparently, though, no one had directly raised the question of whether the 1829 statute remained in force until *Miller v. Conlee* in 1858. In an opinion by Caruthers, the supreme court held that the 1835 constitution superseded the statute. The "other jurisdiction" mentioned in the constitution meant only "such powers as, though not appellate, were absolutely necessary in carrying out and completing" the court's appellate jurisdiction—things such as forfeited recognizances or false returns of process. Thus, in his opinion in *Miller*, Caruthers put the court's stamp of approval on a position he had taken in his compilation of statutes twenty-two years earlier—long before anyone in the state seriously contemplated judicial elections.[19]

The question decided in *Miller* arose in another case at the same term of court. A bank charter granted by the legislature in 1843 authorized the General Assembly, whenever it believed that bank had violated its charter, to direct the supreme court to order the bank to show cause why its charter should not be forfeited. Caruthers again authored the court's opinion. "[I]t was the opinion of the convention," he wrote in *State v. Bank of East Tennessee*, "that the labor and responsibility of correcting errors in the proceedings and judgments of Courts of Law, and the hearing of appeals in Chancery, for the whole State, would afford about as much labor as three men could well perform, without encumbering them with any original jurisdiction." Citing its recent decision in *Miller*, the court declared the challenged section of the bank's charter unconstitutional. Given that *Miller* and *Bank of East Tennessee* involved a single question raised twice at the same term of court, the two cases in effect represented one instance of judicial review.[20]

The elected Tennessee Supreme Court struck down about as many laws between 1854 and 1859 as the appointed court of 1841–1852, but fewer than the appointed court of the 1830s. Given the court's historical volatility, the numbers alone do not speak for a more activist court following the institution of judicial elections. And in light of the foundations of some of the decisions and the consistency demonstrated by McKinney, Totten, and Caruthers, there is not much warrant for concluding that the transition to an elective judiciary accounts for an increase in negative judicial review.

Missouri

The depression that hit Missouri about a year after the national financial panic of 1819 gave rise to the earliest occasions for the use of judicial review there. The panic dampened migration into the new frontier state, drying up a major source of money for Missouri's residents. The state's two banks failed, the value of land plummeted, and everyone from land speculators to farmers to merchants fell on hard times. The General Assembly responded with a series of relief measures, including stays of property executions, exemptions from execution, and abolition of imprisonment for contractual debt. The legislature also established a state loan office that, on receiving security from borrowers, could issue certificates that circulated as currency.[21]

The relief laws provoked an angry debate over their efficacy and validity. The controversy soon made its way into the courts. In February 1822, the St. Louis Circuit Court ruled that the loan office law violated the US Constitution by creating bills of credit and making something other than specie legal tender. In March, the same court held a stay law unconstitutional for impairing the obligations of contract. Around the same time, the Cooper County Circuit Court invalidated the stay law, and in July yet another circuit court struck down the loan office law. Only one decision, on a habeas corpus petition, came down in favor of any of the statutes.[22]

Nathaniel Beverley Tucker, who in 1816 had moved to the Missouri Territory and established himself as a legal and literary figure of note, wrote opinions in at least two of the relief cases, *Missouri v. Lane* and *Glasscock v. Steen*. Tucker's father, the great Virginia jurist and law professor St. George Tucker, as a judge of Virginia's General Court, had maintained in 1793 that "the duty of expounding [the state constitution] must be exclusively vested in the judiciary." In his edition of Blackstone's *Commentaries,* the elder Tucker wrote that "if the legislature should pass a law dangerous to the liberties of the people, the judiciary are bound to pronounce . . . whether such a law be permitted by the constitution." Beverley Tucker's older half-brother was the eccentric, conservative planter and politician John Randolph of Roanoke. During a long and colorful political career Randolph railed against "King Numbers." At the Virginia constitutional convention of 1829–30, he denounced "the all-prevailing principle, that *vox populi vox dei*; aye, Sir, the all-prevailing principle, that Numbers and Numbers alone are to regulate all things in political society."[23]

Beverley Tucker absorbed his father's strictures on the judiciary's role and shared Randolph's distrust of majoritarian democracy. In *Missouri v. Lane,* he took pains to address at length the "monstrous doctrine that courts, though convinced of the unconstitutionality of a statute, are still bound to carry it into effect." Although there were yet, among respectable men, advocates of that doctrine, Tucker insisted that the enforcement by judges of unconstitutional laws made "a mockery and an insult" of their oath to support the constitution. It also promoted anarchy, for if the legislature were not bound by the constitution, the people would not be, either. Not content to rest his argument for judicial review on the authority of Alexander Hamilton, whom he quoted at length, Tucker went on to denounce the "still wilder doctrine" that the constitution was "not a thing fixed and permanent, but fluctuating with the changing will of the majority." The right of the majority to bind the minority, Tucker explained, rested on the minority's consent to be bound. That consent was found in the constitution, which "expressly qualifies the consent, by declaring that in certain cases, and for certain purposes, the will of a mere majority shall not bind."[24]

The Cooper County case, *Bailey v. Gentry,* went up to the supreme court, which affirmed the decision. The supreme court found that the law violated the legal tender and contract clauses of the United States Constitution and the provision of the state constitution that guaranteed justice without delay. Before deciding those issues, though, the court addressed the defendant's "zealous" insistence that the court was required to enforce the law "without regard to the Constitution." Relying on *Marbury v. Madison,* the two-judge majority declared that for courts to "close their eyes on the constitution . . . would subvert the very foundation of all written constitutions."[25] Prorelief forces condemned the court for its "meddling" with the law, but *Niles' Weekly Register* reported that public opinion supported the decision. At one public meeting the participants denounced both the stay law and the loan office law as "demoralizing, impolitic, and unconstitutional."[26]

Having once asserted and explained its authority to pass on the constitutionality of legislation, the Missouri Supreme Court seems never to have felt the need to do so again. The court simply acted on that authority without justifying it. Sometimes the court struck down statutes, sometimes it expressly upheld them, and sometimes it simply ignored the constitutional arguments of counsel. All such cases illustrated the acceptance of judicial review by the judges and the bar.[27]

Missouri's judges did not use their power of judicial review to strike down much legislation before the 1850s. Then the incidence of negative judicial review jumped sharply; the number of cases was small, but the percentage increase was significant.[28] The Missouri court decided some cases on the authority of precedent that predated judicial elections. Consider the marital saga of Isaac Newton Bryson. Two systems of divorce had grown up side by side in early America, judicial and legislative. Statutes established grounds for dissolving marriages and conferred jurisdiction on specified courts to grant divorces. At the same time, legislatures often granted divorces by special acts. Over time, the feeling grew that divorce was really a judicial concern. There was also the practical concern that legislatures were spending far too much time on divorce petitions.[29]

In 1833, the Missouri General Assembly passed a law granting Elvira Gentry a divorce from David Gentry. The Gentry divorce was one of thirty-six granted by the same act (which the legislature passed over the governor's veto). Two years later, the supreme court held that the act violated the separation-of-powers provision of the state constitution. Marriage, said the court, was simply a contractual arrangement; divorce was a remedy for an injury caused by a breach of contract. The constitution conferred upon the courts the power and the duty to afford remedies for injuries to persons, property, or character. A legislative act that attempted to provide the remedy violated the separation of powers expressly established by the constitution.[30]

The decision did not stop the General Assembly from granting lots of divorces. Enter Bryson, a locally prominent merchant in Louisiana, Missouri. Born in South Carolina in 1809, he had moved with his parents to a farm in Pike County, Missouri, in 1816, and launched his mercantile career by clerking for several years in the store of Campbell & Burbridge in Louisiana. In 1838, Bryson married Margaret L. Love, but the love didn't last. In 1845, the General Assembly dissolved the marriage by a special act. Three years after that, Bryson, then thirty-nine, married fifteen-year-old Elizabeth Baird. In the meantime, following the divorce, Margaret had been boarding with Rosanna Campbell. Believing himself to be freed of responsibility for Margaret, Bryson refused to pay Margaret's boarding costs. Campbell sued him and won. The court held, on the authority of *State v. Fry* (the Gentry case), that legislative divorces were unconstitutional.[31]

But that wasn't the end. Margaret sued Bryson for alimony, claiming that Isaac had abandoned her without cause and had refused to support her. Once again, Bryson pleaded the legislative divorce. The judges, now elected, were miffed by Bryson's persistence. In *Bryson v. Bryson* they observed, "it was held, that the general assembly could not constitutionally grant divorces. In *Bryson v. Campbell* . . . the case of the *State* v. *Fry* was approved, and the law regarded as settled. The question is again presented, no doubt, with the hope that, in a change in the judges, there may be a change in the views of the court." But having twice held that the legislature had no authority to grant divorces, and with the tide against legislative divorces running strongly nationwide, it is hard to see how the court, whether elected or appointed, could have changed its mind. The court once again approved its holding in *Fry*.[32]

But still the story continued. Years later, Margaret wanted an increase in alimony, and Bryson for the third time set up the legislative divorce as a defense. In 1869, the court reiterated, again, that such divorces were unconstitutional. Whether Bryson ever legally wed Elizabeth is unclear. A newspaper article on Bryson published in 1905, shortly before his death, says only that he married Elizabeth in 1848 (when he was still legally hitched to Margaret). Isaac and Elizabeth are buried in the Riverview Cemetery in Louisiana, Missouri.[33]

The elected court of the 1850s also struck down another special act of divorce, this one predating statehood. The divorce at issue in *Chouteau v. Magenis* had been granted in 1816 by the territorial legislature. In light of Missouri precedent, and unwilling to say that the territorial legislature had had greater power over divorce than the state legislature, the elected court regarded the legislative divorce as invalid. One judge dissented. The prior decisions, he wrote, were based on a constitution that did not exist in 1816. Moreover, he believed that the weight of American authority held that the granting of a divorce by special act was not an exercise of judicial authority. So, the elected judges split on the issue, but the precedent established by both appointed judges (in *State v. Fry*) and elected judges (in *Bryson v. Campbell* and *Bryson v. Bryson*) made a powerful argument in favor of the court's decision.[34]

Although Missouri did not get a new constitution in the mid-nineteenth century, it did get new constitutional provisions via amendments. One involved the creation of new counties. The rapidly growing populations of the western states induced state legislatures to create counties at a prodigious rate. The proliferation of counties exacerbated the problems of supreme courts that by law had to sit in every county, and it aggravated legislative malapportionment in states in which every county had a right to representation. The establishment of new counties also meant fresh opportunities for the exercise of patronage, a subject of vituperation among proponents of constitutional reform. In Missouri, a constitutional amendment of 1849 prohibited lawmakers from establishing new counties in such a way as to reduce an existing county's physical size to less than twenty square miles or its population to less than the ratio of representation required at that time.[35]

The Missouri amendment soon produced a constitutional controversy. In 1851, the General Assembly created Vernon County out of Bates and Cass counties. Samuel Scott was appointed sheriff of Vernon County pursuant to the act. However, some denizens of a village who thought they stood to lose from the formation of the new county instigated a lawsuit challenging the constitutionality of the legislation. The supreme court agreed, finding that the act had reduced the population of Bates County below the required ratio of representation. The issue would never have arisen before the constitutional amendment and could not have been faced by the appointed court.[36]

Political issues that grew more incendiary in the 1850s also produced occasions for judicial review by Missouri's elected judges. As in other states, excessive drinking gave rise to a crusade in Missouri in the first half of the nineteenth century to restrict or prohibit the sale of liquor. By the 1840s, some counties had gone dry under local option laws. The campaign peaked in 1854 when the General Assembly passed a prohibition act. The governor vetoed the act, and the senate came within one vote of an override. In December 1855, the General Assembly passed a statute regulating dram shops. Among other things, the law prohibited the sale of ardent spirits in quantities of less than a quart. However, the measure was not published in the session laws and was not distributed per statute until a year after its approval by the governor. Perhaps concerned about the constitutionality of prosecutions initiated under the dram shop legislation before December 1856, the legislature in February 1857 relieved defendants from prosecutions for violations committed before December 15, 1856, and directed the circuit courts to dismiss indictments of any such defendants who paid the costs of their pending cases and a two-dollar fee.[37]

When the St. Clair Circuit Court dismissed an indictment against one Sloss under the relief act, the prosecution appealed to the supreme court. The supreme court emphatically declared the 1857 act unconstitutional on separation-of-powers grounds. For one thing, said the court, the act was in effect a legislative pardon, whereas the constitution conferred the pardoning power on the governor. For another, the act infringed on the powers of the judiciary. When a case is pending before a court, declared the judges, the legislature has no authority to direct its disposition. "Here is a prosecution depending in court and the legislature comes in and orders the party to be released from it," they pronounced indignantly. "What is that in effect but entering a judgment of acquittal?"[38]

The court's decision can hardly be attributed to the advent of the elective judiciary. The court's legal reasoning was open to question, but the judges had on their side a Tennessee case based on very similar facts. That decision came down seven years before Tennessee adopted an elective judiciary. Moreover, courts had been seeking to protect their judicial functions from legislative encroachment for a long time—since well before the idea of judicial elections gained a foothold anywhere. For example, when the Maine legislature passed a resolve in 1824 allowing the losing parties in a lawsuit to appeal after the time for appeal had elapsed, the court viewed the resolve as an unconstitutional attempt to set aside a judgment. Vacating judgments, said the court, was a distinctly judicial task.[39]

Even more than prohibition, the growing sectional divide over slavery highlights the significance of the political context within which elected judges rendered some of their most important decisions. Missouri's elective judiciary came into being during the great national crisis of the 1850s, when the question of federal power over slavery threatened to tear the Union apart. Key state court decisions show that the judges' longstanding positions on state rights and federal power shaped their constitutional thinking far more than did the way in which they reached the bench.

Crow v. State and *State v. North*, in which the Missouri Supreme Court invalidated statutes that taxed out-of-state goods, bring home the point that judges did not tailor their views with an eye toward election. Rather, they were elected or defeated *because* of their views—and not necessarily their views on fine points of law. As James Birch observed when he withdrew from the supreme court race in 1851, "each candidate for the station has sufficiently made up his opinion respecting the purposes and powers of government."[40]

The story begins with *Crow*, "the most important litigation" concerning Missouri's tax law and the constitutional requirement that property be taxed according to its value. In 1845, the General Assembly passed another in a line of laws for licensing and taxing merchants. This act required merchants, in order to receive a license to do business, to pay a tax based on the value of merchandise received for sale within the preceding six months, except for the "growth, produce, or manufacture of this state." It also imposed an ad valorem tax on their merchandise, except imported merchandise being offered in its original packaging, at the same rate as the tax on real property. (The original-package exception was meant to comply with *Brown v. Maryland*, a US Supreme Court decision holding that goods imported from foreign countries—and, by implication, good shipped across state lines—remained in interstate commerce as long as the packages in which they had been shipped remained unbroken.) In 1847 and again in 1849, the legislature amended the statute to modify the graduation of the license tax in a way that would bear more heavily on the larger merchants.[41]

The merchants screamed about "double taxation" of their merchandise. Wayman Crow, a "merchant prince of St. Louis" and newly elected Whig state senator, refused to comply with the statute. Convicted in the St. Louis Criminal Court of doing business without a license, Crow and his co-defendants appealed to the supreme court, arguing that the double taxation violated the state constitution's requirement that property be taxed in proportion to its value and that the discrimination against out-of-state goods violated the interstate commerce clause of the federal constitution.[42]

The supreme court at that time consisted of appointed judges Birch, Ryland, and Napton. While dealing with *Crow*, the three judges were also involved with another historic controversy: the *Dred Scott* case. Ryland belonged to the Benton wing of Missouri's badly divided Democratic Party. Benton believed that Congress had the power to outlaw slavery in the western territories. Napton, a diehard, proslavery advocate of state rights, held Benton in low regard. Birch, too, was an anti-Benton, proslavery man sympathetic to the South. In *Dred Scott*, Birch and Napton intended to work a dramatic change in Missouri law. The Missouri court had a history of fairness in handling suits for freedom brought by slaves. However, in the 1840s the growing aggressiveness of abolitionists and the controversy over the extension of slavery into the territories acquired in the Mexican War made staunch proslavery men such as Napton determined to buttress slavery and bring an end to freedom suits. According to Missouri historian Dennis K. Boman, "the charged political atmosphere of state and national politics had prompted Napton and Birch to toss aside all pretense of making a judicial decision."[43]

Before *Dred Scott* could be decided, the first judicial elections in August 1851 deprived Birch and Napton of their seats. In the meantime, though, they along with Ryland had to decide *Crow*. Crow had been convicted in the criminal court in the fall of 1850. The supreme court was anxious to make its position known before the legislature convened in December, and so, in late November, the judges issued a self-admittedly hasty and incomplete split decision striking down the law. Soon thereafter, it scheduled a rehearing to address the issues in greater depth. In March 1851, the judges again declared the act unconstitutional, dividing the same way.[44]

The prospect of elections in August 1851 probably had nothing to do with the judges' ultimate stances on the issue. They had made their positions clear in their first decision, months before final passage of the constitutional amendment that made the judiciary elective. If anything other than strictly legal arguments shaped their opinions, it was the larger politics of federal-state relations. The three judges wrote three separate opinions, each of which was consistent with its author's broader political views. Only Ryland, the Benton Democrat, accepted the argument that the federal constitution prohibited discrimination against out-of-state goods. Birch rested his case against the tax law solely on state constitutional grounds. In the course of his discussion, he warned against reliance on majorities to always do what was right. If legislatures could always be trusted to be wise and virtuous, he said, there would be no need for a constitution. But constitutions were "founded in distrust of [human] infirmities." Constitutions imposed "limits and guaranties which even a majority cannot transcend or impair." As the first example of the need for such protection, Birch posed the action of "an interested and unchecked majority" enacting a law providing "that no citizen should purchase, or sell, or hire, or even own a slave, without obtaining therefor an annual . . . license—paying for it . . . such sum as the legislative wisdom or virtue may enact." Behind that question lay another, one that many in the South were then asking: Without constitutional guarantees, what would prevent an antislavery majority in the North and in Congress from abolishing slavery in the South?[45]

Napton dissented. On the federal question, he dismissed the US Supreme Court's decision in *Brown v. Maryland*, the main precedent relied on by opponents of the Missouri tax law, as of little value. That case, he wrote, "stands by itself—a decision rendered twenty-four years ago—nearly all its principles since doubted or overruled, and narrowed down, and frittered away, until its power for good or evil is gone." To the argument that the law taxed property twice, Napton insisted that the license fee was a tax on an occupation or business, not on property. In upholding the state's taxing power, Napton referred to the state as "an independent sovereignty." As a sovereignty, Missouri "possesses unlimited powers of taxation over all the property and business within her limits, except where the State Constitution has made limitations." While this description of the state may seem like an aside in a lengthy disquisition, it reflected Napton's longstanding, unbending belief in state rights.[46]

A few years after *Crow*, the tax question was back before the court. The General Assembly continued to enact laws that discriminated against out-of-state *manufactured* goods; the ad valorem tax did not apply to the "growth, produce or manufacture" of Missouri or to the "unmanufactured . . . growth or produce" of other states. *Crow* had been decided by the concurrence of Birch and Ryland on state constitutional grounds. When the federal issue returned in *State v. North* in 1858, both those judges were gone from the court. Birch had withdrawn from the supreme court race in 1851, ending his judicial career, and Ryland had failed to finish among the top three vote-getters among the nine candidates in 1857. The voters that year reelected William Scott, put Napton back on the bench after a six-year hiatus, and chose as the third judge the Know Nothing John C. Richardson, a former Whig who was remembered after his death as a "close friend and warm admirer" of Scott.[47]

In *North*, the court once again struck down the law in question in a 2–1 decision, with Scott writing the majority opinion. Napton in dissent remained committed to his state rights views. Scott rested his conclusion on an analysis of pertinent, if not directly conclusive, US Supreme Court decisions. But, with *Dred Scott* having been decided by the Supreme Court and the nation edging closer to civil war, Scott also seems to have been more worried than Napton about the fate of the Union. After declaring the state statute to be in violation of the interstate commerce clause, Scott wrote: "We have not sought this task; it has been forced upon us, and we have entered upon its discharge with a due sense of the responsibility under which we labor. If we have erred, we feel confident that we have erred on the side of safety and in a desire to cherish peace and good-will among the states of the Union."[48]

It is doubtful that Scott was thinking about reelection so early in his term, but if he was, he had a peculiar way of showing it. Prosouthern, state rights feelings had been rising in Missouri.[49] Given the legislature's penchant for enacting discriminatory laws to protect Missouri goods, he must have realized that striking down the law would not have been popular (except, of course, among merchants).[50] His remark about having the task of reviewing the law forced upon the court suggests as much. In any event, neither he nor Napton would get the chance to test his electability again, at least in the near future. After the Civil War broke out, both were removed from office for refusing to take a loyalty oath.[51] Scott died in 1862. Napton would be appointed to fill a vacancy on the court in 1873 and would win election to a full term the following year.

Politics unquestionably played a major, perhaps decisive, role in the judicial elections of 1851 and 1857. But the judges elected in those years did not change their political stripes to curry favor among the voters. They won because of their well-established reputations. Napton was too proslavery and anti-Benton for the voters in 1851 but perfect for the "newly militant, sectionalized climate" of 1857.[52] Scott, another anti-Benton Democrat strong on state rights, suited the new mood too.[53] *Crow* was decided by three appointed judges facing their first elections, *North* by three recently elected judges, but there is no reason to think that any of them would have decided otherwise had the elections amendment not been adopted. The opinions in both cases reflected deeply rooted political values that the coming of elections did not alter.

Louisiana

Judicial review apparently took hold in Louisiana with little opposition. The supreme court claimed the authority to invalidate legislation from the beginning of statehood. "It is no longer a question in the United States, whether unconstitutional acts of the Legislature be of any force and effect," declared the court in 1815. "This state is among those, the

Constitution of which contains an express provision on this subject: 'All laws contrary to this Constitution shall be null and void;' and this Court ... determined it was their province to enquire into and pronounce upon the constitutionality of any law invoked before them."[54]

Nevertheless, the court rarely used its power of judicial review to annul laws before 1840. The elected judges of the 1850s invalidated laws perhaps ten times, compared to four or five in the 1840s.[55] New constitutional provisions account for several decisions in the later decade. Louisiana adopted two constitutions in the span of seven years. The constitution of 1852 retained many of the innovations that had been made just a few years earlier. Provisions that were new in 1845 and that reappeared in 1852 were effectively still new.

The old, appointed court decided *In re Municipality No. 2* in February 1852, months before the constitutional convention met, although by that time the adoption of judicial elections by the forthcoming convention was a foregone conclusion. The case arose under the constitution of 1845, which strengthened property rights by requiring that the government, when taking private property pursuant to its power of eminent domain, compensate the owner in advance rather than indemnify the owner afterwards. The constitution also provided that all laws in force at the time of the constitution's adoption that were not inconsistent with the constitution would continue in effect. The court had no trouble invalidating an 1832 statute that conflicted with the new compensation clause. Although the report of the case includes a "dissenting" opinion by Thomas Slidell, Slidell actually concurred in the judgment and in the finding that the statute violated the advance-compensation provision.[56]

In 1853, after judicial elections took effect, the General Assembly enacted a statute providing for the hearing of district court cases by a member of the bar if the judge recused himself. This was a new procedure; previously, a recused district judge referred the case to the judge of an adjoining district. In *State v. Judge*, the court found the law unconstitutional on the grounds that the 1852 constitution required all judges, even those serving *pro hac vice* (for this occasion), to be elected. Slidell, who had been elected chief justice, wrote the opinion. As we have seen, Slidell was perfectly willing to declare laws unconstitutional even under the appointive system. The following year, on the authority of *State v. Judge*, the supreme court again held the statute unconstitutional.[57]

In *Lafon v. Dufrocq*, the court struck down an act giving mayors judicial authority because, among other things, the constitution of 1845 expressly conferred judicial power on the supreme court, district courts, and justices of the peace. In *Boykin v. Shaffer*, the court held that an act separating two canal companies that previously had been consolidated by legislation violated the provision of the 1845 constitution that prohibited the General Assembly from exercising judicial functions. The separation of the companies and the assignment of assets to each was a partition, which was a traditional judicial act. And if the partition was unconstitutional, the parts of the statute that took away franchises and contractual rights were also unconstitutional for violating the obligations of contract. In support of the last point, the court cited *Montpelier Academy v. George*, an 1840 case in which the appointed court struck down two laws for impairing contractual obligations.[58]

Among the novelties of the 1845 constitution that were kept virtually intact in the 1852 constitution were a requirement that taxation be "equal and uniform throughout the state" and a limitation of every bill to one object expressed in the bill's title. Cases involving these provisions arose during the interlude from 1845 to 1852 and kept appearing after the implementation of judicial elections, allowing for a comparison of the decisions of appointed and elected judges on the same issues.

Uniformity in Taxation

In the early days of the republic, governments relied heavily on property taxes, which they usually imposed on property by type rather than by value. Often, different rates of taxation applied to different types of property. The Jacksonian era witnessed an egalitarian tax-reform movement that spread the ideas of taxation of property according to value and taxation of all types of property uniformly.[59]

Article 127 of the Louisiana constitution of 1845, retained in substance but renumbered Article 123 in the 1852 constitution, required taxation to be "equal and uniform throughout the state." The appointed court first confronted a challenge to a tax under Article 127 in *Second Municipality of New Orleans v. Duncan* in 1847 after the Second Municipality, one of the three sections into which New Orleans was divided between 1836 and 1852, had imposed a special tax on real property and slaves. The court held that the provision, "by its very terms, applies to state, and not to municipal taxes. It provides for the equality and uniformity of taxation *throughout the State*." That remained the court's position throughout the remaining years of the appointive judiciary, with the justices rejecting challenges under Article 127 to locally imposed taxes or the statutes under which they were adopted.[60]

In 1854, the year after Louisiana's first judicial elections, the supreme court twice struck down legislation authorizing municipalities to assess only the properties benefiting from certain improvements. In the first case, *Municipality No. Two v. White*, the majority expressly rejected *Duncan*, dismissing that case's remarks on Article 127 as an *obiter dictum* to which it could not subscribe. "We consider," wrote Justice Abner N. Ogden, "that the Constitution established equality and uniformity to be the principle of taxation throughout the State, in all its subdivisions of local sovereignty."[61]

A few months later, in *Cumming v. Police Jury of Rapides*, Ogden reiterated that position on behalf of the court. The police jury (the governing body) of Rapides Parish had imposed a special tax on a portion of the parish that was prone to flooding in order to defray the costs of embankments and other improvements. Ogden did not deny that the police jury had the authority to levy local taxes, but he insisted that such taxes had to be equal and uniform within the parish. *Municipality No. Two* and *Cumming* would seem to support the thesis that elected judges were more aggressive than appointed judges in their review of statutes and their readiness to strike them down.[62]

But the situation was not so simple. In both *Municipality No. Two* and *Cumming*, Justice Ogden gained the concurrence of Alexander M. Buchanan and Cornelius Voorhies. In the former case, Slidell and James G. Campbell dissented; in the latter, Slidell was absent, and Campbell was gone altogether, having resigned and not yet been replaced. In 1856, by which time Slidell and Ogden were also gone from the bench, the court returned to its original stance. In *Yeatman v. Crandall*, the court, without adverting to *Municipality No. Two* or *Cumming*, concluded that Article 127 "refers to State taxation, in its proper sense, for general or State purposes. When it says that taxation shall be equal and uniform *throughout the State*, it points directly to its object, which is to regulate the mode of filling the State Treasury. It does not take away the power of making local assessments for local improvements, upon the equitable principle that he who reaps the benefit must bear the burden." Furthermore, said the court, an assessment for a local improvement was not even a tax "in the strict legal sense of the term." Buchanan took no part in the decision, but Voorhies explicitly reversed himself. Voorhies noted that five of the seven judges with whom he had sat (all since the advent of judicial elections) had agreed that Article 127 did not apply to special assessments for local improvements.⁶³

The court faced other controversies arising under Articles 127 and 123 during the 1850s. Attorneys wielded these articles against real property assessments, taxes on occupations, license fees, and so on. The court regularly upheld the ordinances or statutes assailed.⁶⁴ In only one instance did it find a statute to be unconstitutional, and that statute had been repealed by the time the decision was rendered.⁶⁵ In separate cases, Ogden and Buchanan wrote opinions for the court sustaining the exercise of the taxing power by the city of New Orleans as consistent with Article 123. Each prompted a concurrence that straightforwardly reaffirmed the principle of *Duncan* that the article did not even apply to municipal taxes.⁶⁶ Given the court's overwhelming support for laws attacked for alleged violations of Article 127 or 123, the two split decisions of 1854 that invalidated legislation appear as anomalies that represented neither an accounting to the electorate nor a new sense of empowerment on the part of elected judges. Interestingly, in 1879, long after judicial elections had been abolished in Louisiana, an appointed court decided that Ogden and Buchanan had been right after all in holding that the uniformity clause applied to local as well as state taxes.⁶⁷

The Object/Title Rule
The Appointed Court

The Louisiana Constitution of 1812 had said nothing of the number of objects a bill could address or the contents of a bill's title. Articles 118 of the 1845 constitution and 115 of the 1852 constitution, worded identically, mandated that every law be limited to "one object" and that the object be expressed in the law's title. The one-object rule, which dates back to ancient Rome, first appeared in this country in the New Jersey constitution of 1844. The concept of clear title grew out of the Yazoo land scandal of 1795, when the bribery-besotted Georgia legislature passed a law with a deliberately misleading title, obscuring the fact that the lawmakers were selling enormous tracts of public land to private parties at shockingly low prices. The goal of the object/title rule was to prevent "legislation by stealth," that is, the sneaking of proposals into law without adequate notice or deliberation.⁶⁸

Four challenges to legislation under Article 118 reached the Louisiana Supreme Court before the first judicial elections in 1853. In 1849, the court invalidated a recently enacted statute with the title: "An act to amend the act entitled, an act to provide for the liquidation of the affairs ... of insolvent corporations, approved the 4th of May, 1847." The problem with the 1848 act was that its title failed to state the purpose of the amendment. (It also failed to set forth the amended law or section of law in full, another constitutional requirement.[69]) The court explained:

> The condition of our statute law was such, at the time of the formation of the constitution, as to impose on the convention the necessity of providing in the constitution itself for the forms of legislation.
>
> The title of an act often afforded no clue to its contents; important general provisions were found placed in acts private or local in their operation; provisions concerning matters of practice or judicial proceedings were sometimes in the same statute with matters entirely foreign to them; the result of which was that, on many important subjects, the statute law had become almost unintelligible, as they whose duty it has been to examine, or to act under, it, can well testify. To prevent any further accumulation to this chaotic mass was the object of the constitutional provisions under consideration.[70]

The court rendered a similar decision the following year. The statute in question, passed in 1848, required that captured runaway slaves, when not returned directly to their owners or employers, be committed to the parish (county) prison rather than to the municipal jail, the traditional "depot" for unclaimed runaways. The legislation bore the title: "An Act to regulate and define the fees to be paid by owners of runaway slaves for the taking up and confinement of the same, etc." Those fees could be substantial. In a dispute over the custody of runaways between Sheriff N. H. Hackett of Orleans Parish and the Second Municipality, the supreme court found the 1848 statute to be in violation of the object/title rule. The purpose of the rule, said the judges, was to oblige the lawmakers "to state the object of every law in its title, according to the understanding of reasonable men." But the title failed to reveal the extensive scope of the act. The court thought it unreasonable to expect a member of the legislature, when the act was called up by its title, to "have any idea of its contents" unless he had previously heard the act read in full. Adding "etc." at the end of the title meant nothing.[71]

Together with *Hackett*, the supreme court decided *Heirs of Duverge v. Salter*. The act, by its title, purported only to give the district courts of

New Orleans jurisdiction over certain landlord-tenant actions. However, the court held that the material parts of the act were procedural in nature, "deeply affecting the privileges of litigants," and that the act therefore violated the title part of the object/title rule. In this case, Slidell dissented. Starting with the principle that no statute should be invalidated unless its unconstitutionality was clear beyond a reasonable doubt, Slidell observed that to confer jurisdiction was to confer the power to hear and determine a cause. The details of how the court would hear and determine the cause did not have to be spelled out in the title. "While the salutary intention of the Constitution should be fairly and substantially carried out," Slidell concluded, it "should not be interpreted by the judiciary with a rigor so strict that it might defeat the power to legislate," which also was granted by the constitution.[72]

The last case under Article 118 to come before the appointed judges involved "an act to provide for the payment of the debts of the municipalities of New Orleans." A taxpayer challenged the act, claiming both that it embraced multiple objects and that the title did not express all of them. The court disagreed. Citing *Hackett*, the majority pointed out that the title had to state the statute's objects only "according to the understanding of reasonable men." The act's various sections, providing for the raising and appropriation of funds to pay the municipalities' debts, were sufficiently connected to pass constitutional muster. In any event, the opinion went on, the taxpayer's liability arose under a section of the act that clearly came within the title; even if the other sections were unconstitutional, the pertinent section remained valid.[73]

In the space of two years, then, Louisiana's four appointed justices heard four cases arising under Article 118. Three times they struck down the challenged statute.

The Elected Court

Louisiana's first judicial elections occurred in 1853. The elected justices, now five in number, quickly faced additional challenges brought under the object/title rule (some under Article 118, others under Article 115 of the new constitution, depending on when the acts were passed).

The objections in three of the cases decided between 1853 and 1860 were too flimsy to merit extended consideration and were summarily dispatched. The other cases required treatment in more depth; two of them divided the court. The first title controversy to come before the court, *Succession of Lanzetti*, involved an act "to provide a homestead for the widow and children of deceased persons." The measure did not in so many words afford a homestead. Rather, it provided for a payment of money to the survivors from the decedent's estate. In an opinion by Slidell, the court found the appellant's argument too hair-splitting. If the court engaged in "a nice and fastidious verbal criticism," wrote Slidell, it would "often frustrate the action of the Legislature" without actually carrying out the intention of the constitution's framers, which was "to prevent that loose legislation which disgraced our statute books." Because the title gave "a reasonable clue" to the act's contents, it substantially complied with Article 118 and was constitutional.[74]

Shortly after *Lanzetti*, the court decided *Lafon v. Dufrocq*. Again, the court was satisfied with "substantial compliance." In fact, the judges set a rather low bar for the legislature, being satisfied with a title that read: "An Act to amend the several Acts relative to the police and government of the town of Baton Rouge." That broad, nonspecific title, said the court, "sufficiently indicates its object, which was to change the laws relative to the police and government of the town of Baton Rouge; this certainly afforded a clue to the contents of the body of the Act."[75]

The relaxed approach did not last. In *State v. Harrison*, the court heard an appeal from the conviction of a slave for killing another slave. The trial court consisted of two justices of the peace and ten slaveowners, organized under "an Act relative to slaves and free colored persons." The court's three-judge majority found the act unconstitutional because it dealt with two distinct classes of people, slaves and free blacks, whose legal statuses were so different that they could not be regarded as a single object. Two members of the court dissented. The two supposedly different classes of people, insisted Justice Henry M. Spofford, constituted "a single, homogeneous class of beings, distinguished from all others by nature, custom and law, and never confounded with citizens of the State." That made them one object, which was sufficiently expressed in the title.[76]

In *Parish of Bossier v. Steele*, the court again struck down a statute for addressing more than one object, and Spofford again dissented from the court's reasoning, although he concurred in the judgment. The act in question was, according to its title, "relative to the payment of expenses incident to the prosecution of criminals." The act provided for payment of the state's expenses in criminal proceedings and for the dispositions of fines and forfeitures collected for the violation of the criminal laws. The majority noted that previously the subjects of the act had been treated in several different statutes with different titles, which it took as evidence that the act dealt with multiple objects. "[S]uppose a citizen wished to ascertain what disposition the laws make of judgments, in favor of the State, for fines and on forfeited bonds, in criminal proceedings," wrote the court. "Would the title of the Act in question give him any clue to the subject? Could he reasonably expect to find the subject treated of under the head of *the payment* of costs or expenses?" The majority did not think so.[77]

Spofford concurred in the judgment on the grounds that statute applied prospectively only; the prosecution in the case had been commenced before the act was promulgated. However, he believed that the two sections of the act were "so interwoven, and relate so naturally to the one main object of the Act" as expressed in the title that it took "too subtle an analysis, to bring it into conflict with Article 115."[78]

In the penultimate antebellum case dealing with Article 115, the court acknowledged that the fifteenth section of an act "relative to Pilots" for the port of New Orleans had nothing to do with the object specified in the title. The rest of the act remained valid, though, and the invalid section was irrelevant to the dispute. In the last such case, a slave convicted of murder pursuant to "an act relative to slaves" argued that the statute contravened Article 115 because of its breadth. The court conceded that the law "treats of crimes committed by slaves and prescribes the penalties; it declares the duties of Justices of the Peace and District Attorneys in relation to the same; regulates the trial and punishment, and provides for the compensation of the owner where slaves are executed; treats of runaways; compels the attendance of witnesses, and declares who may be witnesses in certain cases." However, the justices held that the "general scope" of the statute was clearly enough reflected in its title.[79]

Louisiana's elected judges of the antebellum era decided nine cases brought at least in part under the object/title rule. Six times they flatly rejected challenges to statutes based on the rule, although in one of those cases they invalidated the statute on other grounds. In one instance, the judges noted that a statutory section appeared to violate Article 115 but observed that the section was irrelevant to their decision. The two declarations of unconstitutionality on Article 115 grounds divided the court. In short, the evidence from antebellum object/title cases indicates that the elected judges were *less* likely than their appointed predecessors to declare laws unconstitutional.

Both appointed and elected judges grappled with the new uniform taxation and one-object/clear-title rules, and the elected judges differed among themselves. The method of judicial selection had nothing to do with their jurisprudence. The elected court was no more aggressive, and arguably less so, than its appointed predecessor had been. Any attempt to understand the upswing in the instances of negative judicial review in the 1850s must reckon with these facts. The very existence of so many new restrictions on legislative power seems to have been crucial to the increase in negative judicial review. The adoption of judicial elections, on the other hand, had no apparent effect at all.

CHAPTER 8

Retreat of the South

In 1850, B. Gratz Brown, a twenty-four-year-old lawyer in Missouri, delivered an Independence Day oration that captured the spirit of the Trans-Mississippi West. "Progress is the watchword," he proclaimed. "... Old forms and the husk of ancient errors are passing away, and new modes of thought are coming in upon us. The very mutability of our institutions ... is in itself the strongest assurance to go forward, that we can have.... With the Past we have literally nothing to do, save to dream of it.... We are ourselves at the head and front of all political experience. Precedents have lost their virtue, and all their authority is gone."[1]

Democratic, innovative, unbound by tradition, the West easily accepted judicial elections. Constitutional conventions took place in California in 1849 and in Iowa, Minnesota, and Oregon in 1857. Four conventions, with varying degrees of legitimacy, occurred in Kansas in 1855, 1857, 1858, and 1859. In all five jurisdictions, the cause of judicial elections triumphed (or, in the case of Iowa, further triumphed) without trouble because it fit comfortably within the Jeffersonian-Jacksonian tenor of western political life. Few westerners doubted that white men should be able to vote without having to pay a tax or own a minimum amount of property or that representation in the legislature should be based primarily on population. Every one of the nine Trans-Mississippi state constitutions (as of the outbreak of the Civil War in 1861) enfranchised the adult white male citizenry. With the exception of Louisiana, where the use of total population as the basis of apportionment of the senate favored the slaveholding parishes and where caps on representation discriminated against New Orleans, every Trans-Mississippi state adopted some form of equal representation that rested on the number of white inhabitants or white males as the basis of apportionment. (Minnesota, like Louisiana, used total population. Unlike Louisiana, Minnesota had a miniscule number of black inhabitants and no slaves.) Only Arkansas and Kansas had constitutional requirements that each county be allotted at least one representative, which had the potential to badly skew representation in favor of smaller counties.²

The Jacksonian idea that the people should elect their public officers, including judges, for limited terms met little resistance in the West. The constitutions of California and Texas gave the governor the authority to appoint the secretary of state on the grounds that the secretary was a confidential adviser to the governor. Otherwise, in every state but Arkansas the people elected the chief public officers in all branches of government, not excluding even the Oregon state printer. In Arkansas, the legislature retained the power to appoint the judges of the supreme court and the major state executive officers; but even there, as noted in chapter 6, strong support for the popular election of those officers existed as late as 1859–60.

With Louisiana's adoption of judicial elections in 1852, every then-existing state in the Trans-Mississippi West—Iowa, Missouri, Arkansas, Louisiana, Texas, and California—had at least a partially elective judiciary. From the time of California's admission to the Union in 1850 to the outbreak of the Civil War, every new state (California, Oregon, Minnesota, and Kansas) began with a wholly elective judiciary. Except for Minnesota, where the Mississippi rises, all these new states lay entirely west of the great river. Between 1863 and 1912, Congress would create fourteen more states, all of which elected all their judges and all of which, except West Virginia, emerged from the western territories.

With this history in mind, students of state constitutional development have often observed, as federal judge Jeffrey S. Sutton writes, that "all the states that entered the Union between 1846 . . . and 1959 . . . did so with constitutions that provided for judicial elections of one kind or another. That 113-year run ended in 1959 when Hawaii's constitution provided that the governor would appoint judges with the advice and consent of the Senate."³ Such comments, while true, can leave the impression that the elective principle remained without serious challenge, at least until the Progressive Era. That impression would be wrong. As judicial elections were spreading in the West between 1850 and 1861, some southern states began to question the elective judiciary before it had been fairly tested. A few, on the eve of the Civil War, abandoned it.

The retreat began with the secession conventions of 1861. As the sectional crisis neared its climax, southern state legislatures passed laws providing for popularly elected conventions to decide whether or not their states should secede. Those conventions also proposed or adopted amendments to state constitutions to reflect their states' new relationship with the United States. In some instances, they made other changes as well. Several conventions relegated judicial elections to the dustbin.

The reasons for this reaction against the elective judiciary are not clear. A delegate to the Virginia convention reported that his constituents were sick of "the extended system of petty elections." He had a point, particularly with regard to judicial elections. Where judicial elections did not coincide with general elections, voter turnout for the choice of judges was low. Southern newspapers decried the people's "shameless want of interest in the election of judges," the "extreme apathy" among the populace when it came to electing them, and the people's lack of "knowledge of or interest in the subject." One paper found it "rather singular" that the people needed to be reminded of their right to elect the judges; it blamed the press, in part, for failing to discuss the candidates.[4]

In Georgia, the Macon *Weekly Georgia Telegraph* predicted early in 1859 that that year's elections for superior court judges would be the state's last. According to the paper, the people were "heartily sick and tired of the system of electing Judges." Part of the problem, no doubt, was that in 1856 the legislature moved the elections for superior court judges and prosecutors from the date of the October general election to the first Monday in January. The move may have been an effort to reduce the influence of party politics in judicial elections; the 1855 election in the Blue Ridge Circuit, between a Democrat and a Know Nothing, had been particularly rancorous. (The bitterness sometimes extended to inferior court races as well.) Changing the election date to the first Monday of January must have seemed logical because that's when Georgians already elected their inferior court judges, court clerks, sheriffs, coroners, and local tax collectors. However, the voters chose their constables and justices of the peace on the first Saturday in January. No wonder Georgians were tired of trooping to the polls.[5]

If they even bothered to vote, that is. In Georgia, as in other states where judicial and general elections were conducted on different days, not many voters turned out to elect their judges. Superior court races often went uncontested, which could only have left voters wondering about the point of voting. The *Telegraph's* forecast that the General Assembly would abolish judicial elections sparked some editorial pushback, but it is doubtful that many people, other than editors and judges, cared. Indeed, the *Daily Constitutionalist*, quoting the correspondent of another paper who complained of the harmful effects of having judges wallow in the "dirty pool of politics," came out in favor of the appointment of all judges by the governor, with the advice and consent of the senate.[6]

While the annoyance of frequent contests was a potent argument against them, something bigger may have been behind the turn against judicial elections—the southern defense of slavery. Years before, as we have seen, some southern opponents of judicial elections had warned of the "tyranny of the majority." On its face, fear of an overbearing majority was part and parcel of Jacksonian radicalism. For all their majoritarianism, Jacksonians recognized the potential for abuse inherent in power, regardless of who wielded it. Jackson's solicitor of the treasury, Virgil Maxcy, noting that the "selfish principle" was part of human nature, insisted that "a majority of numbers is no more exempt from it than individuals. The majority will therefore oppress and throw an undue share of the burthens of government upon the minority, or promote its own interest at the expense of the minority, unless there be interposed, for the protection of the latter, some check upon this selfish principle." In the first issue of the *Democratic Review* in 1837, editor John O'Sullivan conceded the plausibility of the antidemocratic argument that "[m]ajorities are often as liable to error of opinion, and not always free from a similar proneness to selfish abuse of power, as minorities." "A strong and active democratic *government*," he declared, ". . . is an evil, differing only in degree and mode of operation, and not in nature, from a strong despotism." Because majorities could no more be trusted with power than minorities, the "best government is that which governs least."[7]

The Jacksonians of the 1830s directed most of their ire against the well-heeled and well-connected who managed to secure legislative favors even in states with free suffrage and equal representation; hence their laissez-faire, limited-government political philosophy. But in the South of the 1850s, it was not majoritarian, limited-government types who worried about tyranny; it was the slaveholding elites and their allies, who feared for the security of their human property. At the high tide of constitutional reform in the late 1840s and early 1850s, emancipation had not been a real possibility, but slaveholders had lost some battles over representation and had fought against the "improper" taxation of slaves. A specific tax on slaves, declared a Kentucky constitutional convention delegate in 1849, was nothing less than "emancipation by direct taxation." As the sectional conflict deepened, desperate planters began to link ad valorem taxation of slaves with abolitionism. A delegate to the Virginia secession convention of 1861 called the tax "an abolition measure in disguise." One North

Carolina planter saw the movement for a tax based on a slave's value as an effort to "revolutionize" the state. "The attempt will be made to carry it in the West," he wrote, "by getting up a furor against the *negroes* in the East. In the East, it is to be urged on the ground of its being a *poor man's law*."[8]

There had never been an idyllic southern society in which all whites were friends. Inequalities of wealth bred resentment of the elites by those lower down on the socioeconomic ladder. The planters and wealthy lawyers who dominated political life distrusted the Upcountry poor whites and non-slaveholding yeomen. The class conflict so evident at the Virginia constitutional conventions of 1829–30 and 1850–51 was typical. "[I]n the eyes of the [North Carolina] gentry," writes historian Paul D. Escott, "a small group of whites was middle class and the rest . . . fell into an unreliable lower class along with free Blacks and slaves." Throughout the South, the distrust on the planters' part deepened along with the sectional crisis. By the late 1850s, the split between slaveholding and non-slaveholding whites had reached "truly troubling proportions." Unionist sentiment remained strong in the Upcountry even as most planters came to believe that slavery could not survive without secession.[9]

However much slaveholders regretted advances toward free suffrage and equal representation (especially when based on the white population), there was no going back on these fundamental democratic principles. But the popular election of judges had been simultaneously more controversial, with arguments on both sides for the good of society, and less important to most people. Slaveholders in the 1850s, particularly after *Dred Scott*, might have looked to an independent judiciary not reliant on the electorate as a bulwark of their interests.

Even more than the majorities within their states, slaveholders railed against the majority of northern "fanatics" who seemed to be bent on their destruction. During the controversy that produced the Compromise of 1850, southerners had repeatedly protested against the "tyranny of a northern majority." As the sectional crisis approached its climax at the end of the decade, the complaint reappeared with force. In 1860, South Carolina fire-eater Robert Barnwell Rhett claimed that northern Democrats had combined with Republicans to thwart the South at every turn, subjecting the South to "the vulgar tyranny of a Northern majority." Rhett meant not only a majority of states but a majority of people, as represented in Congress.[10]

Rhett accused Republicans of trying to exclude slavery from the western territories by congressional action, and he charged northern

Democrats with pursuing the same end through popular sovereignty as expounded by Illinois senator Stephen A. Douglas. Northern Democrats had provided Rhett with ammunition. In voting for the Kansas-Nebraska Act, Democratic congressman William H. English of Indiana declared that his vote for the Kansas-Nebraska Act was not a vote to extend slavery. "The people of these Territories," he insisted, "will never adopt the institution." Even after the *Dred Scott* decision, which seemed to guarantee the right of slaveholders to carry slavery into the territories, Douglas propounded the idea that the people of a territory could keep out slavery by refusing to enact local legislation to protect it. "[W]here in the name of God, have the people ever extended slavery one inch?" asked the Democratic candidate for governor of Ohio in 1859. "I defy any man on the face of the globe to point me out an instance in which they have done it." Rule by popular majority, ever suspect in the eyes of southern conservatives, was coming to seem like a northern plot against the South and slavery.[11]

Critics of judicial elections had always contended that the electioneering necessary to win a place on the bench would sully the judicial robes. Now they buttressed their arguments with a depiction of this "Yankee innovation" as part and parcel of a corrupt and distasteful northern political system. Even in Mississippi, the birthplace of the all-elective judiciary, a newspaper attributed the initial deviation from the appointive principle to the "radical North."[12]

A select committee report at the Virginia secession convention condemned northern society as a sink of corruption, class warfare, irreligion, and divorce. The committee blamed it all on universal white male suffrage and the popular election of government officers. "The former gives a controlling power to men who have the least interest in the community," reasoned the committee, "and the latter renders that power effectual, by giving direction to the legislation and administration of the government." The committee advised that, to secure "[a]n upright and independent judiciary" free from "partizan conflict," judges should be appointed by the governor, with the advice and consent of the senate, to hold office during good behavior. The Virginia constitutional convention of 1850–51, said the committee, had made a grievous error in following the lead of northern politicians; it was time to return to the principles of 1829–30.[13]

By the time the committee issued its report in November, it probably had no members who truly represented the sentiments of the northwestern counties. Those counties were by then in the process of seceding from Virginia. Only two of the committee's original seven members, George W. Summers and Alpheus F. Haymond, hailed from counties that would later be included in the new state. Summers resigned from the convention in May, after it approved the ordinance of secession. Threats of violence forced most of the other delegates from the northwestern counties to flee. Summers was replaced on the committee by Samuel Price, also from western Virginia. Haymond and Price voted against secession, but they stayed with the convention. Haymond later received permission to change his vote. He would go on to serve in the Confederate army. Price would become lieutenant governor of Virginia during the war. Without Summers, the committee probably had no strong voice to oppose its denunciation of democracy and recurrence to conservative principles.[14]

In February 1860, the Alabama legislature adopted a joint resolution directing the governor, in the event of a Republican victory in that year's presidential election, to call an election of delegates to a state convention to "do whatever in the opinion of said Convention, the rights, interests and honor of the State of Alabama requires to be done for their protection."[15] The convention duly met in January 1861. Although the main purpose of the convention was to approve secession, the members created a Committee on the Constitution to consider a variety of constitutional amendments, some of which had nothing to do with secession. Two members of the committee, John Cochran and James D. Webb, along with John T. Morgan, were subsequently named the Committee to Revise the Constitution. All three were lawyers from Alabama's Black Belt, a region of large plantations where slaves outnumbered whites.[16]

The committee submitted a report adverse to the popular election of superior court judges. Stressing the need for an independent judiciary to protect life, liberty, and property, the report insisted that judges must not be beholden to popular majorities. "If a majority of the people must elect the judges by a direct vote, and if the judges may therefore feel secure in deciding questions, great or small, in accordance with the popular will, as expressed in their election, it comes to this at last, that the most sacred rights of the minority may be torn from them by a vote of the people." If constitutions were to be construed by "the representatives of a majority," they would become instruments of destruction wielded by "the most dangerous despotism—an irresponsible voting majority." To give the majority the power not only to make laws but also to construe them, "and shut out even an inquiry into their constitutionality," would be "to create a dangerous despotism."[17]

This reasoning went beyond the usual complaints that trial judges would favor cronies or political supporters in private litigation. The committee feared that elected judges would twist the constitution to serve great ideological ends. Indeed, said the committee, that had already happened. Elected judges in the North, "the mere instruments of popular prejudice," had denied southerners justice "because their robes were placed on their shoulders by the votes of a fanatical people." And now Republicans were "appeal[ing] to the ballot box" to overturn the *Dred Scott* decision and seeking to reform the judiciary to make it bend to the popular will. (After *Dred Scott*, some Republicans sought to "reorganize" the US Supreme Court to ensure that the number of northern judges reflected the North's greater population.) The committee would not cast aspersions on the people of Alabama, whose "high traditional reverence for the law and the judiciary" had led them to elect judges of integrity, so that the "evils of a bad system" were not so obvious in Alabama as in other states; but abuse through the ballot box was sure to come. The committee therefore recommended a constitutional amendment to make all judges except probate judges appointive by the governor, with the advice and consent of the senate.[18]

Notwithstanding the robust anti-election sentiment at the Virginia and Alabama conventions, neither state actually jettisoned judicial elections in 1861. In Alabama, the committee report was made a special order of the day for March 13, but the convention took no further action on it. The constitution adopted on March 20 retained judicial elections for circuit and inferior courts. In Virginia, the referendum on the constitution did not take place until March of 1862, when a relative handful of voters in the war-torn state defeated the constitution by the slimmest of margins. In 1864, a convention of delegates representing a few jurisdictions under federal control adopted a constitution for a "restored" Virginia that provided for appointed judges. That constitution would become, by default, the post-war constitution for the state. In the meantime, the northwestern counties had broken away and drafted a constitution of their own. The new state of West Virginia would enter the Union in 1863 with an elective judiciary.[19]

In other states, the question of constitutional reform, especially with regard to the selection of judges, received little attention in either the published proceedings of the secession conventions or the newspapers. The abolition of the elective judiciary, where it occurred, took place quietly.

The Georgia legislature did not eliminate judicial elections as forecast by the Macon *Telegraph*, but the secession convention dropped the election of superior court judges without recording a vote. Criticism of the move appeared after the fact, but the voters narrowly approved the new constitution. The journal of the Florida convention barely mentioned judicial selection, and the journal of the Texas convention not at all. Those states' constitutions, which were not submitted to the voters, gave the power of appointing judges to the governor, with the advice and consent of two-thirds of the senate.[20]

The Florida convention's chief judicial concern was the creation of one or more courts to exercise the jurisdiction previously belonging to federal courts in the state. Delegate W. S. Dilworth "offered an ordinance to amend the Constitution in the election of Judges of the Supreme and Circuit Courts." The measure was referred to the judiciary committee, but there is no further mention of it in the convention's journal. One study surmises that the 1861 convention abandoned judicial elections due to concerns that "pockets of pro-Union voters" would elect Unionist judges. That is a plausible notion. There was significant pro-Union sentiment in Florida. After the Civil War, as discussed in the epilogue, Republicans controlled the governments of southern states but still worried about anti-Republican district judges.[21]

The Louisiana convention came close to abolishing judicial elections. On March 26, the convention's last day, the members took up proposed amendments to the constitution's article on the judiciary, one of which provided for the appointment of judges by the governor, with the advice and consent of the senate. After first changing the tenure of supreme court judges to good behavior, the delegates agreed to the alter the method of judicial selection from popular election to gubernatorial appointment by a vote of 44–23. This modification was to be submitted to the electorate.[22] When the entire ordinance on the judiciary, as amended, came up for passage, it received a favorable vote of 45–15, but the sixty delegates who participated did not constitute a quorum. With the sergeant at arms unable to locate any of the more than sixty absentees, the constitution retained judicial elections.[23]

In 1860, three of the five southeastern states and all six of the southwestern states had judiciaries that were entirely or partly elective. But the experiment proved to be fragile. By the end of 1861, Georgia had given up on elections for its superior courts, Florida and Texas had abandoned judicial elections entirely, Virginia was in the process of discarding them, Louisiana had come within an ace of eliminating them, and grave doubts about this supposed "Yankee innovation" had been expressed in other southern states. The national crisis had brought popular majorities into disrepute among southern leaders. For the security of their property, they wanted a judiciary independent of the people.

Epilogue

From Reconstruction to Jim Crow

Before the Civil War, the elective judiciary was a democratic reform. Along with the greater causes of free suffrage, equal representation, and democratization of local government, it promised to enhance the power of the people to choose those who would exercise authority on their behalf. Advocates of judicial elections insisted that the appointment of judges by governors or legislatures was unrepublican. They engaged in spirited debates with their adversaries on the subjects of judicial independence and the malevolent effects of politics on justice, but underlying it all was the fundamental principle that the people ought to choose their own agents. The "main motive" for the change to the elective system, wrote one observer, "was not the conviction, that it was the best way to put an end to apparent or real evils. The motive was the wish to be true to the Democratic principle."[1]

The democratic impulse that drove the antebellum push for elected judges was the same, North and South. In both sections, reformers sought to augment the power of the people. That "the people" included blacks only rarely in the North and never in the South did not negate the fact that the constitutional changes occurring in the antebellum period extended democracy. The number of people eligible to vote increased, the clout of underrepresented regions grew, the roster of public officers directly accountable to the electorate expanded. The election of judges was a democratic cause in the Jacksonian tradition.

The war changed the relationship between democracy and the judiciary, especially in the South. Presidents Lincoln and Johnson sought to rebuild the Union with lenient policies for readmission of the southern states to Congress. The southern constitutional conventions during the presidential phase of Reconstruction did little more than repudiate secession and acknowledge the end of slavery. When congressional

Republicans imposed more stringent conditions, including the enfranchisement of blacks, judicial elections in the South became entangled with the racial and political composition of the electorate. Republicans worried about the election of vengeful ex-Confederates in Democratic districts. Democrats (or Conservatives, as Democrats were often called in deference to the former Whigs in their ranks) found the possibility of black judges elected in black-majority districts repugnant. Thanks to the enfranchisement of blacks, to the disenfranchisement of some whites who had served the Confederacy, to the support of whites of both northern and southern origin (the so-called carpetbaggers and scalawags), and to the presence of federal troops, Republicans at first could be confident of controlling southern state governments. Many Republicans therefore favored a judiciary appointed by the governor. For them, the democratic expansion of the electorate led to an undemocratic method of judicial selection.

Democrats had the opposite problem. By the time they regained control of the state governments, the Fifteenth Amendment to the US Constitution prohibited racial discrimination in voting laws. But Democrats would find other ways of restricting the suffrage of blacks—fraud, intimidation, poll taxes, literacy tests, and so on. When the black vote was sufficiently suppressed, when the electorate had been "purified," Democrats would endorse judicial elections. The undemocratic contraction of the electorate enabled a democratic method of choosing judges.

Race relations were bad throughout the South. Most white southerners could not reconcile themselves to the notion of racial equality or even to the idea that blacks deserved to have political rights at all. Tensions were greatest where blacks made up a majority, or close to a majority, of the population and thus could join with carpetbaggers and scalawags to control the government. The higher the black proportion of the population, the less likely a state was to adopt judicial elections. In four states of the former Confederacy—Arkansas, North Carolina, Tennessee, and Texas—blacks constituted less than 40 percent of the total population. North Carolina had the highest proportion of the four with a bit more than one-third. By 1876, all four states had elective judiciaries. (Tennessee had switched to judicial elections in 1853 and never abandoned them.) Five of the six states in which the black population approached or exceeded 50 percent either waited until the Jim Crow era to readopt judicial elections (Florida, Georgia, Louisiana, and Mississippi) or retained an appointive judiciary (South Carolina, which has never elected its judges). The anomaly in this group was Alabama, where blacks were nearly

48 percent of population in 1870. Notwithstanding the highly critical report of the Committee on the Constitution at the Alabama secession convention, the state had not retreated from the popular election of its circuit court judges, and in 1867 the convention held under Congressional Reconstruction extended elections to the supreme court. Virginia fell between the two groups of states, with blacks composing about 42 percent of the total population. Shorn of its western counties by the creation of West Virginia in 1863, Virginia reverted to an appointive judiciary during the war and never relinquished it thereafter.[2]

The Civil War and Reconstruction had no impact on the elective judiciary in the states that stayed with the Union. Those states retained whatever method of judicial selection they had had before the war (popular election in Missouri, Kentucky, and Maryland, appointment by the governor in Delaware). Nor did the turmoil of the times slow the march of the elective principle through newly admitted states. Kansas, West Virginia, and Nevada joined the Union on the eve of or during the war. In Kansas, admitted in January 1861, pro- and antislavery forces held four constitutional conventions between them in the 1850s; every constitution they drafted provided for judicial elections. Congress granted statehood to the disgruntled northwestern counties of Virginia in 1863. West Virginia, the chief source of agitation against Virginia's appointive system at the 1850–51 constitutional convention, embraced the elective judiciary. The Nevada constitutional convention of 1864 accepted judicial elections as a matter of course. A dozen other western territories achieved statehood between 1867 and 1912, all with elective judiciaries.

Judicial Selection under Wartime Reconstruction

The Confederate states did not fit into this narrative of the triumphant march of the elective judiciary. By the end of 1863, Federal forces occupied enough southern territory that President Lincoln felt able to concoct a plan for the restoration of southern states to the Union. (Virginia already had a "restored" government.) The plan required emancipation of the slaves and oaths of allegiance to the United States from 10 percent of the voting population. That population excluded several categories of Confederate government officials and high-ranking military and naval officers.[3]

On January 4, 1864, a constitutional convention met in Arkansas, with delegates from perhaps twenty to thirty of the state's fifty-seven counties. Only five of the represented counties were located in the lowland delta region of the state, where the planters and their allies had dominated political affairs. The rest were in the upland northwest and forested southwest, regions that lacked the delta's relatively sharp social distinctions. The convention's dominant faction, headed by William Fishback of the northwestern county of Sebastian, "was motivated largely by hostility toward the antebellum elite." The delegates extended judicial elections to the supreme court. Why they did so is unclear, although the chairman of the committee that drafted the constitution announced that the committee had, "in the main, reported the old Constitution of the State, with such alterations and amendments as have become necessary by the advancing spirit and genius of the times." For a western state such as Arkansas, supreme court elections accorded with the spirit of the times.[4]

Louisiana, too, saw a constitutional convention in 1864. Representing about two-fifths of the state's parishes, the delegates met under tumultuous political circumstances. With matters related to race and reintegration into the Union dominating the proceedings, judicial selection was of minor concern. However, the delegates did debate the issue, which was of particular interest to the lawyers of New Orleans. Two months before the convention met, the New Orleans *Daily True Delta* reprinted a speech given the previous fall by Michael Hahn, a Republican who would soon be elected governor, in which Hahn had come out against judicial elections. Hahn believed that every member of the New Orleans bar opposed the popular election of judges because of the deleterious effects upon "the ermine from mingling in the strifes of party contests." The state's experience with an elective judiciary, Hahn had declared, had brought every respectable person in the city to favor a change in the mode of judicial selection.[5]

At the convention itself, the delegates devoted several days to an impassioned debate over the elective versus appointive judiciary. Most of the arguments had been heard many times before in the antebellum constitutional conventions in Louisiana and other states, but opponents of the elective judiciary added their fear that existing circumstances made elections especially dangerous. Blaming the advent of the elective judiciary in 1852 on "Slidell, Benjamin and other traitors," R. King Cutler noted the difficulty of knowing who was truly loyal. "In case a Judge of certain proclivities was elected," he warned his fellow delegates, "any of them might simply, for being in Convention, be sentenced out of all proportion to the actual or pretended offence." Or, as another delegate put it, "It might not be a very difficult matter for the secessionists to elect their own men, and then any one of those before him . . . might swing because they had passed the act of emancipation." The advocates of judicial elections had an uphill battle. The reports of the standing judiciary committee and a special judiciary committee provided for the appointment of all judges, down to justices of the peace, by the governor, with the advice and consent of the senate. W. T. Stocker offered a substitute judiciary title that provided for judicial elections. The convention voted on it section by section. When the members got to the elections provision, J. V. Bofill moved a substitute for Stocker's substitute to return the selection of judges to the governor and senate. It passed by a vote of 50–33 and was incorporated into the final document.[6]

Virginia had had a "restored" government since June 1861, when delegates from thirty-seven counties, most of them located in the northwestern region of the state, held a convention and created a new, loyal government. This government, recognized by Lincoln in a message to Congress as the legitimate government of the whole state, functioned to a limited extent in the areas under Union control until the admission of West Virginia as a separate state in 1863. Although the restored government operated in only a small part of Virginia's pre-war territory, with the Union victory it would become the government of the entire state. In early 1864, the General Assembly called for a constitutional convention to accommodate two new realities—the loss of the northwestern counties and the need to abolish slavery. Now that Virginia was free of those democratic northwestern gadflies, the convention returned the state to an appointive judiciary (and restored the taxpayer qualification for voting). The delegates decided not to submit the document to the electorate for ratification.[7]

Judicial Selection under Presidential Reconstruction

After Abraham Lincoln's assassination, Andrew Johnson pursued Reconstruction along lines similar to Lincoln's, although he added the disenfranchisement of ex-Confederates who owned property worth more than $20,000. Johnson recognized the governments established in Louisiana, Arkansas, and Virginia. Tennessee, which had been largely under Union control since 1862, held a state convention in January 1865 that proposed a state constitutional amendment abolishing slavery. An electorate severely truncated by the disenfranchisement of Confederate sympathizers ratified the amendment in February and elected a civilian government to replace the military government that had been headed by Johnson. In 1866, shortly after the legislature ratified the Fourteenth Amendment,

Congress agreed to "readmit" Tennessee to the Union. For the other seven rebellious states, Johnson issued proclamations appointing provisional governors and directing them to call conventions to draft constitutions that would abolish slavery and repudiate Confederate state debts.[8]

Johnson's proclamations, issued between May 29 and July 13, 1865, after Lee's surrender, were addressed to Alabama, Florida, Georgia, Mississippi, North Carolina, South Carolina, and Texas. All seven duly held conventions, the chief purpose of which was to satisfy Johnson's demands. They did not aim to reform state government in other ways. Judicial selection was, as usual, a minor issue. The South Carolina, Mississippi, and Alabama conventions adhered to their states' existing systems (appointive, elective, and mixed, respectively). So did the North Carolina convention, except that it democratized local government by making justices of the peace, and therefore the county courts, elective. However, North Carolina's voters rejected the constitution, so even justices remained appointive. Tennessee continued to operate under its existing constitution, with its elective judiciary. Georgia and Texas returned to their prewar positions, making the superior courts of the former and all the courts of the latter elective. The new constitution of Florida went partway toward restoration of the elective system, applying it to the lower courts but not the supreme court.[9]

The continuation of the elective system in Alabama, Mississippi, and Tennessee, extension in Arkansas, and revival in Florida, Georgia, and Texas could be seen as advances for democracy, except for the unpalatable fact that all the voters would be white. The conventions of 1865 and 1866 did not extend suffrage or other civil or political rights to blacks. The racial restrictions on suffrage were no worse than they had been before the war, but times had changed. Congressional Republicans were not satisfied with southern intransigence on race or with the fact that some of the conventions had refused to repudiate Confederate debts. In the first elections under the new constitutions, southerners elected twenty-five former high-ranking Confederate political or military figures to Congress and even more to their state governments, further inflaming Republican fury.[10] Radical Republicans were not going to watch idly as their military victory turned into electoral defeat.

From Congressional Reconstruction to Redemption

To achieve their goals of legal equality for the freedmen and Republican control of the South, Republicans in Congress enacted two Reconstruction Acts in March 1867.[11] The acts placed all of the former Confederacy except Tennessee under military rule and recognized the existing governments as provisional and subordinate to the military authorities. In order for a state to be readmitted to Congress, it would have to hold a constitutional convention elected by blacks as well as whites, adopt a new constitution that provided for black suffrage, and ratify the Fourteenth Amendment to the US Constitution, passed by Congress in June 1866. In addition to its better-known due process and equal protection clauses, the Fourteenth Amendment disqualified from holding a federal or state civil or military office anyone who, as a federal or state public officer, had taken an oath to support the Constitution and then engaged in insurrection or rebellion against the United States. The Reconstruction Acts barred these individuals from voting for delegates to the state constitutional conventions and from voting on the ratification of the constitutions.

The Reconstruction Acts established a system of voter registration for the convention elections, with federal registrars managing the enrollment of voters. They also required that at least half the registered voters in a state participate in a referendum on the holding of a convention. A combination of disenfranchisement, resentment, and apathy kept an estimated 35–45 percent of the potential white voters from registering. Blacks constituted a majority of the registrants in five states (Alabama, Florida, Louisiana, Mississippi, and South Carolina) and in the unreconstructed states overall. In the elections, fewer than half the whites who registered bothered to vote, a tactic intended to thwart the conventions by keeping the vote total under the required half of registered voters. Of those whites who did vote, half opposed the holding of conventions. Blacks turned out in far higher numbers, and they naturally supported the calling of conventions. Under these circumstances, Republicans won the great majority of seats. Southern whites made up about 57 percent of all the convention delegates, blacks a little over a quarter, and whites from outside the South the remaining 16 percent. Forty percent of the southern white delegates were yeoman farmers.[12]

Historians have described the constitutions drafted by these conventions as "progressive" not only because of their racial egalitarianism but also for their provisions for free public schools, establishment of institutions for orphans and the insane, criminal justice reform, and debt relief in the form of exemptions of homesteads from attachment.[13] The voters ratified all of the new constitutions except those of Alabama and Mississippi, and in those two states, as we will see, the federal government found ways to reverse the results.

The new constitutions reflected the tension between resurgent Jacksonian democracy and political necessity. The constitutional conventions of 1867–69 should have been ideal forums for the adoption of judicial elections. The freedmen were anxious to exercise their newly granted right to vote. Many of the northern delegates came from states where the people elected their judges. And many of the southern whites hailed from Upcountry districts that had long been at odds with the Lowcountry "aristocrats."

However, the Republicans faced a dilemma. They might control the conventions, but they did not control every district in every state. There was no way to ensure that elected judges, sheriffs, and other officers would not try to obstruct the implementation of their policies. To some, the wiser course appeared to be centralization of authority in governors chosen in statewide elections. As long as Republicans outnumbered Democrats in the electorate, they would be able to place their own men on the bench—men who would protect the franchise and other rights of Republicans, black and white.

The conversion or reconversion of judicial selection from appointment to election was closely linked to the extent of the franchise. In general, Republicans were committed to manhood suffrage, Democrats to *white* manhood suffrage. Until blacks could legally be denied access to the ballot, Democrats used extra-legal means to accomplish that goal. Fraud and violence occurred on a wide scale throughout the period of Reconstruction and beyond. Once the Democrats "redeemed" a state from Republican rule, they found politer methods of disenfranchising blacks. During the Jim Crow era, North Carolina historian Stephen B. Weeks identified four methods then being used to restrict black suffrage. The first was centralization, the appointment of key local government officers by the legislature (or, Weeks might have added, by the governor). Centralization prevented local black majorities from controlling county governments and also kept county funds "in the hands of the more conservative and better element of the population"—a suggestion, perhaps, that certain whites could not be trusted with the government either.[14]

Another way to reduce the black vote was to demand the payment of taxes as a prerequisite to voting, a condition sometimes made more burdensome by the imposition of a poll tax and the requirement of a poll-tax receipt as proof of payment. In Arkansas, wrote Weeks, the receipt requirement "works well, and the negro vote is said to be practically eliminated." Other ways to limit the black vote included a complex registration process, byzantine election laws, and educational requirements. Weeks might also have mentioned residency requirements and disqualifications for criminal convictions. "The negro," wrote the Mississippi attorney general, "is known . . . as a nomadic tribe . . . drift[ing] from plantation to plantation and landlord to landlord," and therefore unable to meet the residency qualification. The attorney general further listed a series of crimes, from burglary to bigamy, that were "indigenous to the negro's nature." Labor conditions and law enforcement thus deprived many blacks of the elective franchise.[15]

One way or another, through means legal and illegal, black suffrage was rendered more theoretical than practical. (The same was true for many poor whites.) Once the electorate had been thus "purified," judges could be safely elected.

The States with the Lowest Proportions of Blacks

As observed above, the states with the lowest percentage of blacks in the population were the first to adopt or extend judicial elections during Reconstruction, although in Arkansas and Texas the change would come in stages. (The exception of Alabama is discussed below.) Only a quarter of the populations of Tennessee and Arkansas, according to the 1870 federal census, consisted of blacks. Tennessee still had judicial elections under the constitutional amendment of 1853. Arkansas had gone to an all-elective judiciary at its truncated convention of 1864, but in 1868 it took a step back. The scheme passed by the 1868 convention provided for an appointed chief justice of the supreme court; appointed circuit court judges; associate justices of the supreme court elected at large; and justices of the peace elected by local constituencies. The plan elicited no discussion. A memorial presented to the convention asked that the circuit judges be appointed by the governor because of the partiality and dubious loyalty to the Union of some of the elected judges, but the request provoked only a brief exchange at the time and seems to have been quickly forgotten. Even a long debate over a resolution favoring the extension of the life of the Freedmen's Bureau, in which debate the delegates argued vigorously over whether blacks could get justice in the state's courts, produced no comments on the method of selecting judges. The hybrid plan is hard to fathom, except perhaps as some kind of awkward compromise, but it would not last long.[16]

Arkansas's return to a completely elective judiciary began with the state's "redemption." Most white southerners could not abide the changes taking place under federal supervision and Republican rule, from which they sought to be released. In a sense, redemption began with Tennessee, even though that state had not been subjected to Congressional Reconstruction. In 1865, the Radical legislature limited the franchise to unconditionally loyal men and expressly denied the suffrage to former Confederate soldiers for five years and to Confederate leaders for fifteen years. In 1867, the statute was amended to allow blacks to vote. Nevertheless, after several years of "dismal" government and "wretched excesses" on the part of the administration, and widespread disregard of the statutory franchise restrictions, Democrats regained control of the state government and called a constitutional convention mainly for the purpose of legally restoring the franchise to former rebels. The convention drafted amendments to accomplish this goal and in addition authorized the legislature to impose a poll tax and to make its payment a prerequisite to voting. (The legislature did not levy a poll tax until 1889. Then the statute, together with other election laws, "effectively disposed of the negro vote" and disenfranchised or discouraged from voting many whites as well.) Ratification of the amendments in 1870 ensured the redemption of the state.[17]

Redemption in Arkansas began with the election of Elisha Baxter as governor in 1872. Although a Republican, Baxter found himself drifting toward the Democrats, with whom he had formed an electoral alliance. The political and financial condition of Arkansas at the time was deplorable. Public promotion of railroads and other projects, many of questionable merit, had produced a massive state debt and rising taxes. A gubernatorial contest between the candidates of the regular and reformist wings of the Republican Party had turned into a nasty brawl known as the Brooks-Baxter War that landed in court and had both sides appealing to President Grant for support. Democrats saw this fight as an opportunity. They gained increasing influence over Baxter, the eventual winner, who found them more congenial than his opponents within his own party.[18]

In this atmosphere of political turmoil, corruption, and economic distress, made worse by the nationwide depression of 1873, different parties saw advantages in a proposed constitutional convention. Democrats especially found a convention appealing because they had high hopes of controlling it. Their chances were buoyed by a constitutional amendment, ratified in 1873, that restored the franchise to many thousands of white men who had been disenfranchised in 1868 during Congressional Reconstruction. The Democrats secured the overwhelming majority of convention delegates and proceeded to draft a constitution reminiscent of the Jacksonian constitutions of the 1840s and 1850s. The new instrument placed severe restrictions on state spending, debt, and taxation; reduced the terms of public officers; and made virtually all public offices, including all judgeships, elective.[19]

The fully elective judiciary did not return to Arkansas without debate. Before and during the convention, Democratic newspapers published arguments pro and con. At the convention, delegate Hugh French Thomason offered a resolution to express the convention's intention "to reflect the unmistakable wish of the people, and to adopt a constitution that shall provide for the election by the people of all officers, from governor to township constable." Some delegates objected for various reasons, but the convention passed the resolution, 82–6. The judiciary committee subsequently submitted a report that provided for the election of all judges, and the subject seems to have elicited no serious discussion thereafter.[20]

When it appeared that the convention would vote in favor of an elective judiciary, a white resident of a black-majority county appealed to the white delegates for protection against the election of ignorant men who could barely write their names and knew nothing of the law. He suggested the creation of judicial districts in such a manner as to ensure that they all had majorities of "the honest conservative element." He further called for reducing the jurisdiction of justices of the peace and requiring that the qualifications of judicial candidates be certified by a board of attorneys. One convention delegate went so far as to propose that circuit court judges be elected by the voters of the entire state. The districts ultimately created by the convention appear to have been deliberately drawn to dilute the black vote as much as possible, with the exception of one overwhelmingly black district. The delegates also mandated that a circuit court judge be "learned in the law" and have at least six years of practice under his belt, requirements that would have severely restricted the number of eligible blacks even if fairly applied. Without impinging on black suffrage, the constitution ensured that the elective judiciary would be white.[21]

In Texas, where western democracy had reasserted itself in 1866 and produced a judiciary elected by white voters, the constitutional convention of 1868–69 reversed course. Texas was beset by lawlessness and violence directed at Republicans, black and white. Some district judges elected in 1866 and 1867 were former secessionists who allegedly sympathized with the perpetrators of violence and obstructed the seating of non-whites on juries. With blacks making up less than a third of the state's total population, the moderate Republicans who composed a majority of the delegates at the 1868–69 convention did not want to disenfranchise their Democratic adversaries, as some conventions did, but to attract them to their side. That meant that elections in non-Republican districts could not be made safe. Although neither the convention's journal of proceedings nor contemporary newspapers seem to contain any direct evidence on the point, the concern about the unreliability of local officials may have been the reason that the convention created a strong governor with the power to appoint the judges of the supreme and district courts.[22]

In Texas, as in Arkansas, the Democrats prevailed in the 1872 elections and promptly curtailed the powers of the Republican governor, Edmund J. Davis. In their 1873 campaign platform, they also urged the next legislature to authorize another constitutional convention. Davis denounced that plank as a call for "revolution" by the "titled gentlemen, the generals and judges" of the state Democratic convention. This "nobility," the governor declared, would knock out the section of the bill of rights that condemned secession and acknowledged the supremacy of the US Constitution, bringing Texas into conflict with the national government. And the "nobility" would "apportion the offices among themselves."[23]

The Democratic press beat the drums for a convention, demanding the usual variety of changes, from shorter terms of judicial office to the reduction of salaries of state officials to biennial legislative sessions. The list naturally included the election of all state officers, expressly including judges. The election on August 2 drew a low turnout, but the pro-convention forces had a large majority of those who did vote, and Democrats won seventy-five of the ninety seats.[24]

The delegates convened in Austin on September 6, 1875. On October 20, a fractured judiciary committee submitted its report. There were three minority reports as well. The committee members disagreed over the structure of the judicial system, the jurisdiction of the different courts, and other matters, but all four reports recommended that the judges be elected. Some of the delegates, such as Fletcher Summerfield Stockdale, worried that local majorities characterized by "ignorance and prejudices" would "elect men to the bench who were inimical to the interests of the state." Stockdale's remarks may have been aimed as much at poor city dwellers as at blacks. A leading politician and railroad lawyer, Stockdale belonged to the class of nabobs who would have restricted the right of suffrage. He argued for payment of a poll tax as a qualification for the right to vote. "There had always been that class of men who, possessing nothing themselves, would delight to vote any measure of taxation upon other men," Stockdale declared. "Was it right that these irresponsible and often transient men should be permitted to vote what they pleased upon others? The duty of paying a poll tax abridged no one, but was equal to all." But another delegate made plain his fear of black voters, contending that too many judicial districts would allow for the election of a "negro elected judiciary" in some counties and would turn Democrats against ratification of the constitution.[25]

The convention heard arguments over judicial districts and other court-related issues, but that judges would be elected was never in doubt. The majority of convention delegates had no interest in establishing suffrage restrictions that would disqualify as many whites as blacks[26] and not enough concern about the influence of black voters to create unwieldly judicial districts.

The convention settled on a supreme court and a court of appeals, both elected at large; twenty-six judicial districts, each with an elected district judge; and elected county courts and justices of the peace. The qualifications for judicial office made it likely that no black would become a judge any time soon. Judges of the supreme court and court of appeals had to have been practicing lawyers or judges in Texas for seven years. For district court judges, the requirement was four years. Even county court judges had to be "well informed in the law of the State." There were at the time perhaps two black attorneys in Texas. One of them was a justice of the peace in 1872, earning him the title of Texas's first black judge. But it would be many decades before Stockdale's nightmare of a black district court judge would come true.[27]

The most dramatic turnabout in judicial selection occurred in North Carolina, a state that had never elected its "real" judges and had made justices of the peace elective only in its ill-fated constitution of 1866. Citizens of Davidson County in the west-central part of the state had petitioned the 1866 convention for an elective judiciary, but to no avail. During the 1868 convention, a correspondent from the mountain town of Marshall sent to the *Weekly North-Carolina Standard* "the views, in general, of our western people, concerning the constitutional reforms necessary in our judiciary." Topping the list was the election of public officers, including judges of the supreme and superior courts.[28]

At the 1868 convention, the judiciary committee was so badly divided on the subject of judicial selection that it simply threw the matter into the hands of the convention without making a recommendation. In the discussion that ensued, Joseph H. King charged that all the opposition to the existing appointive system came from non-natives (for example, carpetbaggers) who wanted to win judgeships for themselves. (Two of the delegates who spoke out for judicial elections, David Heaton and Albion W. Tourgée, had touted the experiences of their former states of residence, Ohio and New York.) Native-born Tarheels from the central and western sections of the state rejoined that they were "in favor of electing every officer in the State by the people," one of them adding that his large white constituency was almost unanimously for the election of all officers. Abraham H. Galloway, whom the *Wilmington Journal* identified as "negro" every time it reported his words, also advocated the elective judiciary. He described the judiciary of his southeastern county of New Hanover as "a bastard, born in sin and secession," that saw being black or loyal as a crime and that sent men to the workhouse to prevent them from voting to ratify the constitution.[29]

Attorney J. W. Graham protested against the avalanche of support for the elective principle. "If there is anything in the past history of our State, of which we are justly proud," he declared, "it is the high character, learning and independence of those who have adorned the bench of the Supreme and Superior Courts." The current judges, he continued, gave no cause for complaint, "even from colored persons or those who are called loyal men." Henry M. Ray responded that in his county (Alamance), men had been condemned to death by appointed judges without proper evidence. Attempts to delay a vote on the question failed. The convention went for judicial elections for both courts. The change was part of a much broader democratization of the constitution that established manhood suffrage, abolished property qualifications for legislative office, limited judicial terms to eight years, replaced the county court with elected commissioners, and provided for a free public school system for all children.[30]

The delegates' approval of judicial elections disgusted much of the press. The *Raleigh Register* objected that the people were too ignorant to choose judges and that the elective judiciary had proved bad wherever it had been tried. The *Western Democrat* added that the overabundance of elections to take place under the new constitution would "keep up almost a constant political agitation," when what the people needed was "peace and quiet." The *Tarboro Southerner* saw the vote as a radical assault on the distinguished North Carolina judiciary and predicted that the prospect of "Supreme Court Judges elected by ignorant negroes" would ensure the defeat of the constitution." But in the referendum on the ratification, the voters accepted the document 93,084–74,015.[31]

When the Democrats took control of the General Assembly, they asked the voters to approve another constitutional convention, but the people rejected the idea. The legislators then put a series of constitutional amendments on the ballot, most of which sought to save the state money and to modify the tax laws. These the people approved. Still, in 1875 the legislature called another convention. This time they did not submit the call to a popular referendum. The convention produced thirty proposed amendments, none of them touching judicial elections, although the number of supreme court judges would fall from five to three. One amendment gave the legislature the power to make itself the appointee of township and county officers, which would keep blacks in black-majority counties from controlling local government. (The General Assembly soon followed through.) Another amendment raised the county-residence requirement for voting from thirty to ninety days and barred convicted felons from voting. All of these the voters ratified.[32]

The States with the Highest Proportions of Blacks

According to the 1870 census, blacks made up between 46 and 49 percent of the populations of Florida, Georgia, and Alabama and a majority of the populations of South Carolina, Mississippi, and Louisiana. Of the six states, only Alabama embraced judicial elections for all its courts before 1885. None of the others would do so until the Jim Crow era, when the black vote was legally, effectively, and almost entirely suppressed.

It is not clear why Alabama differed. The composition of the membership of the state's 1867 constitutional convention, the first of the conventions to meet under the conditions imposed by Congress, may have been a factor. A reporter for the *New York Herald* described most of the delegates as possessing little in the way of worldly means (although a modern analysis of the delegates' wealth suggests that they were fairly well-off). Many came from the northern part of the state, which had been a Jacksonian stronghold of yeoman farmers before the Civil War, while the southern Black Belt had been the home of Whiggery. The sectional animosity carried over into the immediate aftermath of the war, as the Upcountry became the seat of Republican radicalism.[33]

The judiciary committee, chaired by Henry C. Semple of Montgomery County in the Black Belt, recommended the appointment of all judges by the governor, with the advice and consent of the senate. (Semple, a former Confederate army officer, signed a protest against the constitution, after which a Republican paper accused him and his fellow signatories of "wag[ing] a war against the negro men of Alabama.") But the convention, on the motion of Thomas M. Peters of Lawrence County in northern Alabama, opted for a judiciary chosen by the General Assembly, 45–36. The next day, the members reconsidered the vote. Thomas Haughey, representing the northern county of Morgan, moved to make the judges elective, while Semple sought to go back to gubernatorial appointment. Semple derided the supporters of elections as "nigger ticklers" who wanted "fat offices" for themselves and were after black votes. The delegates set Semple's substitute aside and passed Haughey's by a vote of 52–29. One reporter observed that "[s]ome of the radical members voted the wrong way, thereby . . . hurting themselves with the 'people.'"[34]

During the post-convention ratification campaign, many newspapers criticized the conferring of the elective franchise on "ignorant negroes." Some predicted that the proposed elective judiciary would mean the end of law and order. The Reconstruction Acts required ratification by a majority of registered voters for the constitution to take effect; so, to forestall the horrors of a black electorate and a Republican constitution, many opponents of the instrument registered to vote and then boycotted the referendum on ratification. A large majority of those who voted, mostly blacks, approved the constitution, but they constituted less than half of the registrants. Congress reacted by passing corrective legislation so that ratification required only a majority of those voting rather those registered and applied it retroactively to Alabama. Upon ratification of the Fourteenth Amendment, Alabama would be fully restored to the Union.[35]

The Democrats regained mastery of the state in 1874 and promptly called for a constitutional convention. The convention made many changes, but it refrained on two key issues, suffrage and judicial selection. The citizenry was too democratic to countenance property or educational qualifications for suffrage, either of which might have disenfranchised whites and both of which the Democratic Party had rejected before the convention met.[36] There was a lot of sympathy for an appointive judiciary, but to turn back the clock on the popular election of public officers might have alienated too many voters and jeopardized ratification.[37] In what might have been a concession to a desire to limit black influence on the judiciary, the delegates capped at eight the number of judicial circuits that the legislature could create without a supermajority vote, with the number of counties per circuit ranging from three to twelve.[38] In 1875, the Democrats redrew the state's congressional district map, putting as many Black Belt counties as possible into the fourth district. They thereby virtually negated the black Republican vote in other districts. When the General Assembly created judicial circuits under the new constitution, it generally followed the lines of the congressional districts; the fourth district and fourth circuit were identical.[39] It was a step toward making election of judges a white affair throughout the state, something that would come to pass when the constitution of 1901 effectively disenfranchised nearly all blacks (and many whites).[40]

Like Alabama, South Carolina, had a high percentage of blacks in its population at the time of Reconstruction—at 58 percent, higher than any other state in the country. Unlike Alabama, South Carolina had never had an elective judiciary. That would not change, regardless of which party controlled the constitutional conventions or the state government. At the 1868 convention, the report on the judiciary provided for the popular election of circuit court judges and justices of the peace. In the brief debate on a motion to amend the report so that the judges would be chosen by the General Assembly, one delegate objected to electioneering by judges who would then be dependent on the will of the people. He also adverted to the opinion of a "distinguished lawyer of New York" that the elective system had worked out badly in the Empire State. "How would it look," asked another delegate, "to see a Judge with a bottle of whiskey in one hand and ballots in the other, begging for the votes of the people?" It would be a "strange spectacle" for South Carolina.[41]

But beyond these objections, raised so often in the mid-century conventions of other states, there was the characteristic problem of Congressional Reconstruction. "[I]n certain portions of the state," observed E. W. M. Mackey, referring to the "upper districts," "the rebels have a majority." The judiciary report required the circuit court judges to "interchange circuits with each other," as the General Assembly provided. "Perhaps," continued Mackey, "the gentleman from Beaufort [Jonathan Wright, a black delegate who had spoken in favor of judicial elections] may find one of these Judges elected by rebel votes coming down to his district and administering justice there." That contingency could be prevented if the legislature, which represented the entire state, selected the circuit court judges. Wright was not convinced, but he was in the minority. The convention voted 65–24 for legislative selection of the circuit judges.[42]

The contretemps over judicial elections didn't end there. An attempt to take the selection of probate judges away from the voters drew an angry reaction from a delegate who was tired of "see[ing] my people robbed of their rights." The probate judges remained elective. But there was no serious assault on the appointment of "real" judges. In 1888, Populist leader Ben Tillman spoke up for the elective judiciary, and from then through about 1900 there was significant support for the idea, but not nearly enough to get a constitutional amendment through the legislature or through the 1895 constitutional convention.[43]

The other states with high concentrations of black residents—Florida, Georgia, and Mississippi—followed more or less the same road to the elective judiciary. Their constitutions adopted under Congressional Reconstruction all provided for judiciaries appointed by the governor with the advice and consent of the senate. After Democrats regained control, fraud, violence, and intimidation kept many blacks away from the polls. At the same time, the promotion of railroads, industry, and commerce by boosters of the "New South" added to the social dislocations that accompanied the end of slavery and gave rise to labor organizations and farmers' alliances. The disorder dismayed the leaders of the New South. They were particularly embarrassed by the lawlessness that characterized southern elections. Preferring to establish white supremacy in law, they sought to restrict black suffrage through constitutional revisions that would not run afoul of the Fifteenth Amendment and possibly trigger a federal reaction. To some, if such measures also disenfranchised poor whites, so much the better. As a Mississippi congressman explained in 1904, "We have disenfranchised not only the ignorant and vicious black, but the ignorant and vicious white as well, and the electorate in Mississippi is now confined to those, and those alone, who are qualified by intelligence and character for the proper and patriotic exercise of this great franchise."[44]

In the presidential phase of Reconstruction, the initial report of the judiciary committee to the Florida constitutional convention provided for the popular election of all judges, restoring the pre-war method of judicial selection. An attempt to change to gubernatorial appointment lost 31–17. However, at some point in the next few days, by a vote not reflected in the journal, the convention decided to give to the governor the power to appoint the supreme court judges. In 1868, at the next stage of Reconstruction, the Republicans reverted to the appointment of all judges, including justices of the peace. Republicans in Florida, as in other states, may have feared that judicial elections would put some obstructionist judges on the bench.[45]

In the mid-1870s, the Democrats took control of the state and soon began agitating for a constitutional convention. In 1880, the voters turned down the opportunity to call a convention, but proponents in the General Assembly persisted. Wanting to rid Florida of the Republican constitution, reduce the governor's powers of appointment, and cut down on public spending, reformers succeeded in having a convention called for 1885.[46]

Five months before the convention met, the *Pensacola Commercial*, which the previous October had recommended a poll tax as a prerequisite to voting, argued at length against universal suffrage on the ground that only those who shared in the burdens of government should participate in its operation. While the paper made its case in general terms, not limiting it to any particular kind of tax or specific class of individuals, its real target was clear enough. The existing constitution, wrote the paper, had been imposed by carpetbaggers "for the sole purpose of perpetuating party rule through the aid of the whole mass of the negroes . . . and throwing the whole burden of supporting the government on the whites, while it relieved ninety-nine one hundredths of the negroes from the payment of all taxes and conferred upon them the unlimited right of franchise." The *Palatka Daily News*, quoting a Philadelphia newspaper, subsequently described the poll tax as "the best means yet devised for controlling the evil of unrestricted suffrage. The ignorant negroes whose votes are largely controlled by unprincipled schemers will not generally exercise a privilege they have to pay for." The subject occasioned considerable debate at the convention; ultimately, the delegates decided to authorize the legislature to make payment of a capitation (poll) tax a prerequisite for voting. In 1889, the legislature did just that.[47]

Before the judiciary committee issued its majority and minority reports, the *Pensacola Commercial* noted the amount of "loose talk" floating around concerning the "propriety of appointing instead of electing judges." The experience of other states, thought the editors, was a sufficient answer to all objections. The *Weekly Floridian*, on the other hand, reprinted items from two other papers urging the convention to reject elections. When the committee's reports came out, before the dispute over the poll tax had been resolved, the majority favored an elective judiciary, the minority an appointive one. In the end, the convention compromised, submitting a new report that provided for the election of the supreme court judges and appointment by the governor of circuit court judges. The members of the supreme court would be elected at large, which meant that, notwithstanding the absence of a poll tax, the black vote would be inconsequential. The appointment of the circuit judges practically guaranteed that any pockets of resistance to Democratic rule would not be able to elect judges beyond the level of the county court. Florida would go on to reduce the black vote through a poll tax, white primaries, and other legal devices, but the 1885 constitution already ensured that the upper levels of the judiciary would be selected by white voters.[48]

The Georgia convention of 1867–68 wrote an appointive judiciary into the constitution, as both the majority and minority reports of the judiciary committee recommended. The minority report urged that "subordinate Judicial officers" be elected, and an amendment to the majority report made justices of the peace elective,[49] but otherwise there seems to have been no debate on the subject at the convention itself or in the press. Following the state's redemption came the predictable calls for a constitutional convention. Not until 1877, though, did the General Assembly put the question of a convention to the people. Those who bothered to vote approved the call. (The turnout was so light that election day in one county was "quiet as a funeral.") The delegates convened in July of that year.[50]

At the convention, a spirited debate took place over the question of judicial selection. The prevailing method of appointment by the governor had its defenders, but supporters of both selection by the General Assembly and election by the people criticized it vehemently. The arguments echoed those that had occurred at the mid-century conventions, but the subject of race also intruded into the discussion. Robert Toombs, former Confederate secretary of state and brigadier general, presented the most intemperate attack on the elective judiciary. The people are sovereign, he conceded, but "[w]ho are the people? It is those in society who are strong enough to form civil government, and to administer its powers. They are not anybody; they are not women, and the children of these are not counted." And "the people" certainly did not include blacks, who were "kind" and "affectionate" but utterly incapable of governing. The federal government, complained Toombs, "has injected into the social organization and political body 500,000 savages, who, whatever their rights, are not fit to exercise the powers of government." Having no faith in the black voter and not much more in the average white voter, Toombs wanted the legislature to elect the judges. The convention as a whole agreed. Ratification of the constitution transferred the power of judicial selection from the governor to the legislature.[51]

Fears about the impact of the black vote were overblown. In 1868, blacks had constituted 51 percent of the electorate but just 14 percent of the delegates at that year's convention. The 1877 convention had no black delegates. As a supporter of judicial elections pointed out, the "different population" that had been "turned loose" on Georgia "have hardly ever controlled an election in this state." Moreover, the new constitution authorized the imposition of a poll tax; required the payment of all taxes due (except for the year of the election) as a qualification for voting; empowered the legislature to establish a system of voter registration; and prohibited from voting any person convicted of certain crimes, including larceny and crimes of moral turpitude. These were all devices used during the Jim Crow era to keep blacks from voting.[52]

A constitutional amendment providing for the election of supreme and superior court judges (and prosecutors, called solicitors general, as well) would eventually result from the confluence of two perceived needs: one, desired by the legal profession, to relieve an overworked supreme court; the other, driven by populists, to have more public officers directly elected by the people. Echoing complaints that had been heard in many states then and for decades earlier, the Savannah *Morning News* asserted that with the election of judges and solicitors general always taking up two to three weeks of the General Assembly's time, selection by the legislators was "certainly the most expensive method that could be devised." Moreover, the lawmakers sometimes chose not the best-qualified men but "the shrewdest wire-pullers and log-rollers."[53]

To deal with these problems, in 1884 Senator William P. Sheffield introduced a constitutional amendment to transfer the appointment of the judges and prosecutors to the governor. The measure passed the senate, but the house failed to act on it. The *Brunswick Herald* denounced gubernatorial appointments, declaring that "[t]he people can attend to that matter better than the Governor." The *Carroll Free Press*, which reprinted the *Herald* article, agreed. During the next legislative session, the house judiciary committee reported unfavorably on another proposal to transfer the appointing power to the governor; at least one representative noted that his constituents wanted judges to be elected by the people.[54]

While the wrangling over the selection of judges was going on, the legislature had another judicial issue to consider. By the early 1880s, court-watchers believed that the supreme court was overburdened. "There is not a dray horse in Georgia worked as hard as the judges of our highest court," commented one paper. "That court is a stepping stone to the grave." But repeated attempts to add more judges to the court foundered on the rock of rural opinion. While "lawyers and litigants" and the "best minds in the state" favored a constitutional amendment to increase the size of the court, the denizens of small towns and farms opposed the creation of more offices. "The people are burdened with taxation and still the cry is more offices, more taxes and more oppression," groused a taxpayer of Cobb County. If the present judges couldn't handle the work, he suggested, they should quit in favor of others who would do the job without complaining. When the amendment failed at the polls, the Savannah *Morning News* blamed the defeat on the statewide "concerted action" of the Farmers' Alliance.[55]

Georgia muddled along into the 1890s with its three-member supreme court appointed by the governor. In 1894, when the house killed a bill to make judges elective, one editor claimed that the main objection to the measure had been the Democrats' fear that Populists would win some judgeships. Around the same time, attorney and former state representative C. N. Featherston suggested that the people would approve an increase in the number of judges if the judiciary were made elective. That is ultimately what happened. In 1895, the General Assembly passed a constitutional amendment that added three judges to the supreme court and provided for the popular election of all the judges. The voters ratified the amendment the following year, together with another amendment that transferred the selection of the state school commissioner from the governor to the people. In 1897, the legislature passed constitutional amendments that extended popular elections to the superior court judges and solicitors general, but not before amending the bill to provide that the judges and prosecutors would be elected by the voters of the whole state rather than of the judicial circuits. The Populists, who might have elected judges in some circuits under the original plan, initially opposed the change, but they eventually threw in the towel and voted for the bill. The voters ratified the amendments the following year.[56]

The potential impact of the black vote on judicial elections seems not to have played a role in the transition to judicial elections. Through most of the 1880s, the pro-business, reform-minded Bourbon Democrats so thoroughly dominated Georgia politics that they often ran for office unopposed. In 1884, a presidential and gubernatorial election year, the *Savannah Morning News* noted the voters' lack of interest in the contests: "Georgia will attend almost exclusively to gathering her crops."[57] Until the rise of populism at the end of the decade, neither the black vote nor the white vote meant much.

Populism gave black voters an important role in the politics of the 1890s by presenting a serious challenge to the ruling Democrats. But by then blacks were being effectively disenfranchised by a poll tax and the spread of the white primary. Through the latter device—the exclusion of blacks from Democratic primary elections—judicial elections became all-white affairs. Virtually complete disenfranchisement came by way of a constitutional amendment ratified in 1908.[58]

As noted above, Louisiana switched to an appointive system of judicial selection in 1864. The state's convention of 1867–68 chose to restore judicial elections for the district courts. Although judicial selection took a distant back seat to suffrage and other issues at all the southern conventions, the *New Orleans Republican* asserted that "great and grave interests" were involved in the question. If the district judges were made elective, the paper claimed, half of them throughout the state would be opposed to Reconstruction, and Radical Republicans would be hard pressed to elect even one. Since Republicans were "morally certain" of electing their state ticket, the paper urged that district judges be appointed by the governor, subject to confirmation by the senate. That mode of selection would ensure that "men of ability and integrity, of unquestionable loyalty, and zealous friends of reconstruction" would fill the judicial seats.[59]

At the convention, the majority report of the committee to draft a constitution provided for the appointment of the supreme, district, and parish (county) court judges by the governor, with the advice and consent of the senate. The minority report recommended the popular election of district and parish court judges. When the judiciary article came up for debate, an amendment to elect the supreme court was quickly tabled by a vote of 38–32. However, a proposal to elect the district courts provoked debate, eliciting the familiar objections from opponents—that politics would determine not only nominations and elections but also the judgments rendered; that the people did not know the qualifications of the candidates; that experience had shown the superiority of independent judges appointed for life (during good behavior). The amendment died by being tabled, but another amendment to make the district judges elective passed 44–32. Upon ratification of the constitution, Louisiana partially reinstated judicial elections. The state would retain this hybrid system for the rest of the nineteenth century.[60]

As Reconstruction came to an end, many white Louisiana Democrats, especially among the planters and their allies, wanted to cement in the constitution the recovery to dominance that they had made during the preceding few years. Together with this desire to firm up white supremacy, complaints about political corruption and state finances helped fuel a successful movement to hold a constitutional convention. The convention of 1879 addressed all these subjects and more.[61]

Judicial selection was not a major issue, but it did make an appearance. The 1868 constitution had required the legislature to create from twelve to twenty judicial districts, in each of which a district judge would be elected by the voters. Long before the convention met, the *Opelousas Courier*, a staunch opponent of the elective judiciary, thought it obvious to "every unprejudiced mind" that the election of judges could not be entrusted to "a vast population . . . but recently emancipated from slavery . . . for the most part incapable of intelligently exercising that important function of citizenship [the elective franchise], easily impressed by the designing politician and easily corrupted." During the convention, the *St. Landry Democrat* editorialized in favor of an elective judiciary on the grounds of democratic principle and of experience (supreme court judges had been "the most cringing tools . . . to the master that appointed them"). The *Courier* responded by noting that a proposal then pending in the convention would create a slew of new judicial districts, in many of which "an ignorant and semi-barbarous constituency [would] have the controlling voice," placing the "personal and property rights of the whole population" in the hands of judges who held their offices "by the favor or caprice of an ignorant and prejudiced class." But "[i]f these semi-ignorant and semi-barbarous voters are sufficiently strong to elect their judges," riposted the *Democrat*, then they would be strong enough to influence the election of the governors and senators who would appoint the judges and who might be equally "depraved." There was simply no sense, concluded the *Democrat*, to "this howl against the right of the people to elect their judges."[62]

What the *Democrat* did not say, and apparently did not intend, was that the solution to the problem might be the restriction of the franchise of the "semi-civilized" portion of the population. In fact, the paper argued that the convention must not have believed in the existence of such barbarians among the voters because if it had it would have qualified the right of suffrage. In the midst of the exchange between the two papers, the convention settled on retaining elections for the district courts only (except in the parish of Orleans, where the district judges would be appointed by the governor) but expanding the number of districts to a minimum of twenty and a maximum of thirty. "[I]t was only by a compromise," according to the *Democrat*, "that the whole system of judiciary was not made elective."⁶³

By the 1890s, the Democratic ascendancy in Louisiana had become threatened by ballot-box stuffing and other forms of political corruption, divisions within the party, and the rise of populism. One proposed reform that had broad support was the Australian ballot, a standardized paper ballot, printed and distributed by the government, that listed all the candidates for all the offices. The use of a standard ballot, instead of the distinctive party ballots handed out by party operatives, would, it was hoped, preserve the secrecy of the vote and thereby guard against intimidation of the voter. But the Australian ballot also amounted to "a de facto literacy test" that would exclude many blacks and poor whites. Democrats alarmed by the strength of the populist People's Party, with its democratic platform and sometime alliances with blacks and Republicans, began to think seriously about restricting the franchise, as had recently been done in neighboring Mississippi.⁶⁴

In 1894, the legislature passed a joint resolution putting a suffrage amendment on the ballot. Under the amendment, a would-be voter had to be able to read the state constitution in his mother tongue or be the owner of real or personal property located in the state and worth at least two hundred dollars. The reason for the amendment was clear; it was intended to disenfranchise most blacks. Supporters gave other reasons as well, such as the abolition of "ballot box stuffing, bribery and intimidation from the polls," but the "danger of negro domination" outweighed all else. As the date for the referendum on the amendment approached, it became evident that the voters would turn it down, probably because it would have disenfranchised some whites along with blacks. The *Lake Charles Commercial*, endorsing the amendment in the name of white supremacy, conceded that about four thousand whites and eighty-five thousand blacks would be disenfranchised but insisted that the whites "ought to be willing to surrender their right of franchise, if by doing so it will save the State from grave peril, and remove a dark stain from Louisiana's good name."⁶⁵

After the election, the *Commercial* blamed the narrowness of the Democratic victory and the defeat of the suffrage amendment on "bribery and corruption" and poor Democratic Party discipline. The paper was disgusted by the "humiliating spectacle of Democratic office seekers begging the negro for his vote." It was imperative, ran the editorial, "to eliminate the corruptible vote from the body politic." The way to do it was to pass a narrowly restrictive Australian ballot law under which delegates to a constitutional convention would be elected. What the paper wanted was "legal relief from the danger of negro domination," not the increasingly ineffective and reprehensible "shot gun" methods "now in vogue." A constitutional amendment restricting black suffrage, the paper editorialized, was "the only way, for the white man legally and righteously to maintain control of governmental affairs and thus ensure the preservation of white civilization."[66]

In July 1896, the General Assembly put the convention question to the voters. The statute restricted the convention's agenda, prohibiting, among other things, any change that would make the Louisiana Supreme Court elective. The limited discussion of judicial elections at the convention, which met in 1898, therefore focused on the lower courts. The district courts were already elective, and the convention kept them that way. The judiciary committee recommended that the intermediate courts of appeals also be made elective, but in the end, it hardly mattered since the convention effectively abolished those courts except in the parish of Orleans. Elsewhere, beginning in 1904, two district judges in each parish would constitute a court of appeals for the parish.[67]

The real purpose of the convention was to take the vote away from blacks. The president of the convention acknowledged as much in his opening address. Another delegate asserted that the convention "interpreted its mandate from the people to be, to disenfranchise as many negroes and as few whites as possible, without violating the prohibition of the fifteenth amendment to the Federal Constitution." The delegates accomplished their mission through a stringent voter registration requirement, alternative education and property qualifications, what amounted to the white primary, and the adoption of the Australian ballot. An 1897 voter registration law aimed at the uneducated had already slashed the number of both black and white registrants drastically. The new constitution cut the figures even further.[68]

Once elections had been "purified," there was no reason not to have an entirely elective judiciary. In the years after the constitutional convention, the judicial system came under fire for its costliness and inefficiency. At the same time, newspapers gave considerable coverage to various forms of direct democracy, such as the initiative and referendum. In this atmosphere of democratic ferment and criticism of the judiciary, the notion that the judges of the supreme court should be popularly elected seemed natural. The New Orleans *Times-Democrat* editorialized in its favor, and a bill to that effect was introduced in the senate and reported on favorably by the judiciary committee. In mid-1904, when a popular political revolution was sweeping Louisiana, public sentiment in favor of an elective supreme court was all but unanimous. The legislature passed an amendment providing for the election of a chief justice and four associates, each for a term of twelve years. The proposed amendment was one of fifteen to be decided upon by the voters at that fall's election. The amendments dealt with a wide range of issues, including the filling of vacancies in public offices by popular election. In November, the voters were not in a simple "yes" mood; they defeated six of the proposed amendments. However, all those that provided for elections passed easily. In 1906, when another amendment created new courts of appeals, the judges of course were to be elected. Once again, the voters approved by a large majority. Louisiana had finally returned to an entirely elective judiciary but with a shrunken white electorate.[69]

Of all the southern states that readopted judicial elections after the Civil War, Mississippi followed the most frustrating path. The constitutional convention of 1868 had established an appointive judiciary with fairly long terms of office (nine years for supreme court judges, six years for judges of the circuit courts). Thanks to a fierce campaign by Democrats, the constitution lost at the polls. Republicans in Washington blamed the defeat on intimidation of black voters, and President Grant ordered a new election. Mississippi Republicans moderated their extreme position on the disenfranchisement of ex-Confederates, and this time the voters ratified the document.[70]

In the early 1880s, a lively debate took place in the press in which Mississippians griped about the courts and blamed the Republicans for forcing on them a system of gubernatorial appointments. The combatants exchanged all the usual arguments for and against judicial elections, but now the issue of race intruded. Opponents insisted that the enfranchisement of ignorant blacks had made elections untenable. Supporters riposted that with Democrats back in the saddle, there was no need for the appointive system.[71]

Advocates of the elective judiciary raised other points as well. One in Oxford claimed that no court had been held in his county for three years; if the judges had to depend on the electorate, he wrote, they would not have ignored the county. Another contended that judges would not take free passes from the railroads if they had to face the voters. But race trumped all. When a resolution to restore judicial elections received a clear majority of votes in the house, but less than the two-thirds required for a constitutional amendment, newspapers applauded the result, saying that such measures should continue to fail until the suffrage was "purified."[72]

The debate over the elective judiciary took place in a state that was politically divided between "agrarians" and "elite reformers." Both sides sometimes found it necessary to appeal to black voters, and neither was happy about it. To make matters worse, whenever one side succeeded in attracting black support, the other responded with fraud or violence. Eliminating blacks from the political process would clean up elections and perhaps clarify the issues by removing the temptation to decry every issue raised by one's opponents as a threat to white supremacy. Agrarians also wanted to change the apportionment of the legislature, which favored black-majority counties represented by white men not generally sympathetic to their concerns.[73]

In 1888, the legislature passed a bill to allow the voters to decide on the calling of a constitutional convention. Governor Robert Lowry vetoed it. The constitution had been drafted by "aliens," said Lowry, but it was essentially the same document as the 1832 constitution. The people of Mississippi held diverse views "on many exciting questions," he continued, "such as an elective judiciary, prohibition, restriction of suffrage, and limiting the office of Governor to one term." Any or all of them could be addressed by constitutional amendments, without producing the "storm of excitement" that a convention would arouse.[74]

In 1890, with Lowry out of office, the lawmakers passed another convention bill. After the forces favoring judicial elections suffered a decisive defeat, one commentator claimed that the question of judicial selection, having been discussed nonstop for fifteen years, was "more largely the cause of calling the convention than any other." But Judge J. B. Chrisman was undoubtedly right when he said that no subject but suffrage—not taxation of corporations, the governor's terms of office, or even the elective judiciary—had been important enough to call a convention. The people, declared Chrisman, had found the elective franchise, "the bed rock upon which the Republic is based[,] . . . so corrupt that it was about to rot." Denouncing the "perjury, ballot-box stuffing, and intimidation" that had characterized elections, the judge proclaimed that only "a moral idiot would be willing to perpetuate white rule by such methods."[75]

The convention proceeded to disenfranchise blacks and many poor whites through a poll tax, a literacy or "understanding" test (requiring the would-be voter to demonstrate that he understood a constitutional provision read to him), the Australian ballot, and a variety of other devices.[76] With the "purification" of the franchise, judicial elections should have followed. However, conservatives controlled the convention, and the elective judiciary lost by a vote of 75–55. The defeat was a major blow to the agrarians, who had serious grievances against the railroads and believed that appointed judges were beholden to the railroads and other influential economic actors.[77]

The new suffrage reality removed the biggest obstacle to judicial elections. As one well-known figure observed in a letter to the editor, "Under our present elective system, ignorance is eliminated from politics, and the governmental constituency is practically upon an intelligent basis—thus rendering political conditions entirely favorable to an elective judiciary." In 1892, a majority of both legislative chambers voted for a constitutional amendment to restore judicial elections to the circuit and chancery courts, but the senate majority was short of the necessary two-thirds.[78]

Over the next few years, the press devoted considerable space to the subject of judicial selection. In 1895, Anselm J. McLaurin, one of the staunchest supporters of the elective judiciary, was elected governor. In his annual message to the legislature in 1898, he endorsed the cause, and soon afterwards both houses passed a constitutional amendment with votes to spare. At the referendum on the measure in November 1899, a large majority voted to ratify. However, the constitution required a majority of all votes cast at the election, not just a majority of votes cast on the issue. Because so many voters had ignored the issue, the amendment failed. When the legislature nevertheless tried to insert the new language into the constitution, the state supreme court declared the action unconstitutional.[79]

In 1902, the General Assembly passed a constitutional amendment to change the ratification requirement so that a majority of those voting on the issue, not those voting at the election, would be enough to ratify. The amendment lost in a low-turnout referendum. So, the bar facing the elective judiciary remained high. But the issue refused to die. It became a major matter in the gubernatorial campaign of 1903. All four candidates favored judicial elections, but Edmund Noel boasted of his consistent record on the subject, while James K. Vardaman, his chief rival and the eventual winner, had previously, as a legislator, voted against them. In the next legislature, the house and the senate passed different versions of a judicial election amendment but failed to reconcile them. Once again, the popular idea went down to defeat.[80]

When the legislature met again in 1906, the house passed a judicial elections amendment by a wide margin, but the senate vote, once again, came up short of two-thirds. That pushed the matter off to 1908. A constitutional amendment to establish an elective judiciary was, of course, introduced, but another approach to the subject overshadowed and contributed to the demise of the proposal. Representative H. M. Quin, apparently frustrated by the repeated failures to amend the constitution despite popular support, tried to circumvent the amendment process by taking a cue from the election of US senators. Although US senators were then chosen by the state legislatures pursuant to the US Constitution, Mississippi law provided that nominations would be made at primary elections. It was an indirect method of having the voters choose the senators. Quin's bill likewise provided for judicial nominations to be made through a primary election, and it required the governor to appoint the winners. (Given that Mississippi was a one-party state, there was no need to choose between the winners of different primaries.) The supreme court soon let it be known in an "informal" opinion that the proposal was unconstitutional, and it was a "foregone conclusion" that Governor Noel, despite being a steadfast supporter of the elective judiciary, would veto the bill on that basis if it passed. The legislature nevertheless passed the bill, which, as ordinary legislation, needed just a simple majority in each chamber.[81]

Noel held the bill without signing it until the session ended, before it could become law without his signature. That left the legislation in limbo until the 1910 session. Soon after the session opened, he issued his veto. The house failed to muster the votes to override, dooming still another attempt to restore the elective judiciary.[82]

Undaunted, the legislators proceeded to introduce two judicial election resolutions, one allowing for the election of circuit judges and chancellors, the other for the election of supreme court judges. The first passed both chambers without much controversy; the second got through the house only. Upon ratification of the first amendment in November, in yet another election with a low turnout, it seemed that Mississippi would finally have elected judges again.[83]

Mississippi being Mississippi, however, nothing could be so simple. A controversy arose over the constitutionality of the amendment. The constitution prohibited rolling two proposed amendments into one; by providing for the election of both circuit judges and chancellors, the argument went, the amendment that the voters ratified had been invalid from the start. The argument over the amendment's constitutionality went on for over a year. Finally, in January 1912, the supreme court declined to give an advisory opinion on the matter, insisting that until the General Assembly incorporated the amendment into the constitution, and someone challenged the amendment through normal legal proceedings, there was nothing for the court to decide.[84]

The legislature responded by duly inserting the amendment into the constitution and enacting legislation for the election of the judges. Governor Earl L. Brewer vetoed the act, making it impossible to hold the elections regardless of the amendment's validity. At a special session in June, the General Assembly resolved to ask Attorney General Ross Collins to bring a lawsuit to test the constitutionality of the amendment. In September, the press reported that Collins would bring a test case in the chancery court of Lee County. In November came the news that Collins had arranged for a friendly suit in Hinds County that brought into question the right of P. Z. Jones, whom Brewer had appointed a district chancellor in January, to hold his office. The latter court ruled against Collins, but the supreme court reversed the decision and declared the constitutional amendment valid.[85]

After years of missteps, Mississippi once again had judicial elections. But the amendment did not include the supreme court. The lawmakers fixed that at their next session. This time the resolution went through without a ruckus. Supreme court justice Sidney M. Smith, working with a joint legislative committee, drafted a set of six amendments designed to relieve the "congestion" in the court. A news report described the expansion of the court from three to six members as "of course" the "most important." That all the judges would be elected was mentioned only incidentally. The committee called for a special election to ratify the amendments to provide the court with immediate relief and to avoid a problem that had doomed previous amendments: the neglect of constitutional issues at a general election. The latter idea did not fly, and in the November election the voters showed "little interest" in the amendments. Nevertheless, each of the supreme court amendments received more than the half of the total votes cast. (Two other amendments failed to get a majority of all the votes.) The legislature inserted in the amendments into the constitution at its next session in 1916.[86]

Mississippi had finally gone all the way back to its pioneering method of judicial selection. It was, on the surface, a democratic reform of the antebellum type. The arguments pro and con had not changed much, except for one thing—the commitment on all sides to white supremacy.

Before the Civil War, the question of race had not figured in the debates over judicial selection. Most blacks in Mississippi then were slaves, and no blacks could vote. After the war, blacks had to be taken into account. Once fraud, intimidation, and finally the law, as written and administered, had "purified" suffrage, old-fashioned Jacksonian democracy was restored—but for the fact that, with most blacks having been effectively disenfranchised by other means, the poll tax may have discouraged more whites than blacks from voting.[87] With what mixed feelings must the soul of Andrew Jackson have witnessed this simultaneously democratic and undemocratic development in the selection of judges!

NOTES

Introduction

1. Alexis de Tocqueville, *Democracy in America*, trans. Arthur Goldhammer (New York: Library of America, 2004), 310; *Lloyd's Weekly Newspaper*, Mar. 11, 1877, 1; Hans A. Linde, "Elective Judges: Some Comparative Comments," *Southern California Law Review* 61, no. 6 (Sept. 1988): 1995–2006; Adam Liptak, "U.S. voting for judges perplexes other nations," *New York Times*, May 25, 2008, www.nytimes.com/2008/05/25/world/americas/25iht-judge.4.13194819.html (accessed Oct. 27, 2024). Tocqueville finished his tour in February 1832, months before the Mississippi constitutional convention of that year met, so in referring to elected judges he probably had justices of the peace and lay associate trial judges in mind. Today, the United States is one of just five countries that elect some of their judges. "Judicial Selection," Judiciaries Worldwide: A Resource on Comparative Judicial Practice, Federal Judicial Center, https://judiciariesworldwide.fjc.gov/judicial-selection. In 2024, an amendment to the constitution of Mexico made all judges in that country elective. "Judicial reform takes effect after AMLO signs it into law," *Mexico News Daily*, Sept. 16, 2024, https://mexiconewsdaily.com/politics/judicial-reform-bill-takes-effect-in-mexico/ (accessed Oct. 26, 2024).

2. *Mississippian*, Feb. 6, 1832, 1; Feb. 13, 1832, 1; *Ohio H.J.* 568 (Reg. Sess. 1833–34) (declaration made in reference to a statute giving to the voters the power to elect prosecuting attorneys); *Mass. D&P*, 2:708 (Foster Hooper); *Richmond Enquirer*, July 23, 1850, 1; *Kentucky Yeoman*, May 17, 1849, 1; *Daily Union*, Dec. 3, 1849, 2.

3. Andrew L. Kaufman, "The First Judge Cardozo: Albert, Father of Benjamin," *Journal of Law and Religion* 11, no. 1 (Feb. 1994): 302–10; D. B. Eaton, *Should Judges Be Elected? Or the Experiment of an Elective Judiciary in New-York* (1873), 7–8. Jeffreys and Scroggs were seventeenth-century English judges with reputations for venality and other unsavory character traits. Eaton mentioned five judges awaiting trial. Charges against at least one were dropped. Matthew P. Breen, *Thirty Years of New York Politics Up-to-Date* (New York, 1899), 399, 404.

4. Emmet O'Neal, "Reorganizing the State Governments," *Constitutional Review* 2, no. 4 (Oct. 1918): 211–12. O'Neal endorsed the plan put forth a few years earlier by law professor Albert M. Kales. See Albert M. Kales, *Unpopular Government in the United States* (Chicago: University of Chicago Press, 1914), 238–51.

5. Walter Clark, "Constitutional Changes Which Are Foreshadowed," *American Law Review* 30, no. 5 (Oct. 1896): 704–5; Walter Clark, "The Election of Federal Judges by the People," *Arena* 32, no. 180 (Nov. 1904): 459.

6. Act of Mar. 6, 1909, 1909 N.D. Laws 84; Act of Feb. 17, 1911, 1911 Ohio Laws 5; Thomas F. McDonald, "Missouri's Ideal Judicial Selection Law," *Journal of the*

American Judicature Society 24, no. 6 (Apr. 1941): 194–98. California actually preceded Missouri in the adoption of merit selection by a few years, but the plan gave the governor the power to name the nominees, from whom a commission would choose the judge. Charles Gardner Geyh, *Who Is to Judge? The Perennial Debate Over Whether to Elect or Appoint America's Judges* (New York: Oxford University Press, 2019), 39–40.

7. Brennan Center for Justice, Judicial Selection: An Interactive Map, https://www.brennancenter.org/judicial-selection-map (last updated Oct. 11, 2022) (fifty-one jurisdictions, including the District of Columbia); Sanford C. Gordon, "Elected vs. Appointed Judges," Democracy Reform Primer Series, Center for Effective Government, University of Chicago, Feb. 20, 2024. Gordon cites a 2002 source for the percentage of state judges facing elections, but the changes in judicial selection since then have been few. The variety of judicial selection methods today is even wider than suggested here. See Matthew J. Streb, "The Study of Judicial Elections," in *Running for Judge: The Rising Political, Financial, and Legal Stakes of Judicial Elections*, ed. Matthew J. Streb (New York: New York University Press, 2007), 6–8.

8. Michael S. Kang and Joanna M. Shepherd, *Free to Judge: The Power of Campaign Money in Judicial Elections* (Stanford, CA: Stanford University Press, 2023); Chris W. Bonneau and Melinda Gann Hall, *In Defense of Judicial Elections* (New York: Routledge, 2009); Richard Lorren Jolly, "Judges as Politicians: The Enduring Tension of Judicial Elections in the Twenty-First Century," *Notre Dame Law Review Online* 92, no. 1 (2016): 71–86; Laura Zaccari, "Judicial Elections: Recent Developments, Historical Perspective, and Continued Viability," *Richmond Journal of Law and the Public Interest* 8, no. 1 (Summer 2004): 138–56; Ronald M. George, "Why state courts—and state-court elections—matter," *Daedalus* 137, no. 4 (Fall 2008): 110–21; Dmitry Bam, "Voter Ignorance and Judicial Elections," *Kentucky Law Journal* 102, no. 3 (2013–2014): 553–99 (quotation at 557).

9. Most historical overviews published after 2012 rely heavily on Jed Handelsman Shugerman, *The People's Courts: Pursuing Judicial Independence in America* (Cambridge, MA: Harvard University Press, 2012). See, for example, Kang and Shepard, *Free to Judge*, 28–32; Jeffrey S. Sutton, *Who Decides? States as Laboratories of Constitutional Experimentation* (New York: Oxford University Press, 2022), 80–87, 93–94; Geyh, *Who Is to Judge?* 28–33.

10. Regional variations in the adoption of judicial elections were noted at least early as 1888 and are remarked on by modern scholars, but they remain largely unexplored. James Bryce, *The American Commonwealth* (London, UK: 1888), 2:117–18; Sutton, *Who Decides?* 81.

11. Shugerman, *People's Courts*, 278, app. B.

12. J. D. B. DeBow, *The Seventh Census of the United States: 1850* (1853), lxi; DeBow, *Statistical View*, 37. De Bow spelled his last name as two words, but it appears on his census publications as one.

13. DeBow *Statistical View*, 38.

14. *Edgefield Advertiser*, Mar. 20, 1850, 1; *Daily National Era*, Apr. 3, 1854, 2; Joseph C. G. Kennedy, *Preliminary Report on the Eighth Census, 1860* (1862) (usually grouping Maryland and Delaware with the middle states and Kentucky and Missouri with the western states); *Centre Democrat*, Oct. 17, 1861, 2; *New York Herald*, Oct.

18, 1861, 4; *Indiana State Sentinel*, Sept. 29, 1862, 2; Alexander H. Stephens, *A Constitutional View of the Late War between the States; Its Causes, Character, Conduct and Results* (1870), 2:174–75. Even the strongly Unionist *Delaware State Journal and Statesman* of Wilmington referred to Delaware as a southern state. July 18, 1862, 2; Sept. 2, 1862, 1.

15. Jefferson to Samuel Kercheval, July 12, 1816, in *The Writings of Thomas Jefferson*, ed. Albert Ellery Bergh, vol. 15 (Washington, DC: Thomas Jefferson Memorial Association of the United States, 1907), 36.

16. Dwight Loomis and J. Gilbert Calhoun, eds., *The Judicial and Civil History of Connecticut* (Boston: The Boston History Company, 1895), 102, 126–30. In 1890, chief judge and former governor of Connecticut Charles B. Andrews said in a speech that after 1784, when the members of the council constituted most of the supreme court of errors, it became "the subject of complaint, that the members of this court were chosen with reference to their qualifications as legislators rather than as judges." "The Supreme Court of Connecticut and the Saturday Night Club of New York," *Medico-Legal Journal* 7, no. 4 (1889–90): 575.

17. Shugerman, *People's Courts*, 27–28.

18. Jefferson to Kercheval, in *Writings of Jefferson*, 34; Robert M. Ireland, *The County Courts in Antebellum Kentucky* (Lexington, KY: University Press of Kentucky, 1972), 1; Act of Feb. 25, 1837, 1836–37 Ill. Laws 176, 177–78; Scott v. Crow, 5 Ill. 183 (1843) (describing the statutory power as ministerial); *Pittsfield Sun*, Mar. 8, 1860, 3; Surrency, *Creation of a Judicial System*, 85–88; Albert Berry Saye, *A Constitutional History of Georgia, 1732–1945* (Athens: University of Georgia Press, 1948), 180.

19. Ohio Const. of 1802, art. III, § 11; Act of Feb. 18, 1804, 1803–4 Ohio Laws 235. Pennsylvania's first constitution provided for the election of justices of the peace. Pa. Const. of 1776, Plan or Frame of Gov't, § 30. Under the next constitution, however, the justices were appointed by the governor. Pa. Const. of 1790 art. V, § 10.

20. Marshall to Charles Simms, June 16, 1784, in *The Papers of John Marshall*, ed. Herbert A. Johnson, vol. 1, *Correspondence and Papers, November 10, 1775–June 23, 1788* (Chapel Hill: University of North Carolina Press, 1974), 124; *Report on the memorial of the Council and House of Representatives of the Territory of Iowa, praying an amendment of the organic law of the Territory*, S. Rep. 37, serial 376, 1 (1841). See also Glenn McNair, *Criminal Injustice: Slaves and Free Blacks in Georgia's Criminal Justice System* (Charlottesville: University of Virginia Press, 2009), 85–87 (describing justices of the peace and their work).

21. Ind. Const. of 1816, art. V, § 7; Mich. Const. of 1835, art. VI, § 4; *Evansville Weekly Journal*, Jan. 7, 1848, 2; *Indiana State Sentinel*, May 23, 1850, 1; Thomas M. Cooley, "Address on Laying the Corner Stone of the New Court House for Lenawee County at Adrian, June 28, 1884," in *Pioneer Collections: Report of the Pioneer Society of the State of Michigan*, 7 (1886): 530.

22. Reynolds v. Sims, 377 U.S. 533, 555 (1964).

23. David N. Mayer, *The Constitutional Thought of Thomas Jefferson* (Charlottesville: University of Virginia Press, 1994), 56–57, 63–64. See Thomas Jefferson, *Notes on the State of Virginia* 2nd Am. ed. (1794), app. 2, 313–332 (Jefferson's proposed constitution for Virginia).

24. Elizabeth Cady Stanton, "Declaration of Sentiments," in *Treacherous Texts: U.S. Suffrage Literature, 1846-1946*, ed. Mary Chapman and Angela Mills (New Brunswick, NJ: Rutgers University Press, 2011), 20–22; *Proceedings of the Ohio Women's Convention, Held at Salem, April 19th and 20th, 1850; With an Address by J. Elizabeth Jones* (1850), 6–8, 10, 14, 16–18, 25.

25. Daniel Walker Howe, *What Hath God Wrought: The Transformation of America, 1815-1848* (New York: Oxford University Press, 2007), 4–5; Gregory S. Alexander, *Commodity and Propriety: Competing Visions of Property in American Legal Thought, 1776-1970* (Chicago: University of Chicago Press, 1997), 101; Joshua A. Lynn, *Preserving the White Man's Republic: Jacksonian Democracy, Race, and the Transformation of American Conservatism* (Charlottesville: University Press of Virginia, 2019), 5, 28–29.

26. James D. Richardson, comp., *A Compilation of the Messages and Papers of the Presidents* (Washington, DC: Bureau of National Literature and Art, 1910), 2:1012; Jackson to John Quincy Adams, Aug. 26, 1821, in *American State Papers: Miscellaneous*, vol. 2 (1834), 802; Richardson, *Messages and Papers*, 2:1153; C. Edward Merriam, *A History of American Political Theories* (1903; repr. New York: MacMillan, 1915), 196–99; *Kentucky Yeoman*, July 12, 1849, 2.

27. Richardson, *Messages and Papers*, 3:1547, 1561.

28. Richardson, *Messages and Papers*, 2:1011; *Chicago Democrat*, July 8, 1835, quoted in Larry D. Kramer, *The People Themselves: Popular Constitutionalism and Judicial Review* (New York: Oxford University Press, 2004), 196; *Evening Post*, Apr. 15, 1835, 2.

29. Richardson, *Messages and Papers*, 2:1012; Robert V. Remini, *Andrew Jackson and the Course of American Freedom, 1822-1832* (New York: Harper & Row, 1981), 189–90; *United States Telegraph* (Washington, DC), Oct. 21, 1826, quoted in W. Stephen Belko, *The Invincible Duff Green: Whig of the West* (Columbia: University of Missouri Press, 2006), 80.

Chapter 1: The Southern Roots of the Elective Judiciary

1. Vt. Const. of 1777, ch. 2, § 27; An Act Directing County Elections, 1781 Vt. Laws (Feb. sess., unpaginated); Vt. Const. of 1793, ch. 2, § 43. Pennsylvania dropped the council of censors in its constitution of 1789, but Vermont retained it until 1870. Paul S. Gillies and D. Gregory Sanford, eds., *Records of the Council of Censors of the State of Vermont* (Montpelier, VT: Vermont Secretary of State, 1991), xin2, xvii.

2. Gillies and Sanford, *Records*, 58; Vt. Const. of 1786, ch. 2, §§ 8–9.

3. Ga. Const. of 1798 art. IV, § 1 (electors); art. I, § 7; art. II, §§ 2 (governor), 12 (secretary of state, surveyor general, treasurer); art. III, §§ 1 (superior and inferior courts), 4 (inferior court justices), 5 (justices of the peace); Act of Dec. 22, 1835, 1835 Ga. Acts49; Ga. Const. of 1798, art. III, § 1 (amended 1835); Act of Dec. 10, 1845, 1845 Ga. Acts 18. In the absence of a supreme court, a convention of superior court judges partially filled its place. See Beverly B. Bates, "Two Courts for the Price of One: The Superior Courts of Georgia and the Convention of Judges, 1797-1845," *Georgia Journal of Southern Legal History*, 2, nos. 1 & 2 (Spring-Summer 1993): 219–46.

4. Act of Feb. 9, 1797, 1797 Ga. Acts 1, 11; Ga. Const. of 1798 art. III, §§ 5, 1. The constitution did not specify who elected the superior court judges, but they had always

been chosen by the General Assembly and continued to be so. Saye, *Constitutional History*, 161.

5. Act of 1812 (no date indicated), 1812 Ga. Acts 125, 126; Ga. Const. of 1798, art. III, §§ 4, 5 (amended 1812). The amendment process did not require a popular referendum, so the constitutional amendment took effect when the legislature passed it for the second time with the necessary majority.

6. Saye, *Constitutional History*, 165–66; Surrency, *Creation of a Judicial System*, 92; Ethel K. Ware, *A Constitutional History of Georgia* (New York: Columbia University Press, 1947), 85n24. The authors of one historical essay on the Georgia constitution do not even mention the amendment. Melvin B. Hill Jr. and G. LaVerne Williamson Hill, *The Georgia State Constitution*, 2nd ed. (New York: Oxford University Press, 2018). Jed Handelsman Shugerman suggests (1) that the legislature wanted to protect a recent, popular debt-relief law from a constitutional challenge by making judges dependent on the voters, and (2) that the US Supreme Court's recent decision in *Fletcher v. Peck*, with an opinion written by Federalist chief justice John Marshall, "reopened the wounds" of the Yazoo land scandal and that Georgia's political leaders wanted a way to get Federalist judges off their state's bench. Jed Handelsman Shugerman, *The People's Courts: Pursuing Judicial Independence in America* (Cambridge, MA: Harvard University Press, 2012), 60–62. In either case, making the county courts elective would hardly have solved the problem as long as superior court judges had the final say. See Ga. Const. of 1798 art. III, § 1; Grimball v. Ross (1808) and State v. Corporation of Savannah (1809), in Thomas U. P. Charlton, *Reports of Cases Argued and Determined in the Superior Courts of the Eastern District of the State of Georgia* (1824; repr., Atlanta: Franklin-Turner, 1907), 175, 235.

7. *Augusta Chronicle and Gazette of the State*, Sept. 26, 1795, 1; *Republican and Savannah Evening Ledger*, Nov. 14, 1811, 2.

8. Act of Dec. 4, 1799, 1799 Ga. Acts (Nov. sess.) 7, 8; Surrency, *Creation of a Judicial System*, 85–88; McNair, *Criminal Injustice*, 87–88; *Columbus Enquirer*, Nov. 13, 1849, 2. Governor Towns's remarks were occasioned by the passage of a law giving inferior courts jurisdiction to try slaves for capital offenses.

9. William O. Lynch, "The Influence of Population Movements on Missouri before 1861," *Missouri Historical Review* 16, no. 4 (July 1922): 509. See generally Floyd Calvin Shoemaker, *Missouri's Struggle for Statehood, 1804–1821* (Jefferson City, MO: Hugh Stevens, 1916).

10. Mo. Const. of 1820 art. III, §§ 2, 4, 6, 10. In Virginia, for example, John Randolph fulminated against "King Numbers" at the 1829–30 constitutional convention. Va. *P&D*, 320. Opponents of equal representation at the state's 1850–51 constitutional convention continued to insist that "property was entitled to protection, and to protection to be secured by representation." Va. *P&D*, 284 (Robert E. Scott).

11. Mo. Const. of 1820 art. III, § 31 (treasurer); art. IV, § 3 (governor), 12 (auditor), 14 (lieutenant governor), 21 (secretary of state), 23 (sheriffs and coroners); art V, § 18 (attorney general). The wording of the section on sheriffs and coroners could have meant that the legislature had authority to regulate the time and manner of election rather than the method of selection itself. The General Assembly quickly embodied the popular election of sheriffs and coroners in statute. Act of Oct. 7, 1820, 1820 Mo. Laws 4.

12. Mo. Const. of 1820 art. V, §§ 1 (supreme court, circuit courts, chancellor), 7

(circuit courts), 12 (inferior courts), 13 (appointment during good behavior), 17 (justices of the peace).

13. Act of Nov. 28, 1820, 1820 Mo. Laws 41, 43; Act of Oct. 31, 1820, 1820 Mo. Laws 6. The act of November 28 established county courts with probate jurisdiction and broad administrative powers over county revenue, elections, roads, bridges, and so on. Within a few years the legislature would confer probate jurisdiction on separate probate courts (appointed by the governor) and leave local government to county courts made up of justices of the peace. Act of Jan. 7, 1825, *Laws of the State of Missouri*, 2 vols. (St. Louis, 1825), 1:269, 271. In 1825, the General Assembly empowered the governor to appoint justices of the peace upon petition of the inhabitants of townships. Act of Jan. 4, 1825, *Laws of Missouri*, 1:469. Ten years later, the legislature provided for the popular election of justices of the peace. Act of Mar. 20, 1835, Mo. R.S. (1840), 344.

14. Marvin R. Cain, *Lincoln's Attorney General: Edward Bates of Missouri* (Columbia: University of Missouri Press, 1965), 1–8, 14–15.

15. Perry McCandless, "McNair, Alexander (1775–1826)," in *Dictionary of Missouri Biography*, ed. Lawrence O. Christensen et al. (Columbia: University of Missouri Press, 1999), 538–40; Walter B. Stevens, "Alexander McNair," *Missouri Historical Review* 17, no. 1 (Oct. 1922): 3–21.

16. Stevens, "McNair," 10; Shoemaker, *Missouri's Struggle for Statehood*, 265–67, 269, 277. Several sources state that McNair favored an elective judiciary, but none provides a source for the assertion. Cain, *Bates*, 13; Perry McCandless, *A History of Missouri, 1820–1860*, vol. 2 of *A History of Missouri*, ed. William E. Parrish (Columbia: University of Missouri Press, 1972), 10; William E. Parrish, Lawrence O. Christensen, and Brad D. Lookingbill, *Missouri: The Heart of the Nation*, 4th ed. (Hoboken, NJ: Wiley-Blackwell, 2020), 69. The skimpy journal of the convention's proceedings makes no mention of an effort to create an elective judiciary. See *Mo. Jour.* (1820).

17. Mo. Const. of 1820 art. XII.

18. Shoemaker, *Missouri's Struggle for Statehood*, 278–80; Lawrence M. Friedman, *A History of American Law*, 4th ed. (New York: Oxford University Press, 2019), 22–23, 118–19. The legislators understood the constitution to require a two-thirds majority of all members elected, but the supreme court would later decide otherwise. State v. McBride, 4 Mo. 303 (1836). The house at that time had forty-three members, meaning that an amendment had to receive twenty-nine favorable votes in order to go to the senate. The votes on judicial salaries, tenure, and appointment were 27–9; on the chancellor's office, 25–10, on supreme court sessions, 22–13; and on removal by address and election of sheriffs and coroners, 18–16. As Friedman explains, hostility toward chancellors in colonial days stemmed from the chancellors' close association with royal authority. In nineteenth-century Missouri, the complaints arose from the expense of maintaining separate chancery (equity) courts and from the complexity of the system of multiple courts each having its own intricate procedural rules. See *Missouri Intelligencer*, July 30, 1822, 1, and *Metropolitan*, July 6, 1847, 1 (letter to the editor from federal judge R. W. Wells).

19. Shoemaker, *Missouri's Struggle for Statehood*, 280–81.

20. Mo. Const. of 1820 art. III, §26; Robert Pierce Forbes, *The Missouri Compromise and Its Aftermath: Slavery and the Meaning of America* (Chapel Hill: University of North Carolina Press, 2007), 110–18; Shoemaker, *Missouri's Struggle for Statehood*, 308–18.

21. W. J. Hamilton, "The Relief Movement in Missouri, 1820–1822," *Missouri Historical Review* 22, no. 1 (Oct. 1927): 80–81; Murray N. Rothbard, *The Panic of 1819: Reactions and Policies* (New York: Columbia University Press, 1962), 42–47; Shoemaker, *Missouri's Struggle for Statehood*, 318.

22. Mo. S.J. 36–37, 57–59 (Reg. Sess. 1828–29); Res. (undated), 1832–33 Mo. Laws 3; McCandless, *History of Missouri*, 97; John Vollmer Mering, *The Whig Party in Missouri* (Columbia: University of Missouri Press, 1967), 19–20. Mering, citing pages 57–59 of the 1828–29 senate journal and 131–39 of the 1828–29 house journal, states that an amendment for the popular election of circuit court judges was also proposed in that session. Neither the senate nor the house journal says anything about popular elections at the cited pages.

On November 28, 1834, with twenty-two members voting, the senate passed ten of the twelve proposed constitutional amendments by votes of 15–7, just enough to meet the constitutional majority of two-thirds. The senators voted for the amendments providing for the popular election of circuit court judges 14–8. Mo. S.J. 59–63 (Reg. Sess. 1834–35). The full senate at that time consisted of twenty-four members. Two-thirds of that number would have been sixteen. When the amendments were challenged in court, the supreme court ruled that the constitution required a favorable vote of two-thirds of the members present, not two-thirds of the members elected. State v. McBride, 4 Mo. 303 (1836). The house journal was unavailable to the author, but according to McCandless "the amendments" received a favorable vote of 64 percent in the house. McCandless, *History of Missouri*, 97. The amendment for the election of court clerks passed the house with 69 percent of the vote (49–22). Mo. R.S. (1840), 34.

23. Act of Jan. 17, 1831, 1830–31 Mo. Laws 30 (also providing for the election of township constables); Act of Mar. 20, 1835, *Mo. R.S. (1840)*, 344; Act of Feb. 11, 1841, 1840–41 Mo. Laws 54, 55; Act of Mar. 15, 1845, 1844–45 Mo. Laws 57, 58; Act of Feb. 6, 1847, 1846–47 Mo. Laws 27, 28–29; Act of Mar. 12, 1849, 1848–49 Mo. Laws 428.

24. Thomas P. Abernethy, *The South in the New Nation, 1789–1819* vol. 4 of *A History of the South*, ed. Wendell Holmes Stephenson and E. Merton Coulter (Baton Rouge: Louisiana State University Press, 1961), 444–75; DeBow, *Statistical View*, 45 (excluding the future state of Alabama for 1810); United States Census Bureau, *Guide to 2010 State and Local Census Geography*, https://www.census.gov/geographies/reference-files/2010/geo/state-local-geo-guides-2010/mississippi.html; Edwin A. Miles, *Jacksonian Democracy in Mississippi* (Chapel Hill: University of North Carolina Press, 1960), 18–19; Susan Dabney Smedes, *Memorials of a Southern Planter* (1887), 67.

25. Miss. Const. of 1817 art. III, §§ 1 (qualified electors include free white male adult citizens enrolled in the militia or who paid a tax), 7 (property qualification for representative), 8 (house apportionment based on the free white population of a county, city, or town), 10 (senate apportionment based on the free white taxable population in a district); 14 (property qualification for senator); art. IV, §§ 3 (property qualification for governor), 14 (secretary of state), 17 (General Assembly to appoint all officers except where constitution provides otherwise), 18 (property qualification for lieutenant governor), 24, (sheriffs, coroners), 25 (treasurer, auditor); art. V, §§ 2 (supreme and superior court judges), 3 (district court judges), 8 (justices of the peace), 9 (good behavior), 11 (court clerks), 14 (attorney general and district attorneys). Pursuant to Article V, §§ 7 and 8, the legislature

established probate courts (appointed by the legislature) and provided for the appointment of justices of the peace (by the governor on recommendation of the county courts). A county court consisted of the probate judge and two associates appointed by the governor. *Miss. R.C.* 19, 27, 71.

26. Act of Feb. 3, 1818, 1817–18 Miss. Acts 219, 223; *Miss. R.C.* 285, 423; Alexander Keyssar, *The Right to Vote: The Contested History of Democracy in the United States*, rev. ed. (New York: Basic Books, 2009), 25. Keyssar's source indicates that some towns had universal white male suffrage, or even suffrage for all free adult males regardless of color, for *municipal* elections. It does not suggest that local election officials ignored the taxpaying requirement for state elections. R. H. Thompson, "Suffrage in Mississippi," *Publications of the Mississippi Historical Society*, vol. 1 (Oxford: Mississippi Historical Society, 1898), 32–34, 36–37. However, another commentator argues that enforcement of the taxpayer requirement elsewhere was lax. Kenneth J. Winkle, "Ohio's Informal Polling Place: Nineteenth-Century Suffrage in Theory and Practice," in *The Pursuit of Public Power: Political Culture in Ohio, 1787–1861*, ed. Jeffrey P. Brown and Andrew R. L. Cayton (Kent, OH: Kent State University Press, 1994), 69, 178–79.

27. Keyssar, *Right to Vote*, 25; *Miss. H.J.* 91 (Reg. Sess. 1830); W. B. Hamilton, "Mississippi 1817: A Sociological and Economic Analysis," *Journal of Mississippi History* 78, nos. 1–2 (Spring-Summer 2016 [originally published 1967]): 7 figures on age distribution for a slightly earlier period but noting that in 1830 45 percent of the nation's population was under sixteen and that Mississippi's population was younger than the nation's); Elizabeth Gaspar Brown, "Husband and Wife—Memorandum on the Mississippi Woman's Law of 1839," *Michigan Law Review* 42, no. 6 (June 1944): 1110–21; Joseph A. Custer, "The Three Waves of Married Women's Property Acts in the Nineteenth Century with a Focus on Mississippi, New York and Oregon," *Ohio Northern University Law Review* 40, no. 2 (2014): 401–5. One study suggests that the poll tax was not sufficiently burdensome to significantly depress voting. In various southern states, the poll tax on white men was not more than one dollar and, in most cases, well under a dollar. Brian Sawers, "The Poll Tax before Jim Crow," *American Journal of Legal History* 57, no. 2 (June 2017): 179–82. (The correct citation for the statute that Sawers cites, at page 181, for the one-dollar Louisiana poll tax is Act of May 3, 1847, 1847 La. Acts 164, 165–66.) In 1844, Louisiana Democrats tried unsuccessfully to establish a poll tax with the aim of *expanding* the electorate ahead of the vote for delegates to the coming constitutional convention. William H. Adams, *The Whig Party of Louisiana* (Lafayette: University of Southwestern Louisiana, 1973), 118.

28. Shugerman, *People's Courts*, 68.

29. Miss. Const. of 1817 art. III, §§ 8–10.

30. *Southern Luminary*, Dec. 27, 1824, 3; *Natchez Gazette*, Sept. 15, 1830, 3. Natchez newspapers complained that the city had suffered from an undercount in the 1826 census, most likely because the census was taken during the "sickly season" when many inhabitants escaped to safer climes. *Natchez Gazette*, Jan. 28, 1826, 2; *Ariel*, Jan. 30, 1826, 221.

31. *The American Almanac and Repository of Useful Knowledge, for the Year 1832* (Boston, 1831), 236.

32. Winbourne Magruder Drake, "The Mississippi Constitutional Convention of

1832," *Journal of Southern History* 23, no. 3 (Aug. 1957): 355–56; Miss. Const. of 1817 art. V, §§ 2, 5; Miles, *Jacksonian Democracy*, 35–36; Act of June 29, 1822, in *Miss. R.C.*, 149; John Hebron Moore, "Local and State Governments in Antebellum Mississippi," *Journal of Mississippi History* 44, no. 2 (May 1982): 105–6. The county courts were created by statute (Act of June 28, 1822, 1822 Miss. Laws [adj. sess.] 10) and could have been modified or abolished altogether by statute.

33. Quitman to J. F. H. Claiborne, Oct. 18, 1830, in J. F. H. Claiborne, *Life and Correspondence of John A. Quitman* (1860), 1:101; *Natchez Gazette*, Oct. 20, 1830, 2. Quitman protested against judges' "decid[ing] upon their own errors," but he could not have been referring to their hearing of appeals from their own decisions. Mississippi's constitution prohibited the judge "whose decision is under consideration" from participating with the other superior court judges in reviewing the case as the supreme court. Miss. Const. of 1817 art. V, § 2.

34. Act of Dec. 15, 1830, 1830 Miss. Laws 38; *Natchez*, July 1, 1831, 214.

35. Drake, "Mississippi Constitutional Convention," 358; *Advocate & Register*, Dec. 23, 1831, 3; *Mississippian*, Feb. 6, 1832, 1; Feb. 13, 1832, 1; Feb. 27, 1832, 1. For Redd's own statement of his political philosophy, when running for secretary of state, see his letter in the *Vicksburg Register*, Sept. 3, 1835, 2. Many years later, Henry S. Foote claimed to have been the first to publicly urge the popular election of judges, although by then he had come to regard the innovation as a mistake. Henry S. Foote, *Casket of Reminiscences* (1874), 347–48.

36. *Mississippian*, Feb. 20, 1832, 3; *Natchez*, May 22, 1832, 163. The point about life tenure was related by an opponent of the elective judiciary who was summarizing the arguments of its supporters.

37. *Natchez*, May 22, 1832, 163.

38. *Advocate & Register*, Sept. 30, 1831, 3; Nov. 11, 1831, 2; Sept. 23, 1831, 2; Nov. 4, 1831, 3.

39. *Natchez*, May 22, 1832, 163; June 8, 1832, 181–82.

40. John A. Quitman, "To the Electors of Adams County," in Claiborne, *Life and Correspondence*, 1:98, 116, 118–19. Quitman went on to point out the flaws of elections, in much the same manner as other, future skeptics.

41. Drake, "Mississippi Constitutional Convention," 361–62.

42. Drake, "Mississippi Constitutional Convention," 359–60; *Advocate & Register*, Sept. 20, 1832, 3; Sept. 27, 1832, 2, 3.

43. *Advocate & Register*, Sept. 27, 1832, 2. The report as printed in the *Advocate & Register* inadvertently omits the word "governor" in relation to the appointment of the supreme court judges and chancellor, but that is clearly what Quitman intended. See Quitman, "To the Electors," 123–24.

44. *Advocate & Register*, Sept. 27, 1832, 3.

45. *Advocate & Register*, Oct. 4, 1832, 2; Oct. 25, 1832, 3.

46. *Advocate & Register*, Sept. 20, 1832, 3; Oct. 4, 1832, 3; Oct. 10, 1832, 2; Drake, "Mississippi Constitutional Convention," 364. While running for convention delegate, Howard told his constituents that he favored the direct election of public officers "in almost all cases." He apparently excepted the judges of the supreme court from the general rule. Howard favored "a distinct and separate" supreme court, but he advocated

the election of circuit court judges without mentioning his preferred method of choosing supreme court judges. N. G. Howard, "To the People of Rankin County," broadside, July 2, 1832, Mississippi Department of Archives and History, https://da.mdah.ms.gov/series/broadsides/detail/520465 (accessed Nov. 25, 2022).

47. Jt. Res. of Feb. 25, 1843, 1842–43 Mo. Laws 9; Dennis K. Boman, *Lincoln's Resolute Unionist: Hamilton Gamble, Dred Scott Dissenter and Missouri's Civil War Governor* (Baton Rouge: Louisiana State University Press, 2006), 28–29; *Boon's Lick Times*, Jan. 11, 1845, 2.

48. Priscilla Bradford, "The Missouri Constitutional Controversy of 1845," *Missouri Historical Review* 32, no. 1 (Oct. 1937): 35–40.

49. McCandless, *History of Missouri*, 239; Mering, *Whig Party*, 135; Act of Feb. 27, 1843, 1842–43 Mo. Laws 26; *Niles' National Register*, Oct. 12, 1844, 82; *Boon's Lick Times*, Nov. 30, 1844, 2; Dec. 28, 1844, 2.

50. *Democratic Banner*, Feb. 8, 1845, 3; Aug. 2, 1845, 4.

51. *Democratic Banner*, Feb. 8, 1845, 3.

52. *Mo. Jour. (1845)*, 47–49, 80. On Leslie, see Frederick W. Baldwin, *Biography of the Bar of Orleans County, Vermont* (1886), 94–96. For his Democratic affiliation, see *Boon's Lick Times*, Aug. 16, 1845, 2.

53. *Mo. Jour. (1845)*, 173, 176, 181–83, 185–86. For Bevitt's political affiliation, see *Democratic Banner*, May 31, 1845, 2.

54. *Mo. Jour. (1845)*, 193–94, 197–98. The motion to reconsider may have been based on the number of absences at the original vote. Seven members had been absent without leave, three with leave, and two due to illness (p. 183). At least one paper blamed absenteeism for the defeat of an earlier attempt to secure the popular election of judges. On Saturday, December 20, when the convention took up Leslie's resolution, a delegate moved a substitute of five sections that provided for the popular election of all judges. The convention tabled it. (pp. 171–72). The *Boon's Lick Times*, which reported the vote to table as 32–29, wrote that the absences had caused the defeat of judicial election but that the motion was expected to "prevail by a small majority" on reconsideration. *Boon's Lick Times*, Dec. 27, 1845, 2.

55. Mo. Const. of 1846 (proposed) art. V, §§ 11, 5. For the proposed constitution, see *Mo. Jour. (1845)*, appendix, 38–56.

56. Bradford, "Missouri Constitutional Controversy," 50–51; *Democratic Banner*, Mar. 28, 1846, 1; *Boon's Lick Times*, Feb. 7, 1846, 2. Critics of the proposed constitution also pointed out a number of other perceived flaws. See the series of articles by "Sanco" in *Boon's Lick Times*, Feb. 7, 1846, 2; Feb. 14, 1846, 2; Feb. 21, 1846, 2.

57. *Boon's Lick Times*, Sept. 12, 1846, 2; Feb. 20, 1847, 2; Mo. S.J. 449–50 (Reg. Sess. 1846–47); Constitutional Amendments, 1846–47 Mo. Laws 4–6; Mo. H.J. 99–100 (Reg. Sess. 1848–49); Mo. S.J. 112 (Reg. Sess. 1848–49); Resolutions, 1848–49 Mo. Laws 8–10.

58. *Glasgow Weekly Times*, Jan. 18, 1849, 2; Mo. H.J. 273, 283, 331, 441 (Reg. Sess. 1848–49); Mo. S.J. 274–76, 363–64 (Reg. Sess. 1848–49); Resolutions, 1848–49 Mo. Laws 3–5.

59. Mo. H.J. 243–44 (Reg. Sess. 1850–51); Mo. S.J. 346 (Reg. Sess. 1850–51); Act of Mar. 3, 1851, 1850–51 Mo. Laws 214 (providing for the election of judges and state executive officers).

60. *N.Y. P&D* 160–61, 307–84; N.Y. Const. of 1846 art. VI, §§ 2, 12, 14, 18; Mich. Const. of 1835 art. VI, § 4; Act of Apr. 15, 1833, in *Mich. Laws* 3:1020, 1024; *Mich. R.S.* 377; Iowa Const. of 1844 (proposed) art. VI, § 4; Iowa Const. of 1846 art. V, § 4. For the dates of ratification in Iowa and New York, see p. 257, note 13.

61. Shugerman, *People's Courts*, 73–74.

62. The composition of state legislatures reflects the mobility of the American population. Around 1830, nearly all the members of the Ohio General Assembly had been born in other states or countries. As late as 1856, fewer than half of Ohio's legislators were natives. And Ohioans themselves kept moving; nearly 20 percent of Indiana's legislators in the period 1851–89 were born in Ohio. David M. Gold, *Democracy in Session: A History of the Ohio General Assembly* (Athens: Ohio University Press, 2009), 49–50. The first territorial legislature of Iowa (1838) was young and of various nativities. The thirty-nine members of the assembly came from a dozen different states, half from the South, all born east of the Mississippi. J. A. Swisher, "The First Territorial Assembly," *The Palimpsest* 20, no. 2 (Feb. 1939): 33–34. See also Guy-Harold Smith, "The Settlement and the Distribution of the Population in Wisconsin," *Transactions of the Wisconsin Academy of Sciences, Arts and Letters* 24 (Madison, WI: The Academy, 1929): 53–107 (reviewing the rapid settlement of Wisconsin by immigrants from many northern and southern states and foreign countries, especially Germany, and movement within the state); Don Harrison Doyle, *The Social Order of a Frontier Community: Jacksonville, Illinois, 1825–70* (Urbana: University of Illinois Press, 1978), 95–97; Frank Lawrence Owsley, *Plain Folk of the Old South* (Baton Rouge: Louisiana State University Press, 1949), 58–60; *A Preservation Plan for St. Louis, Part I: Historic Contexts*, 9: Peopling St. Louis: the Immigration Experience, https://www.stlouis-mo.gov/government/departments/planning/cultural-resources/preservation-plan/Part-I-Peopling-St-Louis.cfm (accessed Oct. 19, 2024).

63. Shugerman, *People's Courts*, 76.

64. Edwin D. Bevitt, quoted in Bradford, "Missouri Constitutional Controversy," 41; *Democratic Banner*, Aug. 2, 1845, 1.

Chapter 2: The South's Northern Tier

1. Donald F. Carmony, *Indiana, 1816–50: The Pioneer Era*, vol. 2 of *History of Indiana* (Indianapolis: Indiana Historical Bureau & Indiana Historical Society, 1998), 403–06; Shugerman, *People's Courts*, 84–86, 121–22, 125; Emily Zackin, "State Constitutional Details and America's Positive Rights," in *Modern Constitutions*, ed. Rogers M. Smith and Richard R. Beeman (Philadelphia: University of Pennsylvania Press, 2020), 99.

2. See David M. Gold, "Judicial Elections and Judicial Review: Testing the Shugerman Thesis," *Ohio Northern University Law Review* 40, no. 1 (2013): 44–48.

3. Samuel Shapiro, "The Conservative Dilemma: The Massachusetts Constitutional Convention of 1853," *New England Quarterly* 33, no. 2 (June 1960): 207–08; Samuel Eliot Morison, *A History of the Constitution of Massachusetts* (Boston: Wright & Potter, 1917), 41–44.

4. Gillies and Sanford, *Records*, 509–10.

244　Notes to Pages 40–43

5. Lowell H. Harrison, *Kentucky's Road to Statehood* (Lexington: University Press of Kentucky, 1992), 7–8, 74, 96–97, 103–14.

6. Harry S. Laver, "'Chimney Corner Constitutions': Democratization and Its Limits in Frontier Kentucky," *Register of the Kentucky Historical Society* 95, no. 4 (Autumn 1997): 339–40, 365–66; Ky. Const. of 1792 art. III, § 1 (suffrage); art. I, § 6 (apportionment of house); art. VI, § 1 (sheriffs and coroners); art. II, § 2 (election of governor); art. I, §§ 10–15 (election of senators); art. II, § 8 (appointment of public officers); art. VI, § 7 (treasurer).

7. *Ky. Stat.*, 1:93–94 (Act of June 28, 1792), 373 (Act of Dec. 17, 1796), 63–65 (Act of June 26, 1792). The act of June 26, 1792, said that the tax commissioners "shall be appointed" without specifying by whom, but the legislature quickly made it clear that the appointments were to be made by the county courts (p. 89, Act of June 28, 1792).

8. Lowell H. Harrison, "John Breckinridge and the Kentucky Constitution of 1799," *Register of the Kentucky Historical Society* 57, no. 3 (July 1959): 209; Robert M. Ireland, *The Kentucky State Constitution*, 2nd ed. (New York: Oxford University Press, 2012), 6–7.

9. Ky. Const. of 1799 art. II, §§ 8 (suffrage), 12 (apportionment of senate), 14 (suffrage, election of senators); art. III, §§ 2 (election of governor), 3 (term of governor), 25 (veto).

10. Ky. Const. of 1792 art. III, § 2 (voting by ballot); Ky. Const. of 1799 art. VI, § 16 (voting *viva voce*, or orally); art. VII, § 1 (emancipation); art. II, § 6 (apportionment).

11. Ky. Const. of 1799 art. IV, § 5 (county courts); art. III, § 31 (sheriffs); art. IV, § 8 (county officers); art. IX, § 1 (requiring a majority of the elected members each house to pass a law calling for a convention within the first twenty days of a regular legislative session, followed by approval of the call by a majority of all citizens eligible to vote for representatives in two successive referenda); Schedule § 6 (constitution effective without ratification).

12. Bennett H. Young, *History and Texts of the Three Constitutions of Kentucky* (1890), 51; *Examiner*, June 2, 1849, 3; Ky. Const. of 1799 art. IX, § 1; Harold D. Tallant, *Evil Necessity: Slavery and Political Culture in Antebellum Kentucky* (Lexington: University Press of Kentucky, 2003), 134.

13. Tallant, *Evil Necessity*, 137–38; *Louisville Daily Journal*, Feb. 7, 1849, 3; Apr. 3, 1849, 2. The *Journal*, which opposed judicial elections, charged Democrats with being opposed to emancipation and for the election of all public officers, while the true popular demand was for an end to life tenure. Similarly, the Friends of Emancipation pointed out the irony of the "violent anti-emancipationists . . . professing great love for the people . . . urging them to take all power—elect every body" while refusing to put the question of emancipation directly to the voters. *Frankfort Commonwealth*, repr. in *Louisville Morning Courier*, May 4, 1849, 1.

14. Young, *History and Texts*, 56–57; Tallant, *Evil Necessity*, 136–37; Ky. Const. of 1799 art. IV, § 10; Gertrude Pettus, "The Issues in the Kentucky Constitutional Convention 1849–1850" (MA thesis, University of Louisville, 1941), 35; Ireland, *Kentucky State Constitution*, 9–10; Ireland, *County Courts*, 85–95; *Ky. D&P*, 311; *Kentucky Yeoman*, Oct. 15, 1846, quoted in William Elsey Connelley and E. M. Coulter, *History of Kentucky*, ed. Charles Kerr (Chicago: American Historical Society, 1922), 2:834.

15. Young, *History and Texts*, 57. Circuit Courts were established in 1802. *Ky. Stat.*, 1:37 (Act of Dec. 20, 1802).

16. Ky. Const. of 1799 art. II, § 6; *Ky. H.J.* 4 (Reg. Sess. 1849–50); Young, *History and Texts*, 59; Frank F. Mathias, "Kentucky's Third Constitution: A Restriction of Majority Rule," *Register of the Kentucky Historical Society* 75, no. 1 (Jan. 1977): 13; *Ky. D&P*, 484–85 (Selucius Garfielde). Louisville had been sending its own representatives to the legislature since 1831. Before the convention, though, the city's citizens complained of unequal representation. Pettus, "Issues," 53–54.

17. *Ky. D&P*, 804, 805–14. The delegates reconsidered the vote on the amendment, deleted the words "except for crime," and repassed the amendment 57–30 (pp. 814–15).

18. *Ky. D&P*, 149, 154, 313, 252. Fifty-four slaves lived at Bullitt's Oxmoor Plantation in 1850, although the family may have owned as many as 120 slaves in all. Andrea S. Watkins, "Oxmoor Plantation," in *The Kentucky African American Encyclopedia*, ed. Gerald L. Smith, Karen Cotton McDaniel, and John A. Hardin (Lexington: University Press of Kentucky, 2015), 392. Proslavery delegates did not necessarily oppose judicial elections, of course. For example, Beverly L. Clarke, who defended slavery (*Ky. D&P*, 923), avowed himself in favor of the elective judiciary (*Ky. D&P*, 23–24).

19. *Ky. D&P*, 246 (William D. Mitchell).

20. *Louisville Morning Courier*, Oct. 29, 1849, 3; *Ky. D&P*, 250.

21. *Ky. D&P*, 251.

22. *Ky. D&P*, 252, 258.

23. *Louisville Morning Courier*, Oct. 30, 1849, 3; *Louisville Daily Journal*, Oct. 29, 1849, 2; *Ky. D&P*, 263–64.

24. *Ky. D&P*, 60, 127, 232–33, 435–37, 651 (court of appeals report), 660–61 (circuit court report), 716 (county court report).

25. *Ky. D&P*, 163–64.

26. *Ky. D&P*, 60, 149 and 211 (Charles A. Wickliffe), 282 (James Guthrie), 200 (Benjamin Hardin), 226 (Squire Turner), 282 (Larkin J. Proctor), 68, 351, 791; Ky. Const. of 1850 art. VII, § 15.

27. Ky. Const. of 1850 art. III, § 25 (state treasurer, auditor, register of the land office, attorney general); art. IV, §§ 4 (court of appeals judges), 11 (court of appeals clerks), 20 (circuit court judges), 30 (county court judges), 34 (justices of the peace), 40–41 (judges, clerks, and marshals of city and town courts); art. VI, §§ 3 (state attorneys, circuit court clerks, and county attorneys, clerks, surveyors, coroners, and jailers), 4 (sheriffs); art. VII, § 23 (president of the board of internal improvements); art. XI, § 2 (superintendent of public instruction); art. II, §§ 35 (debt ceiling), 36 (taxes), 33 (lending of credit), 18 (biennial legislative sessions), 24 (length of legislative sessions), 37 (one-subject rule); *Louisville Morning Courier*, May 30, 1850, 2.

28. *American Republican and Baltimore Daily Clipper*, June 11, 1845, 2 (summarizing a reform agenda recently published in the Baltimore *Republican and Argus*.

29. Robert J. Brugger, *Maryland: A Middle Temperament, 1834–1980* (Baltimore: Johns Hopkins University Press, 1988), 258; Fletcher M. Green, *Constitutional Development in the South Atlantic States, 1776–1860: A Study in the Evolution of Democracy* (Chapel Hill: University of North Carolina Press, 1930), 273; Dan Friedman, *The*

Kentucky State Constitution, 2nd ed. (New York: Oxford University Press, 2012), 9; James Warner Harry, *The Maryland Constitution of 1851* (Baltimore: Johns Hopkins Press, 1902), 17.

30. Act of Feb. 21, 1850, 1849–50 Md. Laws ch. 346 (unpaginated); *Cecil Whig*, May 4, 1850, 1; Green, *Constitutional Development in the South Atlantic States*, 273; Hugh Sisson Hanna, *A Financial History of Maryland (1789–1848)* (Baltimore: Johns Hopkins Press, 1907), 103–25.

31. Md. Const. of 1776 art. XII of amendments (1810) (property qualifications for office) and art. XIV of amendments (1810) (establishment of free suffrage); The Constitution, or Form of Government, §§ 2 (apportionment of house), 14 (election of senators); Brugger, *Maryland*, 22; Harry, *Maryland Constitution*, 20–21; Dan Friedman, *The Maryland State Constitution* (2005; repr. New York: Oxford University Press, 2011), 6.

32. *A Brief Outline of the Rise, Progress, and Failure of the Revolutionary Scheme of the Nineteen Van Buren Electors of the Senate of Maryland, in the Months of September, October, and November 1836* (Baltimore, 1837); Md. Const. of 1776, amendments of 1838, §§ 9–10 (representation), 3 (election of senators), 20 (election of governor), 13 (governor's council), 14 (senate confirmation). See Act of Mar. 10, 1837, 1836–37 Md. Laws ch. 197 (unpaginated), confirmed by Act of Feb 13, 1838, 1837–38 Md. Laws ch. 84 (unpaginated).

33. *American Republican, and Baltimore Daily Clipper*, Feb. 16, 1846, 1; May 3, 1845, 1.

34. J. C. G. Kennedy comp., *Catalogue of the Newspapers and Periodicals Published in the United States, Showing the Town and County in Which the Same Are Published, How Often Issued, Their Character, and Circulation* (New York, 1852), 16; *Sun*, Sept. 25, 1845, 1 (one of a series of articles by "Spectator" under the general title "Reform in State Affairs," most of which dealt with judicial reform and some of which the editors disagreed with); Act of Jan. 11, 1843, 1842–43 Md. Laws ch. 2 (unpaginated); *Sun*, Apr. 11, 1849, 2; *Cecil Whig*, Aug. 3, 1850, 2; Sept. 21, 1850, 2.

35. *Port Tobacco Times, and Charles County Advertiser*, Sept. 11, 1850, 2; *Sun*, Nov. 18, 1850, 4; *Md. D&P*, 2:83 (George Brent), 2:154, 156 (John F. Dent). See also the remarks of William J. Blakistone denouncing the tyranny of numbers as a threat to slavery (*Md. D&P*, 2:50).

36. *Md. D&P*, 2:471, 475.

37. *Md. D&P*, 2:476–77.

38. *Md. D&P*, 2:481; Leonard W. Levy, "Sims' Case: The Fugitive Slave Law in Boston in 1851," *Journal of Negro History* 35, no. 1 (Jan. 1950): 39–74. Chambers's lengthy speech, beginning at *Md. D&P*, 2:468, was reprinted separately as *Speech of Judge Chambers, on the Judicial Tenure, in the Maryland Convention, April, 1851* (Baltimore: 1851). On Chambers, see James A. Pearce, "Address by the President," *Report of the Seventeenth Annual Meeting of the Maryland State Bar Association* (Baltimore: Maryland State Bar Association, 1912): 6–14.

39. *Md. D&P*, 1:239–41, 2:487 (Francis P. Phelps), 512, 492, 503 (for other proposals to substitute the appointment of judges for their election, see 2:486–92); Md. Const. of 1851 art. IV, §§ 4 (court of appeals), 8 (circuit courts), 12 (Baltimore court of common pleas and Baltimore superior court), 13 (Baltimore criminal court), 14 (court clerks), 17

(orphans' court judges), 18 (registers of wills), 19 (justices of the peace and constables); art. IV, § 20 (sheriffs); art. V, § 1 (prosecutors).

40. Md. Const. of 1851 art. II, § 22 (secretary of state); art. VI, § 1 (treasurer); art. VI, § 1 (comptroller); art. VII, §§ 1 (commissioners of public works), 4 (commissioners of lotteries), 6 (commissioners of the land office), 8 (county commissioners), 9 (road supervisors), 10 (surveyors), 11 (wreck-master of Worcester County); art. III, §§ 2–3 (representation; allotting to Baltimore four more delegates than the most populous county but capping the number of delegates at eighty, giving every county at least two delegates, and basing representation on total population, further skewing apportionment in favor of the small slaveholding counties in the southern part of the state), 6 (terms of senators); compare with Md. Const. of 1776, The Constitution, or Form of Government, §§ 15 (senators), 22 (debt), 47 (incorporation), 43 (slavery); Harry, *Maryland Constitution*, 68, 84, 86. The eight counties that voted against ratification were Anne Arundel, Charles, Calvert, Kent, Montgomery, Prince George's, Somerset, and St. Mary's. For the distribution of slaves by county in 1850, see Maryland State Archives, Legacy of Slavery in Maryland, Black Marylanders 1850: African American Population by County, Status & Gender, at http://slavery.msa.maryland.gov/html/research/census1850.html (accessed Oct. 14, 2022).

41. Dubin, *Party Affiliations*, 39; Dubin, *Gubernatorial Elections*, 26–28; Dubin, *Presidential Elections*, 52, 62, 73, 84, 98; Dubin, *Congressional Elections*, 130; Michael F. Holt, *The Rise and Fall of the American Whig Party: Jacksonian Politics and the Onset of the Civil War* (New York: Oxford University Press, 1999), 565–56; Randy J. Holland, *The Delaware State Constitution*, 2nd ed. (New York: Oxford University Press, 2017), 19. Although the Democrats won the congressional election only in 1838, they often lost by very narrow margins.

42. Holt, *Rise and Fall*, 28–30; Junius [Calvin Colton], *The Junius Tracts* (New York, 1844), 31, 89, 91; *New-York Daily Tribune*, Mar, 14, 1845, 1; "The Whig Party, Its Position, and Duties," *American Review* 2, no. 6 (Dec. 1845): 548; "The Convention—Reorganization of the Judiciary," *American Review* 2, no. 5 (Nov. 1845): 474.

43. *The Collected Works of Abraham Lincoln*, ed. Roy P. Basler, vol. 1 (New Brunswick, NJ: Rutgers University Press, 1953), 205; Joseph P. Comegys, *Memoir of John M. Clayton* (1882), 297; Del. Const. of 1831 art. VII, § 3 (compare with Del. Const. of 1792 art. VII, § 4, under which the voters of each county chose two persons for sheriff and two for coroner, and the governor appointed one of them to each office); John A. Fairlie and Charles Mayard Kneier, *County Government and Administration* (New York: Century, 1930), 23–31.

44. Dubin, *Gubernatorial Elections*, 27–28; *Whig Almanac and United States Register for 1847* (New York, 1847), 57 (Sussex County majority for the Democratic congressional candidate in 1846); *Whig Almanac and United States Register for 1851* (New York, 1851), 57 (Sussex County majorities for the Democratic congressional candidates in 1848 and 1850); *Whig Almanac and United States Register for 1853* (New York, 1853), 52 (Sussex County majority for the Whig congressional candidate in 1852); *Whig Almanac for 1851*, 57 (New Castle County majorities for the Democratic congressional and gubernatorial candidates in 1850); *Whig Almanac for 1853*, 52 (New Castle County majorities for the Democratic congressional and presidential candidates in 1852); Holt, *Rise and Fall*, 566.

45. *Smyrna Telegraph*, Jan. 24, 1850, 2; *Blue Hen's Chicken*, Apr. 23, 1852, 2.

46. Del. Const. of 1831 art. IV, § 1 (county tax); art. II, §§ 2 (house), 3 (senate); *Del. S.J.* 3 (Reg. Sess.1853); *Del. H.J.* 3 (Reg. Sess. 1853).

47. *Del. R.S.* 25–26; J. Thomas Scharf, *History of Delaware, 1609–1888* (1888), 2:628–29; Delaware Public Archives, Levy Court, https://archives.delaware.gov/delaware-agency-histories/levy-court-2/. The poll tax went back at least as far as 1796. Act of Feb. 9, 1796, 1796 Del. Laws 1257, 1262.

48. *Blue Hen's Chicken & Delaware Democratic Whig*, Nov. 21, 1845, 3; *Del. H. J.* 129–30 (Reg. Sess. 1847). The column in the *Blue Hen's Chicken & Delaware Democratic Whig* was the third in a series concerning the constitution. Unfortunately, only scattered issues of Delaware newspapers from the 1840s, and not many more from the 1850s, appear to have survived—or, if they have survived, they have not been digitized and made available online. The odd name of this particular newspaper derived from the blue gamecocks that Delaware soldiers kept during the Revolution, leading the soldiers themselves to be called blue hen's chickens. Such, at least, is one oral tradition; there are others. See Herbert Halpert, "The Blue Hen's Chickens," *American Speech* 26, no. 3 (Oct. 1951): 196.

49. *Blue Hen's Chicken & Delaware Democratic Whig*, Mar. 5, 1847, 2.

50. *Blue Hen's Chicken*, Aug. 17, 1849, 2; *Smyrna Telegraph*, Jan. 24, 1850, 2; *Blue Hen's Chicken*, Mar. 8, 1850, 2; Holland, *Delaware State Constitution*, 18.

51. According to a nineteenth-century Delaware historian, in 1846 the owner of the *Blue Hen's Chicken* advocated the transfer of political power in the state from the Whigs to the Democrats. Scharf, *History of Delaware*, 1:456. However, the paper continued to endorse Whig candidates for legislative and other public offices. See, e.g., *Blue Hen's Chicken*, Oct. 27, 1848, 2. By the next year, the paper was claiming to "represent the honest and virtuous of all parties." *Blue Hen's Chicken*, Aug. 17, 1849, 2.

52. Holt, *Rise and Fall*, 564–66; *Del. H. J.* 8, 10 (Reg. Sess. 1851).

53. *Del. H. J.* 159, 164 (Reg. Sess. 1851); Act of Feb. 26, 1851, 1851 Del. Laws 548; Del. Const. of 1831 art. IX.

54. *Blue Hen's Chicken*, Oct. 3, 1851, 2.

55. *Blue Hen's Chicken*, Oct. 3, 1851, 2.

56. *Del. S.J.* pt. 1, 4 (Reg. Sess. 1852); Del. Const. of 1831 art. IX; *Del. D&P*, 165 (Benjamin T. Biggs) and 169 (Caleb Smithers) (giving the number of eligible voters in the state as 12,000–13,000); Act of Feb. 4, 1852, 1852 Del. Laws 631; *Weekly National Intelligencer*, May 1, 1852, 8.

57. *Blue Hen's Chicken*, Apr. 23, 1852, 2. Under the 1792 constitution, the voters chose their representatives annually and their senators triennially, and the legislature met annually. Del. Const. of 1792 art. II, §§ 2–4. The 1831 constitution changed the terms to two years for representatives and four years for senators and provided for biennial sessions. Del. Const. of 1831 art. II, §§ 2–4.

58. *Address of the Whig Convention of Three Hundred Delegates, Assembled at Dover, on the Eighth of June, 1852, To the People of the State of Delaware* (Philadelphia, 1852), 6–7; John A. Munroe, *History of Delaware*, 5th ed. (Newark: University of Delaware Press, 2006), 121–22.

59. *Del. D&P*, 77, 82–83 (corrected report), 95.

60. Del. D&P, 102.
61. Del. D&P, 103–6.
62. Del. D&P, 101–2.
63. Del. D&P, 144.
64. Del. D&P, 182.
65. Del. D&P, 183.
66. Md. D&P, 1:155–61 (John F. Dent); 2:50 (William J. Blakistone); Del. D&P, 197 (Martin W. Bates), 199 (Caleb Smithers), 218 (Caleb Smithers).
67. Del. D&P, 188, 197 (Martin W. Bates), 199 (Caleb Smithers), 195, 196, (Daniel Corbit); Patience Essah, *A House Divided: Slavery and Emancipation in Delaware, 1638–1865* (Charlottesville: University Press of Virginia, 1996), 77, table 5.
68. Del. D&P, 197 (James A. Bayard), 199 (Caleb Smithers); Richard Beeman, *Plain Honest Men: The Making of the American Constitution* (New York: Random House, 2009), 109.
69. Del. D&P, 198.
70. Del. D&P, 197, 213; Del. Const. of 1853 (proposed) art. II, §§ 2–3 (Del. D&P, 303). These sections also capped the number of representatives at thirty-five and the number of senators at half the number of representatives.
71. Ignatius C. Grubb, *The Colonial and State Judiciary of Delaware* (1897), 26–27; Del. Const. of 1831 art. VI, §§ 1–10, 14 (good behavior); art. III, § 8 (governor to make all appointments not otherwise provided for in the constitution).
72. Del. Const. of 1831 art. VI, § 3; Grubb, *Colonial and State Judiciary*, 30–31.
73. Del. D&P, 82.
74. Del. D&P, 83–84.
75. Del. D&P, 143, 151.
76. Del. D&P, 164–79, 175 (Daniel Corbit).
77. Del. D&P, 164.
78. Del. D&P, 164.
79. Del. D&P, 164–66.
80. Del. D&P, 166–67.
81. Del. D&P, 168. Delegates voting in favor of judicial elections included six Whigs (Bell, Biggs, Collins, Hall, Smithers, and McColley), five Democrats (Bates, Houston, Lodge, Smith, and Wilkenson), and five whose affiliations I have not been able to identify (Heverin, Long, Merriken, Springer, and Whitaker). Opponents included six Whigs (Burton, Corbit, Gibbs, Hazzard, Lofland, and Maxwell), one Democrat (Hickman), and three unknowns (Calloway, Jones, and Phillips).
82. Del. D&P, 168.
83. Del. D&P, 171, 169 (Caleb Smithers), 172, 175.
84. Del. D&P, 142, 223–25.
85. Del. D&P, 294–95.
86. Del. D&P, 175–76.
87. Del. D&P, 294; Del. Const. of 1853 (proposed) art. VII, § 14 (Del. D&P, 309).
88. Del. Const. of 1853 (proposed) art. V, §§ 1 (suffrage), 5 (officeholding) (Del. D&P, 306, 307); art. III, § 4 (life tenures) (Del. D&P, 305); art. VII, §§ 14 (judges) (Del. D&P, 309), 24 (justices of the peace) (Del. D&P, 310); art. VIII, §§ 3 (sheriffs,

coroners) (*Del. D&P*, 310), 4 (state attorney general, treasurer, auditor, county registers in chancery, prothonotaries, court clerks, court recorders) (*Del. D&P*, 310–11); art. IV, § 14 (secretary of state, appointed by governor) (*Del. D&P*, 306); art. IX, § 2 (conventions) (*Del. D&P*, 311–12). The draft constitution also required that individual amendments approved by the General Assembly be submitted to a popular referendum at the next general election. Art. IX, § 1 (*Del. D&P*, 311). Under the then-existing constitution, the legislature could amend the constitution by a two-thirds favorable vote in one General Assembly followed by a three-fourths favorable vote in the next General Assembly. Del. Const. of 1831 art. IX.

89. Del. Const. of 1853 (proposed) art. II, § 18 (*Del. D&P*, 304).

90. Del. Const. of 1853 (proposed) art. II, §§ 18, 19 (*Del. D&P*, 304–5); Scharf, *History of Delaware*, 1:318, 360.

91. Richard Lynch Mumford, "Constitutional Development in the State of Delaware, 1776–1897" (PhD diss., University of Delaware, 1968), 272.

92. Mumford, "Constitutional Development," 275–79, 281; Holland, *Delaware State Constitution*, 21.

93. Act of Feb. 24, 1857, 1857 Del. Laws 434; Act of Feb. 16, 1859, 1859 Del. Laws 665; *Smyrna Times*, Jan. 10, 1861, 3; Del. Const. of 1831 art. IX; *Delaware Inquirer*, Dec. 3, 1859, 3; Dec. 10, 1859, 3; Dec. 17, 1859, 2; Dec. 31, 1859, 2.

94. *Jefferson Inquirer*, repr. in *Boon's Lick Times*, Nov. 29, 1845, 2; *Mo. Jour.* (1845) 38–39.

Chapter 3: The Reluctant Southeast

1. Jefferson, *Notes on the State of Virginia*, 168–69.

2. *Richmond Enquirer*, June 12, 1816, 1; *Niles' Weekly Register*, Sept. 7, 1816, 20.

3. Jefferson to John Taylor, July 16, 1816, and Jefferson to Samuel Kercheval, July 12, 1816, in Bergh, *Writings of Jefferson*, 36–39, 45.

4. *Va. P&D*, 436 (Philip P. Barbour), 351–52 (Eugenius M. Wilson), 58 (John R. Cooke), 73–79 (Abel P. Upshur), 320 (John Randolph).

5. John Dinan, *The Virginia State Constitution*, 2nd ed. (New York: Oxford University Press, 2014), 10–11; *Richmond Enquirer*, Mar. 26, 1830, 4; William G. Shade, *Democratizing the Old Dominion: Virginia and the Second Party System, 1824–1861* (Charlottesville: University of Virginia Press, 1996), 70; Va. Const. of 1830 art. III, § 14 (suffrage); art. IV, §§ 1 (governor), 5 (council of state); art. VI (treasurer); art. V, §§ 8 (attorney general, court clerks, sheriffs, coroners, constables), 1 (judicial tenure), 6 (removal).

6. *Staunton Spectator, and General Advertiser*, Mar. 26, 1846, 2 (letter from "A Citizen") and *Richmond Enquirer*, Feb. 20, 1846, 1–2 (speech of Rep. Edmunds) and Oct. 9, 1846, 4 (speech of Rep. McPherson); Julian A. C. Chandler, *Representation in Virginia* (1896), 48–55; Craig Simpson, "Political Compromise and the Protection of Slavery: Henry A. Wise and the Virginia Constitutional Convention of 1850–1851," *Virginia Magazine of History and Biography* 83, no. 4 (1975): 387.

7. James Morton Callahan, *History of West Virginia, Old and New* (Chicago: American Historical Society, 1923), 1:317. "Geography and natural resources define the

Notes to Pages 74–78   251

economy and politics of West Virginia. . . . [T]hose who would become West Virginians developed a separate social, cultural, economic, and political identity." Donald P. Haidel-Markel, ed., *Political Encyclopedia of U.S. States and Regions* (Washington, DC: CQ Press, 2009), 1:335. That West Virginians really felt so distinct from other Virginians is doubted by John Alexander Williams, *West Virginia: A History*, 2nd ed. (Morgantown: West Virginia University Press, 2001), 35–37.

8. Callahan, *History of West Virginia*, 1:322–25.

9. *Richmond Enquirer*, May 28, 1850, 2.

10. *Staunton Spectator*, June 19, 1850, 2 (address of Thomas J. Michie). There was some sentiment, at least implied, at the convention of 1829–30 for the popular election of county court judges (see *Va. P&D*, 528 [Alexander Campbell]), but it seems to have been weak.

11. *Richmond Enquirer*, July 23, 1850, 1 (author identified as "P., Jr." and column headed "No. I"), Aug. 9, 1850, 1 (author identified as "P., Jr." and column headed "The Judiciary. [No. II]."

12. *Staunton Spectator*, Jan. 16, 1850, 2; Jan. 30, 1850, 2; *Richmond Enquirer*, July 30, 1850, 2; Aug. 6, 1850, 2.

13. Dinan, *Virginia State Constitution*, 12, 14–15; Robert P. Sutton, *Revolution to Secession: Constitution Making in the Old Dominion* (Charlottesville: University Press of Virginia, 1989), 116–17, 124, 128–29, 135.

14. *Va. D&P*, 149–50, 352. In July, the convention would vote 78–41 to have supreme court judges elected by people rather than the General Assembly. *Alexandria Gazette*, July 24, 1851, 3.

15. *Va. D&P* 185, 235, 352.

16. *Va.D&P*, 163–68; Va. Const. of 1851 art. VI, §§ 25, 27.

17. Va. Const. of 1851 art. III, § 1 (suffrage); art. IV, §§ 2–5 (representation); art. V, §§ 2, 8, 14; art. VI, §§ 6, 10, 19, 22, 27, 30 (elected officers); Sutton, *Revolution to Secession*, 138.

18. John V. Orth, "North Carolina Constitutional History," *North Carolina Law Review* 70, no. 6 (Sept. 1992): 1762–63, 1769; Theodore Brown Jr., "The Tennessee County Courts under the North Carolina and Territorial Governments: The Davidson County Court of Common Pleas and Quarter Sessions, 1783–1796, as a Case Study," *Vanderbilt Law Review* 32, no. 1 (1979): 352–66. The county courts, called courts of pleas and quarter sessions, were conducted by justices of the peace, who were appointed by the General Assembly. N.C. Const. of 1776, art. XXXIII; Act of May 9, 1777, in *The State Records of North Carolina*, ed. Walter Clark, vol. 24 (Goldsboro, NC: Nash Bros. 1905), 39.

19. William K. Boyd, *The Federal Period, 1783–1860*, vol. 2 of *History of North Carolina* (Chicago: Lewis, 1919), 99–100, 156–57. For a later and somewhat different discussion of western discontent and the passage of the convention bill, see William S. Powell, *North Carolina through Four Centuries* (Chapel Hill: University of North Carolina Press, 1989), 270–78.

20. Act of Jan. 6, 1835, 1834–35 N.C. Laws 3. A supplemental act passed a few days after the original authorized the convention to consider a number of other specific propositions. Act of Jan. 9, 1835, 1834–35 N.C. Laws 6.

21. Orth, "Constitutional History," 1770–73.

22. Boyd, *Federal Period*, 229–31; Marc W. Kruman, *Parties and Politics in North Carolina, 1836–1865* (Baton Rouge: Louisiana State University Press, 1983), 22–24. *Weekly North Carolina Standard*, July 28, 1852, 2; *Semi-Weekly Standard*, Sept. 12, 1857, 3 (reporting a ratification vote of 55,095–19,382 in favor of the amendment). For discussions of the complicated interplay among the issues of internal improvements, suffrage, and representation and its shaping of party positions, see Boyd, *Federal Period*, 288–97; Kruman, *Parties and Politics*, 63–75, 91–103.

23. *North Carolina Standard*, Oct. 28, 1846, 2; *North Carolinian*, Sept. 18, 1847, 3; *North Carolina Standard*, Jan. 23, 1850, 3, Aug. 14, 1850, 2; *North Carolinian*, June 22, 1850, 3; *North Carolina Standard*, Aug. 14, 1850, 2.

24. *Goldsborough Patriot*, quoted in *North Carolina Standard*, June 12, 1850, 2.

25. *Raleigh Star*, quoted in *North Carolinian*, July 13, 1850, 2; Kruman, *Parties and Politics*, 146–47; Holt, *Rise and Fall*, 391–92.

26. N.C. Const. of 1776 amendment of 1835, art. IV, §§ 1–2; amendment of 1857; Orth, "Constitutional History," 1773–74.

27. *Weekly North Carolina Standard*, Jan. 8, 1851, 1; *Fayetteville (NC) Observer*, Feb. 11, 1851, 1.

28. N.C. R.S. 1:117 (coroners), 139 (courts of pleas and quarter sessions), 282 (fairs), 513–14, 591 (peddlers), 535 (river commissioners), 536–47 (roads, ferries, and bridges), 610 (weights and measures); Paul Woodford Wager, *County Government and Administration in North Carolina* (Chapel Hill: University of North Carolina Press, 1928), 16–18; Paul D. Escott, *Many Excellent People: Power and Privilege in North Carolina, 1850–1900* (Chapel Hill: University of North Carolina Press, 1985), 15–19. To "lay off" a river or creek meant, in effect, to designate it as a public highway. See *Gwaltney v. Scottish-Carolina Timber & Land Co.* (N.C. 1892), in *Albany Law Journal* 47 (Mar. 25, 1893): 231–36.

29. *Fayetteville (NC) Observer*, Feb. 11, 1851, 1; Kruman, *Parties and Politics*, 99–102. Some debate over judicial elections continued throughout the 1850s. See, e.g., *Weekly NorthCarolina Standard*, Jan. 28, 1857, 1 (letter in opposition); *Daily Progress*, Nov. 5, 1858, 2 (editorial in favor); *Wilmington Journal*, Oct. 22, 1858, 4 (editorial urging caution). The newspapers noted the introduction of judicial election bills in the General Assembly, none of which came close to passing.

30. Allison Dorothy Fredette, *Marriage on the Border: Love, Mutuality, and Divorce in the Upper South during the Civil War* (Lexington: University Press of Kentucky, 2020), 107–8.

31. On the absence of a strong commercial interest in North Carolina, see Kruman, *Parties and Politics*, 6–8; John Lauritz Larson, *Internal Improvement: National Public Works and the Promise of Popular Government in the Early United States* (Chapel Hill: University of North Carolina Press, 2001), 98–105.

32. John C. Inscoe, *Mountain Masters: Slavery and the Sectional Crisis in Western North Carolina* (Knoxville: University of Tennessee Press, 1989), 177.

33. Cole Blease Graham Jr., *The South Carolina State Constitution: A Reference Guide* (Westport, CT: Praeger, 2007), 13–14; S.C. Const. of 1790 art. I, §§ 3–4 (representation, suffrage), 6–8 (qualifications for office); art II, §§ 2–3 (governor, lieutenant

governor); art. III, § 1 (judicial tenure); art. VI, §§ 1–2 (legislative and other appointments).

34. David Duncan Wallace, *South Carolina: A Short History, 1520–1948* (Columbia: University of South Carolina Press, 1951), 356–60; Manisha Sinha, *The Counterrevolution of Slavery: Politics and Ideology in Antebellum South Carolina* (Chapel Hill: University of North Carolina Press, 2000), 12; William W. Freehling, *The Road to Disunion: Secessionists at Bay, 1776–1854* (New York: Oxford University Press, 1990), 220–22.

35. *Southern Patriot*, repr. in *Sumter Banner*, Jan. 27, 1852, 1; *Charleston Courier*, repr. in *Edgefield Advertiser*, Nov. 28, 1855, 1; *Edgefield Advertiser*, Aug. 6, 1856, 2. Pendleton had been divided into the two judicial districts of Pickens and Anderson years before, but it remained one election district. What the denizens of the district wanted in the 1850s was division into two election districts, each with its own senator. *Charleston Mercury*, Aug. 26, 1852, 2.

36. *Edgefield Advertiser*, Mar. 1, 1854, 2.

37. *Edgefield Advertiser*, July 6, 1854, 2.

38. *Edgefield Advertiser*, Mar. 1, 1854, 2; Americanus [Timothy Ford], *The Constitutionalist: Or, an Enquiry How Far It Is Expedient and Proper to Alter the Constitution of South-Carolina* (Charleston, SC, 1794); John C. Calhoun, *A Disquisition on Government and a Discourse on the Constitution and Government of the United States* (Charleston, SC, 1851); E. H. B., "Political Philosophy of South-Carolina," *Southern Quarterly Review* 7 (n.s.), no. 13 (Jan. 1853): 128. Judicial elections apparently had scattered support in the 1850s, but not enough to get much attention in the newspapers. In a discussion of court reform in the house in 1855, a member said, "The cry of so called popular reform which has swept over other States of this Union, evoking such reckless and unhappy changes in their judicial systems, I trust will never find an echo here. But if frequent changes are made in our judicial system, it will not be long before we will hear the proposition boldly advocated, (as it is now to some extent) of giving the election of judges to the people." *Yorkville Enquirer*, Dec. 6, 1855, 2. For editorial remarks critical of judicial elections, see the *Independent Press*, Oct. 31, 1856, 2.

39. Ga. Const. of 1798 art. II, § 2 (amended 1824); art. I, §§ 4, 8 (amended 1835); Green, *Constitutional Development in the South Atlantic States*, 208–9, 233–40; Anthony Gene Carey, *Parties, Slavery, and the Union in Antebellum Georgia* (Athens: University of Georgia Press, 1997), 124–25; *Southern Recorder*, Nov. 28, 1843, 3; *Federal Union*, Nov. 7 1843, 2.

40. *Daily Constitutionalist*, Nov. 18, 1847, 3; Dec. 21, 1847, 3; *Federal Union*, June 5, 1849, 3; *Georgia Journal and Messenger*, Nov. 14, 1849, 2 ("No one who witnesses the electioneering tricks of the aspirants [for judicial office]—the corruption and the open bargain and sale, which these elections before the Legislature give rise to, can doubt the propriety of some change."). In 1845, the grand jury of Harris County complained that Superior Court judge Joseph Sturgis had repeatedly neglected his duties (*Tri-Weekly Chronicle & Sentinel*, 2), but Sturgis offered a convincing defense (*Columbus Times*, Apr. 9, 1845, 2), and the controversy faded away.

41. Clement L. Vallandigham, *Speeches, Arguments, Addresses, and Letters of Clement L. Vallandigham* (New York: J. Walter, 1864), 86–87.

42. *Daily Constitutionalist*, May 9, 1849, 2; Nov. 25, 1849, 2; *Federal Union* (extra), Nov. 23, 1849, 1.

43. Ga. Const. of 1798, art. III, § 1; *Daily Constitutionalist*, Nov. 29, 1849, 2; *Daily Chronicle & Sentinel*, Dec. 1, 1849, 1; *Daily Constitutionalist*, Nov. 29, 1849, 2. The judiciary committee of Georgia's constitutional convention of 1798 reported an article that expressly stated that the judges of the superior courts were to be appointed by the legislature. However, when James Jackson, Georgia's most powerful politician, offered an extensive amendment to the committee report, the convention went along. The amendment left out the express grant of authority. Albert B. Saye, ed., "Journal of the Georgia Constitutional Convention of 1798," *Georgia Historical Quarterly* 36, no. 4 (Dec. 1952): 385–86.

44. *Constitutionalist and Republic*, Oct. 24, 1851, 1; Act of Jan. 12, 1852, 1851–52 Ga. Acts 85.

45. *Ind. D&P*, 2: 1653 (John S. Newman); Shugerman, *People's Courts*, 138; Bond Almand, "The Supreme Court of Georgia: An Account of Its Delayed Birth," *Georgia Bar Journal* 6, no. 2 (Nov. 1943): 95–110.

46. *Albany Patriot*, Nov. 25, 1853, 2; Ga. Const. of 1798 art. IV, § 15; *Daily Chronicle & Sentinel*, Feb. 17, 1854, 2; *Times & Sentinel Tri-Weekly*, June 3, 1857, 4 (text of the proposed amendment passed in 1856); *Daily Constitutionalist*, Dec. 4, 1857, 3; Dec. 5, 1857, 3. Under the Georgia constitution of 1868, the judges of the supreme and superior courts were appointed by the governor, and under the constitution of 1877 by the General Assembly. Ga. Const. of 1868 art. V, § 9; Ga. Const. of 1877 art. VI, § 2, ¶ 4 and § 3, ¶ 2. By constitutional amendments in 1896 and 1898, the judges of both courts were made elective.

47. Ga. Const. of 1798 art. III, § 3 (amended 1855); Michael J. Ellis, "The Origins of the Elected Prosecutor," *Yale Law Journal* 121, no. 6 (Apr. 2012): 1528–69; Carey, *Parties, Slavery, and the Union*, 123; *Southern Banner*, Dec. 13, 1849, 2. Regarding the federal basis of apportionment, a recent study of the impact of the three-fifths clause on representation in Congress found that, contrary to the claims of abolitionists, the clause gave slave-state representation only a very modest boost that failed to stall the North's growth in power in the House. Michael F. Conlin, *The Constitutional Origins of the American Civil War* (Cambridge, UK: Cambridge University Press, 2019), 87–104.

48. Seth A. Weitz, introduction to *A Forgotten Front During the Civil War Era*, ed. Seth A. Weitz and Jonathan C. Sheppard (Tuscaloosa: University of Alabama Press, 2018), 6; Edward E. Baptist, *Creating an Old South: Middle Florida's Plantation Frontier before the Civil War* (Chapel Hill: University of North Carolina Press, 2002), 2–3, 10; Charles S. Sydnor, *The Development of Southern Sectionalism, 1819–1848*, vol. 5 of *A History of the South*, ed. Wendell Holmes Stephenson and E. Merton Coulter (1948; Baton Rouge: Louisiana State University Press, 1968), 284; Stephanie D. Moussalli, "Florida's Frontier Constitution: The Statehood, Banking & Slavery Controversies," *Florida Historical Quarterly* 74, no. 4 (Spring 1996): 423.

49. Fla. Const. of 1838 art. III, §§ 2–3 (qualifications and election of governor), 14, 23 (appointment of state officers); art. IV, §§ 2–5 (qualifications and election of legislators); art. V, § 9–13, 16–17, 19 (selection of probate officers, justices of the peace, judges, court clerks, attorney general, solicitors, county commissioners); art. VI, § 1 (suffrage);

Act of Dec. 27, 1845, 1845 Fla. Laws (adj. sess.) 88 (militia); Act of Jan. 20, 1828, 1827-28 Fl. Terr. Acts 172 (election of county court clerks, sheriffs, coroners, justices of the peace, surveyors, assessors, collectors of taxes).

50. James M. Denham, "From a Territorial to a State Judiciary: Florida's Antebellum Courts and Judges," *Florida Historical Quarterly* 73, no. 4 (Apr. 1995): 444–45; *Journal of the Proceedings of the Legislative Council, of the Territory of Florida* (Reg. Sess. 1843), 29; Act of Dec. 29, 1845, 1845 Fla. Laws (adj. sess.) 77; Act of July 25, 1845, 1845 Fla. Laws (1st sess.), 14.

51. Fla. Const. of 1838 art. IX, §§ 1–2. On party politics in Florida, see Herbert J. Doherty Jr., *The Whigs of Florida, 1845–1854* (Gainesville: University of Florida Press, 1959). Doherty includes a map showing the political leanings of Florida's counties (p. 64). He notes that apportionment was not a subject of sharp division at the convention (p. 7), and Moussalli ("Florida's Frontier Constitution," 435–36) points to evidence of compromise between the leading factions among the delegates. Data on Florida's population, categorized by county, color, and condition (free or slave) can be found in DeBow, *Seventh Census*, 396–401 (Florida: Table I: Population by Counties—Classification of Ages, Color, and Condition—Aggregates).

52. Fla. Const. of 1838 art. V, §§ 1, 3, 5, 8, 12.

53. Dorothy Dodd, ed., *Florida Becomes a State* (Tallahassee: Florida Centennial Commission, 1945), 334–35; Baptist, *Creating an Old South*, 220–22 (describing the "new" Whig Party in Middle Florida). Between 1830 and 1840, Florida's slave population grew by 66 percent, its nonslave population by 53 percent. Between 1840 and 1850, the figures were 50 percent and 67 percent.

54. Fla. S.J. 12 (Reg. Sess. 1846–47); *Pensacola Gazette*, Sept. 2, 1843, 2; Jan. 20, 1844, 2.

55. Fla. S.J. 10 (Reg. Sess. 1847–48). On December 21, 1847, Democratic senator R. J. Floyd, on the second reading of a proposed constitutional amendment dealing with judicial terms of office, sought to amend the measure to make all judges elective. The senate rejected the motion 11–4. Fla. S.J. 117 (Reg. Sess. 1847–48).

56. Fla. S.J. 9 (Reg. Sess. 1848–49); *Floridian & Journal*, Jan 13, 1849, repr. in *Pensacola Gazette*, Jan. 20, 1849, 2.

57. Fla. Const. of 1838 art. IV, § 1 (amended 1847); art. V, § 12 (amended 1848); art. VI, § 1 (amended 1847); Thomas Brown, *Message of the Governor of Florida to the General Assembly, Nov. 25, A.D. 1850, with the Accompanying Documents* (1850), 4–6 (printed with the house and senate journals for the 1850–51 session; separately paginated).

58. La. P&D, 755.

59. Fla. S.J. 71, 96, 121 (Reg. Sess. 1850–51); Fla. H.J. 134–35, 148–49, 266. The lone dissenter explained that he was not opposed to judicial elections but believed that the proposed amendment had not been published in advance as required by the constitution. Fla. H.J. 266–67 (Reg. Sess. 1852–53).

60. Fla. S.J. 196 (Reg. Sess. 1850–51); Fla. H.J. 247 (Reg. Sess. 1850–51); Fla. S.J. 121, 269–70 (Reg. Sess. 1852–53); Fla. H.J. 266, 284–85 (Reg. Sess. 1852–53); Fla. S.J. 152, 167 (Reg. Sess. 1854–55).

61. Dubin, *Party Affiliations*, 43; *Florida Sentinel*, Oct. 24, 1854, 2.

Chapter 4: The Old Southwest

1. Fred Arthur Bailey, "Charles S. Sydnor's Quest for a Suitable Past," in *Reading Southern History: Essays on Interpreters and Interpretations*, ed. Glenn Feldman (Tuscaloosa: University of Alabama Press, 2001), 105.

2. Sydnor, *Development of Southern Sectionalism*, 283–84.

3. Thomas D. Clark and John G. W. Guice, *The Old Southwest, 1795–1830: Frontiers in Conflict* (1989; Norman: University of Oklahoma Press, 1996), 1; Harold M. Mixon, "Old Southwest," in *The Companion to Southern Literature: Themes, Genres, Places, People, Movements, and Motifs*, ed. Joseph M. Flora and Lucinda H. Mackethan (Baton Rouge: Louisiana State University Press, 2002), 607; James H. Justus, *Fetching the Old Southwest: Humorous Writing from Longstreet to Twain* (Columbia: University of Missouri Press, 2004), 5; DeBow, *Statistical View*, 37–38.

4. The Louisiana constitutional convention of 1852, which adopted judicial elections, dispensed with the services of a reporter. However, the 1845 convention did retain reporters in both English and French. See *La. P&D*, 949. For an exception to the general rule of neglect of the southwestern states, see Chris Klemme, "Jacksonian Justice: The Evolution of the Elective Judiciary in Texas," *Southwestern Historical Quarterly* 105, no. 3 (Jan. 2002): 428–50.

5. Ark. Const. of 1836 art. IV, §§ 2 (suffrage), 4 and 6 (qualifications of legislators), 32 and 34 (apportionment); art. V, §§ 4 (qualifications of governor), 14 and 24 (state officers); art. VI, §§ 7 (judges), 9–10 (county and probate courts), 15–17 (local officers); art. VII, § 3 (atheists). For the statutory powers of the county courts, see E. H. English, *Digest of the Statutes of Arkansas Embracing All Laws of a General and Permanent Character in Force at the Close of the Session of the General Assembly of 1846* (1848), 313.

6. Donald P. McNeilly, *The Old South Frontier: Cotton Plantations and the Formation of Arkansas Society, 1819–1861* (Fayetteville: University of Arkansas Press, 2000), 7, 175–76; Carl H. Moneyhon, *The Impact of the Civil War and Reconstruction on Arkansas: Persistence in the Midst of Ruin* (Baton Rouge: Louisiana State University Press, 1994), 35–58; Ark. Const. of 1836 arts. of amendment I–IV (1846).

7. Ark. Const. of 1836 art. VII, Establishment of Banks, § 1; John Joseph Wallis, Richard E. Sylla, and Arthur Grinath III, "Sovereign Debt and Repudiation: The Emerging-Market Debt Crisis in the U.S. States, 1839–1843" (working papers, National Bureau of Economic Research 2004), 34 (table 3), http://www.nber.org/papers/w10753; *Arkansas State Gazette*, Feb. 17, 1841, 3; Res. of Jan. 9, 1845, 1844–45 Ark. Laws 161; 1846 Ark. Laws 198 (undated ratification of amendments); Ark. Const. of 1836 art. IV, § 35.

8. *Ark. S.J.* 50–51 (Reg. Sess. 1844–45). The senate journal's summary of the petition refers to the election of county court judges generally rather than the presiding judges. However, the justices of the peace who made up the associate judges were already elected.

9. *Ark. S.J.* 60, 67, 146 (Reg. Sess. 1846).

10. *Ark. S.J.* 178–81, 231 (Reg. Sess. 1846); Res. of Dec. 23, 1846, 1846 Ark. Laws 197; Res. of Nov. 25, 1848, 1848–49 Ark. Laws 9. The 1846 house journal is unavailable online, and the house proceedings on the election amendments were not reported in the newspapers that are available online. However, the sentiments of the representatives

are apparent from the unanimous passage by the house of a resolution for the election of county judges and prosecutors. *Arkansas State Gazette*, Dec. 5, 1846, 2.

11. *Ark. S.J.* 75 (Reg. Sess. 1848); *Washington Telegraph*, June 14, 1848, 2, 3; Dec. 6, 1848, 4.

12. *Ark. Digest*, 313.

13. *Ark. Digest*, 306; Ellis, "Origins of the Elected Prosecutor," 1559. The Iowa constitution, which provided for the election of district court judges, was signed by the convention delegates on May 18, 1846, and ratified on August 3, 1846. The legislature passed a law providing for the election of district judges in February, 1847. Act of Feb. 16, 1847, 1846–47 Ia. Laws 66. Under that law, the first judicial elections were to take place at the next regularly scheduled township elections. Township elections occurred on the first Monday in April. Act of Feb. 17, 1842, in *Ia. R.S.* 618. The *Iowa Capitol Reporter* noted the results in some of the judicial races in its issue of May 12, 1847, 2. The New York constitution, signed on October 1, 1846, ratified on November 3, 1846, and effective on January 1, 1847, set the first judicial elections for some time in the period between April and June, 1847. N.Y. Const. of 1846 art. XIV, § 4. The first elections took place on June 7. For the first Michigan election, see *Mich. R.S.* 377.

14. *Ark. Digest*, 301–4; McNeilly, *Old South Frontier*, 81; Diane D. Blair and Jay Barth, *Arkansas Politics and Government*, 2nd ed. (Lincoln: University of Nebraska Press, 2005), 21. For descriptions of county court days in the nineteenth century, see Robert M. Ireland, *Little Kingdoms: The Counties of Kentucky, 1850–1891* (Lexington: University Press of Kentucky, 1977), 90–100; John W. Wayland, *A History of Rockingham County, Virginia* (Dayton, VA: Ruebush-Elkins, 1912), 424–25; Louis Clinton Hatch, *Maine: A History* (1919; Somersworth, NH: New Hampshire Pub. Co., 1974), 723; James Lane Allen, "County Court Day in Kentucky," *Harper's New Monthly Magazine* 79, no. 472 (August 1889): 383–97.

15. *Washington Telegraph*, July 26, 1848, 3; Nov. 22, 1848, 1.

16. *Washington Telegraph*, Dec. 11, 1850, 2; *Arkansas State Gazette and Democrat*, Dec. 3, 1852, 2; *True Democrat*, Jan. 13, 1857, 1; *Arkansas State Gazette and Democrat*, Nov. 24, 1854, 2 (proposed amendment offered in house); Dec. 29, 1854, 3 (proposed amendment taken up in senate, indicating house passage); Act of Feb. 21, 1859, 1858–59 Ark. Laws 314; *Ark. H.J.* 37, 184–85, 198–99 (Reg. Sess. 1860–61).

17. Act of Jan. 10, 1853, 1852–53 Ark. Laws 123; *True Democrat*, July 26, 1854, 2; *Arkansas State Gazette and Democrat*, July 21, 1854, 2.

18. *Arkansas State Gazette and Democrat*, May 26, 1854, 2; Sept. 15, 1854, 2; *Washington Telegraph*, July 26, 1854, 2; *True Democrat*, Sept. 13, 1854, 2; Ark. Const. of 1836 art. X of amendments (1850).

19. J. Mills Thornton III, *Politics and Power in a Slave Society: Alabama, 1800–1860* (Baton Rouge: Louisiana State University Press, 1978), 13.

20. Malcolm Cook McMillan, *Constitutional Development in Alabama, 1798–1901: A Study in Politics, the Negro, and Sectionalism* (Chapel Hill: University of North Carolina Press, 1955), 34, 37; Ala. Const. of 1819 art. III, §§ 4 (qualifications of representatives), 5 (suffrage), 8–10 (representation), 12 (qualifications of senators); art. IV, §§ 4 (qualifications of governor), 14 and 23 (state officers), 24 (sheriffs); art. V, §§ 12 (judges), 15 (court clerks).

21. Ala. Const. of 1819 art. V, §§ 1–3, 8–10; McMillan, *Constitutional Development*, 41.

22. McMillan, *Constitutional Development*, 47–51.

23. McMillan, *Constitutional Development*, 64; Act of Dec. 31, 1822, 1822 Ala. Laws 19; *Ala. Digest (1843)*, 296; *Ala. Digest (1833)*, 98–100, 404–5, 86. The lines of authority set forth in the statute are not clear. The judge of the county court and the county road commissioners together constituted a court for the levying of road taxes, but the general regulation of roads, bridges, and ferries appears to have been transferred from the county courts to the commissioners. However, other statutes conferred separate authority over related matters on the county courts. See, e.g., *Ala. Digest (1833)*, 363–64 (county court's authority to establish or authorize certain ferries, bridges, and causeways).

24. *Alabama Beacon*, Apr. 20, 1850, 2; *Independent Monitor*, Dec. 21, 1842, 2. The text of the proposed amendment is in *Wetumpka Argus*, Aug. 30, 1843, 4.

25. *Wetumpka Argus*, July 12, 1843, 3.

26. *Wetumpka Argus*, July 26, 1843, 2. The paper bears the day and date Wednesday, July 27, 1843. The *Argus* was indeed published weekly on Wednesdays, but July 27, 1843, was a Thursday.

27. *Jacksonville Republican*, July 19, 1843, 2.

28. *Advertiser and State Gazette*, Dec. 26, 1849, 2.

29. *Democrat*, Nov. 20, 1829, 3; Nov. 25, 1830, 2; *Spirit of the Age*, Dec. 14, 1831, 1–2; Act of Jan. 14, 1832, 1831–32 Ala. Laws 19.

30. *Democrat*, July 21, 1847, 3; *Democrat* (Eufaula), Dec. 15, 1847, 2; *Independent Monitor*, Dec. 30, 1847, 3; *Democrat*, Feb. 16, 1848, 1.

31. *Independent Monitor*, Dec. 23, 1847, 3; Ala. S.J. 128 (Reg. Sess. 1847–48); Ala. H.J. 57 (Reg. Sess. 1847–48); *Independent Monitor*, Jan. 6, 1848, 3; "A Voter," Letter to the Editor, *Democrat*, July 11, 1849, 3; Jt. Res. of Mar. 1, 1848, 1847–48 Ala. Laws 444–45.

32. Ala. Const. of 1819 art VI, Mode of Amending and Revising the Constitution; *Independent Monitor*, Jan. 6, 1848, 3; *Southern Advocate*, repr. in *Daily State Guard*, Oct. 19, 1849, 2; Jt. Res. of Jan. 29, 1850, 1849–50 Ala. Laws 485; Act of Feb. 11, 1850, 1849–50 Ala. Laws 24.

33. *Alabama Beacon*, Mar. 30, 1850, 3.

34. *Alabama Beacon*, Jan. 5, 1850, 1; *Southern Advocate*, repr. in *Alabama Beacon*, July 16, 1852, 2; *Alabama Beacon*, July 9, 1852, 2; *Jacksonville Republican*, July 27, 1852, 2 (state officers); *Southern Advocate*, Aug. 18, 1852, quoted in McMillan, *Constitutional Development*, 73.

35. On antebellum politics in Alabama, with extensive treatment of banking and internal improvements but, unfortunately, only brief mention of state constitutional developments, see Thornton, *Politics and Power*.

36. Ala. Const. of 1819 art. IV, Executive Department, § 24 (sheriffs); Act of Dec. 31, 1822, 1822 Ala. Laws 19 (justices of the peace, constables); *Ala. Digest (1843)*, 149 (road commissioners), 568 (tax collectors). Other county officers (coroner, surveyor, treasurer, auctioneers) were appointed. *Ala. Digest (1843)*, 162.

37. See, e.g., *Ala. Code*, 244 (licensing of liquor retailers by probate court), 264 (establishment and licensing of toll bridges and ferries by court of county commissioners).

The code expressly made the courts of county commissioners courts of record, but this "court" was really a board of county commissioners, not a judicial body, as its statutory authority shows (pp. 190–91).

38. *Ala. Digest (1843)*, 288; *Spirit of the Age*, Dec. 14, 1831, 2.

39. Tex. Const. of 1836 art. VI, § 11. Section 11 did not explicitly exclude blacks or Indians, either, but another provision (General Provisions, § 10) denied them citizenship. That females lacked political equality is evident from provisions requiring a petition of one hundred free male inhabitants to establish a new county (art. IV, § 11) and entitling male citizens to hold public office (Schedule § 3).

40. Tex. Const. of 1836 art. I, §§ 5 and 7 (apportionment); art. IV, §§ 6 (district court clerks), 9 (judges); art. VI, § 10 (executive officers); Act of Dec. 20, 1836, *Rep. Tex. Laws*, 1:141 (justices of the peace); Act of Dec. 20, 1837, *Rep. Tex. Laws*, 1:179 (sheriffs), 1:183 (coroners), 1:185 (constables); Act of Dec. 20, 1836, *Rep. Tex. Laws*, 1:148, 1:153 (county courts); Act of Dec. 20, 1836, *Rep. Tex. Laws*, 1:150 (county court clerks).

41. *Tex. Deb. (1845)*, 7; Tex. Const. of 1845 art. III, §§ 1–2 (suffrage), 29 (house apportionment per free population), 31 (senate apportionment per qualified electors); art. IV, §§ 5 (judges), 12 (attorney general, district attorneys), 13 (local officers), 15 (probate judges); art. V, §§ 16 (secretary of state), 19 (notaries), 23 (treasurer, comptroller); Act of May 11, 1846, 1846 Tex. Laws 308 (probate judges).

42. *Texas National Register*, July 17, 1845, 250.

43. *Texas National Register*, Aug. 7, 1845, 276; Aug. 14, 1845, 283. During the convention, Ford regularly contributed signed articles to the *Register*. He and a partner bought the paper in October 1845. W. J. Hughes, *Rebellious Ranger: Rip Ford and the Old Southwest* (Norman: University of Oklahoma Press, 1964), 15–16.

44. *Tex. Deb. (1845)*, 33, 489–90.

45. See *Tex. Deb. (1845)*, 24, 26, 118–32. For a summary of the arguments over popular election, see Annie Middleton, "The Texas Convention of 1845," *Southwestern Historical Quarterly* 25, no. 1 (July 1921): 34–37.

46. Klemme, "Jacksonian Justice," 440–2 (quotation at p. 440). Jt. Res. of Mar. 14, 1848, 1847–48 Tex. Laws 84.

47. E. Bagby Atwood, *The Regional Vocabulary of Texas* (Austin: University of Texas Press, 1962), 7–14; David G. McComb, *The City in Texas: A History* (Austin: University of Texas Press, 2015), 61–62; Klemme, "Jacksonian Justice," 440, 443. The organization of political parties was just under way in Texas. Because the national Democratic Party had favored the annexation of Texas to the United States and because of a widespread belief in "the tenets of the good old Democratic creed," most voters favored the Democrats. On the organization of parties, see Ernest William Winkler, *Platforms of Political Parties in Texas* (Austin: University of Texas, 1916), 11–36 (quotation on p. 23 attributed to *State Gazette*, Dec. 14, 1850). In 1848 and 1852, Texans voted overwhelmingly for the Democratic presidential candidates. Dubin, *Presidential Elections*, 112, 132.

48. Tex. Const. of 1845 art. VII, § 37; *Democratic Telegraph and Texas Register*, Sept. 27, 1848, 2; Klemme, "Jacksonian Justice," 446–48. For samples of pro-amendment newspaper commentary, see Klemme, 445–46.

49. Paul H. Bergeron, *Antebellum Politics in Tennessee* (Lexington: University Press of Kentucky, 1982), 38; Tenn. Const. of 1796 art. I, §§ 2–3 (apportionment), 7

(qualifications of legislators), 26 (poll tax, taxation of town lots); art. II, § 3 (qualifications of governor); art. III, § 1 (suffrage); art. V, §§ 1 (legislature to establish judiciary), 2 (tenure of judges, state attorneys), 10 (court clerks), 12 (justices of the peace); art. VI, § 1 (local officers); art. VIII, § 2 (belief in God); State v. Claiborne, 19 Tenn. 331 (1838); Act of Sept. 1794, 1794 Tenn. (Terr.) Laws 37–38; Act of Apr. 4, 1796, 1796 Tenn. Laws 101; Lewis L. Laska, "A Legal and Constitutional History of Tennessee, 1772-1972," *Memphis State University Law Review* 6, no. 4 (Summer 1976): 587–88. The constitution vested in the legislature the power to appoint all officers mentioned in the constitution whose appointments were not otherwise provided for. Tenn. Const. of 1796 art. VI, § 3. The officers appointed by the General Assembly, either expressly or by virtue of this default provision, included the secretary of state (art. II, § 17), state treasurer (art. VI, § 2), judges, state attorneys (art. V, § 2), and justices of the peace (art. V, § 12). Each court appointed its own clerk (art. V, § 10).

50. Joshua W. Caldwell, *Studies in the Constitutional History of Tennessee*, 2nd ed. (Cincinnati, OH: Robert Clarke, 1907), 169–75; Theodore Brown Jr., "The Formative Period in the History of the Supreme Court of Tennessee, 1796-1835," in *A History of the Tennessee Supreme Court*, ed. James W. Ely Jr. (Knoxville: University of Tennessee Press, 2002), 46–60; Timothy S. Huebner, "Judicial Independence in an Age of Democracy, Sectionalism, and War, 1835-1865," in Ely, *Tennessee Supreme Court*, 63–64; *Messages of the Governors of Tennessee*, vol. 2, *1821-1835*, ed. Robert H. White (Nashville: Tennessee Historical Commission, 1952), 292; Act of Dec. 15, 1831, 1831 Tenn. Laws 76.

51. Laska, "Legal and Constitutional History," 603–4; Williams v. Register, 3 Tenn. 213 (1812); Bank v. Cooper, 10 Tenn. 529 (Special Ct. 1831); Fisher's Negroes v. Dabbs, 14 Tenn. 78 (1834); Huebner, "Judicial Independence," 63–64; N. Houston Parks, "Judicial Selection—The Tennessee Experience," *Memphis State University Law Review* 7, no. 4 (Summer 1977): 622–24.

52. Jonathan M. Atkins, *Parties, Politics, and the Sectional Conflict in Tennessee, 1832-1861* (Knoxville: University of Tennessee Press, 1997), 4; Laska, "Legal and Constitutional History," 602–3; Robert Cassell, "Newton Cannon and the Constitutional Convention of 1834," *Tennessee Historical Quarterly* 15, no. 3 (Sept. 1956): 224–25.

53. *National Banner, and Daily Advertiser*, Mar. 3, 1834, 3; Feb. 21, 1834, 2. Cobbs was one of three candidates vying for a place at the convention who, in remarks published in this issue of the *Banner*, opposed judicial elections

54. *Nashville Republican and State Gazette*, Aug. 7, 1834, 2; Caldwell, *Constitutional History*, 213; Tenn. Const. of 1835 art. VI, §§ 3–4.

55. Laska, "Legal and Constitutional History," 584, 584n98, 607; Tenn. Const. of 1835 art. I, § 4 (religious qualification); art. II, §§ 5–6 (apportionment), 9–10 (property qualifications for legislators), 28 (taxation); art. III, § 3 (property qualification for governor); art. IV, § 1 (suffrage); art.VI, § 15 (justices of the peace, constables); art. VII, § 1 (sheriffs, trustees, registers).

56. Milton Henry, "What Became of the Tennessee Whigs?" *Tennessee Historical Quarterly* 11, no. 1 (Mar. 1952): 57; Tenn. Const. of 1835 art 11, § 3. Control of the General Assembly swung back and forth between the parties during period 1835-1853. See Dubin, *Party Affiliations*, 176.

57. Tenn. Const. of 1835 art. XI, § 3; *Daily Union*, Jan. 6, 1848, 1. Polk may have been mistaken. The General Assembly did pass a resolution proposing a constitutional amendment in 1844 (Jt. Res. of Jan. 25, 1844, 1843–44 Tenn. Laws 177), but it does not appear that the amendment was passed in either the previous or subsequent legislature as required for placement on the ballot. However, Polk noted that some individuals believed that even a single passage of an amendment by the legislature triggered the six-year ban. That could have induced a delay of agitation for a judicial-elections amendment until 1847.

58. Johnson to Elbridge G. Eastman, May 27, 1849, in *The Papers of Andrew Johnson*, vol. 1., *1822–1851*, ed. LeRoy P. Graf and Ralph W. Haskins (Knoxville: University of Tennessee Press, 1967), 509; *Daily Union*, Mar. 16, 1849, 2; James Phelan, *History of Tennessee: The Making of a State* (Boston 1888), 428. Newspapers around the country commented on the suspiciousness of the election of the US senator by the Tennessee legislature. See, e.g., *New-York Daily Tribune*, Nov. 3, 1845, 2; *Richmond Enquirer*, Nov. 4, 1845, 1, 2.

59. *Daily Union*, Nov. 20, 1847, 2; *Republican Banner*, Oct. 31, 1845, 2; *Republican*, Nov. 7, 1845, at 2; *Tri-Weekly Nashville Union*, Jan. 20, 1846, 2; *Republican Banner*, Jan. 23, 1846, 2; *Daily Union*, Nov. 17, 1847, 2.

60. Tenn. H.J. 108–9 (Reg. Sess. 1847–48), 108–9; *Daily Union*, Dec. 6, 1847, 1. Ballew also stated that Missouri elected its judges, which was true at that time only for justices of the peace, justices of the county courts, and probate judges. For Ballew's political affiliation, see Robert M. McBride and Dan M. Robison, *Biographical Directory of the Tennessee General Assembly*, vol. 1, *1796–1861* (Nashville: Tennessee Historical Commission, 1975), 26.

61. Tenn. H.J. 500 (Reg. Sess. 1847–48); *Daily Union*, Jan. 8, 1848, 1. For Pepper's political affiliation, see McBride and Robison, *Biographical Directory*, 578.

62. Tenn. H.J. 670–71, 846 (Reg. Sess. 1847–48); Tenn. S.J. 596–97 (Reg. Sess. 1847–48); *Messages of the Governors of Tennessee*, vol. 4, *1845–1857*, ed. Robert H. White (Nashville: Tennessee Historical Commission, 1952), 301–2.

63. Tenn. H.J. 60–61 (Reg. Sess. 1849–50); *Daily Union*, Jan. 6, 1848, 1.

64. Tenn. H.J. 96–97 (Reg. Sess. 1849–50).

65. Tenn. H.J. 269–70 (Edmund Cooper), 361–62 (Reg. Sess. 1849–50). Cooper also proposed that all judges be elected by the voters, an idea that the house accepted via Polk's amendment.

66. Tenn. H.J. 371, 704 (Reg. Sess. 1849–50); Tenn. S.J. 642–45; 676–77 (Reg. Sess. 1849–50). The creation of new counties had been a contentious issue at Tennessee's 1834 constitutional convention. Citizens often wanted to form new counties so that judicial proceedings and other county business would be closer to home. However, the creation of a new county affected everything from legislative representation to land values, making the subject one of perpetual conflict. The constitution of 1835 significantly reduced the minimum size of new counties but imposed other requirements and included numerous special provisions for individual counties. Compare Tenn. Const. of 1796 art. IX, § 4 with Tenn. Const. of 1835 art. X, § 4.

67. *Daily Union*, Sept. 27, 1849, 2. The *Union* thought the one pro-election Whig

paper might have been the Memphis *Enquirer* or *Eagle*. In fact, the *Eagle* had editorialized in favor of judicial elections a few weeks earlier. *Weekly Memphis Eagle*, Sept. 6, 1849, 1.

68. *Tenn. S.J.* 644 (Reg. Sess. 1849–50); *Tenn. H.J.* 371 (Reg. Sess. 1849–50). The party affiliations of senators and representatives for the 1849–50 session are in the *Knoxville Register*, Aug. 25, 1849, 2.

69. Tenn. Const. of 1835 art. XI, § 3; *Tenn. H.J.* (Reg. Sess. 1851–52), 259; *Tenn. S.J.* 239 (Reg. Sess. 1851–52); *Fayetteville (TN) Observer*, Nov. 18, 1851, 2, July 21, 1853, 2; *Nashville Gazette*, Aug. 3 or 4, 1853, quoted in Huebner, "Judicial Independence," 87; *Nashville Union and American*, Oct. 13, 1852, 2. For Bate's Democratic affiliation, see William S. Speer, ed., *Sketches of Prominent Tennesseans* (Nashville, 1888), 153. As a delegate to the 1870 Tennessee constitutional convention, Bate was still opposed to judicial elections. *Tenn. Jour.*, 205, 208. Huebner calls the *Gazette* nonpartisan, but Tennessee historian Robert H. White says it was a Whig paper. *Messages of the Governors*, 4:361. *Gazette* was a common name for Whig papers in the mid-nineteenth century, just as *Argus* was for Democratic papers.

70. Sydnor, *Development of Southern Sectionalism*, 284–85; Judith K. Schafer, "The Political Development of Antebellum Louisiana", in *Louisiana: A History*, ed. Bennett H. Wall and John C. Rodrigue, 6th ed. (Chichester, UK: Wiley Blackwell, 2014), 139; La. Const. of 1812 art II, §§ 4 (qualifications of representatives), 8 (suffrage), 10 (senate districts), 12 (qualifications of senators); art. III, §§ 2 (election of governor), 4 (qualifications of governor), 9 (judges, sheriffs), 19 (secretary of state); art. IV, §§ 5 (judicial tenure), 7 (attorney general), 9 (treasurer); art. VII, § 1 (amendments).

71. Schafer, "The Territorial Period", *Louisiana: A History*, 125; Roger W. Shugg, *Origins of Class Struggle in Louisiana: A Social History of White Farmers and Laborers during Slavery and After, 1840–1875* (Baton Rouge: Louisiana State University Press, 1939), 18; Judith K. Schafer, "Reform or Experiment? The Constitution of 1845", in *In Search of Fundamental Law: Louisiana's Constitutions, 1812–1974*, ed. Warren M. Billings and Edward F. Haas (Lafayette: Center for Louisiana Studies, University of Southwestern Louisiana, 1993), 21, 26; Frank Towers, *The Urban South and the Coming of the Civil War* (Charlottesville: University of Virginia Press, 2004), 79; Holt, *Rise and Fall*, 116.

72. *Remarks on the Propriety of Calling a Convention to Amend the Constitution of the State of Louisiana* (1841), quoted in Schafer, "Reform or Experiment?" 23; Schafer, "Political Development," 140–41.

73. John M. Sacher, *A Perfect War of Politics: Parties, Politicians, and Democracy in Louisiana, 1824–1861* (Baton Rouge: Louisiana State University Press, 2003), 104; *Baton Rouge Gazette*, July 25, 1840, 2; Jan. 16, 1841, 2; Jan. 30, 1841, 2; Act of Jan. 30, 1841, 1841 La. Laws (1st sess.) 5. The 1840 elections produced a divided General Assembly, but the party affiliations of the members can be hard to identify. According to Michael J. Dubin, the election produced a senate consisting of eight Whigs, eight Democrats, and one of unknown affiliation and a house of twenty-six Whigs, fourteen Democrats, and ten whose affiliation could not be ascertained. Dubin, *Party Affiliations*, 76.

74. Sacher, *Perfect War of Politics*, 107.

75. *Baton-Rouge Gazette*, Aug. 6, 1842, 1; Aug. 13, 1842, 2; Oct. 29, 1842, 2;

John B. Kleinpeter (candidate for convention delegate) to J. C. Patterson, May 23, 1844, *Baton-Rouge Gazette*, May 25, 1844, 2 (for Kleinpeter's Whig affiliation, see *Baton-Rouge Gazette*, June 29, 1844, 2); Dec. 2, 1843, 1; Sacher, *Perfect War of Politics*, 111, 255; Whig editor quoted in Perry Howard, *Political Tendencies in Louisiana*, rev. ed. (Baton Rouge: Louisiana State University Press, 1971), 48.

The political composition of the convention has been difficult to determine. The New Orleans *Picayune* reported that "the democrats have a majority in the Convention, although it should be remembered that to this body several of the members were elected without reference to party predilections." Based on "very imperfect" returns, the paper reported a membership of thirty-three Whigs and forty-two Democrats, leaving two seats unaccounted for. *Daily Picayune*, July 14, 1844, 2. A later report by the *Baton-Rouge Gazette* found thirty-nine Whigs and thirty-eight Democrats, counting among the latter one "conservative" delegate whom both parties had supported against a "radical" opponent. *Baton-Rouge Gazette*, July 27, 1844, 2. Louisiana historians similarly disagree. One writes that among the delegates there were forty-two Democrats, thirty-two Whigs, and three of unknown affiliation (Sacher, *Perfect War of Politics*, 112), while another reports thirty-nine Democrats, thirty-six Whigs, one "probable Democrat," and one "non-partisan" (Adams, *Whig Party of Louisiana*, 144). Others state that the Whigs had a majority of one. W. Lee Hargrave, *The Louisiana State Constitution* (1990; New York: Oxford University Press, 2011), 6; Marius M. Carriere Jr., *The Know Nothings in Louisiana* (Jackson: University Press of Mississippi, 2018), 23. For present purposes, the important fact is that the Whigs, who generally opposed judicial elections, had enough Democratic allies on this point to ensure the defeat of the elective judiciary.

76. *La. Deb.*, 941 (Charles M. Conrad), 302 (Solomon W. Downs), 945 (Duncan Farrar Kenner), 125 (Miles Taylor). Some of Louisiana's banks were "improvement banks," which financed such "improvements" as waterworks and hotels as well as the canals and railroads that are typically thought of as internal improvements. Other so-called banks were primarily construction companies that received banking powers. George D. Green, *Finance and Economic Development in the Old South: Louisiana Banking, 1804–1861* (Stanford, CA: Stanford University Press, 1972), 16, 33. However, it does not appear that the state financed or subscribed to the stock either type of bank.

77. Sydnor, *Development of Southern Sectionalism*, 261–63 (quotation at 261).

78. Charles Gayarré, *History of Louisiana*, vol. 4, *The American Domination*, 2nd ed. (New Orleans, 1879), 660; Stephen A. Caldwell, *A Banking History of Louisiana* (Baton Rouge: Louisiana State University Press, 1935), 102; Sacher, *Perfect War of Politics*, 113. On the troubles of the banks following the panic, see generally Caldwell, *Banking History*, 60–83.

79. La. Const. of 1845 tit. VI, arts. 113, 114, 121, 122; Schafer, "Reform or Experiment?" 35; Sacher, *Perfect War of Politics*, 112.

80. [Gustavus Schmidt], "On the Administration of the Law in Louisiana," The Supreme Court and Its Decisions, *Louisiana Law Journal*, 1, no. 4 (Apr. 1842): 151, 156–57; Mark Fernandez, "From Chaos to Continuity: Early Reforms of the Supreme Court of Louisiana, 1845–1852," *Louisiana History* 20, no. 1 (Winter 1987): 20–23.

81. La. Const. of 1845 tit. IV, arts. 63 (supreme court jurisdiction), 64 (chief justice, supreme court tenure, salaries), 76, (district court salaries), 77 (district court tenure), 81 (justices of the peace), 82 (district court clerks), 83 (sheriffs, coroners); La. Const. of 1812, art. III, § 9 (judges, sheriffs); Act of Sept. 5, 1812, 1812 La. Laws 40 (justices of the peace); Act of Jan. 21, 1814, 1814 La. Laws 4 (coroner); Act of Mar. 24, 1840, 1840 La. Laws 72, 73 (creation of new parish authorizing district judge to appoint clerk).

82. *La. P&D*, 740–41 (James F. Brent), 741–43 (Amasa Read). When Brent died in 1847, newspapers described him as one of the Louisiana Democratic Party's "most influential members." *Concordia Intelligencer*, July 10, 1847, 2; *National Whig*, July 27, 1847, 3. Read, brother of Ohio Supreme Court judge Nathaniel C. Read, was a Democratic representative in the Louisiana legislature in 1846 and a congressional candidate in 1847. *Baton Rouge Gazette*, Oct. 11, 1845, 2; July 31, 1847, 2.

83. *La. P&D*, 744–45 (James F. Brent).

84. *La. P&D*, 747–48.

85. *La. P&D*, 748.

86. *La. P&D*, 748.

87. *La. P&D*, 749–51.

88. *La. P&D*, 755–58. On Quitman's changing views on the elective judiciary, see Robert E. May, *John A. Quitman: Old South Crusader* (Baton Rouge: Louisiana State University Press, 1985), 52–57.

89. La. Const. of 1845 tit. II, arts. 8 (representation in house), 10–11 (suffrage), 15–16 (representation in senate); tit. IV, arts. 64 (supreme court tenure), 77 (district court tenure), 81 (justices of the peace election and tenure), 82 (district court clerks), 83 (sheriffs, coroners); *La. P&D*, 844 (Bernard de Marigny); Hargrave, *Louisiana State Constitution*, 8 ("Under the new constitution, the twelve parishes in the black belt had as many representatives as twenty white parishes with twice the number of freemen"); Schafer, "Political Development," 141. According to the federal census of 1840, New Orleans had 29 percent of the state's total population (102,193 inhabitants out of 352,411 in the state) and 37 percent of its white population (59,272 out of 158,457), but the constitution of 1845 limited the city to 20 percent of the state's representatives and 12.5 percent of its senators. See Sacher, *Perfect War of Politics*, 115 (proportion of legislators from New Orleans).

90. Sacher, *Perfect War of Politics*, 115; Wayne M. Everard, "Louisiana's 'Whig' Constitution Revisited: The Constitution of 1852," in *In Search of Fundamental Law: Louisiana's Constitutions, 1812–1974*, ed. Warren M. Billings and Edward F. Haas (Lafayette: Center for Louisiana Studies, University of Southwestern Louisiana 1993), 37–39; Howard, *Political Tendencies*, 69; Joe Gray Taylor, *Louisiana: A History* (New York: Norton, 1984), 69, 71; "Southern and Western Rail-road Convention," *De Bow's Review of the Southern and Western States*, o.s. 12 (Mar. 1852): 314; John G. Van Deusen, *The Ante-Bellum Southern Commercial Conventions* (Durham, NC: Duke University Press, 1926), 21–38.

91. *Daily Crescent*, May 15, 1849, 2; June 9, 1849, 2.

92. "Teche," letter to the editor of the *Daily Crescent*, repr. in *Planters' Banner*, Nov. 8, 1849, 3; *Southern Sentinel*, Oct. 3, 1849, 2; Oct. 31, 1849, 2.

93. Dubin, *Party Affiliations*, 76; Everard, "Louisiana's 'Whig' Constitution," 40–41; Act of Mar. 20, 1850, 1850 La. Laws 177; *Planters' Banner*, Feb. 14, 1850, 2. The house of representatives wanted to make a host of other offices elective as well, from the state engineer to weighers of hay, but the senate refused to go along. *Daily Crescent*, Mar. 15, 1850, 2; Mar. 18, 1850, 1.

94. Sacher, *Perfect War of Politics*, 161–64, 167; Everard, "Louisiana's 'Whig' Constitution," 41; *Southern Sentinel*, Nov. 29, 1851, 2; Res. of Feb. 11, 1852, 1852 La. Laws 14; Act of Feb. 23, 1852, 1852 La. Laws 57; *Southern Sentinel*, Feb. 14, 1852, 2. Contrary to the *Southern Sentinel*, Dubin says that the senate was evenly divided 16–16 and the Whigs controlled the house 54–43. *Party Affiliations*, 76. Judith K. Schafer writes that the Whigs had much Democratic support for the call for a convention (Schafer, "Political Development", 142), while Michael F. Holt maintains that Whigs called the convention over the opposition of Democrats (Holt, *Rise and Fall*, 736). According to Everard, the division was more between urban and rural members than between Whig and Democratic members, with rural Democrats providing the "meager opposition." Everard, "Louisiana's 'Whig' Constitution," 41–42. Two years earlier, writes Sacher, the Whig house had passed a convention bill but the Democratic senate had defeated it (p. 164).

95. Everard, "Louisiana's 'Whig' Constitution," 42–43; Schafer, "Political Development," 142; Holt, *Rise and Fall*, 736, 1121n37.

96. Sacher, *Perfect War of Politics*, 167–68, 229–30; Green, *Finance and Economic Development*, 132–35; La. Const. of 1852, tit. II, art. 10 (suffrage); tit. VI, arts. 109–10 (debt for internal improvements), 118 (creation of banks by special or general acts). Public offices made elective by the 1852 constitution included the secretary and treasurer of state (tit. III, art. 57), supreme court justices (tit. IV, art. 64), justices of the peace (tit. IV, art. 78), clerks of the inferior courts (tit. IV, art. 79), sheriffs and coroners (tit. IV, art. 80), inferior court judges (tit. IV, art. 81), the attorney general and district attorneys (tit. IV, art. 83), commissioners of the board of public works (tit. VII, art. 130), and the superintendent of public education (tit. VIII, art. 135). At the convention, 20–25 percent of Democrats voted with the Whigs on banking and internal improvements. Everard, "Louisiana's 'Whig' Constitution," 43.

97. *La. Jour. (1852)*, 33, 58, 61 (adoption of articles providing for the election of supreme and inferior court judges without debate or roll calls), 54–56.

98. Sacher, *Perfect War of Politics*, 169–70.

99. *Daily Crescent*, Sept. 21, 1852, 1.

Chapter 5: Explaining the Rise of Judicial Elections

1. Eaton, *Should Judges Be Elected?*, 70, 72.

2. Harlan F. Stone, "The Issues Involved in the Methods of Selecting and Removing Judges," *Proceedings of the Academy of Political Science in the City of New York* 3, no. 2 (Jan. 1913): 77; Learned Hand, "The Elective and Appointive Methods of Selection of Judges," *Proceedings of the Academy of Political Science in the City of New York* 3, no. 2 (Jan. 1913): 82–83; James Willard Hurst, *The Growth of American Law: The Law Makers* (Boston: Little, Brown, 1950), 140; Evan Haynes, *The Selection and Tenure of Judges* (Newark, NJ: National Conference of Judicial Councils, 1944), 100–1.

3. Caleb Nelson, "A Re-Evaluation of Scholarly Explanations for the Rise of the Elective Judiciary in Antebellum America," *American Journal of Legal History* 37, no. 2 (Apr. 1993): 192, 219.

4. David M. Gold, *The Great Tea Party in the Old Northwest: State Constitutional Conventions, 1847–1851* (New Orleans: Quid Pro, 2015); *Ill. Deb.* 124 (Zadoc Casey); *Ind. D&P*, 1:645 (Daniel Read); *Ohio D&P*, 1:469 (Henry Gregg).

5. Michael F. Holt, *The Rise and Fall of the American Whig Party: Jacksonian Politics and the Onset of the Civil War* (New York: Oxford University Press, 1999), 66–67; Joseph W. Pearson, *The Whigs' America: Middle-Class Political Thought in the Age of Jackson and Clay* (Lexington: University Press of Kentucky, 2020), 142–43; *New-York Daily Tribune*, Nov. 29, 1845, 2. For examples of Democratic support for publicly funded internal improvements, free common schools, and prohibition, see, respectively, *Ohio D&P*, 2:123 (James Louden), *Indiana State Sentinel*, July 30, 1846, 4 and June 10, 1848, 2, and Jon Sterngass, "Maine Law," in *Alcohol and Temperance in Modern History: A Global Encyclopedia*, ed. Jack S. Blocker Jr., David M. Fahey, and Ian R. Tyrell (Santa Barbara, CA: ABC-CLIO, 2003), 2:393. (The legislature that passed the original Maine Law of 1851 had huge Democratic majorities in both houses. *Eastern Argus*, Sept. 21, 1850, 2.)

6. Eaton, *Should Judges Be Elected?* 5, 1; Patrick Winston Dunn, "Judicial Selection in the States: A Critical Study with Proposals for Reform," *Hofstra Law Review* 4, no. 2 (Winter 1976): 279; Shugerman, *People's Courts*, 76, 101.

7. *Ky. D&P*, 252–53 (William D. Mitchell), 277 (Francis M. Bristow), 663 (William R. Thompson); *Del. D&P*, 167 (Benjamin T. Biggs); *N.Y. D&P (C&S 1846)*, 591 (Horatio J. Stow), 588 (Conrad Swakhamer).

8. Kermit L. Hall, "The Judiciary on Trial: State Constitutional Reform and the Rise of an Elected Judiciary, 1846–1850," *Historian* 45, no. 3 (May 1983): 337–54.

9. Nelson, "Re-Evaluation," 202–3, 207; Hall, "Judiciary on Trial," 348, 350.

10. Hall, "Judiciary on Trial," 341–43.

11. Hall "Judiciary on Trial," 350, 344; James A. Henretta, "The Strange Birth of Liberal America: Michael Hoffman and the New York Constitution of 1846," *New York History* 77, no. 2 (Apr. 1996): 151–76; *Ohio D&P*, 1:430–31, 551, 2:622–23; Shugerman, *People's Courts*, 115–16; W. S. Metcalfe, "Peter Hitchcock," *Ohio Law Bulletin*, 51, no. 30 (July 23, 1906): 274; Joseph A. Ranney, "Ryan, Edward G.," in *The Yale Biographical Dictionary of American Law*, ed. Roger K. Newman (New Haven, CT: Yale University Press, 2009), 474–75; Alfons J. Beitzinger, *Edward G. Ryan: Lion of the Law* (Madison: State Historical Society of Wisconsin, 1960), 14–25; *Wisc. Conv.*, 591–96 (Ryan quotation at p. 595).

12. For example, Hall writes that "[m]oderates criticized the repeated inability of the judiciary to strike down legislative measures creating ruinous debt through ill-conceived programs of internal improvements, sustaining the vested rights of corporations and expanding state-backed banking activity. Moderates applauded governmental intervention in the economy, but they denounced the legislature's uncontrolled spending and unwillingness to serve a diverse body of economic interests." Hall, "Judiciary on Trial," 350, text at n60. One source cited by Hall in note 60 (*New Constitution*, May 19, 1849,

38) criticizes the legislature for running up debt, but it says nothing about the judiciary, provides no information to indicate that the anonymous author was a "moderate," and was written before the convention.

13. Hall gives *Ohio D&P*, 1:657 as his source (Hall, "Judiciary on Trial," 344n30), but the quotation is not there. A search of the entire two volumes of published debates as they appear in Google Books and the HathiTrust Digital Library also comes up empty.

14. *Mass. D&P*, 1:7; Hall, "Judiciary on Trial," 350 (Keyes alleged quotation). Hall's footnote ("Judiciary on Trial," 350n61) cites *Mass. D&P*, 2:770. Jed Shugerman also notes his inability to find the Keyes quotation. Shugerman, *People's Courts*, 326n45. Other examples of nonexistent quotations in Hall's article include an oft-repeated one supposedly from *The Old Guard* of Kentucky ("if the dogs could vote," p. 341), a second from the Ohio convention ("little aristocrats," p. 348), and a third from the Indiana convention ("revolution in law," p. 352). I am grateful to Katie Henning and her colleagues at the Special Collections Research Center, Margaret I. King Library, University of Kentucky, for paging through every issue of *The Old Guard*, a journal published in 1850 to oppose ratification of Kentucky's proposed constitution.

15. Nelson, "Re-Evaluation," 199–203, 207–8; Shugerman, *People's Courts*, 115–16; Geyh, *Who Is to Judge?*, 32–33; David Lyle, "A Norm No More: Elected Officials' Lack of Deference to State Courts," *New York University Law Review Online* 93 (Mar. 2018): 55–56.

16. Shugerman, *People's Courts*, 12–13.

17. Shugerman, *People's Courts*, 84–86, 125, 278, app. B.

18. Shugerman, *People's Courts*, 121–22.

19. "The New Constitution of New York," *Law Reporter* 9, no. 11 (Mar. 1847): 482; Charles Z. Lincoln, *The Constitutional History of New York*, vol. 2, *1822–1894* (Rochester, NY: Lawyers Co-Operative Pub. Co., 1906), 140. Shugerman, too, acknowledges the importance of judicial reform as a motivating factor in the calling of the convention. Shugerman, *People's Courts*, 93, 95.

20. Mo. H.J. (Reg. Sess. 1836–37), 36; J. Christopher Schnell, "Chicago Versus St. Louis: A Reassessment of the Great Rivalry," *Missouri Historical Review* 71, no. 3 (Apr. 1977): 251–52.

21. Schnell, "Chicago Versus St. Louis," 252–57; John W. Million, *State Aid to Railways in Missouri* (Chicago, 1896), 7, 36–38, 65, 67–114; Act of Feb. 11, 1839, 1838–39 Mo. Laws 68; Act of Feb. 15, 1841, 1840–41 Mo. Laws 96; Mering, *Whig Party in Missouri*, 146–47.

22. Shugerman, *People's Courts*, 85–100.

23. *N.Y. D&P (B&A 1846)*, 672–73; *Ohio D&P*, 2:181 (Samuel Humphreville); *Federal Union*, June 5, 1849, 3.

24. *Ky. D&P*, 171 (R. N. Wickliffe); *Ohio D&P*, 2:216 (William Sawyer).

25. *Ohio D&P*, 1:689 (Benjamin Stanton); *Washington Telegraph*, June 14, 1848, 2; *Md. D&P*, 2:477 (Ezekiel F. Chambers).

26. Shugerman, *People's Courts*, 94–95; Eaton, *Should Judges Be Elected?* 72.

27. Peter J. Galie and Christopher Bopst, *The New York State Constitution*, 2nd ed. (New York: Oxford University Press, 2012), 15–18; Gold, *Great Tea Party*; New

268 Notes to Pages 142–148

Constitution, May 5, 1849, 1; *Joliet Signal,* Mar. 30, 1847, 2; *Detroit Free Press,* Apr. 7, 1848, 2; *Hillsdale Whig Standard,* Oct. 2, 1849, 2.

28. *Arkansas State Gazette and Democrat,* June 9, 1854, 2; *Examiner,* June 2, 1849, 3.

29. Miss. Const. of 1832 art. IV, § 2; Mo. Const. of 1820, art. VI of amendments (1851); Tex. Const. of 1845 art. IV, § 5; *Tex. Digest,* 30; Act of Jan. 1, 1853, 1852–53 Fla. Laws 189; Ky. Const. of 1850 art. IV, § 3; Res. of Feb. 1, 1850, 1849–50 Tenn. Laws 566; La. Const. of 1852 tit. IV, § 62; Md. Const. of 1851 art. IV, § 4; Va. Const. of 1851 art. VI, § 10; Ohio Const. of 1851 art. IV, § 11; Cal. Const. of 1849 art. VI, § 3; Ind. Const. of 1851 art. VII, § 2; Iowa Const. of 1857 art. V, § 3; Kan. Const. of 1861 art. III, §2; Act of Apr. 17, 1852, 1852 Wis. Laws 597; Minn. Const. of 1857 art. VI, § 3; Ill. Const. of 1848 art. V, § 3; Mich. Const. of 1850 art. VI, § 2; N.Y. Const. of 1846 art. VI, § 2; Pa. Const. of 1838 art. V, § 2 (amended 1850).

30. Northern New England had a democratic political culture, with free suffrage and acceptable if not equal representation. For example, the constitutions of Maine and Vermont bestowed the franchise on all adult male citizens, with no property, taxpaying, religious, or even racial qualifications, and they imposed no such qualifications for holding office. Me. Const. of 1819 art. II, § 1; art. IV, pt. 1, § 4; art. IV, pt. 2, § 6; Vt. Const. of 1793 ch. I, art. 8; ch. II, §§ 8, 10, 18. The Vermont constitution gave the right to vote to "freemen," but it conferred the privileges of freemen on all adult males "of a quiet and peaceable behaviour" who met the one-year residency requirement. Vt. Const. of 1793 ch. II, § 21. The system of legislative representation in Vermont, based on towns rather than population, was far from equal, but most Vermonters seemed satisfied with it. See note 32.

31. *Sun,* July 27, 1849, 1; Jan 2, 1850, 4.

32. Gillies and Sanford, *Records,* 374, 509; *Burlington Free Press,* Jan. 11, 1850, 2 (constitutional convention's rejection by a vote of 218–9 of proposal that towns be represented in the house approximately according to population); Eli A. Glasser, "Government and the Constitution (1820–1917)," in *Commonwealth History of Massachusetts: Nineteenth Century Massachusetts, 1820–1889,* vol. 4 ed. Albert Bushnell Hart, (New York: States History Co., 1930), 21.

33. Act of December 15, 1830, 1830 Miss. Laws 117.

Chapter 6: Electing the Judges

1. *New-York Daily Tribune,* Apr. 27, 1847, 2. The *Tribune* referred to the elections forthcoming on May 31 because that was the date set by the bill that provided for judicial elections then pending in the legislature. See *Brooklyn Daily Eagle,* Mar. 19, 1847, 2. The bills that finally passed, one dealing with elections in New York County and the other with elections in the rest of the state, fixed the date as June 7. Act of May 12, 1847, 1847 N.Y. Laws (1st sess.) 279; Act of May 12, 1847, 1847 N.Y. Laws (1st. sess. 306).

2. "Ithuriel," letter to the editor, *New-York Daily Tribune,* May 1, 1847, 2; *New York Herald,* June 8, 1847, 2; *Sunday Dispatch,* June 13, 1847, 2.

3. *Point Coupee Democrat,* Oct. 23, 1858, 2; *New Orleans Daily Crescent,* Mar. 17, 1853, 1; *Alexandria Democrat,* repr. in *Opelousas Courier,* Dec. 8, 1855, 2.

4. *Republican Banner,* Sept. 17, 1858, 2; *Nashville Union and American,* Dec. 2,

1855, 3; Kermit L. Hall, "Progressive Reform and the Decline of Democratic Accountability: The Popular Election of State Supreme Court Judges, 1850–1920," *American Bar Foundation Research Journal*, 9, no. 2 (Spring 1984): 352–53.

5. *Jeffersonian Republican*, Sept. 26, 1850, 2; *Cadiz Sentinel*, repr. in *Spirit of Democracy*, Sept. 29, 1849, 2.

6. *Georgia Telegraph*, Oct. 11, 1853, 2; *Georgia Jeffersonian*, Apr. 14, 1853, 2; *Georgia Journal and Messenger*, Aug. 1, 1855, 2; *Times and Sentinel Tri-Weekly*, Mar. 12, 1856, 3; *Albany Patriot*, Nov. 4, 1858, 2.

7. N.Y. Const. of 1846 art. XIV, §§ 1, 2, 4; Va. Const. of 1850 art. VI, § 16; Jt. Res. of Jan. 29, 1850, 1849–50 Ala. Laws 485; Ark. Const. of 1836 art. IV, § 8; Act of Dec. 29, 1848, 1848–49 Ark. Law 49; La. Const. of 1852 tit. IV, art. 82; Res. of Feb. 1, 1850, 1849–50 Tenn. Laws 566; Act of Jan. 12, 1852, 1851–52 Ga. Acts 85; Act of Mar. 1, 1856, 1855–56 Ga. Acts 140; Mo. Const. of 1820 art. III, § 8; art. VI, § 1 (amended 1851).

8. *Richmond Enquirer*, Aug. 9, 1850, 1.

9. Joseph P. Smith, ed., *History of the Republican Party in Ohio* (1898), 1:40. Smith includes the figures for almost all of the races of the 1850s. His vote totals differ slightly from those reported in the newspapers. For the Indiana returns, see *Indiana State Sentinel*, Nov. 18, 1852, 2; *Evansville Daily Journal*, Nov. 2, 1854, 3; *Indiana Daily State Sentinel*, Nov. 2, 1858, 2.

10. *Southern Reformer*, Feb. 9, 1846, 2.

11. *Vicksburg Tri-Weekly Whig*, Jan. 10, 1852, 2; *Mississippian and State Gazette*, Nov. 21, 1851, 3. On Scott and Guion as Whigs, see *Southern Reveille*, May 19, 1852, 1. In 1850, Guion was elected vice president of the newly formed State Rights Association. *Mississippian*, Aug. 2, 1850, 2.

12. Va. Const. of 1850 art. VI, §§ 2, 10; *Richmond Enquirer*, May 25, 1852, 4; *Texas Republican*, Oct. 25, 1851, 2; Act of Feb. 2, 1856, 1855–56 Tex. Laws 69; *Richmond Reporter*, July 12, 1856, 2; *Dallas Herald*, Aug. 16, 1856, 2; *Athens Post*, June 9, 1854, 2; *Memphis Daily Appeal*, Sept. 3, 1858, 2; Dennis K. Boman, *Abiel Leonard, Yankee Slaveholder, Eminent Jurist, and Passionate Unionist* (Lewiston, NY: Mellen, 2002), 177; *Glasgow Weekly Times*, Jan. 4, 1855, 2.

13. *Pointe Coupee Democrat*, Oct. 30, 1858, 2. A Whig paper made a similar complaint about Democratic partisanship in judicial elections but without suggesting a change in the date of judicial elections as a solution. *Planters' Banner*, June 30, 1853, 2.

14. *Republican Banner*, Sept. 17, 1858, 2.

15. *Spirit of Democracy*, Aug. 13, 1851, 2; *Gallipolis Journal*, July 10, 1851, 2; *Indiana State Sentinel*, May 6, 1852; May 13, 1852, 2.

16. For examples of announcements of availability, see *Nashville Union and American*, Mar. 31, 1854, 2; *Memphis Daily Appeal*, Aug. 13, 1858, 3. For the change from nonpartisan to partisan announcements in Louisiana, compare the nonpartisan announcements in the *Southern Sentinel*, June 16, 1855, 2, with the openly partisan announcements in *Feliciana Democrat*, Jan. 1, 1859, 2.

17. Larry D. Kramer, *The People Themselves: Popular Constitutionalism and Judicial Review* (New York: Oxford University Press, 2004), 209; Richard Drew, "The Surge and

Consolidation of American Judicial Power: Judicial Review in the States, 1840–1880" (paper presented at the annual meeting of the American Political Science Association, Chicago, IL, Sept. 2, 2004), 24; Shugerman, *People's Courts*, 140–4.

18. *Ohio D&P*, 1:683; *Vermont Watchman & State Journal*, Mar. 23, 1855, 2; Shugerman, *People's Courts*, 106.

19. *Weekly National Intelligencer*, July 17, 1847, 4; *Liberty Tribune*, repr. in *Glasgow Weekly Times*, July 24, 1851, 2; *Richmond Enquirer*, Aug. 9, 1850, 1.

20. "Madison," letter to the editor, *New Constitution*, June 23, 1849, 116. See also Silvana R. Siddali, *Frontier Democracy: Constitutional Conventions in the Old Northwest* (New York: Cambridge University Press, 2016), 188–89 (disgust with the idea of party judges in the Old Northwest, especially Illinois). An elderly Roger B. Taney would have disagreed. In 1857, the eighty-year-old chief justice, fearing the country was on the road to perdition, saw the "continually recurring Elections by the people of every Office—small and great" as a source of instability and loss of respect for authority. He thought that few public officers, including judges, "dared to do their duty, for fear of offending those who elected them, and thereby losing the offices which gave them bread." G. P. R. James to George William Frederick Villiers, May 30, 1857, in Robert L. Paquette, "The Mind of Roger Taney: New Light on the *Dred Scott* Decision," *Academic Questions* 29, no. 1 (Mar. 2016): 47.

21. The closer a decision was to election time, the more likely a judge might have been to decide the case with the election in mind. In 1987, Otto Kaus, a former justice of the California Supreme Court, said, "I'm afraid the era of retaining judges on the basis of their character, without tallying up their votes, is a thing of the past. There's no way a judge is going to be able to ignore the political consequences of certain decisions, especially if he or she has to make them near election time." Paul Reidinger, "The Politics of Judging," *American Bar Association Journal* 73, no. 5 (Apr. 1987): 58.

22. Joel H. Silbey, *The American Political Nation, 1838–1893* (Stanford, CA: Stanford University Press, 1991), 60, 120; Eugene H. Roseboom, *The Civil War Era: 1850–1873*, vol. 4 of *The History of the State of Ohio*, ed. Carl Wittke (Columbus: Ohio State Archaeological and Historical Society, 1944), 349–50.

23. The five successful candidates were William Daniel, Richard C. L. Moncure, Green B. Samuels, John J. Allen, and George H. Lee. *Richmond Enquirer*, June 15, 1852, 2 (listing the electees without reference to party). All of the winners are identified in one source or another as Democrats except for Allen, a Whig from Botetourt County in western Virginia. For Allen's political affiliation, see S. S. P. Patteson, "The Supreme Court of Appeals of Virginia," pt. 2, *Green Bag* 5, no. 8 (Aug. 1893): 364.

24. Geo. W. Atkinson and Alvaro F. Gibbens, *Prominent Men of West Virginia* (1890), 212 (Joseph Johnson); Holt, *Rise and Fall*, 623.

25. Henry Plauché Dart, "The History of the Supreme Court of Louisiana," *Louisiana Historical Quarterly* 4, no. 1 (Jan. 1921): 35–36; *True American*, Feb. 5, 1839, 2; Act of Feb. 2, 1839, 1839 La. Laws 4; "Judges of the Supreme Court during the Time Embraced by this Volume," 14 La. iii (1840).

26. Associate Judge George Rogers King resigned from the court in 1850. *Concordia Intelligencer*, Jan. 26, 1850, 2. His successor, Isaac T. Preston, died on July 5, 1852, nine

months before the first popular election for supreme court justices. Dart, "Supreme Court of Louisiana," 39.

27. La. Const. of 1852 tit. IV, arts. 62–65, 82; *Southern Sentinel*, Apr. 9, 1853, 2 (low turnout). For nonpartisan announcements of candidacies, see *Southern Sentinel*, Feb. 26, 1853, 2; *Daily Comet*, Mar. 4, 1853, 2; *Daily Picayune*, Feb. 23, 1853, 4. For conventions declining to nominate supreme court candidates, see *Southern Sentinel*, Feb. 26, 1853, 2 (nomination for chief justice); *Planters' Banner*, Dec. 11, 1852, 2 (state tickets). For newspapers calling for the election of the best men, see *Southern Sentinel*, Feb. 26, 1853, 2; Mar. 5, 1853, 2; *Planters' Banner*, Mar. 17, 1853, 2; *Daily Comet*, Mar. 11, 1853, 2.

28. Sacher, *Perfect War of Politics*, 222–27, 232. The victorious supreme court candidates were Thomas Slidell (chief justice), Cornelius Voorhies, Alexander M. Buchanan, Abner N. Ogden, and James G. Campbell. The Whig candidates included Christian Roselius, Edwin T. Merrick, Edward Simon, Thomas J. Cooley, and Thomas H. Lewis.

29. Sacher, *Perfect War of Politics*, 249; *American Patriot*, June 2, 1855, 2; June 23, 1855, 2; July 7, 1855, 2; *Daily Comet*, May 1, 1853, 2; *Opelousas Patriot*, Apr. 7, 1855, 2.

30. *New Orleans Daily Crescent*, Mar. 28, 1857, 2; Apr. 6, 1857, 1; *Houma Ceres*, Mar. 21, 1857, 2; *New Orleans Daily Crescent*, Apr. 8, 1857, 2; *South-Western*, Sept. 22, 1858, 2; *Daily Delta*, Oct. 7, 1858, 1; *Opelousas Courier*, Mar. 19, 1859, 2. The independent candidate in 1858 was John Ray. In 1855, a faction of the American Party nominated Ray for governor in place of the regularly chosen nominee. *Opelousas Courier*, Oct. 6, 1855, 2. Ray denounced the move and expressed his support for the original selection. *Thibodaux Minerva*, Oct. 20, 1855, 2. In the only other supreme court race in the 1850s, Henry M. Spofford defeated Isaiah Garrett and O. N. Ogden in 1854. *South-Western*, Oct. 25, 1854, 2. Spofford would be a Democrat after the Civil War, but his antebellum political affiliation is unknown. Both Garrett and Ogden were Whigs, although Garrett opposed Winfield Scott's candidacy for president in 1852 and Ogden would associate himself with the American (Know Nothing) Party by 1855. On Garrett, see *Daily Picayune*, Sept. 5, 1844, 2; *Daily Delta*, July 31, 1852, 1. On Ogden, see *Daily Crescent*, July 30, 1849, 2; *Opelousas Patriot*, Aug. 11, 1855, 2.

31. Tenn. Const. of 1835 art. VI, §§ 2–3; Dubin, *Party Affiliations*, 176; Timothy S. Huebner, "Judicial Independence in an Age of Democracy, Sectionalism, and War, 1835–1865," in *A History of the Tennessee Supreme Court*, ed. James W. Ely Jr. (Knoxville: University of Tennessee Press, 2002), 67–68. For Turley's political affiliation, see Russell Fowler, "William B. Turley," in *The Tennessee Encyclopedia of History and Culture*, https://tennesseeencyclopedia.net/entries/william-b-turley/; Polk to Daniel Graham, Nov. 3, 1845, in *Correspondence of James K. Polk*, vol. 10, July–December 1845, ed. Wayne Cutler. (Knoxville: University of Tennessee Press, 2004), 341. Reese was a Whig, although that label would not yet have been used in Tennessee in 1835. John W. Green, *Lives of the Judges of the Supreme Court of Tennessee, 1796–1947* (Knoxville, TN: Archer & Smith, 1947), 97–98. For Green's Whig sympathies, see *Nashville Union*, Nov. 29, 1842, 2. Catron lost his seat on the state supreme court, but his fidelity to the president did not go unrewarded. On Jackson's last day in office, he appointed Catron to the United States Supreme Court, where Catron remained until his death nearly three decades later. Huebner, "Judicial Independence," 68.

32. Dubin, *Party Affiliations*, 176. Elections for the legislature were held in August; the new General Assembly convened in October. Tenn. Const. of 1835 art. II, §§ 7–8.

33. Huebner, "Judicial Independence," 84–85. McKinney hardly participated in politics, but in 1836 he was a presidential elector for Hugh Lawson White, a former Jacksonian who had turned against Jackson. John Trotwood Moore and Austin P. Foster, *Tennessee: The Volunteer State, 1769–1923*, ed. John Trotwood Moore (Chicago: S. J. Clarke, 1923), 2:175. Upon McKinney's appointment to the supreme court a newspaper identified him as a Whig. *Indiana State Sentinel*, Nov. 25, 1847, 1. See also *Nashville Union and American*, Apr. 23, 1869, 2 (identifying McKinney as a Whig when appointed to the supreme court).

34. Huebner, "Judicial Independence," 88. The General Assembly created the Common Law and Chancery Court of the City of Memphis in February 1850 (Act of Feb. 2, 1850, 1849–50 Tenn. Acts 83) and promptly elected Turley to the judgeship (*Republican Banner and Nashville Whig*, Feb. 8, 1850, 2).

35. Ely, *Tennessee Supreme Court*, 341. For Totten as a Democrat, see Samuel H. Laughlin to James K. Polk, Dec. 25, 1843, in *Correspondence of Polk*, 394.

36. For Caruthers's political affiliation, see Andrew R. Dodge and Betty K. Koed, eds., *Biographical Directory of the United States Congress, 1774–2005* (Washington, DC: Government Printing Office, 2005), 794. See also *Nashville Union and American*, Apr. 23, 1869, 2 (identifying Caruthers as a Whig when appointed to the supreme court).

37. Huebner, "Judicial Independence," 89.

38. *Nashville Union and American*, Nov. 12, 1853, 2; Tenn. S.J. 178 (Reg. Sess. 1853–54). According to the senate journal, the vote for Caruthers was 87–2, so either the Democrats saw no point in fighting for a lost cause or Caruthers had genuine bipartisan support.

39. Tenn. Const. of 1835 art. VI, §§ 2 and 3, as amended 1853; *Nashville Union and American*, May 13, 1854, 2; *Athens Post*, June 9, 1854, 2; *Daily Nashville True Whig*, Aug. 25, 1855, 3; *Nashville Union and American*, Dec. 14, 1855, 2 (party affiliations of candidates in the 1855 elections); Ely, *Tennessee Supreme Court*, app. 1, 334; *Memphis Daily Appeal*, July 8, 1858, 2; *Daily Union*, Apr. 12, 1847, 2; Aug. 7, 1847, 2 (Wright elected to the state house of representatives as a Democrat); *Fayetteville (TN) Observer*, Sept. 2, 1858, 2; *Memphis Daily Appeal*, Sept. 3, 1858, 2 (last-minute candidacy of Elijah Walker against Wright, denounced by Democrats as a Know Nothing trick); *Nashville Union and American*, Dec. 2, 1855, 3; *Nashville Patriot*, Sept. 3, 1858, 3.

40. Mo. H.J. 119–20, 147–48 (Reg. Sess. 1850–51).

41. Mo. Const. of 1820, art. V, §§ 13–14. For the identification of Scott, McBride, and Napton as anti-Benton Democrats, see William Barclay Napton, *The Union on Trial: The Political Journals of Judge William Barclay Napton, 1829–1883*, ed. Christopher Phillips and Jason L. Pendleton (Columbia: University of Missouri Press, 2005), 101.

42. *Glasgow Weekly Times*, Feb. 8, 1849, 1. Napton identified Ryland as a Benton Democrat. Napton, *Union on Trial*, 101–2.

43. Dubin, *Party Affiliations*, 108, 110nn2–3; Holt, *Rise and Fall*, 561.

44. *Western Union*, July 31, 1851, 2; *St. Joseph Gazette*, July 2, 1851, 2.

45. *Liberty Tribune*, repr. in *Glasgow Weekly Times*, July 24, 1851, 2; *Western Union*, July 31, 1851, 2; Napton, *Union on Trial*, 102, 102n43; *St. Joseph Gazette*, July 2, 1851, 2.

46. *Glasgow Weekly Times*, July 31, 1851, 2.

47. *Glasgow Weekly Times*, Oct. 2, 1851, 2; Christopher Phillips, "Introduction: The Making of a Southerner: William Barclay Napton, 1808–1883," in Napton, *Union on Trial*, 49; *Glasgow Weekly Times*, Nov. 23, 1854, 2; Boman, *Leonard*, 177; *Glasgow Weekly Times*, Jan. 4, 1855, 2; *St. Joseph Commercial Cycle*, Feb. 2, 1855, 4.

48. *Missouri Statesman*, Sept. 12, 1856, 3; *Glasgow Weekly Times*, Sept. 3, 1857, 3; *Glasgow Weekly Times*, June 23, 1859, 3; Aug. 18, 1859, 3. In 1856 the American Party won eight of thirty-three seats in the senate and twenty-five of 133 seats in the house. The Whigs had been reduced to just four seats in each house. Dubin, *Party Affiliations*, 108. The two Democrats elected to the supreme court in 1857 were Scott and Napton. Dennis K. Boman identifies Richardson as a former Whig who had joined the Know Nothing (American) Party. Boman, *Lincoln's Resolute Unionist*, 95n4. Boman does not give a source for this identification, but a newspaper correspondent reporting from Randolph County noted that "all the Americans voted for Richardson." *Glasgow Weekly Times*, Aug. 6, 1857, 3.

49. *McArthur Democrat*, Sept. 23, 1858, 1. Attempts by political or commercial groups to get judicial candidates to state their opinions on the constitutionality of legislation that had been passed or proposed on the controversial subjects of slavery and prohibition led judicial candidates and newspaper editors to deny the propriety of such interrogatories. See, e.g., *Raftsman's Journal*, Sept. 20, 1854, 2; *Daily American Organ*, Oct. 23, 1855, 2; *New York Herald*, Oct. 24, 1855 (morning ed.), 1.

Chapter 7: Elected Judges and Judicial Review

A portion of chapter 7 was originally published in slightly different form as "Judicial Review in the Mid-Nineteenth Century: The Laboratory of Louisiana," *Journal of Southern Legal History* 30 (2022): 69–101. Reprinted by permission.

1. John Kobler, *Ardent Spirits: The Rise and Fall of Prohibition* (New York: Putnam, 1973), 29, 76, 85; Ernest Cummings Marriner, *The History of Colby College* (Waterville, ME: Colby College Press, 1963), 61; Daniel Dorchester, *The Liquor Problem in All Ages* (New York, 1884), 539; *Bangor Daily Whig and Courier*, Mar. 16, 1837, 2 and Mar. 21, 1837, 2.

2. State v. Learned, 47 Me. 426 (1859); Jed Handelsman Shugerman, "Appendices accompanying *Harvard Law Review* article: 'Economic Crisis and the Rise of Judicial Elections and Judicial Review'" (2010).

3. James M. Rosenthal, "Massachusetts Acts and Resolves Declared Unconstitutional by the Supreme Judicial Court of Massachusetts," *Massachusetts Law Quarterly* 1, no. 4 (Aug. 1916): 301–18; Edward S. Corwin, "The Extension of Judicial Review in New York: 1783–1905," *Michigan Law Review* 15, no. 4 (Feb. 1917): 285; Elijah W. Miles, "The Origin and Early Development of Judicial Review in Indiana, 1816–1855" (PhD diss., Indiana University, 1962), 168–69; Richard Drew, "The Surge and Consolidation of American Judicial Power: Judicial Review in the States, 1840–1880" (paper

presented at the annual meeting of the American Political Science Association, Chicago, IL, Sept. 2, 2004), 38, table 1; Shugerman, *People's Courts*, 278, app. B.

4. Corwin, "Extension of Judicial Review," 285; Morton J. Horwitz, *The Transformation of American Law, 1780–1860* (Cambridge, MA: Harvard University Press, 1977), 259–66, 346n6 (1977) (quotation at 259); Miles, "Judicial Review in Indiana," 108–9. Greg Sergienki rejects Horwitz's analysis, arguing instead that the rise in negative judicial review in New York stemmed from a constitutional change that removed senators (all of them) from the state's highest court. According to Sergienko, the senators, who far outnumbered the court's "professional" judges, tended to uphold legislation that they had passed. When they were gone from the court, the professional judges struck down much more legislation. Greg Sergienko, "A Body of Sound Practical Common Sense: Law Reform through Lay Judges, Public Choice Theory, and the Transformation of American Law," *American Journal of Legal History* 41, no. 2 (Apr. 1997): 175–224.

5. Drew, "Surge and Consolidation," 20, 24; Larry D. Kramer, *The People Themselves: Popular Constitutionalism and Judicial Review* (New York: Oxford University Press, 2004), 209; Kermit L. Hall, "Judicial Independence and the Majoritarian Difficulty," in *The Judicial Branch*, ed. Kermit L. Hall and Kevin T. McGuire (New York: Oxford University Press, 2005), 60, 66.

6. Jed Handelsman Shugerman, "Economic Crisis and the Rise of Judicial Elections and Judicial Review," *Harvard Law Review* 123, no. 5 (Mar. 2010): 1061–1150. This article's argument was subsequently incorporated into *The People's Courts*. Shugerman does not claim that judicial candidates pandered to the voters. In fact, he contends that for a variety of possible reasons—the expansion of vested rights theory, the independence afforded by judicial elections, the fragmentation of politics, a disenchantment with democracy after experiencing the electoral process, and so on—judges exhibited the same disgust with legislatures that had prompted the turn to elections in the first place. Shugerman, *People's Courts*, 128–40. Still, Shugerman maintains that "judicial elections did not merely coexist with judicial review. . . . [A]ntilegislature sentiments and judicial elections were mutually reinforcing. Judicial elections harnessed those sentiments and made them more influential to judges." Shugerman, *People's Courts*, 125.

Caleb Nelson noted that "the rise of the elective judiciary paralleled the rise of judicial review" and that mid-nineteenth-century constitutional convention delegates who favored judicial elections tended to see judicial review "as a restraint on the power of government." Caleb Nelson, "A Re-Evaluation of Scholarly Explanations for the Rise of the Elective Judiciary in Antebellum America," *American Journal of Legal History* 37, no. 2 (Apr. 1993): 204–5. However, he did not link the two observations causally; the actual practice of judicial review lay outside the scope of his article.

7. Shugerman, *People's Courts*, 278, app. B. Richard Drew's numbers are different, perhaps due to a different method of counting cases, but he too finds that Indiana and New York accounted for far more cases than other states. In his eight-state study, Drew reports ninety cases in the 1850s (not all decided by elected courts) in which judges struck down state statutes, forty-eight of them (53 percent) from Indiana and New York. Drew, "Surge and Consolidation," 38, table 1.

8. Barbara Kritchevsky, "Justiciability in Tennessee, Part One: Principles and

Limits," *Memphis State University Law Review* 15, no. 1 (Fall 1984): 10–17; Shugerman, *People's Courts*, 52–53, 278, app. B.

9. Theodore Brown Jr., "The Formative Period in the History of the Supreme Court of Tennessee, 1796–1835," in *A History of the Tennessee Supreme Court*, ed. James W. Ely Jr. (Knoxville: University of Tennessee Press, 2002), 46–47; Cornet v. Winton's Lessee, 10 Tenn. 143 (1826).

10. Brown, "Formative Period," 48, 51–54.

11. Brown, "Formative Period," 55–56; *Messages of the Governors*, 2:379.

12. Brown, "Formative Period," 56; Fisher's Negroes v. Dabbs, 14 Tenn. 119, 142 (1834); Bank of the State v. Cooper, 10 Tenn. 599 (1831).

13. Gotcher v. Burrows, 28 Tenn. 585 (1848) (McKinney); Maury County v. Lewis County, 31 Tenn. 236 (1851) (Totten); Clack v. White, 32 Tenn. 540 (1852) (Totten; McKinney dissenting on the constitutional question). Concurrences are not noted in the Tennessee reports of the time. But since Caruthers was on the bench for *Clack* and McKinney dissented on the constitutional question, Caruthers must have sided with Totten.

14. In *Greenfield v. Dorris*, 33 Tenn. 548 (1853), Dorris had conveyed real property to one McCombs in trust as security for the payment of certain debts. Two years later, McCombs sold the property to Greenfield. In the interim, the General Assembly passed a law determining who was entitled to rent when property was sold under a deed of trust. The court found that the statute was an impairment of the preexisting contract (the deed of trust) and therefore unconstitutional as to that contract. The court did not declare the statute unconstitutional as to contracts entered into after its enactment.

Shugerman lists eleven cases in which a transitional or elected Tennessee court struck down statutes in the 1850s, but in one of them, *Town of Morristown v. Shelton*, 38 Tenn. 24 (1858), the court did not declare a statute unconstitutional.

15. In *Rice v. Alley* (1853), one of the transition cases, the court did not declare a statute unconstitutional; rather, it noted that it had already held the act unconstitutional in "*White v. Settle*, at Nashville, 1852." The citation was incorrect. The court did decide a case called *White v. Suttle*, 31 Tenn. 169 (1851), in Nashville during the December 1851 term, but that case did not involve the statute in question. However, the court struck down the statute in *Clack v. White*, 32 Tenn. 540 (1852), during the December 1852 term. So, in *Rice*, the same judges who had invalidated the statute before the adoption of judicial elections reaffirmed their position afterward.

16. Tenn. Const. of 1835, art. I, § 8; Mayor and Aldermen of Alexandria v. Dearmon, 34 Tenn. 104, 120–22 (1854); Budd v. State, 22 Tenn. 483, 491 (1842).

17. Tenn. Const. of 1835, art. X, § IV; Gotcher v. Burrows, 28 Tenn. 585 (1848) (McKinney); Maury County v. Lewis County, 31 Tenn. 235 (1851) (Totten); Marion County v. Grundy County, 37 Tenn. 490 (1858).

18. Brown, "Formative Period," 8–10; Miller v. Conlee, 37 Tenn. 432, 435 (1858).

19. Miller v. Conlee, 37 Tenn. 432, 434–35 (1858).

20. State v. Bank of East Tennessee, 37 Tenn. 573, 576 (1858).

21. McCandless, *History of Missouri*, 23–26.

22. Hamilton, "Relief Movement," 80–81. Hamilton identifies the cases as *Missouri v. Lane* (St. Louis Cir. Ct., 18 Feb. 1822), *Fulkerson v. Devore* (St. Charles Cty. Cir. Ct.,

July 1822), *Glasscock v. Steen* (St. Louis Cir. Ct., Mar. 1822), the habeas case brought by Steen (Mar. or Apr., 1822), and the Cooper County case (Cooper Co. Cir. Ct., Mar. 1822). For opinions in *Glasscock* and *Lane*, see *Niles' Weekly Register*, supp. to vol. 22 (appended to vol. 23, Sept. 1822–Mar. 1823), 121–29.

23. Missouri v. Lane, *Niles' Weekly Register*, supp. to vol. 22, 124–29 (St. Louis County Cir. Ct., 1822); Glasscock v. Steen, *Niles' Weekly Register*, supp. to vol. 22, 121–24 (St. Louis County Cir. Ct., 1822); Kamper v. Hawkins, 3 Va. 20, 79 (Gen. Ct. 1793); St. George Tucker, *Blackstone's Commentaries: With Notes of Reference, to the Constitution and Laws, of the Federal Government of the United States; and of the Commonwealth of Virginia* (1803), 1:357; Va. P&D, 316, 313 (John Randolph). On St. George Tucker and judicial review, see Jessica K. Lowe, "Guarding Republican Liberty: St. George Tucker and Judging in Federal Virginia," in *Signposts: New Directions in Southern Legal History*, ed. Sally E. Hadden and Patricia Hagler Minter (Athens: University of Georgia Press, 2013), 111–33. On the conservatism of Nathaniel Beverley Tucker and John Randolph, see Adam L. Tate, *Conservatism and Southern Intellectuals, 1789–1861: Liberty, Tradition, and the Good Society* (Columbia: University of Missouri Press, 2005), 20–29, 139–46.

24. Missouri v. Lane, *Niles' Weekly Register*, supp. to vol. 22, 125–27.

25. Bailey v. Gentry, 1 Mo. 164, 165–66, 168 (1822). The third judge, the same one who had granted the habeas petition, dissented. He believed that the law was constitutional, but he did not dispute the court's power to decide the issue. Brown v. Ward, 1 Mo. 209, 209 (1822) (Jones, J., dissenting).

26. Hamilton, "Relief Movement," 81; *Niles' Weekly Register*, June 8, 1822, 226.

27. Cases striking down statutes include *State v. Stein*, 2 Mo. 67 (1828) and *Mattison v. State*, 3 Mo. 421 (1834). Cases upholding statutes include *Rector v. Price*, 1 Mo. 198 (1822), *Tracy v. State*, 3 Mo. 3 (1829), *McGunnegle v. State*, 6 Mo. 367 (1840), and *Freleigh v. State*, 8 Mo. 606 (1844). Among the decisions ignoring the arguments of counsel are *Evans v. Wilder*, 5 Mo. 313 (1838) and *Guelbreth v. Watson & Hildeburn*, 8 Mo. 663 (1844).

28. Shugerman reports one decision in the 1840s and eight decisions in the 1850s, making for an eight-fold increase. "Appendices," 57–58. One of the 1850s cases, *Butler v. Chariton County*, 13 Mo. 112 (1850), which Shugerman lists as a transition case, was decided in the January 1850 term, before the Sixteenth General Assembly ratified the judicial election amendment. On the other hand, Shugerman missed *Crow v. State*, which, having been decided during the court's March 1851 term, truly was a transition case. Technically, the one decision from the 1840s, *Bryson v. Campbell*, did not strike down an act of the legislature. The suit was for the cost of boarding the defendant's wife following a legislative divorce, and the court reaffirmed the principle of an earlier decision that legislative divorces were unconstitutional. But the act granting the divorce was not at issue. That would come in a subsequent case.

29. For general divorce statutes and special acts granting divorces in Missouri in both the territorial and early statehood periods, see Henry S. Geyer, *A Digest of the Laws of Missouri Territory* (1818), 169–72; Act of Jan. 17, 1825, *Laws of Mo.*, 1:329; Act of Dec. 22, 1818, 1818 Mo. Laws (Oct., Nov., and Dec. sessions, 1818), 66; Acts of Jan. 16 and Jan. 21, 1829, 1828–29 Mo. Laws 65.

30. Act of Feb. 11, 1833, 1832–33 Mo. Laws. 130, 131–32; *Missouri Intelligencer and Boon's Lick Advertiser*, Feb. 2, 1833, 2; State *ex rel.* Gentry v. Fry, 4 Mo. 120 (1835).

31. *The History of Pike County, Missouri* (Des Moines, IA, 1883), 676–77; Act of Feb. 24, 1845, 1844–45 Mo. Laws (local) 85; Bryson v. Campbell, 12 Mo. 498 (1849). Some of the information in this paragraph is from Ancestry.com. For the history of the Bryson divorce litigation, see Henry N. Ess, *A Treatise on the Power of Special Taxation* (Kansas City, MO: Pipes-Reed, 1907), 330–33.

32. Bryson v. Bryson, 17 Mo. 590, 591 (1853). In 1853 the General Assembly adopted a constitutional amendment expressly prohibiting legislative divorces.

33. Bryson v. Bryson, 44 Mo. 232 (1869); *St. Louis Republic*, Aug. 6, 1905, pt. 3, 8.

34. Chouteau v. Magenis, 28 Mo. 187 (1859).

35. Isidor Loeb, "Constitutions and Constitutional Conventions in Missouri," in *Mo. Jour. (1875)*, 17; Mo. Const. of 1820, amendment of 1849. A "ratio of representation" is the number of people required for a legislative district to have a representative. It is usually determined by dividing the whole population of a state by the number of districts. In the nineteenth century, it was typically subject to other requirements. For example, a county might have been entitled to a representative even if its population fell below the ratio.

36. Act of Feb. 17, 1851, 1850–51 Mo. Laws 188; *The Old Settlers' History of Bates County, Missouri* (1897), 16–17; State *ex rel.* Douglass v. Scott, 17 Mo. 521 (1853).

37. Marie George Windell, "The Background of Reform on the Missouri Frontier," *Missouri Historical Review* 39, no. 2 (Jan. 1945): 174–77; Marie George Windell, "Reform in the Roaring Forties and Fifties," *Missouri Historical Review* 39, no. 3 (Apr. 1945): 305–11; State v. Sloss, 25 Mo. 291 (1857) (indicating the failure to publish and distribute the law as required). The dram-shop act (Act of Dec. 13, 1855) appears in *Mo. R.S. (1856)*, 1:682.

38. State v. Sloss, 25 Mo. 291, 295 (1857).

39. State v. Fleming, 26 Tenn. 152 (1846); Lewis v. Webb, 3 Me. 326 (1825). On the court's reasoning in *Sloss* and similar decisions in other states, see Henry Wiehofen, "Legislative Pardons," *California Law Review* 27, no. 4 (May 1939): 371–86 and Max Radin, "Legislative Pardons: Another View," *California Law Review* 27, no. 4 (May 1939): 387–97. For a forceful defense of judicial powers against legislative encroachment, by a legislatively appointed court, see G. *& D. Taylor and Co. v. Place*, 4 R.I. 324 (1856).

40. Crow v. State, 14 Mo. 237 (1851); State v. North, 27 Mo. 464 (1858); *Glasgow Weekly Times*, July 31, 1851, 2. Birch believed that a "political" rather than a "strictly legal" test should be applied to the selection of a judicial candidate. That the voters did just that is evidenced by the straight-ticket voting in Ohio and Indiana. The voters were more interested in judicial candidates' political views and affiliations than in their legal acumen.

41. Frederick N. Judson, *A Treatise Upon the Law and Practice of Taxation in Missouri* (Columbia, MO: E. W. Stephens, 1900), 40; Mo. Const. of 1820 art. XIII, § 19; Act of Mar. 25, 1845, *Mo. R.S. (1845)*, 737–38; Brown v. Maryland, 5 U.S. 419 (1827); Act of Feb. 13, 1847, 1847–48 Mo. Laws 97; Act of Mar. 12, 1849, 1848–49 Mo. Laws 68. An ad valorem tax is a tax based on the value of the taxed item.

42. Clayton Keith, "Medical History of Pike County," in *History of Pike County*, 406; *St. Louis Globe-Democrat*, May 11, 1885, 10; Mo. Const. of 1820 art. XIII, § 19.

43. Boman, *Lincoln's Resolute Unionist*, 68–75, 82.

44. *St. Louis Intelligencer*, repr. in *Adventure*, Oct. 4, 1850, 2 (upholding the indictment); *Missouri Whig*, Nov. 28, 1850, 1; *Adventure*, Dec. 6, 1850, 2; Crow v. State, 14 Mo. 237 (1851).

45. *Crow*, 14 Mo. at 260 (Birch, J.). For a discussion of how the politics of sectionalism during this period played out in tax cases in the US Supreme Court, see Austin Allen, *Origins of the Dred Scott Case: Jacksonian Jurisprudence and the Supreme Court, 1837–1857* (Athens: University of Georgia Press, 2006), 110–15.

46. *Crow*, 14 Mo. at 338, 324 (Napton, J., dissenting).

47. Act of Dec. 11, 1855, in *Mo. R.S. (1856)*, 2:1073; L. C. Krauthoff, "The Supreme Court of Missouri," *Green Bag* 3, no. 4 (Apr. 1891): 180.

48. State v. North, 27 Mo. at 482. If Scott was indeed concerned about the Union, his feelings would hardly have been unique among state rights Democrats. In his inaugural address of October 1857, Governor Robert M. Stewart, an anti-Benton Democrat, declared that Missourians loved the Union and remained loyal to it even as they insisted on the constitutional rights of their state. In his outgoing message of January 1861, he continued to assert that Missourians would hold to the Union as long as possible, "both on account of the blessings they have derived from the Union, and the untold and unimagined evils that will come with its dissolution." Buel Leopard and Floyd C. Shoemaker, eds., *The Messages and Proclamations of the Governors of the State of Missouri* (Columbia: State Historical Society of Missouri, 1922), 3:62–63, 144–45. Arkansas, on Missouri's southern border, remained attached to the Union until the firing on Fort Sumter. Jack B. Scroggs, "Arkansas in the Secession Crisis," *Arkansas Historical Quarterly* 12, no. 3 (Autumn 1953): 179–224.

49. McCandless, *History of Missouri*, 282–86.

50. The new bill taxing out-of-state merchandise passed both the house and the senate on a first reading. *Mo. H.J.* 168 (Adj. Sess. 1855); *Mo. S.J.* 194 (Adj. Sess. 1855). Neither journal records the vote. The expedited procedure and absence of a roll call suggests general agreement among the legislators and the probable popularity of the act. In 1850, after the supreme court's first decision in *Crow*, a newspaper claimed that the "farmers and mechanics," having become aware of the "one sided legislation," had nothing but disdain for lawmakers who would seek popularity by oppressing one class of the community so as to reduce the taxes of another. *Adventure*, Dec. 6, 1850, 2. That the farmers and mechanics had such tender regard for the merchants, especially the merchant princes of St. Louis, may be doubted. Farmers had already been exempted from the license and tax requirement for their retail sale of iron, nails, leather, or other specified items that they had acquired in a direct exchange for "any article of produce" they had grown. Act of Feb. 6, 1847, 1846–47 Mo. Laws 97. The 1855 act incorporated this exemption.

51. J. F. D. [John Forrest Dillon], "The Missouri Supreme Judgeship," *American Law Register*, n.s., 4, no. 12 (Oct. 1865): 707.

52. Christopher Phillips, "Introduction: The Making of a Southerner: William Barclay Napton, 1808–1883," in William Barclay Napton, *The Union on Trial: The Political*

Journals of Judge William Barclay Napton, 1829–1883, ed. Christopher Phillips and Jason L. Pendleton (Columbia; University of Missouri Press, 2005), 49, 57.

53. By 1857, Scott's reputation as a staunch advocate of state rights had long been secure. See his opinion in *Scott v. Emerson*, 15 Mo. 576 (1852), which, on appeal to the US Supreme Court, became *Scott v. Sandford*, the *Dred Scott* case. One of the men appointed to the supreme court when Scott and his fellow judges resigned rather than take the loyalty oath later wrote of Scott, "We do not know that he was a disunionist, but he unquestionably sympathized with the Confederacy." W. V. N. [William Van Ness] Bay, *Reminiscences of the Bench and Bar of Missouri* (1878), 327.

54. Poutz v. Duplantier, 2 Mart. (o.s.) 178 (1812); Johnson v. Duncan, 3 Mart. (o.s.) 530, 538 (1815). See also Le Breton v. Morgan, 4 Mart. (n.s.) 138, 140–41 (1826); Syndics of Brooks v. Weyman, 3 Mart. (o.s.) 9, 12 (1813).

55. Shugerman lists four instances of negative judicial review in the 1840s, two by the appointed court in 1850–51, one by the transitional court, and eleven by the elected judges. "Appendices," 44–45. However, Shugerman overlooked *Montpelier Academy v. George*, 14 La. 395 (1840). The "transition" case, *In re Municipality No. 2*, 7 La. Ann. 72 (1852), was decided in February 1852, more than four months before the constitutional convention even met. Another decision, *Maranthe v. Hunter*, 11 La. Ann. 734 (1856), did not declare a statute unconstitutional. The act in question in *Maranthe* had already been held invalid in *State v. Harrison*, 11 La. An. 722 (1856), one of the other decisions on Shugerman's list.

56. *In re Municipality No. 2*, 7 La. Ann. 72 (1852); La. Const. of 1845 tit. VI, art. 109; tit. IX (Schedule), art. 142.

57. Act of Apr. 28, 1853, 1853 La. Laws 211; Act of June 1, 1846, 1846 La. Laws 113; State v. Judge, 9 La. Ann. 62 (1854); Hayes v. Hayes, 10 La. Ann. 642 (1855).

58. Lafon v. Dufrocq, 9 La. Ann. 350 (1854); Boykin v. Shaffer, 13 La. Ann. 129, 135–36 (1858); Montpelier Academy v. George, 14 La. 395 (1840).

59. Glenn W. Fisher, "History of Property Taxes in the United States," in *EH.Net Encyclopedia* (Robert Whaples ed., 2002), https://eh.net/encyclopedia/history-of-property-taxes-in-the-united-states/.

60. Second Municipality of New Orleans v. Duncan, 2 La. Ann. 182, 183 (1847); Charity Hosp. v. Stickney, 2 La. Ann. 551 (1847); Lafayette v. Cummins, 3 La. Ann. 673 (1848); Buffington v. Dinkgrave, 4 La. Ann. 548 (1849); Bordelon v. Lewis, 8 La. Ann. 472 (1852).

61. 9 La. Ann. 446, 451 (1854).

62. Cumming v. Police Jury of Rapides, 9 La. Ann. 503 (1854). In *Cumming*, the court held unconstitutional the local taxing ordinance, not the statute under which the ordinance had been passed. However, the statute had expressly authorized the tax. Act of Feb. 29, 1848, 1848 La. Acts 15. By implication, the statute itself was also unconstitutional. The next year, Ogden, with the concurrence of Buchanan and Voorhies, upheld an ordinance that assessed the owners of property in front of which streets had been paved for part of the expense of the paving. Since all similarly situated property owners were taxed alike, wrote Ogden, the ordinance did not violate Article 123. Slidell and Spofford concurred in the result but continued to insist that Article 123 did not apply to local taxes. City of New Orleans v. Elliott, 10 La. Ann. 59 (1855).

63. Yeatman v. Crandall, 11 La. Ann. 220, 220–22 (1856) (Voorhies, J., concurring, at 222).

64. State v. Widow & Heirs of Poydras, 9 La. Ann. 165 (1854); State v. Rebassa, 9 La. Ann. 305 (1854); State v. Lathrop, 10 La. Ann. 398 (1855); Municipality No. Two v. Dubois, 10 La. Ann. 56 (1855); Bolte v. City of New Orleans, 10 La. Ann. 321 (1855); City of New Orleans v. Elliott, 10 La. Ann. 59 (1855); City of New Orleans v. Commercial Bank of New Orleans, 10 La. Ann. 735 (1855); Surgi v. Snetchman, 11 La. Ann. 387 (1856); *In re* New Orleans Draining Co., 11 La. Ann. 338 (1856); Charity Hospital v. De Bar, 11 La. Ann. 385 (1856); City of New Orleans v. Staiger, 11 La. Ann. 68 (1856); City of New Orleans v. Turpin, 13 La. Ann. 56 (1858); Wallace v. Shelton, 14 La. Ann. 498 (1859). This list does not include cases in which the court simply ignored arguments of counsel based on Article 127. See, e.g., Police Jury *ex rel.* New Orleans, Opelousas & Great W. R.R. v. Succession of McDonogh, 8 La. Ann. 341 (1853); Bolte v. City of New Orleans, 10 La. Ann. 321 (1855).

65. State v. Merchants' Ins. Co., 12 La. Ann. 802 (1857). The court found that a tax levied by state law on insurance companies in New Orleans for the benefit of fire companies in that city violated Article 123. The court rejected analogies to *Yeatman* (because the tax was not a quid pro quo for special benefits received by the taxed party) and to occupational licensing fees (because licensing was an exercise of the police power and not of the taxing power). In *Police Jury of the Parish of Orleans, Right Bank of the Mississippi River v. Nougues*, 11 La. Ann. 739 (1856), the court found that a tax levied by a police jury violated the principle of equality and uniformity, but the basis for invalidating the taxing ordinance was that the ordinance was not within the police jury's statutory authority.

66. City of New Orleans v. Elliott, 10 La. Ann. 59 (1855) (Ogden; Slidell, joined by Spofford, concurring); City of New Orleans v. Commercial Bank of New Orleans, 10 La. Ann. 735 (1855) (Buchanan; Spofford concurring). Buchanan and Spofford kept up their sparring in *Merchants' Insurance Company*, 12 La. Ann. 802, with Spofford writing for the court and Buchanan concurring. In *Mayor and Board of Selectmen v. City of Baton Rouge*, 15 La. Ann. 208 (1860), in which the court, per Voorhies, dismissed the question of whether a municipal assessment complied with the uniformity requirement on the grounds that it was not a tax, Buchanan took no part in the decision, "having dissented in *Yeatman v. Crandall*." 15 La. Ann. at 209.

67. State *ex rel.* S. Bank v. Pilsbury, 31 La. Ann. 1 (1879).

68. Millard H. Ruud, "No Law Shall Embrace More Than One Subject," *Minnesota Law Review* 42, no. 3 (Jan. 1958): 389–92.

69. La. Const. of 1845 tit. VI, art. 120.

70. Walker v. Caldwell, 4 La. Ann. 297, 298 (1849).

71. Act of Mar. 17, 1826, 1825–26 La. Laws 90; Act of Mar. 16, 1848, 1848 La. Laws 66; State v. Hackett, 5 La. Ann. 91 (1850). Article 31 of the constitution required that each bill be read three times in each house unless the rule was suspended by a supermajority vote.

72. Heirs of Duverge v. Salter, 5 La. Ann. 94, 96 (Slidell, C.J., dissenting at 98).

73. Municipality No. 3 v. Michoud, 6 La. Ann. 605, 608 (1851). On rehearing, the court annulled its judgment and decreed a new one, but not for reasons related to Article

118. 6 La. Ann. 608 (1851). Rost and Slidell dissented from the new decree, apparently not on constitutional grounds. It is not clear how two out of four judges, less than a majority, could have reversed the court's initial decision. The issue in *Michoud* was the same as in *Third Municipality of New Orleans v. Ursuline Nuns*, 2 La. Ann. 611 (1847), which had been decided on statutory grounds.

74. Arnoult v. City of New Orleans, 11 La. Ann. 54 (1856); State v. Waples, 12 La. Ann. 343 (1857); State v. Jumel, 13 La. Ann. 399 (1858); Succession of Lanzetti, 9 La. Ann. 329, 333 (1854). Slidell's position in *Lanzetti* was consistent with his dissent in *Heirs of Duverge*, discussed at pages 185–86, which predated judicial elections.

75. Lafon v. Dufrocq, 9 La. Ann. 350, 351 (1854). The court struck down the statute in question on other grounds.

76. State v. Harrison, 11 La. Ann. 722 (headnote), 725 (Spofford, J., dissenting).

77. Parish of Bossier v. Steele, 13 La. Ann. 433, 435 (1858).

78. Parish of Bossier v. Steele, 13 La. Ann. at 435 (Spofford, J., concurring).

79. Williams v. Payson, 14 La. Ann. 7 (1859); State v. Henry, 15 La. Ann. 297, 297 (1860).

Chapter 8: Retreat of the South

1. *River Times*, Aug. 19, 1850, 1.

2. The antebellum constitutions of the western states are included in Francis Newton Thorpe, comp. and ed., *The Federal and State Constitutions, Colonial Charters, and Other Organic Laws of the States and Territories Now or Heretofore Forming the United States of America*, 7 vols. (Washington, DC: GPO, 1909), available at the Online Library of Liberty, https://oll.libertyfund.org/titles/thorpe-the-federal-and-state-constitutions-7-vols. Thorpe omits the secession constitutions of the southern states as well as most constitutions that failed to take effect for one reason or another. However, he includes all four proposed constitutions of Kansas. His version of the one that became law, drafted at Wyandotte in 1859, incorporates amendments adopted through 1905. The original Wyandotte constitution, together with the other three, can be found at the website of the Kansas Historical Society, https://www.kshs.org/kansapedia/kansas-constitutions/16532. In Minnesota, the Republican and Democratic delegates at the constitutional convention of 1857 produced two separate constitutions. The differences were small—mostly matters of punctuation—but it was impossible to say that there was an official version. For a "verified" text based on a comparison of the two documents, accompanied by a table showing the differences, see William Anderson, *A History of the Constitution of Minnesota, with the First Verified Text* (Minneapolis: University of Minnesota, 1921), 207–75.

3. Sutton, *Who Decides?* 81.

4. *Richmond Enquirer*, Nov. 22, 1861, 4; *Point Coupee Democrat*, Oct. 23, 1858, 2; *New Orleans Daily Crescent*, Mar. 17, 1853, 1; *Nashville Union and American*, Dec. 2, 1855, 3; *Floridian*, repr. in *Pensacola Gazette*, Sept. 24, 1853, 2.

5. *Weekly Georgia Telegraph*, Jan. 4, 1859, 2; Act of Mar. 1, 1856, 1855–56 Ga. Acts 140; *Atlanta Daily Examiner*, July 25, 1855, 2; *Atlanta Weekly Intelligencer and Cherokee Advocate*, June 29, 1855, 2; *Southern Recorder*, Oct. 9, 1855, 2; Ga. Code, 146, 501, 507, 655, 657. Confusion caused by the change of date for the election of superior court judges may have added to the disenchantment with judicial elections. The

statute was unclear as to the year in which January elections were to begin, which raised the possibility that the statute unconstitutionally extended some judges' terms of office. *Daily Sun*, Dec. 19, 1856, 2; *Southern Watchman*, Dec. 18, 1856, 3; *Columbus Daily Times*, Oct. 28, 1858, 2.

6. *Times & Sentinel Tri-Weekly*, Jan. 9, 1857, 2; *Georgia Journal and Messenger*, Dec. 24, 1856, 2; *Columbus Daily Times*, Jan. 11, 1859, 2 *Daily Constitutionalist*, Nov. 16, 1859, 2.

7. Virgil Maxcy, "Mr. Maxcy's Oration," *Examiner and Journal of Political Economy* 1, no. 7 (Oct. 30, 1833): 102; John O'Sullivan, "Introduction," *United States Magazine and Democratic Review* 1, no. 1 (Oct. 1837): 3, 6.

8. *Ky. D&P*, 854 (Philip Triplett); *Richmond Enquirer* (semiweekly), Nov. 1, 1861, 1; Kenneth Rayner to Ruffin, Mar. 6, 1860 in *The Papers of Thomas Ruffin*, ed. J. G. de Roulhac Hamilton, vol. 3 (Raleigh: North Carolina Historical Commission, 1920), 72; Donald C. Butts, "The 'Irrepressible Conflict': Slave Taxation and North Carolina's Gubernatorial Election of 1860," *North Carolina Historical Review* 58, no. 1 (Jan. 1981): 44–66.

9. Escott, *Many Excellent People*, 7; Keri Leigh Merritt, *Masterless Men: Poor Whites and Slavery in the Antebellum South* (Cambridge, UK: Cambridge University Press, 2017), 178. See generally William L. Barney, *Rebels in the Making: The Secession Crisis and the Birth of the Confederacy* (New York: Oxford University Press, 2020), 192–252; Daniel W. Crofts, *Reluctant Confederates: Upper South Unionists in the Secession Crisis* (Chapel Hill: University of North Carolina Press, 1989), 153–63; Wallace Hettle, *The Peculiar Democracy: Southern Democrats in Peace and Civil War* (Athens: University of Georgia Press, 2001), 47–52.

10. Conlin, *Constitutional Origins*, 82–133; *Charleston Mercury*, May 17, 1850, 2; *Spirit of the South*, Nov. 26, 1850, 2; *Richmond Enquirer*, Feb. 1, 1850, 2; *Charleston Daily Courier*, June 6, 1850, 4.

11. Cong. Globe app., 33rd Cong., 1st Sess., 609 (1854) (William H. English); Rodney O. Davis and Douglas L. Wilson, eds., *The Lincoln-Douglas Debates* (Urbana: University of Illinois, Press, 2008), 44–45, 58; *Daily Ohio State Journal*, Sept. 21, 1859, 3. On English and the debate over popular sovereignty among northern Democrats, see Elliott Schimmel, *The Center Could Not Hold: Congressman William H. English and His Antebellum Political Times* (Ocala, FL: Atlantic Publishing, 2020).

12. *Eastern Clarion*, Mar. 22, 1861, 4. As early as 1850, a writer in Maryland calling himself "Planter" asserted that the popular election of judges originated with radical northern Democratic barnburners who had since joined with abolitionist Whigs under the name of Free Soilers. *Port Tobacco Times, and Charles County Advertiser*, May 29, 1850, 1.

13. Doc. No. 33 (report of a select committee on amendments to the constitution), 6, 12–13, in *Va. Jour.* (separately paginated).

14. *Richmond Enquirer* (semiweekly), May 31, 1861, 2; William A. Link, *Roots of Secession: Slavery and Politics in Antebellum Virginia* (Chapel Hill: University of North Carolina Press, 2003), 243; *Alexandria Gazette*, June 24, 1863, 2; Granville Davisson Hall, *The Rending of Virginia, a History* (Chicago: Mayer & Miller, 1902), 526, 540; Bernard L. Butcher, ed., *Genealogical and Personal History of the Upper Monongahela*

Valley, West Virginia (New York: Lewis Historical Pub. Co., 1912), 2:529; Eva G. Maloney, "The Prices of Greenbrier," *West Virginia Historical Magazine Quarterly* 5, no. 2 (Apr. 1905): 137. On Summers, see Crofts, *Reluctant Confederates*, 26–28, 263–64.

15. Jt. Res. of Feb. 24, 1860, 1859–60 Ala. Laws 685, 686.

16. Ala. Jour. (1861), 49, 118–19, 142; Lewy Dorman, *Party Politics in Alabama from 1850 through 1860* (Tuscaloosa: University of Alabama Press, 1995), 13.

17. Ala. Jour. (1861), 178, 179–81. According to the convention journal, the report was made on behalf of the Committee on the Constitution. However, Morgan made the report, and he sat only on the smaller committee.

18. Ala. Jour. (1861), 182–84. For efforts to reorganize the Supreme Court, see *New York Herald*, Apr. 12, 1857, 4 (recommendation of a New York State joint legislative committee); *National Era*, Feb. 18, 1858, 26 (bill introduced by US senator William Seward).

19. Ala. Jour. (1861), 184; Ala. Const. of 1861 art. V, § 11; Henry Thomas Shanks, "Conservative Constitutional Tendencies of the Virginia Secession Convention," in *Essays in Southern History*, ed. Fletcher Melvin Green (Chapel Hill: University of North Carolina Press, 1949), 28, 45–46; Va. Const. of 1864 art. VI, § 1; W. Va. Const. of 1863 art. VI, §§ 4, 7. The Alabama constitution was not submitted to the people for ratification. The West Virginia constitution was drafted in 1861 but amended to provide for the emancipation of slaves before West Virginia's admission as a state in 1863.

20. *Southern Watchman*, Apr. 3, 1861, 3; *Southern Recorder*, Aug. 27, 1861, 3; Fla. Const. of 1861 art. V, § 10, in *Constitution or Form of Government for the People of Florida, as Revised and Amended at a Convention of the People Begun and Holden at the City of Tallahassee on the Third Day of January, A.D. 1861, together with the Ordinances Adopted by Said Convention* (Tallahassee, 1861), 13; Tex. Const. of 1861 art. IV, § 5, in John Sayles, *The Constitutions of the State of Texas, with the Reconstruction Acts of Congress, the Constitution of the Confederate States, and of the United States, Annotated*, 3rd ed. (1888), 235.

21. Fla. Proc. 23, 30; Walter W. Manly II, ed., *The Supreme Court of Florida and Its Predecessor Courts, 1821–1917* (Gainesville: University Press of Florida, 1997), 191; John F. Reiger, "Secession of Florida from the Union: A Minority Decision?" *The Florida Historical Quarterly* 46, no. 4 (Apr. 1968): 358–68.

22. La. Jour. (1861), 94, 100.

23. La. Jour. (1861), 93–94, 100–1, 310, 314. The rules of the convention did not specify the number needed to make a quorum, but they did refer to "Jefferson's Manual" and "Cushing's work on Parliamentary Law" as authorities when the rules were silent (p. 27). According to Cushing, a majority of all the members of a body constituted a quorum if the rules did not specify otherwise. Luther S. Cushing, *Manual of Parliamentary Practice: Rules of Proceeding and Debate in Deliberative Assemblies*, 7th ed. (1848; Boston, 1861): 17–18. There were more than 120 delegates (La. Jour. [1861], 5) so the sixty who voted on the judiciary article were less than a quorum.

Epilogue: From Reconstruction to Jim Crow

1. Hermann von Holst, *The Constitutional and Political History of the United States*, vol. 3, *1846–1850. Annexation of Texas—Compromise of 1850*, trans. John J.

Lalor and Paul Shorey (Chicago, 1881), 155. Von Holst was a German historian who had decided to become an American citizen. Albert Bushnell Hart, "Hermann von Holst," *Political Science Quarterly* 5, no. 4 (Dec. 1890): 677–87.

2. There was considerable interest in an elective judiciary in Virginia at the end of the nineteenth century. The constitutional convention of 1901 witnessed some lively debates on the subject. See, e.g., *Richmond Dispatch*, Dec. 12, 1901, 10; Dec. 13, 1901, 2, 5. However, the elective judiciary never came close to adoption.

3. Proclamation No. 11, 13 Stat. 737 (Dec. 8, 1863).

4. Thomas S. Staples, *Reconstruction in Arkansas, 1862–1874* (New York: Columbia University, 1923), 24–25; Dallas T. Herndon, ed., *Centennial History of Arkansas* (Chicago: S. J. Clarke, 1922), 1:286–87; George H. Thompson, *Arkansas and Reconstruction: The Influence of Geography, Economics, and Personality* (Port Washington, N.Y.: Kennikat Press, 1976), 18, 27 (map of Arkansas showing the counties and regions); Moneyhon, *Impact of the Civil War*, 160; *Ark. Jour.*, 17.

5. John Rose Ficklen, *History of Reconstruction in Louisiana (through 1868)* (Baltimore: Johns Hopkins Press, 1910), 68 (nineteen of forty-eight parishes represented); *Daily True Delta*, Feb. 12, 1864, 1.

6. *La. Deb.*, 281–333; *New-Orleans Weekly Times*, May 28, 1864, 5. The remarks as recorded in the *Debates* were somewhat different but to the same effect. *La. Deb.*, 291, 292–93 (R. King Cutler); 295, 297 (T. B. Thorpe). J. R. Terry challenged Cutler's comments regarding the responsibility of Slidell and Benjamin for the elective judiciary, noting that both had favored appointed judges (pp. 316–17). For the committee reports, the substitutes offered, and the judicial selection article as finally adopted, see *La Deb.*, 74, 369, 372–73, 384–85, 637.

7. Brent Tarter, *Constitutional History of Virginia* (Athens: University of Georgia Press, 2023), 85–90; Va. Const. of 1864 art. 4, § 1. The justices of the peace, who made up the county courts, were made elective. Art. VI, §§ 24, 26.

8. Lewis L. Laska, "Legal and Constitutional History of Tennessee," 621–25, 627–28; Proclamations Nos. 38, 39, 41, 42, 43, 46, 47, 13 Stat. 760–71 (May 29–July 13, 1865).

9. S.C. Const. of 1865 art. III, § 1; Miss. Const. of 1865 art. IV, §§ 2, 11, 16, 23; Ala. Const. of 1865 art. V, § 11; N.C. Const. of 1866 art. IV, §§ 7, 11; John V. Orth, "Constitutional History," 1776; Ga. Const. of 1865 art. IV, §2, ¶ 1; Tex. Const. of 1866 art. IV, §§ 2, 5, 15; Fla. Const. of 1865 art. V, §§ 8, 9, 10, 11, 13.

10. James M. McPherson and James K. Hogue, *Ordeal by Fire: The Civil War and Reconstruction*, 4th ed. (New York: McGraw-Hill, 2010), 543–44.

11. Act of Mar. 2, 1867, 14 Stat. 428; Act of Mar. 23, 1867, 15 Stat. 2.

12. McPherson and Hogue, *Ordeal*, 580; Richard L. Hume and Jerry B. Gough, *Blacks, Carpetbaggers, and Scalawags: The Constitutional Conventions of Radical Reconstruction* (Baton Rouge: Louisiana State University Press, 2008), 12, 15, 24 (table 2.2).

13. McPherson and Hogue, *Ordeal*, 581; Eric Foner, *Forever Free: The Story of Emancipation and Reconstruction* (New York: Knopf, 2005), 143–44; Keyssar, *Right to Vote*, 73.

14. Douglas R. Egerton, *The Wars of Reconstruction: The Brief, Violent History of America's Most Progressive Era* (New York: Bloomsbury, 2014); Stewart E. Tolnay and E. M. Beck, *A Festival of Violence: An Analysis of Southern Lynchings, 1882–1930*

(Urbana: University of Illinois Press, 1995); Stephen B. Weeks, "The History of Negro Suffrage in the South," *Political Science Quarterly* 9, no. 4 (Dec. 1894): 692.

15. Weeks, "History of Negro Suffrage," 692–99; *Jackson Daily News*, Feb. 16, 1911, 5.

16. Ark. D&P, 595–98 (report of the Committee on the Constitution), 203–5, 427–49, 454–71. The hybrid plan as incorporated into the committee report seems to have been accepted without discussion.

17. Act of June 5, 1865, 1865 Tenn. Laws 32; Act of Feb. 25, 1867, 1866–67 Tenn. Laws (2nd adj. sess.) 26; Laska, "Legal and Constitutional History," 625, 631–32, 636–37; Act of Apr. 8, 1889, 1889 Tenn. Laws 145, 168 (poll tax); Act of Apr. 4, 1889, 1889 Tenn. Laws 414 (voter registration); Act of Apr. 4, 1889, 1889 Tenn. Laws 364 (Australian ballot; the Dortch Law); *Nashville Banner*, Nov. 11, 1890, 4.

18. Walter Nunn, "The Constitutional Convention of 1874," *Arkansas Historical Quarterly* 27, no. 3 (Autumn 1968): 182; Thompson, *Arkansas and Reconstruction*, 97–169.

19. Nunn, "Constitutional Convention of 1874," 182; Thompson, *Arkansas and Reconstruction*, 110, 113–14, 160–61.

20. Rodney Waymon Harris, "Arkansas's Divided Democracy: The Making of the Constitution of 1874" (PhD diss., University of Arkansas, Fayetteville, 2017), 76–82, 86, 90; *Fort Smith Herald*, July 25, 1874, 2; *Daily Arkansas Gazette*, Aug. 7, 1874, 1.

21. *Daily Arkansas Gazette*, Aug. 2, 1874, 3; *Southern Standard*, July 25, 1874, 2; *Daily Arkansas Gazette*, Aug. 7, 1874, 1; Ark. Const. of 1874 art. VII, § 16. Arkansas had only a handful of black lawyers in the nineteenth century. J. Clay Smith Jr., *Emancipation: The Making of the Black Lawyer, 1844–1944* (Philadelphia: University of Pennsylvania Press, 1993), 321–28; Arkansas Black Lawyers, https://arkansasblacklawyers.uark.edu/index.html.

22. Randolph B. Campbell, "The District Judges of Texas in 1866–1867: An Episode in the Failure of Presidential Reconstruction," *Southwestern Historical Quarterly* 93, no. 3 (Jan. 1990): 357–77; Eric Foner, *Reconstruction: America's Unfinished Revolution, 1863–1877* (1988; repr. New York: Perennial Classics, HarperCollins, 2002), 324; Charles William Ramsdell, "Reconstruction in Texas" (PhD diss., Columbia University, 1910), 227; Tex. Const. of 1869 art. V, §§ 2, 6.

23. Seth Shepard McKay, *Making the Texas Constitution of 1876* (Philadelphia: University of Pennsylvania, 1924), 39–40; *Daily Democratic Statesman*, Sept. 10, 1873, 4; *Galveston Daily News*, Sept. 17, 1873, 3.

24. McKay, *Making the Texas Constitution*, 59, 67–68 (quoting the Austin *State Gazette*, Aug. 24, 1875), 73–74.

25. *Tex. Jour. (1875)*, 406; McKay, *Making the Texas Constitution*, 90; *Tex. Deb. (1875)*, 386; Patrick G. Williams, "Suffrage Restriction in Post-Reconstruction Texas: Urban Politics and the Specter of the Commune," *Journal of Southern History* 68, no. 1 (Feb. 2002): 31–64; *Tex. Deb. (1875)*, 176, 424 (J. W. Whitfield).

26. The convention did restrict suffrage by excluding from the electorate "all paupers supported by any county" and, in any municipal election "to determine expenditure of money or assumption of debt," anyone who did not pay property taxes in the municipality. Tex. Const. of 1876 art. VI, §§ 1, 3.

27. Tex. Const. of 1876 art. V, §§ 2, 5, 7, 15, 18; John G. Browning and Carolyn Wright, "We Stood on Their Shoulders: The First African American Attorneys in Texas," *Howard Law Journal* 59, no. 1 (Fall 2015): 59–64.; John G. Browning and Carolyn Wright, "Undaunted: William A. Price, Texas' First Black Judge and the Path to a Civil Rights Milestone," *Thurgood Marshall Law Review* 43, no. 2 (Spring 2019): 583–596.

28. *Weekly North-Carolina Standard*, June 13, 1866, 1; Feb. 26, 1868, 1.

29. *N.C. Jour.*, 180; *Wilmington Journal*, Feb. 21, 1868, 1. The pro-election speakers from central and western North Carolina included Isaac Kinney of Davidson County; Jacob Ing of Nash County; Mark May, representing Macon, Clay, and Cherokee Counties, and John Q. A. Bryan of Caldwell County. They had support from Abraham Congleton of the eastern county of Carteret.

30. *Wilmington Journal*, Feb. 21, 1868, 1; N.C. Const. of 1868 art. II, §§ 9–10 (compare with N.C. Const. of 1866 art. II, §§ 7–8, imposing property qualifications for legislative office); art. IV, § 26 (judicial elections; compare with N.C. Const of 1866 art. IV, §§ 1, 3, 4, giving the General Assembly the power to choose the judges for tenure during good behavior); N.C. Const. of 1868 art. VI, § 1 (suffrage; compare with N.C. Const. of 1866 art. II, §§ 9–10, imposing a taxpayer qualification to vote for legislators); art. IX, § 2 (public schools). Under the constitution of 1866, justices of the peace manned the county courts. The justices were elected by the same voters who elected the state legislators (i.e., taxpayers) for terms of six years. N.C. Const. of 1866 art. IV, §§ 7, 11. Under the new constitution, the broader electorate chose both the county commissioners and the justices of the peace, the latter for terms reduced to two years. N.C. Const. of 1868 art. VII, §§ 1, 5. The 1866 constitution appeared in the *Tri-Weekly Standard*, July 3, 1866, 1, 4.

31. *Raleigh Register*, repr. in the *Western Democrat*, Feb. 18, 1868, 2; *Western Democrat*, Feb. 18, 1868, 3; *Tarboro Southerner*, Feb. 27, 1868, 2; J. G. de Roulhac Hamilton, *Reconstruction in North Carolina* (New York: Columbia University Press, 1914), 286.

32. Orth, "Constitutional History," 1781–84; Act of Feb. 27, 1877, 1876–77 N.C. Laws 226. For a synopsis of the amendments, see the *Era*, Oct. 28, 1875, 2. The constitution as amended is in the *Observer*, Nov. 17, 1876, 1, 4. The ratification vote was reported in the *Charlotte Democrat*, Dec. 16, 1876, 2.

33. *New York Herald*, Nov. 29, 1867, 7; Hume and Gough, *Blacks, Carpetbaggers, and Scalawags*, 77–78; Theodore Henley Jack, *Sectionalism and Party Politics in Alabama, 1819–1842* (Menasha, WI: George Banta Pub. Co, 1919), 66, 85; Michael W. Fitzgerald, "Radical Republicanism and the White Yeomanry during Alabama Reconstruction, 1865–1868," *Journal of Southern History* 54, no. 4 (Nov. 1988): 565–96. According to McMillan, most of the scalawags came from northern Alabama. McMillan, *Constitutional Development*, 133. Hume and Gough found that three-fifths of the southern white delegates (scalawags) and 43.4 percent of all the delegates came from the upland regions (the Tennessee Valley, Mountain, and Piedmont regions) of the state. Hume and Gough, *Blacks, Carpetbaggers, and Scalawags*, 97, table 4.2.

34. McMillan, *Constitutional Development*, 141; *Northern Alabama: Historical and Biographical* (1888), 599; *Selma Daily Messenger*, Dec. 12, 1867, 2; *Daily State Sentinel*, Dec. 12, 1867, 2; *Ala. Jour. (1867)*, 163–64, 168–69; *Montgomery Weekly Advertiser*, Dec. 3, 1867, 1.

35. McMillan, *Constitutional Development*, 161, 168–74.

36. *Montgomery Weekly Advertiser*, July 21, 1875, 3; McMillan, *Constitutional Development*, 201.

37. McMillan, *Constitutional Development*, 200.

38. Ala. Const. of 1875 art. VI, § 4. Previously, the number of counties per circuit had ranged from three to eight (Ala. Const. of 1867 art. VI, § 4) and from three to six (Ala. Const. of 1861 art. V, § 4). Several new counties were formed after the Civil War.

39. Act of Feb. 13, 1875, 1874–75 Ala. Laws 115; Act of Jan. 31, 1879, 1878–79 Ala. Laws 80; *Alabama Beacon*, Feb. 1, 1879, 1; McMillan, *Constitutional Development*, 221–22. The cap on the number of circuits would cause practical problems by the 1890s. McMillan, *Constitutional Development*, 246.

40. McMillan, *Constitutional Development*, 352–53.

41. *S.C. Proc.*, 260–61, 618 (C. P. Leslie), 619 (B. F. Randolph).

42. *S.C. Proc.*, 260, 617–19, 621–22.

43. *S.C. Proc.*, 635, 637 (S. G. W. Dill); S.C. Const. of 1868 art. IV, § 20; *Times and Democrat*, Aug. 8, 1888, 1; *Sumter Daily Item*, repr. in *Greenville Daily News*, July 4, 1900, 6; *Fairfield News and Herald*, Oct. 3, 1900, 2; *Bamberg Herald*, Oct. 25, 1900, 2; *Yorkville Enquirer*, Jan. 19, 1898, 3; Jan. 26, 1898, 3; *Abbeville Press and Banner*, Nov. 27, 1895, 8.

44. Edwin DuBois Shurter, *Oratory of the South from the Civil War to the Present Time* (New York: Neale Pub. Co., 1908), 260–1.

45. *Fla. Jour. (1865)*, 53, 76, 145; Fla. Const. of 1868 art. VI, §§ 3, 7, 9, 15.

46. Edward C. Williamson, "The Constitutional Convention of 1885," *Florida Historical Quarterly* 41, no. 2 (Oct. 1962): 117.

47. *Pensacola Commercial*, Oct. 4, 1884, 2; Jan. 7, 1885, 2; *Palatka Daily News*, July 1, 1885, 1 (quoting the *Philadelphia Record*); Fla. Const. of 1885 art. VI, § 8; Act of May 25, 1889, 1889 Fla. Laws 13.

48. *Pensacola Commercial*, June 27, 1885, 2; *Weekly Floridian*, July 9, 1885, 2; *Fla. Jour. (1885)*, 241, 246, 436–37; Robert Cassanello, "The Right to Vote and the Long Nineteenth Century in Florida," *Florida Historical Quarterly* 95, no. 2 (Fall 2016): 215–16.

49. *Ga. Jour.*, 435–36.

50. Ga. Const. of 1868 art. V, § 9, ¶ 1; *Ga. Jour.*, 109, 111–12, 435–36; *Union and Recorder*, Jan. 22, 1873, 2; Act of Feb. 26, 1877, 1877 Ga. Laws 26; *Daily Constitution*, June 29, 1877, 1; June 14, 1877, 1.

51. *Ga. Deb.*, 223–24; Ga. Const. of 1877 art. VI, §2, ¶ 4; art. VI, § 3, ¶ 2. Justices of the peace remained elective. Art. VI, § 7, ¶ 3.

52. Hume and Gough, *Blacks, Carpetbaggers, and Scalawags*, 140, table 5.1; Ellen Garrison, "Reactionaries or Reformers? Membership and Leadership of the Georgia Constitutional Convention of 1877," *Georgia Historical Quarterly* 90, no. 4 (Winter 2006): 510; *Ga. Deb.*, 222 (James R. Brown); Ga. Const. of 1877 art. II, § 1, ¶ 2 (suffrage); art. II, § 2, ¶ 1 (registration, prohibition of criminals from voting); art. VII, § 2, ¶ 3 (poll tax). Neither the poll tax nor the requirement that taxes due had to be paid for a person to vote was new. For an example of a poll tax imposed by the legislature, see *Ga. Code*, 131. For the payment of taxes due as a prerequisite for voting, see Ga. Const. of 1798 art. IV, § 1; Ga. Const. of 1868 art. II, § 2.

53. *Savannah Morning News*, Nov. 10, 1884, 2.

54. *Atlanta Constitution*, Nov. 14, 1884, 3; Dec. 6, 1884, 3; *Brunswick Herald*, repr. in *Carroll Free Press*, Jan. 2, 1885, 2; *Savannah Morning News*, Sept. 2, 1885, 1.

55. *Atlanta Constitution*, Sept. 18, 1883, 3; *Atlanta Constitution*, Aug. 28, 1888, 6; *Columbus Enquirer-Sun*, Aug. 28, 1888, 1; *Marietta Journal*, Sept. 6, 1888, 6; *Morning News*, Oct. 5, 1888, 2.

56. *North Georgia Citizen*, Nov. 22, 1894, 2; *Newnan Herald & Advertiser*, Sept. 3, 1909, 3 (Featherston obituary); *Hustler of Rome*, Oct. 15, 1894, 7; Act of Dec. 16, 1895, 1895 Ga. Laws 15; *Atlanta Constitution*, Dec. 6, 1897, 1; *Macon Telegraph*, Dec. 11, 1897, 3; Act of Dec. 21, 1897, 1897 Ga. Laws 16; *Morning News*, Oct. 14, 1898, 2.

57. *Savannah Morning News*, Sept. 16, 1884, 2.

58. William F. Holmes, "Populism in Black Belt Georgia: Racial Dynamics in Taliaferro County Politics, 1890–1900," *Georgia Historical Quarterly* 83, no. 2 (Summer 1999): 242–66; John Dittmer, *Black Georgia in the Progressive Era, 1900–1920* (Urbana: University of Illinois Press, 1977), 94–104.

59. *New Orleans Republican*, Jan. 17, 1868, 2.

60. *La. Jour. (1867–68)*, 90–1, 103–4, 153, 158 (William Brown, proposing to substitute art. 91 of the minority report); *New-Orleans Times*, Jan. 15, 1868, 2; Jan. 18, 1868, 2; *La. Jour. (1867–68)*, 162, 163–64 (W. R. Crane amendment).

61. Hargrave, *Louisiana State Constitution*, 13–14.

62. La. Const. of 1868, tit. IV, art. 83; *Opelousas Courier*, Oct. 6, 1877, 1; July 19, 1879, 1; *St. Landry Democrat*, July 12, 1879, 1; July 26, 1879, 1.

63. La. Const. of 1879 arts. 107, 109, 130; *St. Landry Democrat*, July 26, 1879, 1.

64. *Daily Picayune*, Nov. 4, 1891, 4; Keyssar, *Right to Vote*, 86.

65. Jt. Res. No. 200 (undated), 1894 La. Laws 259; *Weekly Messenger*, Mar. 7, 1896, 4; *Lake Charles Commercial*, Feb. 22, 1896, 2; Mar. 7, 1896, 2; Apr. 11, 1896, 2.

66. *Lake Charles Commercial*, Apr. 25, 1896, 2; Feb. 22, 1896, 2.

67. Act of July 7, 1896, 1896 La. Laws 85; La. Const. of 1898 art. 99.

68. *The Convention of '98. A Complete Work on the Greatest Political Event in Louisiana's History, and a Sketch of the Men Who Composed It* (New Orleans, 1898), 15; Thomas J. Kernan, "The Constitutional Convention of 1898 and Its Work," *Proceedings of the Louisiana Bar Association. 1898–1899* (New Orleans, 1899), 57; La. Const. of 1898 arts. 197–98, 200, 212; Donna A. Barnes, *The Louisiana Populist Movement, 1881–1900* (Baton Rouge: Louisiana State University Press, 2011), 228–38.

69. *Times-Democrat*, May 9, 1902, 6; *Shreveport Journal*, June 3, 1902, 8; *Shreveport Times*, June 13, 1902, 7; *Lafayette Advertiser*, July 6, 1904, 3; June 29, 1904, 2; Act of July 6, 1904, 1904 La. Laws 306; *Lafayette Advertiser*, Nov. 30, 1904, 3; Act of July 10, 1906, 1906 La. Laws 227; *Shreveport Journal*, Nov. 19, 1906, 8.

70. Miss. Const. of 1868 art. VI, §§ 2, 3, 11; Hume and Gough, *Blacks, Carpetbaggers, and Scalawags*, 94–95.

71. *Weekly Clarion*, Sept. 8, 1881, 2; *Clarion*, Feb. 21, 1883, 4; June 13, 1883, 4.

72. *Oxford Eagle*, June 14, 1883, 2; *Clarion*, June 20, 1883, 3; *Greenville Times*, Feb. 23, 1884, 2.

73. Stephen Cresswell, *Rednecks, Redeemers, and Race: Mississippi after Reconstruction, 1877–1917* (Jackson: University Press of Mississippi, 2006), 110–12, 120–21.

74. *Clarion-Ledger*, Jan. 26, 1888, 2.

75. Act of Feb. 5, 1890, 1890 Miss. Laws 53; *Daily Commercial Herald*, Oct. 11, 1890, 2; *Brookhaven Leader*, Sept. 11, 1890, 2.

76. Cresswell, *Rednecks, Redeemers, and Race*, 119–20, 124.

77. *Clarion-Ledger*, Oct. 16, 1890, 3; Creswell, *Rednecks, Redeemers, and Race*, 99–102, 122.

78. *Daily Clarion-Ledger*, Jan 31, 1896, 3; *Daily Commercial Herald*, Mar. 6, 1892, 6; *Weekly Democrat*, Mar. 16, 1892, 6.

79. *Vicksburg Evening Post*, Jan. 4, 1898, 1; Jan. 18, 1898, 1; *New South*, Jan. 29, 1898, 4; *Grenada Sentinel*, Nov. 25, 1899, 2; State *ex rel.* McClurg v. Powell, 77 Miss. 543 (1900).

80. S.C.R. No. 7, Feb. 20, 1902, 1902 Miss Laws (spec. sess.) 199; *Meridian Press*, Nov. 16, 1902, 1; *Jackson Evening News*, Apr. 2, 1903, 1; *Water Valley Progress*, Aug. 1, 1903, 1; *Weekly Corinthian*, Mar. 9, 1904, 1; *Clarion-Ledger*, Mar. 15, 1904, 3.

81. *Vicksburg American*, Feb. 21, 1906, 6; *Jackson Evening News*, Feb. 21, 1906, 7; *Jackson Daily News*, Feb. 29, 1908, 3; *Miss. Code*, 1041; *Columbus Commercial*, Feb. 25, 1908, 4; *Vicksburg Evening Post*, Feb. 20, 1908, 1; *Jackson Daily News*, Mar. 14, 1908, 3; *Simpson County News*, Feb. 27, 1908, 3 (Quin bill passed house 63–26); *Vicksburg American*, Mar. 14, 1908, 1 (Quin bill passed senate 23–15).

82. *Jackson Daily News*, Mar. 21, 1908, 2; Miss. Const. of 1890 art IV, § 72; *Jackson Daily News*, Jan. 7, 1910, 8; *Hattiesburg News*, Feb. 17, 1910, 5.

83. *Vicksburg Evening Post*, Mar. 23, 1910, 1; *Jones County News*, Apr. 8, 1910, 6; *Jackson Daily News*, Nov. 21, 1910, 4; S.C.R. No. 17, 1912 Miss. Laws 449.

84. *Hattiesburg News*, June 24, 1911, 1; Sept. 1, 1911, 1; Miss. Const. of 1890 art. XV, § 273; *Vicksburg Evening Post*, Jan. 30, 1912, 1.

85. S.C.R. No. 17, 1912 Miss. Laws 449; *Jackson Daily News*, Mar. 18, 1912, 4; S.C.R. No. 3, 1914 Miss. Laws 569 (spec. sess. 1913); *Jackson Daily News*, Sept. 6, 1913, 8; *Semi-Weekly Leader*, Jan. 22, 1913, 4; *Lexington Advertiser*, Nov. 7, 1913, 4 (requiring P. Z. Jones to show that his judicial appointment was valid); *Vicksburg Evening Post*, Jan. 2, 1914, 1; *Jackson Daily News*, Feb. 9, 1914, 1, 3.

86. *Jackson Daily News*, Feb. 1, 1914, 16; *Starkville News*, Nov. 6, 1914, 2; *Semi-Weekly Leader*, Nov. 7, 1914, 1; *Grenada Sentinel*, Nov. 13, 1914, 1; *Tallahatchie Herald*, Dec. 3, 1914, 4; H.C.R. No. 18, Jan. 15, 1916, 1916 Miss Laws 214 (election of supreme court judges).

87. *Times-Democrat*, Mar. 8, 1898, 4.

SELECTED BIBLIOGRAPHY

Although the notes contain references to many secondary works, the significant facts and arguments presented in this book are drawn almost entirely from primary sources, including census reports, state constitutions, the published proceedings of state constitutional conventions, statutes, legislative journals, court cases, and newspapers.

Population Data

Most of the population statistics come directly or are extrapolated from the *The Seventh Census of the United States: 1850* (Washington, DC, 1853), prepared under the supervision of the superintendent of the census, J. D. B. De Bow. (De Bow spelled his last name as two words, but it appears as one on his census publications.) Of particular interest is Table I: Population of the United States Decennially from 1790 to 1850. Demographic data for cities, including their rankings by population size, may be found at a web page of the Boston University Physics Department: http://physics.bu.edu/~redner/projects/population/cities/.

De Bow also oversaw the publication of *Statistical View of the United States* (Washington, DC, 1854), cited in the notes as DeBow, *Statistical View*. Other sources of population data, typically referred to just once in the notes, are cited in full.

Constitutions

Most of the constitutions and constitutional amendments cited in the notes can be found at multiple websites. One convenient, nearly complete source is Francis Newton Thorpe, comp. and ed., *The Federal and State Constitutions, Colonial Charters, and Other Organic Laws of the States and Territories Now or Heretofore Forming the United States of America*, 7 vols. (Washington, DC: Government Printing Office, 1909). This compilation is available online at the Online Library of Liberty website and the HathiTrust Digital Library. Thorpe does not include proposed constitutions that the voters rejected or the constitutions produced by the secession conventions. He includes constitutional amendments but overlooks the amendments in Florida and Texas that provided for judicial elections. The sources for items omitted by Thorpe are indicated in the notes.

A typical feature of state constitutions was a division into articles, designated by Roman numerals, and sections, designated by Arabic numerals. However, some constitutions deviated from this pattern. I used Roman numerals for articles and Arabic numerals for sections in all cases, even for constitutions that used a different system. For constitutions that did not follow the common article-and-section scheme, the citations include different or additional information.

Constitutional Convention Proceedings

The published proceedings of some state constitutional conventions include the debates of the delegates. In other states, only an official journal was published, although debates could sometimes be found in newspapers. Most of the debates and journals can be found online at websites such Google Books, HathiTrust, or Internet Archive or at state or university websites. The following list, arranged alphabetically by state and chronologically where there is more than one entry for a state, includes the debates and journals referred to in the notes, followed by the abbreviations used in the citations. A URL is provided for the hard-to-find journal of the Alabama secession convention of 1861.

Alabama

Journal of the Constitutional Convention of the State of Alabama. 1861. Ala. Jour. (1861). Available at https://digital.archives.alabama.gov/digital/collection/constitutions/id/125/ (original title page missing).

Smith, William R. *The History and Debates of the Convention of the People of Alabama, Begun and held in the City of Montgomery, on the seventh Day of January, 1861.* Montgomery, AL, 1861. Ala. Deb. (1861).

Official Journal of the Constitutional Convention of the State of Alabama, Held in the City of Montgomery, Commencing on Tuesday, November 5th, A. D. 1867. Montgomery, AL: 1868. Ala. Jour. (1867).

Arkansas

Journal of the Convention of Delegates of the People of Arkansas. Assembled at the Capitol, January 4, 1864. Little Rock, AR, 1870. Bound with the journals of the Arkansas house of representatives for the sessions of 1864 and 1865. Ark. Jour.

Debates and Proceedings of the Convention which Assembled at Little Rock, January 7th, 1868. Little Rock, Ark., 1868. Ark. D&P.

Delaware

Sutton, Richard, rptr. *Debates and Proceedings of the Constitutional Convention of the State of Delaware.* Dover, DE: 1853. Del. D&P.

Florida

Proceedings of the Convention of the People of Florida, at Called Sessions, Begun and Held at the Capitol in Tallahassee, on Tuesday, February 26th, and Thursday, April 18th, 1861. Tallahassee, FL, 1861. Fla. Proc.

Journal of Proceedings of the Convention of Florida. Begun and Held at the Capital of the State, at Tallahassee, Wednesday, October 25th, A. D. 1865. Tallahassee, FL, 1865. Fla. Jour. (1865).

Journal of the Proceedings of the Constitutional Convention of the State of Florida, which Convened at the Capitol, at Tallahassee, on Tuesday, June 9, 1885. Tallahassee, FL, 1885. Fla. Jour. (1885).

Georgia

Journal of the Proceedings of the Constitutional Convention of the People of Georgia, Held in the City of Atlanta in the Months of December, 1867, and January, February and March, 1868. Augusta, GA, 1868. Ga. Jour.

Small, Samuel W., rptr. *A Stenographic Report of the Proceedings of the Constitutional Convention Held in Atlanta, Georgia, 1877.* Atlanta, GA, 1877. Ga. Deb.

Illinois

Coles, Arthur Charles, ed. *The Constitutional Debates of 1847.* Springfield: Illinois State Historical Library, 1919. Ill. Deb.

Indiana

Fowler, H., rptr. *Report of the Debates and Proceedings of the Convention for the Revision of the Constitution of the State of Indiana.* 2 vols. Indianapolis, IN, 1850. Ind. D&P.

Kentucky

Sutton, R., rptr. *Report of the Debates and Proceedings of the Convention for the Revision of the Constitution of the State of Kentucky.* Frankfort, KY, 1849. Ky. D&P.

Louisiana

Ker, Robert J., rptr. *Proceedings and Debates of the Convention of Louisiana Which Assembled at the City of New Orleans January 14, 1844* [sic]. New Orleans, LA, 1845. La. P&D.

Journal of the Convention to Form a New Constitution for the State of Louisiana. New Orleans, LA, 1852. La. Jour. (1852).

Official Journal of the Proceedings of the Convention of the State of Louisiana. New Orleans, LA, 1861. La. Jour. (1861).

Bennett, Albert P., rptr. *Debates in the Convention for the Revision and Amendment of the Constitution of the State of Louisiana.* New Orleans, LA, 1864. La. Deb.

Official Journal of the Proceedings of the Convention for Framing a Constitution for the State of Louisiana. New Orleans, LA, 1867–1868. La. Jour. (1867–68).

Maryland

Debates and Proceedings of the Maryland Reform Convention to Revise the State Constitution. 2 vols. Annapolis, Md., 1851. Md. D&P.

Massachusetts

Fowler, Harvey, rptr. *Official Report of the Debates and Proceedings in the State Convention, Assembled May 4th, 1853, to Revise and Amend the Constitution of the Commonwealth of Massachusetts.* 3 vols. Boston, MA, 1853. Mass. D&P.

Missouri

Journal of the Missouri State Convention. St. Louis, MO, 1820. Mo. Jour. (1820).

Journal of the Convention of the State of Missouri. Jefferson City, MO, 1845. Mo. Jour. *(1845).*

Loeb, Isidor, and Floyd C. Shoemaker, eds. *Journal [sic] Missouri Constitutional Convention of 1875.* Columbia: State Historical Society of Missouri, 1920. Mo. Jour. *(1875).*

New York

Carter, Nathaniel H. and William L. Stone, rptrs., and Marcus T. C. Gould, stenographer. *Reports of the Proceedings and Debates of the Convention of 1821, Assembled for the Purpose of Amending the Constitution of the State of New-York.* Albany, NY, 1821. N.Y. P&D.

Croswell, S. and R. Sutton, rptrs. *Debates and Proceedings in the New-York State Convention, for the Revision of the Constitution.* Albany, NY, 1846. N.Y. D&P (C&S 1846).

Bishop, William G. and William H. Attree, rptrs. *Report of the Debates and Proceedings of the Convention for the Revision of the Constitution of the State of New-York, 1846.* Albany, NY, 1846. N.Y. D&P (B&A 1846).

North Carolina

Journal of the Constitutional Convention of the State of North-Carolina, at Its Session 1868. Raleigh, NC, 1868. N.C. Jour.

Ohio

Smith, J. V., rptr. *Report of the Debates and Proceedings of the Convention for the Revision of the Constitution of the State of Ohio.* 2 vols. Columbus, OH, 1851. Ohio D&P.

South Carolina

Woodruff, J., rptr. *Proceedings of the Constitutional Convention of South Carolina, Held at Charleston, S. C., beginning January 14th and ending March 17th, 1868.* Charleston, SC, 1868. S.C. Proc.

Tennessee

Journal of the Proceedings of the Convention of Delegates Elected by the People of Tennessee, to Amend, Revise, or Form and Make a New Constitution for the State. Nashville, TN, 1870. Tenn. Jour.

Texas

Weeks, Wm. F., rptr. *Debates of the Texas Convention.* Houston, 1846. Tex. Deb. *(1845).*

Winkler, Ernest William, ed. *Journal of the Secession Convention of Texas, 1861.* Austin: Austin Printing Co., 1912. Referred to in the text, but not cited in the notes.

Journal of the Constitutional Convention of the State of Texas, Begun and Held at the City of Austin, September 6th, 1875. Galveston, TX, 1875. Tex. Jour. *(1875).*

McKay, Seth Shepard, ed. *Debates in the Texas Constitutional Convention of 1875.* Austin: University of Texas, 1930. Tex. Deb. *(1875).*

Virginia

Proceedings and Debates of the Virginia State Convention, of 1829–30. Richmond, VA, 1830. *Va. P&D.*

Bishop, Wm. G., rptr. *Register of the Debates and Proceedings of the Va. Reform Convention.* Richmond, VA, 1851. *Va. D&P.*

Journal of the Acts and Proceedings of a General Convention of the State of Virginia, Assembled at Richmond, on Wednesday, the Thirteenth Day of February, Eighteen Hundred and Sixty-One. Richmond, VA, 1861. *Va. Jour.*

Wisconsin

Quaife, Milo M., ed. *The Convention of 1846.* Madison: Wisconsin Historical Society, 1919. *Wisc. Conv.*

Legislative Materials

The notes include numerous citations to state session laws (the laws passed at individual sessions of a legislature). The titles of the volumes containing session laws vary from state to state in referring to the legislative work product: Laws, Acts, Acts and Resolves, Public Laws, and so on. In these notes, all are referred to as Laws. Each citation includes the date of the act or resolution, the year of the session, and the page on which the measure begins (Act of June 5, 1865, 1865 Tenn. Laws 32). Occasionally, the citation also includes the page on which the part of the measure cited may be found. Resolutions are cited similarly, except that they are abbreviated as Res., Jt. Res. (joint resolution), H.C.R. (house concurrent resolution), or S.C.R. (senate concurrent resolution).

Citations to legislative journals include the state, chamber, journal page, and session. The abbreviations *H.J.* and *S.J.* refer to the house and senate journals, respectively. In almost all cases, the session referred to is a regular session of the legislature. A typical citation: *Mo. S.J.* 59–63 (Reg. Sess. 1834–35).

Some of the notes refer to compilations of statutes. The following list includes all the cited compilations, arranged alphabetically by state and then chronologically where there is more than one entry for a state, followed by the abbreviations used in the citations.

Alabama

Aiken, John G. *A Digest of the Laws of the State of Alabama.* Philadelphia, 1833. *Ala. Digest (1833).*

Clay, C. C. *A Digest of the Laws of the State of Alabama.* Tuskaloosa, 1843. *Ala. Digest (1843).*

Ormand, John J., Arthur P. Bagby, and George Goldthwaite. *The Code of Alabama.* Montgomery, 1852. *Ala. Code.*

Arkansas

English, E. H. *Digest of the Statutes of Arkansas Embracing All Laws of a General and Permanent Character in Force at the Close of the Session of the General Assembly of 1846.* Little Rock, 1848. *Ark. Digest.*

Delaware

Revised Statutes of the State of Delaware. Dover, 1852. Del. R.S.

Georgia

Hotchkiss, William A. *Codification of the Statute Law of Georgia, including the English Statutes of Force.* Savannah. 2nd ed. Augusta, 1848. Ga. Code.

Iowa

Revised Statutes of the Territory of Iowa. Iowa City, 1843. Ia. R.S.

Kentucky

Littell, William. *The Statute Law of Kentucky.* 4 vols. Frankfort, 1809–14. Ky. Stat.

Michigan

Laws of the Territory of Michigan. 4 vols. Lansing, 1871–84. Mich. Laws.
The Revised Statutes of the State of Michigan. Detroit, 1846. Mich. R.S.

Mississippi

Poindexter, George, ed. *The Revised Code of the Laws of Mississippi.* Natchez, 1824. Miss. R.C.
The Mississippi Code of 1906 of the Public Statute Laws of the State of Mississippi. Nashville: Brandon Printing Co., 1906. Miss. Code.

Missouri

Geyer, Henry S. *A Digest of the Laws of Missouri Territory.* St. Louis, 1818.
Laws of the State of Missouri. 2 vols. St. Louis, 1825. Laws of Mo.
The Revised Statutes of the State of Missouri. 2nd ed. St. Louis, 1840. Mo. R.S. *(1840).*
Jones, William Claude, supt. *The Revised Statutes of the State of Missouri.* St. Louis, 1845. Mo. R.S. *(1845).*
Hardin, Charles H. *The Revised Statutes of the State of Missouri.* Jefferson City, 1856. Mo. R.S. *(1856).*

North Carolina

Clark, Walter, ed. *The State Records of North Carolina.* Vol. 24, *Laws 1777–1788.* Goldsboro, NC: Nash Bros. 1905. N.C. St. Rec.
Nash, Frederick, James Iredell, and William H. Battle, eds. *The Revised Statutes of the State of North Carolina.* 2 vols. Raleigh, 1837. N.C. R.S.

Tennessee

Caruthers, R. L., and A. O. P. Nicholson. *A Compilation of the Statutes of Tennessee, of a General and Permanent Nature, from the Commencement of the Government to the Present Time.* Nashville, 1836. Tenn. Stat.

Texas

Laws of the Republic of Texas. 2 vols. Houston, 1838. Rep. Tex. Laws

Oldham, Williamson S., and George W. White. *A Digest of the General Statute Laws of the State of Texas.* Austin, 1859. Tex. Digest.

Court Cases

Citations to most of the judicial decisions referred to in the notes take the traditional legal format. A few decisions were reported in newspapers. A citation includes the name of the case, the volume of reports, the abbreviation of the series of reports, and the page on which the case begins. If no court is indicated before the year, the decision was issued by the highest court of the state. A typical example is Greenfield v. Dorris, 33 Tenn. 548 (1853). A citation may also include the specific page on which language is quoted or a point of law is mentioned in the text. If the text refers to a concurring or dissenting opinion, the name of the judge concurring or dissenting is also noted.

Newspapers

In writing this book, I made extensive use of newspapers. Most of them were found on the Chronicling America and Newspapers.com websites. Others I located in online newspaper archives for individual states, such as Georgia Historic Newspapers (University System of Georgia), Hoosier State Chronicles (Indiana State Library), and Missouri Digital Newspapers (State Historical Society of Missouri). Newspapers often changed their names. Anyone using Newspapers.com should be aware that the name under which a paper is catalogued by that service is not necessarily the one that appears on the paper's masthead. In my citations to newspapers, I used the name on the p. 1 masthead (which sometimes differed from the name on the editorial page). A reader who wishes to look up a cited source might want to search by date, key word, and state, omitting the name of the paper.

The following list contains the names of all the newspapers cited in the notes. If a newspaper reprinted an item from another paper, the note includes the name of the original newspaper and the one that did the reprinting, but the list below includes only the latter. Where the city or state of publication is not clear from the name, I added that information in parentheses. Newspapers called the *Democrat* were published in Eufaula and Huntsville, both in Alabama. In the notes, all citations are to the Huntsville paper except where Eufaula is specified. Both Tennessee and North Carolina had papers called the *Fayetteville Observer*. The state is identified in the notes.

Abbeville (SC) Press and Banner
Adventure (St. Joseph, MO)
Advertiser and State Gazette (Montgomery, AL)
Advocate & Register (Vicksburg, MS)
Alabama Beacon (Greensboro, AL)
Albany (GA) Patriot
Alexandria Gazette (DC until Sept. 3, 1846; VA thereafter)

American Patriot (Clinton, LA)
American Republican and Baltimore Daily Clipper
Ariel (Natchez, MS)
Arkansas State Gazette (Little Rock)
Arkansas State Gazette and Democrat (Little Rock)
Athens (TN) Post
Atlanta Constitution
Atlanta Daily Examiner
Atlanta Weekly Intelligencer and Cherokee Advocate
Augusta (GA) Chronicle and Gazette of the State
Bamberg (SC) Herald
Bangor (ME) Daily Whig and Courier
Baton Rouge (LA) Gazette
Blue Hen's Chicken (Wilmington, DE)
Brookhaven (MS) Leader
Brooklyn Daily Eagle
Boon's Lick Times (Fayette, MO)
Burlington (VT) Free Press
Carroll Free Press (Carrollton, GA)
Cecil Whig (Elkton, MD)
Centre Democrat (Bellefonte, PA)
Charleston (SC) Daily Courier
Charleston (SC) Mercury
Charlotte (NC) Democrat
Chicago (IL) Democrat
Clarion (Jackson, MS)
Clarion-Ledger (Jackson, MS)
Columbus (MS) Commercial
Columbus (GA) Daily Times
Columbus (GA) Enquirer
Columbus (GA) Enquirer-Sun
Columbus (GA) Times
Concordia Intelligencer (Vidalia, LA)
Constitutionalist and Republic (Augusta, GA)
Daily American Organ (Washington, DC)
Daily Arkansas Gazette (Little Rock)
Daily Chronicle & Sentinel (Augusta, GA)
Daily Clarion-Ledger (Jackson, MS)
Daily Comet (Baton Rouge, LA)
Daily Commercial Herald (Vicksburg, MS)
Daily Constitution (Atlanta, GA)
Daily Constitutionalist (Augusta, GA)
Daily Crescent (New Orleans, LA)
Daily Delta (New Orleans, LA)
Daily Democratic Statesman (Austin, TX)

Daily Nashville True Whig
Daily Ohio State Journal (Columbus)
Daily Picayune (New Orleans)
Daily Progress (Newbern, NC)
Daily State Guard (Wetumpka, AL)
Daily State Sentinel (Montgomery, AL)
Daily Sun (Columbus, GA)
Daily True Delta (New Orleans)
Daily Union (Nashville)
Dallas Herald
Delaware Inquirer (Wilmington)
Delaware State Journal and Statesman (Wilmington)
Democrat (Eufaula, AL)
Democrat (Huntsville, AL)
Democratic Banner (Bowling Green, MO)
Democratic Telegraph and Texas Register (Houston)
Detroit Free Press
Eastern Argus (Portland, ME)
Eastern Clarion (Paulding, MS)
Edgefield (SC) Advertiser
Era (Raleigh, NC)
Evansville (IN) Daily Journal
Evansville (IN) Weekly Journal
Evening Post (New York)
Examiner (Louisville, KY)
Fairfield News and Herald (Winnsboro, SC)
Fayetteville (NC) Observer
Fayetteville (TN) Observer
Federal Union (Milledgeville, GA)
Feliciana Democrat (Clinton, LA)
Florida Sentinel (Tallahassee)
Fort Smith (AR) Herald
Gallipolis (OH) Journal
Galveston Daily News
Georgia Jeffersonian (Griffin)
Georgia Journal and Messenger (Macon)
Glasgow (MO) Weekly Times
Greenville (MS) Times
Greenville (SC) Daily News
Grenada (MS) Sentinel
Hattiesburg (MS) News
Hillsdale (MI) Whig Standard
Houma (LA) Ceres
Hustler of Rome (Georgia)
Independent Monitor (Tuscaloosa, AL)

Independent Press (Abbeville, SC)
Indiana Daily State Sentinel (Indianapolis)
Indiana State Sentinel (Indianapolis)
Iowa Capitol Reporter (Iowa City)
Jackson (MS) Daily News
Jackson (MS) Evening News
Jacksonville (AL) Republican
Jeffersonian Republican (Stroudsburg, PA)
Joliet (IL) Signal
Jones County News (Ellisville, MS)
Kentucky Yeoman (Frankfort)
Knoxville (TN) Register
Lafayette (LA) Advertiser
Lake Charles (LA) Commercial
Lexington (MS) Advertiser
Lloyd's Weekly Newspaper (London, UK)
Louisville Daily Journal
Louisville Morning Courier
Macon (GA) Telegraph
Marietta (GA) Journal
McArthur (OH) Democrat
Memphis Daily Appeal
Meridian (MS) Press
Mississippian (Vicksburg)
Mississippian and State Gazette (Jackson)
Missouri Intelligencer (Franklin)
Missouri Intelligencer and Boon's Lick Advertiser (Columbia)
Missouri Statesman (Columbia)
Missouri Whig (Palmyra)
Montgomery (AL) Weekly Advertiser
Morning News (Savannah, GA)
Nashville Banner
Nashville Patriot
Nashville Republican and State Gazette
Nashville Union
Nashville Union and American
Natchez
Natchez Gazette
National Banner, and Daily Advertiser (Nashville, TN)
National Era (Washington, DC)
National Whig (Washington, DC)
The New Constitution (Columbus, OH)
Newnan (GA) Herald & Advertiser
New Orleans Daily Crescent
New Orleans Republican

Selected Bibliography 301

New-Orleans Times
New-Orleans Weekly Times
New-York Daily Tribune
New York Herald
New York Times
Niles' National Register (Baltimore, MD)
Niles' Weekly Register (Baltimore, MD)
North Carolina Standard (Raleigh)
North Carolinian (Fayetteville)
North Georgia Citizen (Dalton)
Observer (Raleigh, NC)
Opelousas (LA) Courier
Opelousas (LA) Patriot
Oxford (MS) Eagle
Palatka (FL) Daily News
Pensacola Commercial
Pensacola Gazette
Pittsfield (MA) Sun
Planters' Banner (Franklin, LA)
Pointe Coupee Democrat (False River, LA)
Port Tobacco Times, and Charles County (MD) Advertiser
Raftsman's Journal (Clearfield, PA)
Republican and Savannah Evening Ledger
Republican Banner (Nashville, TN)
Republican Banner and Nashville Whig
Richmond (VA) Dispatch
Richmond (VA) Enquirer
Richmond (TX) Reporter
River Times (Fort Winnebago, WI)
Savannah Morning News
Selma (AL) Daily Messenger
Semi-Weekly Leader (Brookhaven, MS)
Semi-Weekly Standard (Raleigh, NC)
Shreveport Journal
Shreveport Times
Simpson County News (Mendenhall, MS)
Smyrna (DE) Telegraph
Southern Banner (Athens, GA)
Southern Luminary (Jackson, MS)
Southern Recorder (Milledgeville, GA)
Southern Reveille (Port Gibson, MI)
Southern Sentinel (Plaquemine, LA)
Southern Standard (Arkadelphia, AR)
Southern Watchman (Athens, GA)
South-Western (Nashville, TN)

Spirit of Democracy (Woodsfield, OH)
Spirit of the Age (Tuscaloosa, AL)
Spirit of the South (Eufaula, AL)
St. Joseph (MO) Commercial Cycle
St. Joseph (MO) Gazette
St. Landry (LA) Democrat
St. Louis (MO) Globe-Democrat
St. Louis (MO) Republic
Starkville (MS) News
Staunton (VA) Spectator
Staunton (VA) Spectator, and General Advertiser
Sumter Banner (Sumterville, SC)
Sun (Baltimore, MD)
Sunday Dispatch (New York)
Tallahatchie Herald (Charleston, MS)
Tarboro (NC) Southerner
Texas National Register (Washington, TX)
Texas Republican (Marshall, TX)
Thibodaux (LA) Minerva
Times and Democrat (Orangeburg, SC)
Times-Democrat (New Orleans, LA)
Times & Sentinel Tri-Weekly (Columbus, GA)
Tri-Weekly Chronicle & Sentinel (Augusta, GA)
Tri-Weekly Nashville Union
Tri-Weekly Standard (Raleigh, NC)
True American (New Orleans, LA)
True Democrat (Little Rock, AR)
Union and Recorder (Milledgeville, GA)
Vermont Watchman & State Journal (Montpelier)
Vicksburg (MS) American
Vicksburg (MS) Evening Post
Vicksburg (MS) Register
Vicksburg (MS) Tri-Weekly Whig
Washington (AR) Telegraph
Water Valley (MS) Progress
Weekly Clarion (Jackson MS)
Weekly Corinthian (Corinth, MS)
Weekly Democrat (Natchez, MS)
Weekly Floridian (Tallahassee)
Weekly Georgia Telegraph (Macon)
Weekly Memphis Eagle
Weekly Messenger (St. Martinville, LA)
Weekly National Intelligencer (Washington, DC)
Weekly North-Carolina Standard (Raleigh, NC)
Western Democrat (Charlotte, NC)

Western Union (Hannibal, MO)
Wetumpka (AL) Argus
Wilmington (NC) Journal
Yorkville (SC) Enquirer

Election Data

Newspapers are useful sources of information on nineteenth-century judicial elections. For other election-related data for that time, Michael J. Dubin's books are valuable. The full bibliographical information and abbreviations for the volumes referenced in the notes are:

Party Affiliations in the State Legislatures: A Year by Year Summary, 1796–2006. Jefferson, NC: McFarland, 2007. *Party Affiliations.*
United States Congressional Elections, 1788–1997: The Official Results of the Elections of the 1st through 105th Congresses. Jefferson, NC: McFarland, 1998. *Congressional Elections.*
United States Gubernatorial Elections, 1776–1860: The Official Results by State and County. Jefferson, NC: McFarland, 1998. *Gubernatorial Elections.*
United States Presidential Elections, 1788–1860: The Official Results by County and State. Jefferson, NC: McFarland, 2002. *Presidential Elections.*

INDEX

Adcock, Jacob 117
Alabama: apportionment in, 93, 95, 103, 107; constitution of 1819 of, 103; constitutional conventions of, 197–98 (1861), 215 (1867), 216 (1875); county courts in, 104–5, 106–7, 108; demographics of, 102–3, 202–3; elective judiciary in, 103–9, 197–98, 203, 216; elective judiciary in, retreat from, 197–98; internal improvements in, 107; judicial tenure in, 103, 105, 108; justices of the peace in, 104–5; probate courts in, 106, 107, 108; public debt in, 98; public officers, election of, 97–98, 99, 101–2, 106, 108; slavery and apportionment in, 93; suffrage, black and elective judiciary in, 216–17; suffrage, white, in 85, 103
apportionment. *See* equal representation; specific state
Arkansas: apportionment in, 95, 97; constitution of 1838 of, 97; constitutional conventions of, 203–4 (1864), 209 (1868), 210–11 (1874); constitutional reform agendas in, 98, 101–2; county courts in, 98–99, 100; demographics of, 97, 202; and elective judiciary in, 98–102, 204, 210; judicial tenure in, 102; public debt in, 98, 210; sectionalism (intrastate) in, 203–4; suffrage, black and elective judiciary in, 211–12; suffrage, white, in 95, 97, 102
associate judges: election of, as harbinger of elective judiciary, 145; whether "real" judges, 10

Ballew, David W., 116–17
Ballou, DeWitt C., 34
Barth, Jay, 100
Bate, Humphrey R., 119

Bates, Edward, 18–19
Bates, Frederick, 18
Bates, Martin D., 59, 66, 67
Baxter, Elisha, 210
Bayard, James A., 60–62, 69
Benjamin, Judah P., 204
Benton, Thomas Hart, 158, 160
Bergeron, Paul H., 112
Bevitt, Edwin D., 32
Biggs, Benjamin T., 62, 64, 65–66, 67
Bilbo, Theodore, 95
Birch, James H., 159, 160, 177–78, 179
Blair, Diane D., 100
Bofill, J. V., 205
Boggs, Lilburn W., 138
Boman, Dennis K., 178
Breckinridge, John, 41
Brent, George, 50
Brent, James F., 92, 123–25
Brewer, Earl L., 231
Brooks, Joseph, 210
Brown, B. Gratz, 191
Brown, Thomas, 91
Bryson, Isaac Newton, 173–74
Buchanan, Alexander M., 156
Buckner, Robert H., 124
Buford, Jefferson, 106
Bullard, Henry A., 154
Bullitt, William C., 44–45
Burton, R. M., 114

Calhoun, John C., 84
California, 6–7, 137, 142, 191, 192
Campbell, James G., 183
Carleton, Henry, 154
Caruthers, Robert L., 157, 168, 169, 170, 171
Catron, John, 156–57
Chambers, Ezekiel F., 50–52, 140

Chrisman, J. B., 228
Clark, Walter, 3
Clark, William, 19
Clarke, G. W., 99
Clayton, John M., 55, 57, 58, 69
Cobbs, R. L., 114
Cochran, John, 197
Cole, James L., 156
Collier, Henry W., 105
Collins, Ross, 231
Connecticut, 8, 27, 144
Cooley, Thomas M., 10
Corbit, Daniel, 59, 65–66, 67
Corwin, Edward S., 164
county courts: judges of as harbingers of elective judiciary, 145; judges of, whether "real" judges, 8. *See also* under specific state
Crow, Wayman, 177
Cutler, R. King, 204

Davis, Edmund J., 212
Davis, Garrett, 44, 45–46
De Bow, James 6–7, 71
Delaware; apportionment in, 55–57, 58–59 60–63; conservatism of, 54–55; constitutional convention of 1852–53, 56–69; constitutional reform agendas in, 55, 57, 58; constitutions of, 54–55, 55–56, 63 (1831), 68–69 (proposed 1853); demographics of, 62; and elective judiciary in, 53–54, 57, 64–69; internal improvements in, 68; judicial tenure in, 57, 58–59, 63, 64, 66, 67, 68, 69; justices of the peace in, 55; public debt in, 39, 68; public officers, election of, 55, 56, 57; sectionalism (intrastate) in, 55, 61; slavery and apportionment in, 61; suffrage in, 55–56, 57, 58, 59–60, 63
democracy: definition of, 10–13; elective judiciary, relationship to, 143; Jacksonian, 11–13; Jeffersonian, 10. *See also* apportionment under specific state; majority rule; suffrage under specific state
demographics, relationship to elective judiciary, 35–36, 143–44. *See also* demographics under specific state
Dent, John F., 50
Dilworth, W. S., 199

Dixon, Archibald, 44
Douglas, Stephen A., 196
Drew, Richard, 164–65

Eaton, Dorman B., 2, 131, 133, 141
elective judiciary: as an American phenomenon, 1–2; common features in early appearances of, 35–37; current status of, 3–4; early instances of, 8–10, 15, 16–17, 34–35; and judicial review, 6, 163–89; Progressive Era views on, 2–3; after Reconstruction, 218–32; during Reconstruction, 203–18, 223–24, 227; regional diversity in adoption of, 5–7; retreat from, antebellum, 192–200; southern roots of, 16–37; spread of, 4–5, 191–92, 203; in Trans-Mississippi West, 191–92. *See also* under specific state
elective judiciary—arguments for and against: in Alabama, 104, 197–98; in Arkansas, 99, 211; in Delaware, 64, 65–66; in Florida, 91; in Georgia, 86, 193–94, 219, 220, 222; in Kentucky, 46; in Louisiana, 123–25, 204–5, 223; in Maryland, 51–52; in Mississippi, 26–28, 196, 227–28; in Missouri, 31–32; in North Carolina, 80–81, 213–14; in South Carolina, 216; in Tennessee, 114, 115, 116–18; in Texas, 110, 111; in Virginia, 74–75, 76, 193, 196
elective judiciary—explanations for advent and spread of: democratic culture, importance of, 136, 143; demographics, importance of, 143–44; diversity among states as obstacle for, 140–41; economic crisis, importance of, 136–40; election of lowest-court justices as harbingers of, 144–45; Jacksonian populism as, 131, 141; Jacksonian suspicion of government, as, 132–33; moderate lawyers at constitutional conventions, influence of, 134–36; New York precedent, influence of, 133
English, William H., 196
equal representation: definition of, 10; as component of democratic culture, 10, 23, 36–37; in early state adopters of judicial elections, 36. *See also* apportionment under specific state

Escott, Paul D., 195
Eustis, George, 154–55
Everard, Wayne M., 128

Falconer, Thomas P., 28
Featherston, C. N., 222
Fishback, William, 204
Florida: apportionment in, 89, 93; constitution of 1838 in, 88–89, 93; constitutional conventions of, 199 (1861), 219–20 (1885); county courts in, 89; demographics of, 88, 90, 202; and elective judiciary in, 90–92, 218; elective judiciary in, retreat from, 199; judicial tenure in, 89, 90, 91, 142; justices of the peace in, 88; probate judges in, 88; public officers, election of, 88–89, 92–93; slavery and apportionment in, 89, 93; suffrage, black and elective judiciary in, 219–20; suffrage, white, in 88, 90
Foote, Henry S. 1, 150
Ford, John S., 110
free suffrage: definition of, 10; as component of democratic culture, 10, 23; in early state adopters of judicial elections, 36. *See also* suffrage; suffrage under specific state
Fugitive Slave Law, 7, 154

Galloway, Abraham H., 214
Gamble, Hamilton, 160
Garland, Rice, 154
Garrott, I. W., 106
Georgia: apportionment in, 85, 88; constitutional conventions of, 220 (1867, 1877); county (inferior) courts in, 17; democratic reforms in, 85; demographics of, 202; and elective judiciary, 16–17, 85–88, 220–22; elective judiciary in, retreat from, 193, 199; judicial tenure in, 16; public officers, election of, 85, 87–88; slavery and apportionment in, 16, 88; suffrage, black and elective judiciary, 220–23
Geyh, Charles Gardner, 4
Graham, J. W., 214
Grant, Ulysses S., 210, 227
Greeley, Horace, 132
Green, Fletcher M., 49
Green, Nathan, Sr., 156, 157

Greenleaf, Daniel, 29
Guion, John I., 150

Hahn, Michael, 204
Hall, Kermit L., 4, 131, 148; on judicial review, impact of judicial elections on, 139, 165; on moderate lawyers, influence of on rise of elective judiciary, 134–36
Hand, Learned, 131
Harris, Isham G., 157
Harris, William R., 157
Harry, James Warner, 49, 53
Haughey, Thomas M., 216
Hawaii, 192
Hayes, Rutherford B., 1
Haymond, Alpheus F., 197
Haynes, Evan, 131
Heaton, David, 214
Herron, Andrew S., 130
Hitchcock, Peter, 135
Hoffman, Michael, 135, 139
Holden, William H., 79
Holt, Michael F., 128
Horwitz, Morton J., 164
Howard, Nathaniel G., 29
Humphreville, Samuel, 139
Hunt, Ezra, 31, 32
Huntsman, Adam, 113
Hurst, James Willard, 131

Illinois: constitutional convention of 1847 in, 132; election of probate judges in, 145; election of public officers in, 141, 142; elective judiciary in, example for other states, 79, 86; internal improvements in, 39; judicial tenure in, 142
Indiana: associate judges elected in, 10, 145; constitutional convention of 1850–51 in, 132; internal improvements in, 39; judicial elections, partisanship in, 150, 151; judicial review in, 164–65, 274n7; judicial tenure in, 142; straight-ticket voting in, 149
internal improvements, debt from, as impetus for constitutional reform, 39, 136–39. *See also* internal improvements under specific state; public debt under specific state
Iowa: constitutions of 1844 (proposed) and 1846, 54, 137; demographics in, 35;

district court judges, election of, 35, 145, 257n13; elective judiciary, early adopter of, 35, 36, 100; judicial tenure in, 142; justices of the peace in Territory of, 9; supreme court judges, election of, 144, 191

Jackson, Andrew: 1, 115, 120, 157, 232; on equality, 11–12; on majority rule, 12; on rotation in office, 12
Jefferson, Thomas: 27, 65, 71, 72; on county courts in Virginia, 8–9, 72; on the elective judiciary, 8, 27, 72; on representation, 10–11, 71–72; on suffrage, 10, 71; on the Virginia constitution of 1776, 71–72
Johnson, Andrew, 157, 201, 205–6
Jones, P. Z., 231
judicial elections: dates of, 148–50, 193; and judicial review, 152–54; nominations for, 148, 151–55, 159, 223, 226, 230; and political partisanship in, 148–52, 154–61; and straight-ticket voting, 149–50; and uncontested races, 150–51; voter indifference towards, 147–51, 157, 193. *See also* specific state
judicial review: explanations for increase in, 164–65; increase in, 163–64; in New England, 163; in the South, 165–66. *See also* specific state
judicial tenure. *See* under specific state
judiciary: definition of, 8–10; place of non-"real" judges in, 8–10.
justices of the peace: administrative powers of, 8–9; election of, as harbinger of elective judiciary, 144–45; and first debate over judicial elections, 144; judicial powers of, 9; whether "real" judges, 8–9. *See also* judiciary; specific state
Justus, James H., 96

Kansas, 92, 142, 191, 192, 203
Kansas-Nebraska Act, 7, 84, 85, 92, 196
Kent, Edward, 163
Kentucky: apportionment in, 40, 41, 44, 48, 69; constitutional convention of 1849 in, 41–48; constitutional reform agenda in, 42–44; constitutions of, 40–41 (1792), 41–43 (1799), 48 (1849); county courts in, 41–43, 48; demographics of, 40, 41; and elective judiciary in, 44–48; judicial reform demands in, 41, 43–44; judicial review in, 44–45, 166; judicial tenure in, 42, 45, 48, 142; majoritarianism at constitutional convention of 1849 in, 44–46; public debt in, 48; public officers, election of, 40–41, 43, 48; slavery and apportionment in, 42, 44; slavery at constitutional convention of 1849 in, 42–45; suffrage in, 41

Keyes, Edward, 135
King, Austin A., 159
King, Joseph H., 213
Kramer, Larry, 165

Land, Thomas T., 156
Lea, James N., 156
Leonard, Abiel, 160
Leslie, Miron, 32
Lincoln, Abraham, 201, 203, 205
Lodge, William C., 69
Lofland, James R., 60, 64, 67, 69
Louisiana: apportionment in, 121, 126–27, 128, 129–30; constitutional conventions of, 120–25 (1844–45), 127–29 (1852), 199 (1861), 204–5 (1864) 223 (1867–68), 224–25 (1879), 226 (1898); constitutions of, 119–20 (1812), 122–23, 125–27 (1845), 128–30 (1852); demographics of, 120, 202; and elective judiciary in, 121, 123–25, 127–29, 205, 223; elective judiciary, retreat from, 199–200; internal improvements in,122–23, 126–27, 128–29, 138; judicial elections and political affiliation in, 149, 151, 154–56; judicial elections, public indifference towards, 147; judicial problems in, 123; judicial review in, 166, 124–25, 127, 180–89; judicial tenure in, 120–21, 124–27, 129, 142, 223, 227; justices of the peace in, 126; public debt in, 122–23, 129, 138; public officers in, election of, 121, 126, 127; sectionalism (intrastate), in 120; slavery and apportionment in, 126, 128, 129–30, 191; suffrage, black and elective judiciary in, 224–26; suffrage, white, in 119, 121, 126, 127, 128
Lowry, Robert, 228
Lucas, William, 76

Mackey, E. W. M., 217
Maine, 144, 163, 165, 166, 176
majority rule: and democracy, 12, 72, 194; rejection of, in principle, 73, 84–85, 172; and sectional conflict, 195–96; as threat to slavery, 44–45, 51, 61, 78, 92–93, 194–95; "tyranny" of and judicial elections in, 27, 52, 197–98. *See also* apportionment; specific states
Marmaduke, Meredith M., 31
Martin, François Xavier, 154
Marvin, William, 89
Maryland: apportionment in, 49–50, 53, 69; constitutional convention of 1850–51 in, 48–52; constitutional reform agenda in, 48–49; constitutional revisions of 1836–37, 49–50; constitutions of, 50 (1776), 53 (1851); demographics of, 50; and elective judiciary, 50–53; internal improvements in, 49, 53; judicial review in, 166; judicial tenure in, 50, 51–52, 52–53, 142; and majority rule, 50–52; public debt in, 49, 53; public officers in, election of, 48, 51, 53; sectionalism (intrastate), 49, 50; slavery and apportionment in, 50; suffrage in, 49
Mason, Samson, 135
Massachusetts: constitutional convention of 1853 in, 1–2, 5, 40, 135–36; demographics of, 144; judicial review in, 164; judicial tenure in, 144
Maxcy, Virgil, 194
Mayfield, James S., 111
McBride, Priestly H., 158, 159
McClung, James W., 106
McGirk, Mathias, 158
McKinney, Robert J., 157, 168, 169, 171
McLaurin, Anselm J., 229
McNair, Alexander, 18–19
Medary, Samuel, 141
Merrick, Edwin T., 155
Merriken, Richard N., 59
Michigan: elective judiciary, early adopter of, 10, 35, 100; internal improvements in, 39; judicial tenure in, 142; public officers in, election of, 141, 142
Miles, Elijah W., 164
Minnesota, 142, 191, 192

Mississippi: apportionment in, 23–24, 35, 69, 95; constitution of 1817 in, 22–25; constitutional conventions of, 25–30, 35 (1832), 227 (1868), 228–29 (1890); constitutional reform agenda in, 25; county courts in, 25; demographics of, 22, 202; and elective judiciary, 1, 25–28, 227–31; elective judiciary in, retreat from, 196; example of cited in other states, 46, 79, 117, 118, 124, 125, 133; judicial elections and straight-ticket voting in, 149–50; judicial problems in, 24–25; judicial review in, 165; judicial tenure in, 23, 26–29, 142, 227; sectionalism (intrastate), 22; suffrage, black and elective judiciary in, 227–28; suffrage, white, in 23, 95
Missouri: apportionment in, 18, 30, 31, 33, 35, 69; constitution of 1820 of, 16–17; constitutional conventions of, 17–19 (1820), 30–33, 69 (1845–46); county courts in, 22; demographics of, 17; and elective judiciary, 19, 21, 31–34, 69; internal improvements in, 138–39; judicial elections and political affiliation in, 158–61; judicial reform in, 30, 34; judicial review in, 20–21, 166, 171–80; judicial tenure in, 18–21, 30–34, 142, 158–60; justices of the peace in, 22; probate courts in, 22; suffrage in, 18
Moore, Francis, Jr., 112
Moore, Gabriel, 105
Morgan, John T., 197
Morphy, Alonzo, 154
Moseley, William D., 90, 91
Murphy, William M., 107

Napton, William B., 158, 159, 160, 177–78, 179–80
Nebraska, 92
Neeson, James, 76
Nelson, Caleb: 4, 133; on elective judiciary, moderate-lawyer explanation for rise of, 134; on elective judiciary, suspicion of official power and rise of, 131–32, 134; on judicial review, impact of judicial elections on, 139
Nevada, 203
New Jersey, 144, 184
New Hampshire, 144

New York: constitutional conventions in, 34, 144–45 (1821), 136, 137, 141 (1845); demographics of, 35, 144; and elective judiciary in, 34–35, 100, 144; elective judiciary in, adoption of as trigger for spread of, 36, 131, 133–34, 136, 139; example of cited in other states, 46, 66, 74, 79, 134, 139, 117–18, 214; impeachment of elected judges in, 2; internal improvements in, 5, 39, 136, 141; judicial elections in, public indifference towards, 147; judicial review in, 139, 164–65, 273n4, 274n7; judicial tenure in, 142; public debt in, 136, 141; senators as judges in, 8

Nicholas, George, 40
Nicholson, A. O. P., 169
Noel, Edmund, 229, 230
North Carolina: apportionment in, 77–78; constitutional conventions of, 77–78, 79 (1835), 206 (1865), 213–14 (1868); constitutions of, 77 (1776), 206 (1865); county courts in, 77, 80–81, 206; demographics of, 81, 144, 202; and elective judiciary, 78–82, 214; judicial tenure in, 214; justices of the peace in, 80–81, 206; and majority rule, 77; sectionalism (intrastate) in, 77, 78, 80–82, 195; slavery and apportionment in, 78; suffrage in, 77, 78, 80; Virginia, compared to, 77
North Dakota, 3
Nuttall, Elijah F., 47

Ogden, Abner N., 183, 184
Ohio: example of cited in other states, 214; internal improvements in, 39, 137; judicial elections in, 3, 149, 150; judicial problems in, 5, 137; judicial review in, 140, 152; judicial tenure in, 142; justices of the peace in, 9; public debt in, 132; public officers, election of, 1, 141
Old Southwest: definition of, 96; democratic constitutions of, 95–96
O'Neal, Emmet 2–3
Oregon 6, 191, 192
O'Sullivan, John, 194

Pennsylvania: constitution of 1776, 15; demographics of, 144; example of cited in other states, 65, 118; and judicial elections, 148; judicial tenure in, 142–43
Pepper, William W., 116
Peters, Thomas M., 216
Polk, Edwin, 115, 117–18
Porter, Benjamin F., 106
Preston, William, 47
Price, Samuel, 197
probate judges: election of, as harbinger of elective judiciary, 145; whether "real" judges, 8–9, 107. *See also* specific state

Quin, H. M., 230
Quitman, John A., 25, 27, 28, 65, 92, 125

Randolph, John, 172
Ranney, Rufus P., 135
Ray, Henry M., 214
Read, Amasa, 123–24
"real" judges: definition of, 8; exclusions from definition of, 8–10. *See* judiciary
Reconstruction Acts, 206–7, 216
Reemelin, Charles, 152
Reese, William B., 156, 157
regional diversity, significance of for elective judiciary, 5–6, 35–36, 39–40, 140–41. *See also* sectionalism
representation, legislative. *See* apportionment under specific state
Rhett, Robert Barnwell, 195–96
Rhode Island, 5, 11, 40, 144
Richardson, John C., 160, 179
Robb, James, 126
Roberts, Oran, 112
Rosenthal, James M., 164
Ross, William, 57
Rost, Adolph, 154
Rusk, Thomas J., 109, 111
Ryan, Edward, 135
Ryland, John F., 159, 160, 177, 178–79

Schafer, Judith K., 120, 128
Scott, Charles, 150
Scott, William, 158, 159, 160, 179–80
sectionalism, 7, 70, 176–80, 195–97
sectionalism (intrastate). *See* specific state
Semple, Henry C., 215–16
Sharkey, William L., 124
Sheffield, William P., 221

Shugerman, Jed Handelsman: 4, 135; on economic crisis, impact of on rise of elective judiciary, 136–37; on judicial review, extent of, 164, 165–66; on judicial review, impact of judicial elections on, 136, 152, 165, 274n6; on New York, influence of on rise of elective judiciary, 133, 136, 139
side judges. See associate judges
Simon, Edward 154
slavery: definition of the South and, 7–8, 39, 71; definition of democracy and, 11; judicial independence and, 51–52; judicial review and, 176–79, 180, 182, 187–88; majority rule and, 92–93; retreat from elective judiciary and, 194–96, 205. See also apportionment and slavery under specific state
Slidell, Thomas. 155, 181, 183, 186–87, 204
Smith, James H., 64
Smith, Sidney M., 231
Smithers, Caleb, 61, 62, 65, 67
South: definition of, 6–8; conservatism of, 142–43; slavery as distinguishing feature of, 7–8, 71
Southeast, definition of, 71
South Carolina: apportionment in, 82–85; constitution of 1790, 82–83; constitutional convention of 1868, 217; constitutional reform agenda in, 83–84; demographics of, 82, 202; and elective judiciary, 217–18; judicial tenure in, 82; and majority rule, 84–85; sectionalism (intrastate) in, 82–84; slavery and apportionment in, 83; suffrage in, 82–83
Southwest. See Old Southwest
Spofford, Henry M., 156, 187–88
Stephens, Alexander H., 7
Stewart, James E., 76
Stockdale, Fletcher Summerfield, 212–13
Stocker, W. T., 205
Strawbridge, George, 154
suffrage—black: under Congressional Reconstruction, 202, 207–8; under Presidential Reconstruction, 206, 207; restriction of, methods of, 208–9, 223; in Tennessee, 112. See also suffrage, black and elective judiciary in, under specific state
suffrage—white: under Congressional Reconstruction, 207–8; under Presidential Reconstruction, 205. See also free suffrage; suffrage under specific state
Summers, George W., 197
Sutton, Jeffrey S., 192
Swan, Joseph, 154
Sydnor, Charles S., 95, 119

Taylor, Joseph W., 106
Tennessee: apportionment in, 95, 112–13, 115; constitutional convention of 1834 in, 114–15; constitutions of, 112–13 (1796), 114–15 (1835); county courts in, 113; demographics of, 113, 202; and elective judiciary, 114–19; judicial elections and party affiliation in, 156–58; judicial elections, public indifference toward, 147–48; judicial reform in, 113–19, 167–68; judicial review in, 166–71; judicial tenure in, 113, 114, 115, 118, 142; public officers in, election of, 113, 115, 117, 118; suffrage, black, in, 112; suffrage, black and elective judiciary in, 210; suffrage, white, in, 95, 112, 115
Texas: apportionment in, 95, 109; constitutional conventions of, 109, 110–11 (1845), 211–12 (1868–69), 212–13 (1875); constitutions of, 109 (1836), 110 (1845); county courts in, 109; demographics of 109, 111–12, 202; and elective judiciary, 110–12, 211; elective judiciary, retreat from, 199; judicial tenure in, 110, 111, 142, 212; justices of the peace in, 190, 110; suffrage in, 95, 109
Tharp, William, 56, 57
Thomason, Hugh French, 211
Tillman, Ben, 218
Tocqueville, Alexis de, 1
Tompkins, George, 158
Toombs, Robert, 220
Totten, Archibald W. O., 157, 168, 169, 171
Tourgée, Albion W., 214
Trousdale, William, 117
Tucker, Nathaniel Beverley, 171–72
Tucker, St. George, 171–72
Turley, William B., 156, 157

Vallandigham, Clement, 86
Van Buren, Martin, 12, 90, 157
Vardaman, James K., 229

Vermont: demographics of, 144; and elective judiciary in, 15; judicial review in, 152; judicial tenure in, 15; legislative representation in, 144, 268n30; public officers, election of, 40; suffrage in, 268n30

Virginia: apportionment in, 71–72, 73–74, 75–76, 77; constitutional conventions of, 72–74 (1829–30), 74–76 (1850–51), 196–97 (1861), 205 (1864); constitutions of, 71–72 (1776), 73 (1830), 77, 150 (1851); county courts in, 72, 75–76; democratization, calls for, 72–73; demographics, 73, 81, 203; and elective judiciary, 74–77, 196–97, 203, 205; elective judiciary in, retreat from, 193, 196–97, 198, 200; internal improvements in, 74; judicial review in, 166; judicial tenure in, 73, 142, 196; justices of the peace in, 72, 76, 77; and majority rule, 72, 73; public officers in, election of, 76–77; sectionalism (intrastate) in, 72–74, 75–76, 81, 196–97; slavery and apportionment in, 77; suffrage, 71–73, 77

Voorhies, Cornelius, 183

Walker, Joseph M., 127
Walker, Robert J., 25
Ward, Thomas, 70
Webb, James D., 197
Weeks, Stephen B., 208–9
West Virginia: demographics of future state of, 73, 74, 81; elective judiciary in, 198, 203; separate identity of future state of, 74, 81; statehood of, 192, 203
White, Hugh Lawson, 157
Wickliffe, Charles A., 47
Winston, William O., 104
Wisconsin, 54, 86, 142
Wise, Henry A., 74, 81
Wood, George, T. 112
Woodson, Silas, 46
Wright, Archibald, 157
Wright, Jonathan, 217

Young, Bennett H., 42, 43
Young, William C., 111